Solving the Frame Problem

Solving the Frame Problem

A Mathematical Investigation of the Common Sense Law of Inertia

Murray Shanahan

The MIT Press

Cambridge, Massachusetts

London, England

© 1997 Massachusetts Institute of Technology

This book was set in Times by the author and was printed and bound in the United States of America.

Library of Congress Cataloging-in-Publication Data

Shanahan, Murray.
   Solving the frame problem: a mathematical investigation of the common sense law of inertia / Murray Shanahan.
      p. cm.—(Artificial intelligence)
   Includes bibliographical references and index.
   ISBN 0-262-19384-1 (hardcover: alk. paper)
   1. Artificial intelligence. 2. Logic. 3. Knowledge representation (Information theory). I. Title. II. Series: Artificial intelligence (Cambridge, Mass.)
Q390.S53 1997
006.3'3—dc20   96-27555
                                                 CIP

In the course of our conversations Russell would often exclaim: "Logic's hell!"

— Ludwig Wittgenstein, *Culture and Value*

Contents

Series Foreword

Artificial intelligence is the study of intelligence using the ideas and methods of computation. Unfortunately, a definition of intelligence seems impossible at the moment because intelligence appears to be an amalgam of so many information-processing and information-representation abilities.

Of course psychology, philosophy, linguistics, and related disciplines offer various perspectives and methodologies for studying intelligence. For the most part, however, the theories proposed in these fields are too incomplete and too vaguely stated to be realized in computational terms. Something more is needed, even though valuable ideas, relationships, and constraints can be gleaned from traditional studies of what are, after all, impressive existence proofs that intelligence is in fact possible.

Artificial intelligence offers a new perspective and a new methodology. Its central goal is to make computers intelligent, both to make them more useful and to understand the principles that make intelligence possible. That intelligent computers will be extremely useful is obvious. The more profound point is that artificial intelligence aims to understand intelligence using the ideas and methods of computation, thus offering a radically new and different basis for theory formation. Most of the people doing work in artificial intelligence believe that these theories will apply to any intelligent information processor, whether biological or solid state.

There are side effects that deserve attention, too. Any program that will successfully model even a small part of intelligence will be inherently massive and complex. Consequently, artificial intelligence continually confronts the limits of computer-science technology. The problems encountered have been hard enough and interesting enough to seduce artificial intelligence people into working on them with enthusiasm. It is natural, then, that there has been a steady flow of ideas from artificial intelligence to computer science, and the flow shows no sign of abating.

The purpose of this series in artificial intelligence is to provide people in many areas, both professionals and students, with timely, detailed information about what is happening on the frontiers in research centers all over the world.

J. Michael Brady

Daniel G. Bobrow

Randall Davis

Preface

Works in the style of the present book are a curious mixture. They use a method that dates back at least twenty-three centuries to the time of Euclid, namely the presentation of axioms, and the demonstration of certain theorems that follow from those axioms through rigorous proof. Yet this method is employed in the service of a project that is quintessentially modern: the attempt to endow computers with a degree of intelligence.

At the time of writing, the field of artificial intelligence is healthily volatile, and many researchers are calling into question this mixture of ancient and modern. This style of research, so the argument goes, rests on outdated assumptions about the role and importance of representation in intelligence. Alternative paradigms abound, and I'm sympathetic to many of the new ideas that have been advanced by the champions of these paradigms. But the existence of this book testifies to my conviction that the intellectual tradition of the logician, ancient as it is, has a vital role to play in the future of our quintessentially modern field.

I have chosen to organise this book so that work on the frame problem is presented as an unfolding story, rather than as a body of theory which is to be learned by rote. Accordingly, the order of presentation of the material is different from what would be found in a normal text book. Standard material about default reasoning, for example, is not to be found lumped together in a single chapter, but is presented bit by bit, as it's needed to illustrate a particular technique. I hope the Index and Contents will render the book useful as a reference text despite this. The order I've chosen reflects the development of thinking in the field, and is more or less chronological in the core chapters, with the exception of Chapter 11 which opens with a jump backwards in time to the origins of logic programming.

My reason for arranging the book in this way is that I believe the history of attempts to solve the frame problem is extremely instructive. It isn't an arbitrary record of failures which culminates in the discovery of a truth which, with hindsight, seems obvious. Rather, it seems to me to reflect a natural order of enquiry. The dead ends that people have investigated are much more than mistakes. They're obvious possibilities, which any thinker engaged in studying the frame problem is wont to investigate. A deep understanding of the knowledge representation issues surrounding the frame problem can only be acquired by getting a feel for the space of mathematical possibilities and where they lead.

The style of work I have adopted emphasises the individual example. It can be argued that an approach to the frame problem can only properly be assessed by establishing formal correspondences with a more abstract formal framework that encompasses a large class of examples. According to this argument, appeals to intuition through single example scenarios are suspect. Without denying the importance of establishing correspondences between different formal frameworks, I would contend that the field is constrained by appeals to intuition until its formalisms are deployed in the design of working systems. After all, any abstract framework that is used to assess an approach to the frame problem is itself open to assessment. How do we know that the abstract framework itself is correct? Only by appealing to our intuitions in an examination of its performance on a judiciously chosen set of representative examples.

The book is not intended as a comprehensive survey of attempts to solve the frame problem, so I hope I haven't offended anyone whose favourite attempt at a solution (their own, for example) has been left out. I've concentrated exclusively on work in the non-modal tradition, and I'm conscious that, even within that tradition, the material presented seems to centre on a Stanford/Imperial axis. Even so, there's been more than enough to write about.[1] I'm convinced that most of the fundamental ideas and principles used to tackle the frame problem in the context of the situation calculus and the event calculus are universally applicable. But this conjecture merits a proper investigation.

With the usual caveat that they're not to be held responsible for the book's inevitable flaws, I would like to acknowledge my intellectual debt to three individuals whose influence on my work has been enormous. I was first introduced to the frame problem as an undergraduate in one of Bob Kowalski's lectures on artificial intelligence at Imperial College. By the end of the lecture I thought I'd solved it. That was a dozen years ago. That I now have a keener perspective on the whole cluster of issues surrounding the problem is thanks in part to the many hours of discussion and debate I've enjoyed with Bob since I returned to Imperial as a postdoctoral researcher after three years as a Ph.D. student at Cambridge.

In 1988, my first year back at Imperial, I visited Vladimir Lifschitz at Stanford University. At the time, I was immersed in the culture of logic programming. The frame problem seemed straightforward from a logic programming point of view. I'm grateful to Vladimir for drawing my attention to the many issues in the area of reasoning about action that hadn't been addressed by the logic programming community at the time. His criticism and support of my work since then have been of tremendous value. His own work in the field exemplifies a degree of thoroughness and rigour I'm still striving to emulate.

Finally, in recent years I've enjoyed many discussions with John McCarthy. Parts of this book were written during two visits to Stanford, at John's invitation, one in April 1994 and the other in March 1995. John's indirect influence on the book is all pervading. In a sense, the book follows the trajectory of his ideas over several decades, from the inception of artificial intelligence as a field, through the invention of the situation calculus and the discovery of the frame problem, to his work on circumscription and its application to common sense reasoning, and on to his recent ideas on context.

Over the years, I have benefited from numerous discussions on the topics covered in this book. With apologies to anyone I may have forgotten, my thanks go to: Chitta Baral, John Bell, Craig Boutilier, Saša Buvač, Keith Clark, Tom Costello, Marc Denecker, Charles Elkan, Kave Eshghi, David Etherington, Chris Evans, Michael Gelfond, Pat Hayes, Tony Kakas, Neelakantan Kartha, Bob Kowalski, Hector Levesque, Vladimir Lifschitz, Fangzhen Lin, John McCarthy, Rob Miller, Javier Pinto, Ray Reiter, Mark Ryan, Fariba Sadri, Erik Sandewall, Pierre-Yves Schobbens, Len Schubert, Marek Sergot, Yoav Shoham, Mikhail Soutchanski, and Kristof Van Belleghem. Special thanks are due to Tom Costello, Jacinto Dávila, Hisashi Hayashi, Neelakantan Kartha, François Levy, Rob Miller, Steve Moyle, Joachim Quantz and Mark Ryan for proofreading various parts of the text, and to Deborah Cantor-Adams at MIT Press for suggesting numerous improvements in style and layout.

Thanks are also due to the following organisations and institutions: the Engineering and Physical Sciences Research Council of Great Britain (EPSRC), who, by awarding me a five year research fellowship, gave me the time and freedom necessary to write such a book; the Department of Computing at Imperial College, London, where most of the book was written; and the Department of Computer Science at Queen Mary & Westfield College, London, where the book was completed.

The book is organised as follows. Everything before Chapter 4 is introductory. The introduction and Chapter 1 set the intellectual context, Chapter 2 covers background logical material, and Chapter 3 describes the frame problem and the Hanks-McDermott problem. Based on the situation calculus, Chapters 4 to 8 present various techniques for overcoming the Hanks-McDermott problem, namely chronological minimisation, causal minimisation, state-based minimisation, and monotonic approaches. Chapters 9 and 10 cover the topic of narratives and event occurrence minimisation in the situation calculus.

Chapters 11 to 13 depart from the representational medium of classical predicate calculus, and present the paradigm of logic programming, emphasising the application of negation-as-failure to the frame problem. Chapters 12 and 13 also introduce the event calculus, which is the focus of attention for the rest of the book. Chapters 14 and 15 reconstruct the event calculus using full predicate calculus with circumscription instead of logic programming.

Chapter 16 demonstrates the advantages of abandoning the stricture that the scope of circumscription should be the whole theory, and offers simple solutions to the frame problem for both the situation calculus and the event calculus that exploit this possibility. Finally, Chapter 17 addresses the topic of explanation, or reasoning from effects to causes, in the context of the assimilation of observation sentences.

Notes

1. I recall a workshop in which Pat Hayes proposed a fine of $1000 for every researcher who invents a new logic.

Introduction

The frame problem is a difficulty that arises when we attempt to represent the effects of actions and events in formal logic. It concerns the apparent need to represent large numbers of intuitively obvious facts about things that do not change when actions are performed. Exactly why this difficulty has turned out to be such a challenge to the research community is the subject matter of the body of this book, starting from Chapter 1. My aim in this introduction is to set the frame problem in its intellectual context. Why is it that many (but by no means all) researchers in the field of artificial intelligence (AI) believe that its solution is vital to the realisation of AI's goals? To answer this question, we have to ask what those goals are, and how they might be achieved.

1 Why Is the Frame Problem Important?

It's common to find the assertion at the beginning of introductory AI textbooks that AI's goals are twofold.[1] Of course, the definition of these two goals varies from author to author. But there is broad agreement. Here is my attempt to characterise AI's twin objectives.[2]

The primary objectives of the field of artificial intelligence are,

- Objective One: To engineer artefacts capable of performing tasks which, if performed by a human, would be said to demand intelligence, and

- Objective Two: To arrive at a scientific understanding of the principles underlying intelligent behaviour, as manifest in humans, in animals, and especially in the products of AI's first objective.

How should we measure progress in achieving these two objectives? Let's consider a couple of examples. Suppose I could purchase a robot, unpack it in my kitchen, and then watch as it successfully completed the task of making me a cup of tea. An important attribute of this imagined robot is that it wouldn't be equipped with any inbuilt capacity for dealing with my kitchen's peculiar features. It would be equally capable of making a cup of tea in my neighbour's kitchen, which is fitted out very differently from mine and which contains its own distinctive collection of tools and utensils.

This would be evidence of splendid progress towards Objective One. Such a robot is far beyond the capabilities of present day technology. While we know how to build robots that can perform certain tasks in very carefully designed environments, we still have little idea how to endow a machine with enough common sense to cope with an environment as unfamiliar and idiosyncratic as the average kitchen. Most adult humans, on the other hand, though they might have difficulty matching a computer's ability to simulate weather patterns or calculate the trajectory of a satellite, would have little difficulty making me a cup of tea in my kitchen, given the requisite cultural background.

Here's another example. Suppose that when I arrived at my desk in the morning I could hold a conversation, by voice or via the keyboard, with a program that scanned the daily newspapers (assuming these are available on-line). I could ask this imaginary program about the week's events and receive intelligible, accurate, and useful replies, in a natural language such as English. This too would be evidence of remarkable progress towards Objective One. While we have some idea how to write programs that can process natural language in a limited way, and while some attempts have been made to formalise and encode the large amounts of common sense knowledge that seem to go into the interpretation of the written and spoken word, we are still very far from being able to construct a program which would come as close to passing the Turing test as this hypothetical system.

Objective One is the vision that drives most AI work forwards. But we needn't try to pin it down any more precisely here, because the frame problem only arises when we take Objective Two seriously.

Objective Two, that of arriving at a scientific understanding of the principles underlying intelligent behaviour, might turn out to be even more elusive than Objective One. For example, it may turn out that, while we can engineer intelligent artefacts in a highly principled way and give a clear and precise account of how and why they work, no such account is forthcoming for messy biological products, such as human beings. Worse than this, it may turn out that even engineered intelligent artefacts have to be cobbled together in an unprincipled way, and we may be unable to explain even their workings in any detail. This would be an unfortunate outcome, because only systems whose design is based on sound, well understood principles can be easily validated, maintained, and modified.

But the hope of most researchers in AI is that a principled understanding of intelligent behaviour, at least in so far as that behaviour is the product of good engineering, is indeed possible. And a commonly held belief among these researchers is that this understanding will appeal to the idea of symbolic representation. The best way to account for intelligent behaviour, so the argument goes, is to interpret it as the product of *correct reasoning* on *correct representation*.[3] Furthermore, since intelligent behaviour involves performing actions in or reasoning about a changing world, such as the environment of my kitchen or the world of current affairs, these representations will be largely concerned with actions and events and their effects.

Now the question arises of how we should understand the notions of correct representation and correct reasoning. Since we're in the business of finding fundamental principles, we should expect an account of these concepts that's rigorous and scientific. This is where the frame problem comes in. The best, indeed the only real candidate we have for explicating the concepts of correct representation and correct reasoning, is formal logic. Therefore, since actions and events feature so prominently in our representations, we need to understand how to represent actions and events and their the effects in formal logic. This leads inevitably to the frame problem, as we'll see in Chapter 1.

To recap, the argument rests on the following two main premises, both of which are controversial.

- The best way to understand intelligent behaviour is as the product of correct reasoning on correct representation.

- The best way to explicate the notions of correct representation and correct reasoning is through formal logic.

Many AI researchers who would accept the first of these premises would reject the second. Some AI researchers would reject both. Let me review some of the arguments put forward in this debate.

2 The Role of Representation in Artificial Intelligence

For much of its brief history, the field of artificial intelligence has been dominated by one idea: that of representation. What exactly does it mean to attempt the design of an intelligent artefact based on the idea of representation?

To begin with, as suggested by my choice of examples in the last section, it's useful to distinguish two kinds of artefacts that AI research can produce: disembodied problem solving or natural language systems whose only interaction with the world is through their human operators, and robots that interact directly with their physical environment.[4] What it means for the design of a disembodied problem solving or natural language system to be based on the idea of representation is different from what that means for the design of a robot. Let's consider the role of representation in the design of disembodied systems first.

Let me attempt to clarify what is meant by correct reasoning and correct representation in such a system with an example. Imagine a program which is supposed to store knowledge about a given subject, and answer queries based on that knowledge. Suppose knowledge is represented by the program as a collection of formulae of predicate calculus. For example, suppose the program's collection includes the following two formulae.

$$\text{Mortal}(x) \leftarrow \text{Human}(x)$$

$$\text{Human}(\text{Socrates})$$

The language of predicate calculus is formally defined in such a way that we can easily imagine a variety of ways of encoding such sentences and recording them in the memory of a computer. As a sequence of bits stored in the computer's memory, of course, the encoded version of these sentences is no different from any other sequence of bits. What makes it a representation is the interpretation imposed on it by the program's designer.

There are two levels of interpretation in this particular case. First, the designer interprets particular sequences of bits as predicate calculus formulae. Then the designer interprets these formulae as representing knowledge.

In this particular case, suppose the designer imposes the following interpretation on the predicate calculus formulae encoded in the program.

- The symbol "Socrates" stands for Socrates, the philosopher.

- The formula "Mortal(α)" denotes the fact that α is mortal.

- The formula "$\rho 1(x) \leftarrow \rho 2(x)$" denotes the fact that, for any α, whenever $\rho 2(\alpha)$ is true, $\rho 1(\alpha)$ is also true.

Now we can answer with precision the question of what it means for the program's representations to be correct. The program's representations are correct if, wherever they include a sequence of bits that the designer interprets as representing a given fact, that fact is true. In other words, in this example, the program's representations are correct if Socrates is indeed human, and if indeed all humans are mortal.[5]

We're also in a position to answer the question of what it means for the program to perform correct reasoning. The program's reasoning is correct if it manipulates its representations in a way that preserves their correctness. To clarify this answer, let's continue with the example.

Imagine that a query to our hypothetical AI program is also represented as a predicate calculus formula. In order to answer a query, the program applies *modus ponens* to every pair of formulae in its collection to which *modus ponens* can be applied, and repeats this process until it either finds the formula question, in which case it answers "YES" or until it cannot add any more new formulae, in which case it answers "NO". In other words, it executes the following algorithm, given a query Q and a collection of predicate calculus formulae S.

Y := FALSE; N := FALSE
Repeat
    Find any two formulae in S of the form $\rho 1(x) \leftarrow \rho 2(x)$ and $\rho 2(\alpha)$
        such that $\rho 2(\alpha)$ is not in S
    If no two such formulae exist **Then** N := TRUE
    Else If Q is $\rho 1(\alpha)$ **Then** Y := TRUE
    Else add $\rho 1(\alpha)$ to S
Until Y or N
If Y Then Write("YES")
Else Write("NO")

Given the formulae in the current example and the query Mortal(Socrates), the algorithm terminates after two iterations with the answer "YES". Given the query Mortal(Fred), it terminates with the answer "NO". The final step in constructing an account of a program's working success is to interpret its output. In this case, we interpret a "YES" answer as the assertion that the formula in the query does follow from the program's knowledge, and a "NO" answer as the assertion that it doesn't.

Since *modus ponens* is a valid rule of inference, its computational analogue in the above algorithm does indeed preserve the correctness of the program's representations. To summarise, the program functions as intended, giving right answers to queries, and it does so because it performs correct reasoning on correct representation.

Of course, this example is extraordinarily simple and clean. Few real AI programs reflect such puritan design values. Even in those that do, implementation details may hide the design. But however complex a program is, whether or not its reasoning is deductive, whether or not logic is its representational formalism, if its working success can be accounted for in terms similar to those above, then its design is vindicated on scientific and engineering grounds.

3 The Limits of the Representational Approach

The argument of the last section leaves open a crucial question. What are the limits of what can be accomplished through design based on representation? The claim was simply that such design offers the possibility of a rigorous account of the success of a program. The question of these limits leads naturally into a discussion of Newell and Simon's *physical symbol system hypothesis* [Newell & Simon, 1976]. This in turn will lead on to a discussion of the role of representation in robotics.

In their 1976 Turing Award address, Newell and Simon advanced the following hypothesis.

> *The Physical Symbol System Hypothesis.* A physical symbol system has the necessary and sufficient means for general intelligent action. [Newell & Simon, 1976, p. 116]

Despite strenuous efforts to define what they mean by a physical symbol system, Newell and Simon fail to make this concept entirely clear in their paper. Equating symbols (or structures of symbols) with representations, I will take it to mean a system whose working success (or otherwise) is accountable for in terms of the correctness of its representations and the correctness of its reasoning, in the style of the example of the last section.

The hypothesis has two parts. It claims both necessity and sufficiency. Let me begin by commenting on the first part of the hypothesis, namely the claim that a physical symbol system has the necessary means for intelligent action.[6] This is a very strong claim. Reformulated, it means that all intelligent action is generated by physical symbol systems. So humans and animals, to the extent that they're capable of intelligent action, are physical symbol systems.

This claim is fraught with difficulties. To begin with, it's not clear to what extent it's possible to isolate a component of human activity that can usefully be interpreted as intelligent action. Furthermore, in the absence of a designer to explain the workings of the biological brain, the verification of the claim in the case of humans and animals might demand a feat of reverse engineering which is beyond our capabilities. Perhaps a scientific understanding of the principles underlying intelligent behaviour is realistically attainable only for AI's own products.

For present purposes, it's the sufficiency claim which is of most interest, anyway. The sufficiency claim begs the question mooted at the beginning of this section, namely what are the limits of what can be achieved through design based on representation. Several authors have argued that the limits are quite narrow, disappointingly so for AI researchers who take the representational approach.

One example of such an argument is to be found in Fodor's monograph *The Modularity of Mind* [1983]. While Fodor's main target is the computational approach to cognitive science, his argument is equally potent when applied to the question of the limits of what can be engineered based on representation. The argument rests on an architectural assumption of modularity. In particular, Fodor distinguishes *input systems* from *central systems*.

> Input systems function to get information into the central processors;
> specifically, they mediate between transducer outputs and central
> cognitive mechanisms by encoding the mental representations which
> provide domains for the operations of the latter. [Fodor, 1983, p. 42]

> Central systems look at what the input systems deliver, and they look
> at what is in memory, and they use this information to constrain the
> computation of "best hypotheses" about what the world is like.
> [Fodor, 1983, p. 104]

It's worth noting here that a disembodied problem solver or natural language
system often comprises nothing but central systems, in Fodor's terms. Input
systems are concerned with perception. Disembodied systems aren't required to
perceive the world directly at all. Instead, the human operator can supply
information directly to the machine.

According to Fodor's argument, central systems have a dangerous property,
which renders them insusceptible to theoretical understanding.

> . . . there seems to be no way to delimit the sorts of informational
> resources which may affect, or be affected by, central processes of
> problem solving. [Fodor, 1983, p. 112]

To put it another way, there are no constraints on what facts might be relevant
to the computation of "best hypotheses about what the world is like".[7] In
engineering terms, this makes it hard to imagine an efficient computational
mechanism for implementing central systems, if that mechanism's design has to
be based on the manipulation of representations. This makes it difficult to
conceive of a central system as a physical symbol system at all (even though the
relationship between its input and output may be described by a computable
function). This in turn suggests that the representational approach to designing an
artefact that exhibits intelligent behaviour may be the wrong one. Perhaps
intelligence simply shouldn't be thought of in terms of representation.

I'm not going to offer a reply to this argument, because it rests on an
empirical assumption. Perhaps we can, after all, design an efficient
computational mechanism, based on the idea of manipulating representations,
that doesn't limit the information brought to bear on a particular reasoning
process to such an extent that intelligent behaviour becomes impossible. If the
issue is be purely one of efficiency, then we can employ a battery of computing
techniques, such as indexing and parallel processing, to help us. Only further
research can resolve the issue.

4 The Role of Representation in Robotics

Similarly, only further research can settle the debate begun by Brooks [1991a], [1991b], who argues that the conceptual tools of traditional artificial intelligence research, such as knowledge representation, planning, and problem solving, "cannot account for large aspects of what goes into intelligence". Instead, Brooks advocates an approach in which "there is no central model maintained of the world" and "there is no central locus of control" [Brooks, 1991b].

The basis of Brooks's argument is a powerful critique of traditional AI. The rot set in, according to Brooks, right from the start, at the Dartmouth conference in 1956, where,

> . . . there was a general acceptance of the use of search to solve problems, and with this there was an essential abandonment of any notion of situatedness. [Brooks, 1991b, p. 574]

Situated systems, on the other hand,

> . . . do not deal with abstract descriptions, but with the here and now of the world directly influencing the behavior of the system. [Brooks, 1991b, p. 571]

The field of artificial intelligence has carried the legacy of its original "abandonment of any notion of situatedness" ever since.

> Traditional artificial intelligence has adopted a style of research where the agents that are built to test theories of intelligence are essentially problem solvers that work in a symbolic abstract domain. [Brooks, 1991b, p. 583]

While Brooks fails to acknowledge that problem solvers working in symbolic abstract domains might be of independent interest, the main criticism he levels at traditional AI is valid. Foundational work in artificial intelligence carries on as if it will one day be applicable to the construction of situated, embodied systems. Yet this assumption of applicability is rarely tested.

A research programme that relies on untested assumptions and that is willing to forego the need for empirical validation is destined to fall into self-perpetuating pointlessness. According to Brooks, signs of a total collapse into decadence are to be found in the field of knowledge representation.

> [The field of knowledge representation] concentrates much of its energies on anomalies within formal systems which are never used for any practical task. [Brooks, 1991b, p. 578]

Since this book concentrates entirely on anomalies within formal systems, this remark deserves some comment. The study of these formal systems can be justified in at least three ways. First, as has already been pointed out, disembodied problem solvers working in symbolic domains are of independent interest, and to the extent that the formal systems in question relate to the representations used in such problem solvers, they are worthy of investigation. Second, if logic has any value as a discipline at all, then the formal systems themselves are of independent interest. Third, and most importantly, it's not yet clear that robots cannot be built whose design is based on the idea of correct reasoning on correct representation. If such design is possible, foundational work in knowledge representation will have fulfilled its original purpose.

But is such design possible? One of the purest example of mobile robot design based on the principles of correct reasoning and correct representation was the Shakey project carried out at SRI in the late Sixties and early Seventies [Nilsson, 1984]. Shakey was a wheeled robot that operated in a specially constructed static environment comprising uniformly painted, geometrically regular blocks. Using off-board computing facilities, it employed edge detection techniques to process the images received from an on-board video camera, in order to construct a logic-based representation of its environment. This information was in turn processed by the STRIPS planning program [Fikes & Nilsson, 1971], which searched for sequences of actions the robot could perform to achieve a given goal, such as to construct a stack of blocks.

Using Shakey as an example, we can address the question of what it means for the design of a robot to appeal to the ideas of correct representation and correct reasoning. In part, the story is the same as for disembodied systems. It's clear that we can encode formulae of predicate calculus and store them in the memory of a computer to be used by the program that controls the robot. In the case of a robot like Shakey, a collection of such formulae will be used to represent the current state of the environment. For example, suppose the following formulae are part of the representation of the current state.

At(Block1,5,5)

At(Robot,10,10)

As in the disembodied state, the designer interprets such sentences as representing knowledge. For Shakey, this knowledge concerns the current state of the robot's environment, which we'll assume to be a flat plane (on which a suitable co-ordinate system has been overlaid), containing a number of blocks, each with a unique colour. Here's a possible interpretation.

- The symbol "Block1" stands for the red block.

- The symbol "Robot" stands for the robot.

- The formula "At(w,x,y)" denotes the fact that w is located at co-ordinates $\langle x,y \rangle$.

Defining what it means for a representation to be correct is straightforward, and echoes the definition for the disembodied case. The representations employed by the program controlling the robot are correct if, wherever they include a sequence of bits which the designer interprets as representing a given fact, that fact is true. In other words, for the present example, the robot's representation is correct if the red block is indeed at co-ordinates $\langle 5,5 \rangle$, and the robot is indeed at co-ordinates $\langle 10,10 \rangle$.

What does it mean for the program controlling the robot to perform correct reasoning? Suppose that, as well as a representation of the current state of the robot's environment, the program keeps a record of its current goal, which is represented as another predicate calculus formula ϕ. Furthermore, suppose that alongside a collection of formulae representing the current state of the robot's environment, the program includes a collection of formulae representing the effects of actions. Let Σ be the combination of these two collections of formulae.

Now suppose the program executes an algorithm that searches for a collection of formulae Δ describing a sequence of actions such that ϕ logically follows from the combination of Σ and Δ. Having found such a sequence, the program carries it out, by sending appropriate instructions to the robot's motors and actuators. Since these actions are determined by the application of an algorithm that is provably correct, the robot's behaviour can be said to be the product of correct reasoning.

For example, ϕ could represent the goal that the robot is holding the red block. Σ could include formulae representing the fact that picking up a block w results in the robot holding w, so long as the robot is in the same location as w, and the fact that moving to a location $\langle x,y \rangle$ results in the robot being at the location $\langle x,y \rangle$. Then Δ could be the sequence of actions: move to $\langle 5,5 \rangle$, then pick up Block1.

Give or take a few details, this description fits Shakey fairly well. All we need to complete the story is an account of how the instruction to execute an action as inherently complicated as "move to location $\langle x,y \rangle$" is translated into actual wheel movements, and an account of how digitised images from a video camera are translated into formulae as inherently complicated as "At(Block1,$\langle 5,5 \rangle$)". This is where we run into difficulty. Because while such an account is possible for Shakey, it's not clear that such an account will be possible in general.

Shakey is proof that robotic design based on the principle of correct reasoning on correct representation is possible. However, although the Shakey project was very successful in its own terms, it's frequently criticised on the grounds that its methodology doesn't carry over to the construction of robots that have to operate in less controlled environments. As Brooks puts it,

> [Shakey] only worked because of very careful engineering of the environment. . . . The objective reality of the environment was quite simple, and the mapping to an internal model of that reality was also quite plausible. [Brooks, 1991b, p. 577]

Even though later work relaxed the requirement, adopted by Shakey's designers, for representation to be based on logic the approach to representation exemplified by work on the Shakey project pervades the whole field of artificial intelligence, according to Brooks.

> Over the years within traditional artificial intelligence, it has become accepted that [agents which operate in the world] will need an objective model of the world with individuated entities, tracked and identified over time — the models of knowledge representation that have been developed expect and require such a one-to-one correspondence between the world and the agent's representation of it. [Brooks, 1991b, p. 583]

The last two quotes from Brooks's paper mark the limits of his critique. They both beg questions that require further research to answer.

- Can the ideal of robot design based on correct reasoning and correct representation be applied to robots that work in realistic environments? artificial intelligence has only had twenty five years to address this question. Perhaps it will require another twenty five. Perhaps it will take another century.

- To what extent does design based on correct reasoning and correct representation have to mimic the architecture of Shakey? There's no reason why it has to entail "a one-to-one correspondence between the world and the agent's representation of it". Indeed, much work in knowledge representation concerns incomplete and partial information.

To address these questions, artificial intelligence researchers who base their work on representation need to take up the gauntlet thrown down by their critics, and close the gap that's opened up between theory and practice. (See the Cognitive Robotics work described in [Lespérance, *et al.*, 1994] and [Shanahan, 1996a]). Perhaps this will involve architectures that differ radically from Shakey's, but that nevertheless employ representation at their core in a way which is susceptible to kind of theoretical analysis that the field of knowledge representation advocates.

5   The Role of Logic in Knowledge Representation

Even if we accept that intelligent behaviour is best understood as the product of correct reasoning on correct representation, we might call into question the significance of formal logic to this principle. Indeed, researchers have been calling its significance into question ever since it was first proposed as medium for knowledge representation in the Fifties [McCarthy, 1959].

The argument for the fundamental importance of logic in knowledge representation is very simple, and its two steps are summed up in the following two quotations from papers by Pat Hayes.

> One of the first tasks which faces a theory of representation is to give some account of what a representation or representational language means. Without such an account, comparisons between representations or languages can only be very superficial. Logical model theory provides such an analysis. [Hayes, 1977, p. 559]

> . . . virtually all known representational schemes are equivalent to first-order logic (with one or two notable exceptions, primarily to do with non-monotonic reasoning). [Hayes, 1985a, p. 4]

As pointed out by Moore [1982], the overall claim of such an argument is weaker than the claim that the language of formal logic itself should be used as a representational formalism in AI programs. The claim is simply that the underlying meaning of any representational scheme is supplied by logical model theory. The closer the actual representational formalism is to the language of logic, of course, the easier it is to uncover this meaning. In practice though, for many reasons, the actual formalism used in a program may not be close to logic at all.

Hayes himself presents powerful arguments supporting the reducibility to logic claim in certain cases [Hayes, 1977]. The justification (reminiscent of Kant) for the claim that all *possible* representation schemes are reducible in this way is that,

- In so far as the world is comprehensible at all, it must be composed of objects standing in various relations to one another, and these fundamental components (objects and relations) correspond the fundamental components of the language of formal logic, and

- Facts concerning the relations in which individuals stand to each other can only be combined in a fixed number of ways, corresponding to the connectives of formal logic.

In other words, there's only one serious objection to the whole argument, which is also nicely summarised by Hayes.

> One might argue that [the account of meaning given by model theory] is mistaken. Perhaps the real world isn't like that, does not consist of individuals with relations between them. [Hayes, 1977, p. 560]

To be pedantic here, the question is not what the real world is actually like, but rather how it is talked about by the builders of AI programs and robots whose designs are based on representation. So, to paraphrase the point, perhaps it isn't appropriate, for the purposes of designing representations, to talk about the real world as if it consists of individuals with relations between them. No conclusive argument to this effect has yet been put forward, although *analogical representations* [Gardin & Meltzer, 1989] potentially offer an alternative foundation to that on which logical representation is based.[8]

Despite the clarity of the argument for the importance of logic to knowledge representation, it has been necessary for a major figure in the field to publish a paper every few years advancing essentially the same argument, albeit from a different angle [Hayes, 1977], [Moore, 1982], [Nilsson, 1991]. Part of the reason for this is a widespread misunderstanding of the so-called "logicist" approach to AI, according to which logicists subscribe to one or more articles of doctrine. In particular, according to the caricature,

- Logicists believe that all reasoning is deduction,

- Logicists want to formalise all the common sense knowledge required for intelligent behaviour before they write any programs, and

- Logicists use model theory to explicate the concept of belief.

All of these views have been identified with the logicist approach to AI. For example, the first two doctrines are presented as basic tenets of logicism by repentant logicist Drew McDermott [1987b] (before he criticises them in the same paper). Birnbaum [1991] attributes the third view to the logicist position and bases many of his criticisms on this.

The basic argument for the importance of logic in knowledge representation — that an account is required of the meaning of our representations, and that all (or most) representational formalisms reduce to logic — doesn't depend in any way on these three articles of doctrine. However, the accusation that advocates of logic believe all reasoning to be deduction is pertinent here, as I want to conclude this discussion with some remarks about the relevance of model theory to the notions of correct reasoning and correct representation.

It's clear that model theory, by giving a formal account of the meaning of a representation, also provides a foundation for deciding when a representation is correct (as illustrated in the examples of Sections 2 and 4). What is less clear, however, is the role of logic and model theory in supplying a formal account of the correctness of reasoning. A commitment to the use of logic and model theory in such an account suggests an associated commitment to the view that all reasoning is deduction.

As Quine puts it, "predicate logic markedly expedites the business of settling what follows from what and what does not" [Quine, 1987]. In any given logic, what follows from what is described by that logic's consequence relation. Defining a logic's consequence relation is one of the chief purposes of model theory. As such, model theory underpins deductive reasoning, and has nothing to say on the subject of non-deductive forms of inference, such as abduction, induction, or analogical reasoning.

So it would seem that model theory has only limited use in supplying a formal account of correct reasoning. Many examples of correct inferences, in the sense that they lead to rational action, are non-deductive. In their reply to [McDermott, 1987b], McCarthy and Lifschitz argue that "the question is not which inferences are deduction, but which inferences can be usefully carried out by deduction" [McCarthy & Lifschitz, 1987]. But I want to take a different tack, which is to claim that deductive inference underpins many forms of non-deductive inference. According to this view, the point is not to augment a collection of axioms or modify a logic in order to transform non-deductive inference into deductive inference, but rather to change the way the logic is used.

This perspective has been taken, explicitly or implicitly, by many researchers. To name just a few examples, Davies and Russell [1987] give a logic-based account of analogical reasoning along these lines, Poole [1988] presents default reasoning in similar terms,[9] temporal explanation is treated this way in [Shanahan, 1989], and Muggleton [1991] takes a logic-based approach to inductive learning. In each case, the deductive consequence relation plays a central role in the precise specification of the form of non-deductive reasoning in question, although in each case the specification contains plenty of additional information pertaining to how that consequence relation is deployed.[10]

Let me illustrate the principle of changing the way the logic is used rather than changing the logic, using temporal explanation (reasoning from effects to causes) as an example. Given a background theory Σ and a collection Γ of observations to explain, an abductive approach would seek an explanation for Γ in the form of a consistent collection Δ of hypotheses such that Γ is a logical consequence of the combination of Σ and Δ. In order to be a realistic specification for this form of abductive inference, however, further constraints have to be placed on the form of Δ. For example, Δ might be constrained to mention only certain predicates, and to be minimal in some sense with respect to other potential explanations.

So, to summarise, the argument for logic has three main steps.

- We need to supply an account of what the representations used in AI programs mean. In logic, model theory provides the basis for such an account.

- Almost all representational formalisms are equivalent to first-order logic.

- A model-theoretic account of the meaning of a representational formalism pins down the notion of correct representation for that formalism. It can also play a central role in pinning down the notion of correct reasoning, even if that reasoning is non-deductive.

If we accept this argument, we are lead naturally to consider the question of how the effects of actions and events are to be represented in logic. Then we are only a short step from encountering the frame problem.

Notes

1. See, for example, [Genesereth & Nilsson, 1987] or [Winston, 1992].
2. I'll leave pedantic discussion of the exact meaning of terms like "intelligence" to others. Most human endeavours proceed happily without precise definitions of their aims, and there's no reason why AI research should be an exception.
3. Getting back to Objective One, it can also be argued that the *most* intelligent behaviour will be the product of correct reasoning on correct representation. Or,

to put it another way, "The most versatile intelligent machines will represent much of their knowledge declaratively" [Nilsson, 1991].

4. We can imagine other kinds of intelligent artefact, as well.

5. This exercise is clearly influenced by Tarski-style model theory, which I will later argue for as a basis for all such accounts of the correctness of a representation.

6. I'll drop the word "general" from now on, and assume a degree of robustness and versatility to be inherent in the idea of intelligence.

7. Fodor goes on to cite the frame problem as a symptom of this difficulty. However, he takes the term to mean something different from what I take it to mean (see Section 1.12).

8. I can see no reason why analogical and logical representation schemes shouldn't both contribute to the design of a system, however.

9. McCarthy's circumscription can also be thought of as an example of the approach I'm advocating.

10. McDermott [1987b] attacks this methodology, but like many of the respondents to that paper, I find his arguments unconvincing. I see no point in rehearsing the arguments here.

Solving the Frame Problem

1 What Is the Frame Problem?

This chapter presents an informal overview of the frame problem: what it is, the various ways in which it might be tackled, and the criteria for a good solution. Along the way, the situation calculus is introduced, which is one of the two main formalisms for reasoning about change that will be used in this book, the other being the event calculus. Also, because it underlies one of the major approaches to the frame problem, the basic idea of a non-monotonic formalism for default reasoning is presented. More formal treatment of these topics is postponed for later chapters. At the end of the chapter, I briefly touch on the perspective various philosophers have brought to bear on the frame problem.

1.1 Describing the Non-Effects of Actions

The frame problem, first described by McCarthy and Hayes [1969],[1] arises when we attempt to describe the effects of actions or events using logic.[2] In a nutshell, the problem is this. If we write our description using classical logic, as well as describing what changes when a particular kind of action is performed or a particular kind of event occurs, we also have to describe what does *not* change. Otherwise, we find that we cannot use the description to draw any useful conclusions. For example, if our description includes the fact that painting the walls of my office changes their colour, we also have to include facts such as the following.

- Painting the walls does not alter their shape.

- Painting the walls does not change my hairstyle.

- Painting the walls does not precipitate a General Election.

- Painting the walls does not make the Sun rise.

It's clear that this list could go on indefinitely. Indeed, it turns out that when we use the straightforward apparatus of classical first-order logic in the most obvious way to describe the effects of actions, the description of what does not change is considerably larger than the description of what does change. Yet facts about what does not change like those above are usually a matter of common sense. Surely when we describe the effects of actions, we should be able to concentrate on what changes, and be able to take what does not change for granted. The frame problem is the problem of constructing a formal framework that enables us to do just this.[3]

1.2 Introducing the Situation Calculus

To see the problem more clearly, let's study an example expressed in the situation calculus, which is one of the oldest and best-known formalisms for representing the effects of action in artificial intelligence. The situation calculus, first described in 1963 by John McCarthy in an unpublished memo [McCarthy, 1963], which was later incorporated in [McCarthy & Hayes, 1969], will feature prominently in this book, and later I will present it more formally and in more depth. But for now, we only need to know the basics. The situation calculus ontology includes *situations*, which can be thought of as snapshots of the world, *fluents*, which take on different values in different situations and can be thought of as time-varying properties, and *actions*, which change the values of fluents.

In addition, the language of the situation calculus includes a predicate symbol Holds and a function symbol Result. We write Holds(f,s) to denote that fluent f is true in situation s, and we write Result(a,s) to denote the situation that obtains when action of type a is preformed in situation s.[4] Now we can write formulae to describe the effects of actions. The example domain[5] I will use here is the Blocks World, which inspired much early work on planning in AI, and which is often used to introduce the frame problem. The Blocks World comprises a number of stackable cube-shaped blocks on a table. The task is to describe the effects of moving these blocks from one place to another.

To do this, we introduce two fluents. We write On(x,y) to denote that block x is on y, where y is either another block or the table. And we write Clear(x) to denote that there's room for a block on top of x, where x is either a block or the table. (The table is always "clear", in this sense.) Figure 1.1 shows an example situation, which will be denoted S0.

This is how S0 is represented.

Holds(On(C,Table),S0)

Holds(On(B,C),S0)

Holds(On(A,B),S0)

Holds(On(D,Table),S0)

Holds(Clear(A),S0)

Holds(Clear(D),S0)

Holds(Clear(Table),S0)

Let the conjunction of these formulae be denoted Σ.[6] Notice that this is not a complete description of the situation depicted in Figure 1.1, because only positive information has been included. These formulae, so long as they are interpreted as formulae of classical logic, don't allow us to draw any conclusions of the form $\neg$ Holds(On(x,y),S0) or $\neg$ Holds(Clear(x),S0). But we wouldn't have any use for negative conclusions like this in the present example anyway. The frame problem concerns something else, as we will see shortly.

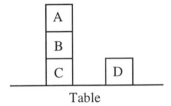

Table

Figure 1.1: A Blocks World Configuration

A single action type Move is introduced next. We write Move(x,y) to denote the action (type)[7] of moving block x to y. So Result(Move(A,D),S0) is the situation that comes about when block A is moved onto block D in situation S0, shown in Figure 1.2.

Now we have to write formulae that capture the effect of Move actions on the fluents On and Clear. These formulae, which are called *effect axioms*, should enable us, for example, to predict the outcome of a sequence of actions. They will have to take into account the *preconditions* of a Move action, that is to say the fluents that have to hold when an action is performed for it to be successful. For example, to move block x onto block y, both x and y have to be clear.

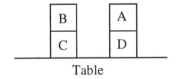

Table

Figure 1.2: Another Blocks World Configuration

Holds(On(x,y),Result(Move(x,y),s)) ← Holds(Clear(x),s) ∧
Holds(Clear(y),s) ∧ x≠y ∧ x≠Table

Holds(Clear(z),Result(Move(x,y),s)) ← Holds(Clear(x),s) ∧
Holds(Clear(y),s) ∧ Holds(On(x,z),s) ∧ y≠z ∧ x≠y

Let the conjunction of these formulae be denoted Δ. Again, these two axioms only take into account positive information, which is all we need for now, to see how the frame problem arises. Let's consider the result of moving A to D in S0. Taken together, Δ and Σ entail many of the conclusions we would expect. For example, we have,

$$\Delta \wedge \Sigma \vDash \text{Holds(On(A,D),Result(Move(A,D),S0))}$$

$$\Delta \wedge \Sigma \vDash \text{Holds(Clear(B),Result(Move(A,D),S0))}.$$

1.3 Frame Axioms

Although many of the conclusions we would expect are present in the logical consequences of Δ ∧ Σ, many conclusions we would like to be able to draw are absent. For example, although B is on C in S0, and moving A to D doesn't change this fact, we do *not* have,

$$\Delta \wedge \Sigma \vDash \text{Holds(On(B,C),Result(Move(A,D),S0))}$$

In other words, although we have captured what does change as the result of an action, we have failed to represent what *doesn't* change. We want to capture the *persistence* of fluents that are unaffected by an action. To do this, we have to add some *frame axioms*.

For example, for the On fluent, we need,

$$\text{Holds(On(v,w),Result(Move(x,y),s))} \leftarrow \text{Holds(On(v,w),s)} \wedge x{\neq}v$$

This frame axiom says that if v was on w before moving x onto y then it's still on w afterwards (so long as v isn't the block being moved). Now, with the addition of this formula to Δ , we can show Holds(On(B,C),Result(Move(A,D),S0)). We need a similar frame axiom for the Clear fluent.

$$\text{Holds(Clear(x),Result(Move(y,z),s))} \leftarrow \text{Holds(Clear(x),s)} \wedge x{\neq}z$$

So far this doesn't seem to be much of a problem. The need for the two frame axioms might be slightly surprising, and perhaps we would prefer not to have to make explicit such common sense facts, but they don't seem to be too much of a burden. Since logic demands their presence, we should feel comfortable about them. However, let's consider what happens if we add an extra action and an extra fluent to the Blocks World domain.

Let Colour(x,c) denote the fact that block x has colour c, and let Paint(x,c) denote the action of painting block x colour c. Painting is always successful, which is to say it has no preconditions. Now we have the following formula in addition to those in Δ.

$$\text{Holds(Colour(x,c),Result(Paint(x,c),s))}$$

Suppose the description of S0 is the same as in Σ, but all the blocks are red.

$$\text{Holds(Colour(x,Red),S0)}$$

Let Δ' and Σ' denote respectively the new domain description and the new description of S0. Moving a block doesn't affect its colour. But as we might now expect, without an extra frame axiom, we can't show,

$$\Delta' \wedge \Sigma' \vDash \text{Holds(Colour(A,Red),Result(Move(A,D),S0))}$$

We need a frame axiom that says that a block's colour persists through a move action, and one that says that a block's colour isn't affected by painting another block.

$$\text{Holds(Colour(x,c),Result(Move(y,z),s))} \leftarrow \text{Holds(Colour(x,c),s)}$$

$$\text{Holds(Colour(x,c1),Result(Paint(y,c2),s))} \leftarrow \text{Holds(Colour(x,c1),s)} \wedge x{\neq}y$$

Unfortunately, the addition of the Paint action forces us to add extra frame axioms for the other fluents, On and Clear.

$$\text{Holds(On(x,y),Result(Paint(z,c),s))} \leftarrow \text{Holds(On(x,y),s)}$$

$$\text{Holds(Clear(x),Result(Paint(y,c),s))} \leftarrow \text{Holds(Clear(x),s)}$$

Now we have a domain description that comprises nine formulae, six of which are frame axioms. In general, because most fluents are unaffected by most actions, every time we add a new fluent we are going to have to add roughly as many new frame axioms as there are actions in the domain, and every time we add a new action we are going to have to add roughly as many frame axioms as there are fluents in the domain. To put this point another way, the total number of frame axioms required for a domain of n fluents and m actions will be of the order of n × m.

1.4 Towards a Solution

This is the frame problem. How can we represent the effects of actions in a formal, logical way without having to write out all those frame axioms? There are many ways to respond to this question. I want to focus on four types of response.

- Who cares? When we can easily write a procedure that generates the right conclusions, why should we bother with descriptions in formal logic?

- Perhaps the problem is an artefact of the situation calculus. A different formalism might not require frame axioms at all.

- Perhaps the problem results, not so much from the underlying formalism, but more from the style of representation being used. Maybe we should look for a different way to express the same knowledge, without employing lots of frame axioms.

- Perhaps the problem is inherent in classical logic. Perhaps a non-monotonic logic will help.

I will consider each of these responses in turn. The first two will only occupy us for a few paragraphs each, but the second two will be the subject of the rest of the book. The first of the responses, which has planning programs like STRIPS [Fikes & Nilsson, 1971] in mind, has already been addressed in the introduction, but the following quote by Drew McDermott summarises my own position on this question.

> [Since 1970] no working AI program has ever been bothered at all by the frame problem. . . . The original frame problem is, in fact, of interest mainly to a fringe group, those who believe that logical analyses are relevant to building knowledge representations. [McDermott, 1987a]

A more radical version of the first response might reject the assumptions inherent in the phrases "generates the right conclusions" and "building knowledge representations". The behaviour-based approach to AI [Brooks, 1991a], [Brooks, 1991b] emphasises the construction of working artefacts whose behaviour is not the product of explicit reasoning about explicit representations. This perspective has also been discussed in the introduction, so I won't get into the issue again here.

Some authors have tried to distinguish a *logical* or *epistemological* aspect of the frame problem from a *computational* aspect [McDermott, 1987a], [Kowalski, 1992]. The computational aspect is to efficiently infer what is true in a situation without having to examine a large number of frame axioms. If we were to use a theorem prover to infer what is true in a given situation, as in the early work of Green [1969], this would indeed be a problem. But, at least for simple planning applications, as suggested by McDermott in the above quote, the STRIPS approach can be used: a situation is stored as a list of fluents, a list that can simply be added to and deleted from when actions are performed.

If logic programming is used for planning, whose philosophy is much closer to Green's theorem proving approach than to STRIPS, the computational aspect of the frame problem can still arise. When Kowalski and Sergot [1986] remark that their event calculus "was developed largely to overcome the frame problem", it is the computational aspect they have in mind. They suggest that "the explicit deduction" that "a relationship that holds in a situation and is not affected by an event continues to hold in the following situation" is "so computationally inefficient as to be intolerable". They purport to solve the problem "by qualifying relationships with time periods instead of with global situations".

This is all I have to say about the so-called computational aspect of the frame problem. The focus of this book is the logical aspect, in other words the original frame problem as described by McCarthy and Hayes [1969]. In what follows, some remarks about implementation techniques and algorithms for reasoning about change will be made. But I don't consider implementation issues to be directly related to the frame problem itself.

The approach suggested by the second response in the above list, namely to junk the situation calculus in favour of some other formalism, has been pursued by various authors. For example, Hayes [1985a], [1985b] introduces a formalism based on what he calls *histories*. He declares that "the frame problem as usually defined just doesn't crop up" with histories, because "there aren't any states or state-to-state functions in the language" [Hayes, 1987].

It's very difficult to construct a watertight argument against the view that the frame problem can be overcome by finding the right formalism for representing change. However, experience has shown that the frame problem arises in much the same guise whatever formalism is used. Yoav Shoham's book *Reasoning about Change: Time and Causality from the Standpoint of Artificial Intelligence* [1988] tackles the problem as it manifests itself in a variant of Allen's interval-based formalism [Allen, 1984]. In later chapters, we will see how it arises with the event calculus [Kowalski & Sergot, 1986]. And contrary to the impression given by Hayes's remarks, the frame problem arises with his histories formalism too. As pointed out by McDermott [1987b], Hayes inadvertently employs a form of default reasoning about the beginnings and endings of histories in his examples.

1.5 Making Frame Axioms More Compact

The third response in the list is more promising, and researchers have been pursuing alternative ways to represent change that don't require frame axioms ever since the frame problem's discovery (see the early work of Hayes [1971], [1973], for example).[8]

Perhaps we can find a more succinct way of expressing the information in the frame axioms, while remaining in the realm of classical, first-order logic, and without modifying the situation calculus significantly. To begin with, note that all frame axioms have a similar form, which is,

$$\text{Holds}(\beta,\text{Result}(\alpha,s)) \leftarrow \text{Holds}(\beta,s) \wedge \Pi$$

where β is a fluent, α is an action, and Π is a conjunction. So, instead of repeating this form over and again, we can use the following *universal frame axiom*.

$$\text{Holds}(f,\text{Result}(a,s)) \leftarrow \text{Holds}(f,s) \wedge \neg \, \text{Affects}(a,f,s)$$

Then, for every old style frame axiom, we have to write a negated atomic Affects formula. For the Blocks World example, including block painting, we have,

$$\neg \, \text{Affects}(\text{Move}(x,y),\text{On}(v,w),s) \leftarrow x \neq v$$

$$\neg \, \text{Affects}(\text{Paint}(z,c),\text{On}(x,y),s)$$

$$\neg \, \text{Affects}(\text{Move}(y,z),\text{Clear}(x),s) \leftarrow x \neq z$$

$$\neg \, \text{Affects}(\text{Paint}(y,c),\text{Clear}(x),s)$$

$$\neg \, \text{Affects}(\text{Move}(y,z),\text{Colour}(x,c),s)$$

$$\neg \, \text{Affects}(\text{Paint}(y,c2),\text{Colour}(x,c1),s) \leftarrow x \neq y.$$

With these frame axioms, we can draw exactly the same conclusions as before. But although each frame axiom has a slightly more compact form, the burden is the number of frame axioms, not their size. An enormous number of small axioms is almost as troublesome as an enormous number of slightly larger axioms. And we will still require of the order of $n \times m$ of these concise frame axioms to represent a domain of n fluents and m actions.

Once again, it is hard to avoid the feeling that these frame axioms are all a matter of common sense. We shouldn't have to say anything more than what does change, taking what does not for granted. For the Blocks World example, we might even be tempted to write just the following formulae,

$$\text{Affects}(\text{Move}(x,y),\text{On}(x,z),s)$$

$$\text{Affects}(\text{Move}(x,y),\text{Clear}(y),s)$$

$$\text{Affects}(\text{Paint}(x,c1),\text{Colour}(x,c2),s)$$

and expect the right results to follow.[9] But of course, from these formulae alone, we cannot draw any conclusions of the form $\neg$ Affects(a,f,s). So they will not allow us to conclude the persistence of fluents that we require. In fact, all formulae of the form Affects(a,f,s) which we would like to be true are already consequences of Σ plus the universal frame axiom. It's not positive Affects formulae we need to be able to infer, it's negative ones. However, if we employ an implication in place of the simple negation used in the set of six Affects formulae, we can indeed cut the number of formulae down to three. The resulting three formulae resemble the *completions* of the three above formulae.

$$\text{Affects}(a,\text{On}(x,z),s) \to a = \text{Move}(x,y)$$

$$\text{Affects}(a,\text{Clear}(x),s) \to a = \text{Move}(x,y)$$

$$\text{Affects}(a,\text{Colour}(x,c2),s) \to a = \text{Paint}(x,c1)$$

These three formulae are stronger than the previous six.[10] For example, as well as including the previous six negations among their logical consequences, they also entail,

$$\neg \text{Affects}(\alpha,\text{Colour}(x,c),s)$$

where α is any new action. However, they do permit us to draw the conclusions we want for the present example. Formulae of this kind were first introduced by Haas [1987], and are known as *explanation closure axioms*.[11] Explanation closure axioms are an effective substitute for frame axioms, and are much more succinct. They form the basis of a whole class of so-called monotonic solutions to the frame problem, which will be discussed in later chapters.

Unfortunately though, the frame problem will not succumb as easily to a solution using explanation closure axioms as the simple example used in this chapter suggests. A valid solution to the frame problem has to be applicable to a wide variety of representation problems. While explanation closure axioms form the basis of a potential solution, much work has to be done to see how they can be applied to complicated domains, as we will see.

1.6   Criteria for a Solution to the Frame Problem

This brings us to consider what the criteria are for an acceptable solution to the frame problem. This in turn will lead us to consider the approach suggested by the fourth and final response in the list, namely to move beyond classical logic with its monotonic consequence relation.

I will offer three criteria that a satisfactory solution to the frame problem should meet.

- Representational parsimony

- Expressive flexibility

- Elaboration tolerance

We have touched on each of these three themes already. But the main emphasis of the discussion so far has been on *representational parsimony*. This is the essence of the frame problem. The criterion of representational parsimony insists that a representation of the effects of actions should be compact. Without trying to quantify this compactness precisely, a reasonable guideline is that the size of the representation should be roughly proportional to the complexity of the domain, where a good indication of the complexity of the domain is the total number of actions plus the total number of fluents. Clearly the naive use of frame axioms violates this criterion, since it results in a representation roughly proportional to the product of the total number of actions and the total number of fluents.

The use of explanation closure axioms puts us on the path to a solution that meets the criterion of representational parsimony. But as hinted at the end of the last section, we need to work a little harder to be convinced that this approach will carry over to more complicated domains. That is to say, we have to see that the proposal meets the second criterion, that of *expressive flexibility*. What is meant by a more complicated domain here is not simply one with a larger number of fluents and actions, but rather one with features that demand a little extra thought before they can be represented. In particular, a domain may feature,

- Ramifications,

- Concurrent actions,

- Non-deterministic actions, and

- Continuous change.

An action will have *ramifications* beyond its immediate effects if we have to take into account *domain constraints*. A domain constraint (sometimes called a *state constraint*) is simply a constraint on what combinations of fluents may hold in the same situation. For example, suppose we say that three blocks constitute a stack if they are on top of each other, like A, B, and C in Figure 1.1. Let's introduce a new fluent Stack(x,y,z) to denote that blocks x, y, and z are a stack. We could write effect axioms for Stack like those previously written for On, Clear and Colour. But alternatively, we can represent Stack via a domain constraint, with the following formula.

$$\text{Holds(Stack}(x,y,z),s) \leftarrow x \neq \text{Table} \wedge \text{Holds(On}(y,x),s) \wedge \text{Holds(On}(z,y),s)$$

Notice that this formula makes no mention of the Result function. Rather, it describes a logical relationship that has to hold between fluents that are true in the same situation. The relationship here is a simple implication, but the possibility of arbitrarily complicated domain constraints makes the task of solving the frame problem much harder. It certainly offers a challenge to monotonic approaches based on explanation closure axioms. In later chapters, we will see how the approach rises to the challenge.

In the Blocks World examples considered so far, no two actions are ever performed at the same time. But *concurrent* or *simultaneous* actions and events are ubiquitous in everyday life. A real playpen full of wooden blocks can contain more than one real child, each with two hands, giving rise to the possibility of many blocks being moved at once.

For a long time, many authors took it for granted that the situation calculus was too ontologically impoverished to be able to represent concurrent action. The use of the Result function seems, at first sight, to preclude anything but a totally ordered sequence of actions. This fallacy was finally laid to rest by Gelfond, Lifschitz and Rabinov [1991] who showed how to extend the situation calculus to cope with concurrent action. Other formalisms, such as the event calculus, can readily represent concurrency. A good solution to the frame problem should not fall apart when simultaneous actions and events are introduced.

Another feature of complicated domains that can trouble a potential solution to the frame problem is the presence of *non-deterministic actions* or actions whose effects are not completely known. For example, when we toss a coin, we know it will come down either heads or tails, but we cannot say which. It is possible to distinguish various kinds of non-determinism, and a solution to the frame problem worthy of the name should be able to handle them all.

Finally, we have the issue of *continuous change*. Needless to say, continuous change is also ubiquitous in everyday life: speeding cars, scudding clouds, jostling people, rising temperatures, filling vessels. In the Situation calculus representations of the Blocks World given so far, all change is discrete. This doesn't mean that the change being represented is discrete, but rather that a representation that treats it as discrete is a convenient abstraction. However, often discreteness is not a convenient abstraction because the continuous variation of some quantity is the salient feature of the domain in question.

Continuous change is particularly hard to represent in the situation calculus, and this is one of the motivations for studying the event calculus, in which continuous change can be represented without too much difficulty. Later chapters will address this important issue in some depth. As with each of the tricky features of complicated domains discussed here, it would embarrassing if a proposed solution to the frame problem were unable to cope with continuous change.

1.7 Elaboration Tolerance

The final criterion in the list is *elaboration tolerance*, a term that is due to McCarthy [1988]. Put simply, a representation is elaboration tolerant to the extent that the effort required to add new information to the representation is proportional to the complexity of that information.[12] In particular, to augment a situation calculus theory with a new action that directly affects, say, n fluents, might require the addition of roughly n new sentences, but it should not necessitate the complete reconstruction of the old theory. Rather, facts about the effects of the new action should be gracefully absorbed into the old theory.[13]

Ideally elaboration tolerance would mean that a new sentence could be appended directly to the old theory to yield the new one. Appending a single sentence to a theory is the simplest possible modification of that theory.[14] Let's examine this idea in the context of the three explanation closure axioms for the Blocks World presented earlier. Here they are again.

$$\text{Affects}(a,\text{On}(x,z),s) \rightarrow a = \text{Move}(x,y)$$

$$\text{Affects}(a,\text{Clear}(x),s) \rightarrow a = \text{Move}(x,y)$$

$$\text{Affects}(a,\text{Colour}(x,c2),s) \rightarrow a = \text{Paint}(x,c1)$$

As mentioned before, these axioms are rather strong. For any new action α they entail, for example,

$$\neg \text{Affects}(\alpha,\text{Colour}(x,c),s).$$

To see that this can be a source of problems, we need to be a little less sloppy about negative information than we have been so far. Recall that the domain theories Δ and Δ', and the descriptions Σ and Σ' of S0 were not intended to yield conclusions of the form $\neg$ Holds(On(x,y),s) or $\neg$ Holds(Clear(x),s). And the same was true for the Colour fluent. From $\Delta' \wedge \Sigma'$, we couldn't draw any conclusions of the form $\neg$ Holds(Colour(x,c),s). Let's introduce a domain theory Δ'' and a new description Σ'' of S0 that, at least for the fluent Colour, take into account both positive and negative information. First we have Δ''. It's the same as Δ', but with one extra formula.

$$\text{Holds(On(x,y),Result(Move(x,y),s))} \leftarrow \text{Holds(Clear(x),s)} \wedge$$
$$\text{Holds(Clear(y),s)} \wedge x \neq y \wedge x \neq \text{Table}$$

$$\text{Holds(Clear(z),Result(Move(x,y),s))} \leftarrow \text{Holds(Clear(x),s)} \wedge$$
$$\text{Holds(Clear(y),s)} \wedge \text{Holds(On(x,z),s)} \wedge y \neq z \wedge x \neq y$$

$$\text{Holds(Colour(x,c),Result(Paint(x,c),s))}$$

$$\neg \text{Holds(Colour(x,c1),Result(Paint(x,c2),s))} \leftarrow c1 \neq c2$$

The new formula simply says that a block loses its old colour after being painted, unless of course it happens to be painted the same colour as before. The new description Σ'' of S0 is the same as Σ', except that it says that red is the only colour the blocks have in S0, something not made explicit before.[15]

$$\text{Holds(On(C,Table),S0)}$$

$$\text{Holds(On(B,C),S0)}$$

$$\text{Holds(On(A,B),S0)}$$

$$\text{Holds(On(D,Table),S0)}$$

$$\text{Holds(Clear(A),S0)}$$

$$\text{Holds(Clear(D),S0)}$$

$$\text{Holds(Clear(Table),S0)}$$

$$\text{Holds(Colour(x,c),S0)} \leftrightarrow c = \text{Red}$$

A better universal frame axiom is needed now, one that can cope with the persistence of negative as well as positive information. The new axiom simply says that a fluent has the same value (true or false) after an action as before it, unless that action affects that fluent.

$$[Holds(f,Result(a,s)) \leftrightarrow Holds(f,s)] \leftarrow \neg Affects(a,f,s) \qquad (F1)$$

With the same explanation closure axioms as before, we get the same consequences as before from this new theory, plus the extra ones we would expect of the form $\neg Holds(Colour(x,c),s)$.

Now, with elaboration tolerance in mind, let's see what happens when we extend this Blocks World theory. To augment the theory with a new action that affects the colour of blocks, such as Bleach(x) which makes a block white, it isn't enough just to append the following obvious effect axioms to the theory.

$$Holds(Colour(x,White),Result(Bleach(x),s))$$

$$\neg Holds(Colour(x,c),Result(Bleach(x),s)) \leftarrow c \neq White$$

This is a start. But, as usual, we also have to take care of fluents that don't change when a Bleach action takes place. Unfortunately, we can't do this just by appending a new explanation closure axiom to cater for the new action. There is now something wrong with the old explanation closure axioms. We now have, for example,

$$\neg Holds(Colour(A,White),S0).$$

And this means the new action is inconsistent with the existing explanation closure axioms, since they entail,

$$\neg Affects(Bleach(A),Colour(A,c),S0).$$

To see this, we just have to consider Result(Bleach(A),S0). The new effect axiom about Bleach tells us,

$$Holds(Colour(A,White),Result(Bleach(A),S0))$$

which, from (F1) and $\neg Holds(Colour(A,White),S0)$, yields,

$$Affects(Bleach(A),Colour(A,White),S0)$$

which is a contradiction.

So it's not enough simply to augment the old explanation closure axioms. They have to be taken apart and reconstructed. Note that, in the face of incomplete information about what can affect a fluent, the option of simply getting the explanation closure axioms right in the first place isn't available to us. To remain safely agnostic in the face of incomplete information isn't an option either, since agnosticism might lead to total inaction.

For the current example, the necessary reconstruction isn't difficult. We simply replace the old axiom,

$$\text{Affects}(a,\text{Colour}(x,c2),s) \rightarrow a = \text{Paint}(x,c1)$$

by the following new one.

$$\text{Affects}(a,\text{Colour}(x,c2),s) \rightarrow [a = \text{Paint}(x,c1) \lor a = \text{Bleach}(x)]$$

However, when the domain includes actions with ramifications, the task of reconstructing explanation closure axioms to take into account new actions and fluents becomes much harder, as we will see in later chapters. Recall that, ideally, we would like the task of updating a theory of action with facts about a new action or a new fluent to be a trivial matter of appending those facts to the existing theory.

1.8 Non-Monotonic Solutions

The goal of elaboration tolerance seems to be impossible to achieve if we remain in the realm of classical logic, with its monotonic consequence relation. A logic is *monotonic* if, for any conjunction of formulae Γ and any two formulae δ and ϕ, $\Gamma \vDash \phi$ implies $\Gamma \land \delta \vDash \phi$. In other words, a logic is monotonic if it guarantees that adding a new fact can never make an old consequence go away.

The monotonicity of classical logic presents us with a dilemma. On the one hand, as we have seen, so that we can infer the persistence of a fluent when it is not affected by an action, we need to be able to infer the *necessary* conditions under which that fluent is affected by an action. This is the reason for frame axioms or explanation closure axioms. On the other hand, we want to admit the possibility of actions or fluents we don't yet know about (or even unknown effects of known actions). In other words, we want to admit the possibility that we don't really know all the necessary conditions for a fluent to be affected by an action.

Yet the monotonicity of classical logic means that the necessary conditions that were inferred prior to our knowledge of a new action (or new fluent or new effect) will still be inferable whatever new formulae we append to the old theory, new formulae that in this case will concern a previously unknown opportunity for an action to affect a fluent. Elaboration tolerance demands that we simply append the new information to the old theory, but the monotonicity of classical logic guarantees that this will result in inconsistency.

Perhaps we will have to move to a non-monotonic logic. But if we relinquish the monotonicity of classical logic, what do we expect from our new consequence relation? Within artificial intelligence, the study of non-monotonic consequence relations and their applications is synonymous with the study of formal techniques for *default reasoning*. That is to say, it is the study of how we can formalise the process of jumping to conclusions that are reasonable in the absence of information to the contrary, but that are not strictly warranted by known facts. These conclusions are then only assumed to be true by *default*. They are *defeasible* conclusions. Later information may invalidate them without giving rise to inconsistency, hence the non-monotonicity.

How does this idea of default reasoning apply to the frame problem? Let's re-examine the troublesome axioms in our running example in the light of the preceding discussion. The original theory included the formulae,

$$Holds(Colour(x,c),Result(Paint(x,c),s))$$

$$\neg\, Holds(Colour(x,c1),Result(Paint(x,c2),s)) \leftarrow c1 \neq c2$$

$$Affects(a,Colour(x,c2),s) \rightarrow a = Paint(x,c1).$$

The addition of the Bleach action gave us the following formulae instead.

$$Holds(Colour(x,c),Result(Paint(x,c),s))$$

$$\neg\, Holds(Colour(x,c1),Result(Paint(x,c2),s)) \leftarrow c1 \neq c2$$

$$Holds(Colour(x,White),Result(Bleach(x),s))$$

$$\neg\, Holds(Colour(x,c),Result(Bleach(x),s)) \leftarrow c \neq White$$

$$Affects(a,Colour(x,c2),s) \rightarrow [a = Paint(x,c1) \vee a = Bleach(x)]$$

Note that the effect axioms are only added to. Learning about the Bleach action doesn't invalidate the effect axioms we already had. It's only the explanation closure axiom that has to be revised. We can think of the effect axioms as representing what we truly know, while the explanation closure axiom is just a *conjecture*. It isn't strictly warranted by what we know, but it's a reasonable conclusion to jump to in the absence of information to the contrary. In the face of incomplete information, an agent is forced to jump to conclusions if it's going to act at all.

Let's try to be a little more precise about what conclusions we want to adopt by default and when we want to adopt them. As previously pointed out, positive information about Affects is a consequence of the effect axioms and the universal frame axiom (F1). We have,

$$Affects(Paint(x,c1),Colour(x,c2),s) \leftarrow c1 \neq c2$$

$$Affects(Bleach(x),Colour(x,c),s) \leftarrow c \neq White$$

which is equivalent to,

$$\text{Affects(a,Colour(x,c2),s)} \leftarrow [a = \text{Paint(x,c1)} \wedge c1 \neq c2] \vee$$
$$[a = \text{Bleach(x)} \wedge c2 \neq \text{White}].$$

So we already know sufficient conditions for what affects Colour. All we really want to do now is to *assume that the sufficient conditions are also the necessary conditions*. In other words, we want to adopt the only-if complement of this implication, by default.

$$\text{Affects(a,Colour(x,c2),s)} \rightarrow [a = \text{Paint(x,c1)} \wedge c1 \neq c2] \vee$$
$$[a = \text{Bleach(x)} \wedge c2 \neq \text{White}]$$

It's easy to see that the explanation closure axiom follows from this. The extra strength of this formula is in fact illusory, because it only concerns actions that in fact have no effect: painting a block the same colour it was before or bleaching a block that's already white.

1.9   The Common Sense Law of Inertia

More generally, we would like to be able to write down just the effect axioms, declare the default assumption that "nothing else changes", and then appeal to some non-monotonic formalism to work out the consequences. Since the early Eighties, there have been several candidates for such a formalism. Two of the most common are *default logic* [Reiter, 1980] and *circumscription* [McCarthy, 1980]. Logic programming's *negation-as-failure* [Clark, 1978] is another candidate, so long as its semantics is properly defined.

Circumscription will feature prominently in this book, and it will be presented in some detail in the next chapter. For the moment I'll just introduce the basic idea, and outline its application to solving the frame problem. Circumscription allows us to declare that the extensions of certain predicates are to be *minimised*. Consider a conjunction of formulae Γ from which we can show $P(A)$, but from which we cannot show either $P(x)$ or $\neg P(x)$ for any x other than A. It follows from the circumscription of Γ minimising P, written CIRC[Γ ; P], that $P(x)$ is false for any x unless Γ demands that it is true. So, for example, $\neg P(B)$ will follow from CIRC[Γ ; P] although it doesn't follow directly from Γ.

It should be obvious that the way to apply circumscription to the frame problem is to minimise the predicate Affects. This is exactly what McCarthy recommends in [McCarthy, 1986] (although he calls the predicate Ab rather than Affects,[16] where Ab is short for "abnormal"). However, minimising Affects (or Ab) in a naive way yields counter-intuitive results for very simple examples. The most famous such example is the so-called Yale shooting scenario, devised by Hanks and McDermott [1987]. The problem that Hanks and McDermott discovered is one of the main subjects of the next chapter, and attempted solutions to it will be described in detail in later chapters.

One way to think of a non-monotonic solution to the frame problem is as a formalisation of the *common sense law of inertia*. In the vaguest possible terms, the common sense law of inertia states that,

Inertia is normal. Change is exceptional.

One component of this common sense law is the following default rule.

Normally, given any action (or event type) and any fluent, the action doesn't affect the fluent.

The following default rule, which concerns the actual occurrence of events (or the performance of actions), is another of its components.

Normally, given any action (or event type) and any time point, there's no instance of that action at that time point.

As a scientific claim, the common sense law of inertia wouldn't stand up to much scrutiny. But it's much better thought of, not as a statement about the world, but either as a useful representational device or as a strategy for dealing with incomplete information. Let's examine these two interpretations in turn.

According to the first interpretation, a formalisation of the common sense law of inertia declares that change is the exception in the representation of which it forms a part. Let me try to make this a little more precise, focusing on the first of the two components of the law described above. For any agent, a certain set of fluents are *salient*, in the sense that knowledge of the behaviour of those fluents is desirable if the agent is to make rational decisions about how to act. Similarly, a certain set of actions are salient. At any time and for any action, the set of fluents that are salient for an agent can be partitioned into a number of subsets, given the state of the agent's knowledge.

A. The salient fluents that are known or assumed to change value.

B. The salient fluents that are known or assumed to persist.

C. The salient fluents whose behaviour is unknown.

Similarly, a representation can adopt one of three stances on the behaviour of a given fluent when a given action is performed. Either,

1. The representation insists that the fluent changes its value,

2. The representation insists that the fluent persists, or

3. The representation is neutral about the behaviour of the fluent.

If the representational language is classical (monotonic) logic, the default stance — the stance adopted in the absence of any explicit information about the effect of a given action on a given fluent — is necessarily the third of these: the representation is neutral about whether or not the action affects the fluent. So the underlying logical substrate is one of neutrality. Neutrality is implicit, and violations of neutrality have to be made explicit.

The common sense law of inertia makes the second stance in the list the default, thereby inverting figure and ground, so to speak. In the absence of any information about a given fluent and a given action, the common sense law of inertia forces the assumption that the action does not affect the fluent. In the presence of the common sense law of inertia, the underlying logical substrate is one of persistence. Persistence is implicit, and violations of persistence (of both sorts)[17] have to made explicit.

According to the second interpretation, the common sense law of inertia is not just a convenient representational device, but is (also) a strategy for dealing with *incomplete information*, specifically incomplete information about the effects of actions and the occurrence of events. Roughly speaking, the strategy is this: if it is not known that an action affects a fluent (or that an event occurs at a given time), assume that it doesn't. Incomplete information is a key feature of the *common sense informatic situation* that any intelligent agent has to confront [McCarthy, 1989], and strategies for dealing with it are an important topic of study within AI. On this view, it's a virtue of non-monotonic approaches to the frame problem that they are able to distinguish between those fluents that are known to persist and those that are merely assumed to persist, although the possibility of explicitly declaring the persistence of a fluent is never exploited in this book when non-monotonic approaches are under discussion.

To many researchers, solving the frame problem is the task of constructing a formalism for reasoning about action that incorporates the common sense law of inertia, however this is interpreted. The common sense law of inertia offers representational parsimony (it's much easier to explicitly describe A and C than A and B) and elaboration tolerance (it's much easier to update an explicit description of A and C than an explicit description of A and B), and incorporates a strategy for handling incomplete information. The task at hand, then, is to render the informal characterisation above into mathematically precise language, so that it can be usefully employed in the principled construction of intelligent artefacts.

1.10   Monotonic Versus Non-Monotonic Solutions

I want to conclude this introduction to non-monotonic approaches to the frame problem by discussing the question of when a proposal is genuinely non-monotonic and when it isn't. The definition of monotonicity seems clear enough, but it still leaves room for debate when it comes to particular proposals.

Let's take circumscription for example. The formal definition of circumscription, which we will encounter in the next chapter, tells us that the circumscription of a formula Γ is a sentence of second-order logic. The consequence relation for second-order logic is classical and monotonic. So in what sense is circumscription non-monotonic?

McCarthy himself remarks,

> Circumscription is not a non-monotonic logic. It is a form of non-monotonic reasoning augmenting ordinary first-order logic. [McCarthy, 1980]

Circumscription preserves monotonicity to the extent that it appeals to a classical consequence relation. But it is non-monotonic in the sense that, given a predicate P, it does not guarantee that for any conjunction of formulae Γ and any two formulae δ and ϕ, CIRC[Γ ; P] $\vDash \phi$ implies CIRC[$\Gamma \wedge \delta$; P] $\vDash \phi$.

Let's introduce a slightly more general definition of monotonicity to make this more precise. We will consider the relationship between *sets* (not conjunctions) of sentences Γ and the sentences ϕ that follow from Γ in a logical system. If ϕ follows from Γ according to that system, I will write $\Gamma \triangleright \phi$. A logical system is *monotonic* if for any two sets of formulae Γ_1 and Γ_2 where $\Gamma_1 \supset \Gamma_2$ and any formula ϕ, $\Gamma_1 \triangleright \phi$ implies $\Gamma_2 \triangleright \phi$.

For classical logic, for example, we have,

$$\Gamma \triangleright \phi \text{ if and only if } \text{Conj}[\Gamma] \vDash \phi$$

where Conj[Γ] is the conjunction of all the sentences in G. So classical logic is monotonic according to the new definition. For circumscription minimising the predicate P, we have,

$$\Gamma \triangleright \phi \text{ if and only if } \text{CIRC}[\Gamma ; P] \vDash \phi$$

which means that circumscription is non-monotonic. Note that the circumscriptive approach to the frame problem outlined above achieves elaboration tolerance, because all we have to do when we learn of new actions or fluents is append the new effect axioms to the old theory, which is to say we add them to the set Γ, and the circumscription takes care of the rest.

Finally, let's reconsider the so-called monotonic solutions to the frame problem that use explanation closure axioms. If they are to achieve elaboration tolerance, they must specify some function Exp[Γ] that automatically generates explanation closure axioms from the effect axioms in Γ. That is to say, Exp[Γ] will comprise Γ plus the necessary explanation closure axioms. This is indeed the strategy adopted by authors such as Reiter who have taken the "monotonic" approach to its limits [Reiter, 1991], [Lin & Reiter, 1994].

But in what sense does this still constitute a monotonic solution? For Exp, we have the following.

$$\Gamma \vartriangleright \phi \text{ if and only if } Exp[\Gamma] \vDash \phi$$

As in circumscription, the $\vartriangleright$ relation appeals to a classical, monotonic consequence relation. But, as should be clear by now, it will not meet the new definition of monotonicity. The addition of a new effect axiom will in general falsify explanation closure sentences that were true beforehand. The main difference between the "monotonic" approaches and the avowedly non-monotonic approaches reduces to this: monotonic approaches[18] that attempt to meet the criterion of elaboration tolerance end up incorporating a tailor-made non-monotonic mechanism for solving the frame problem, while the non-monotonic approaches use off-the-shelf, general purpose default reasoning formalisms.[19]

1.11 Explanations, Qualifications, and Narratives

A number of issues in the field of reasoning about action are so closely related to the frame problem that no discussion of the frame problem can ignore them. In particular, this section will introduce,

- Explanation, or reasoning about the past,

- The qualification problem, and

- Narratives and event occurrence minimisation.

The focus of this chapter so far has been on reasoning forwards in time from causes to effects, a mode of reasoning which is often called *temporal projection*, or *prediction*, in the literature. The converse operation, in other words reasoning from effects to causes, is called *explanation*, or *postdiction*, or sometimes simply "reasoning about the past".

Explanation has its own set of issues. An especially important one from the point of view of this book is how proposals to solve explanation problems interact with proposals to solve the frame problem. This interaction should be seamless and trouble-free, which is to say we don't want a solution to the frame problem which rules out a satisfactory solution to the problem of finding explanations. A much discussed benchmark problem in this context is the so-called stolen car scenario [Kautz, 1986], which will receive attention in due course.

Another issue that has been the subject of a lot of thought is the *qualification problem*. The qualification problem is easily muddled up with the frame problem itself since, like the frame problem, it concerns the effects of actions, and default reasoning techniques seem to be needed to overcome it. But it is important to separate the two.

The essence of the qualification problem is this. How can we be sure that all the preconditions that we have built in to our effect axioms are all the preconditions there are? In the same way that we can learn of new actions and fluents, we can learn of new preconditions for actions. For example, in the Blocks World, we may discover that some blocks are stuck to the table.

We would like our theory to be elaboration tolerant with respect to this sort of new information as well as information about new actions and fluents. Once again, we can use a default reasoning technique like circumscription to formalise the assumption that the known preconditions of each action are the only preconditions. The qualification problem isn't a major theme of this book, but remarks about it are sprinkled throughout the text where appropriate.

The final issue I want to talk about here is that of narratives, which will be treated fairly thoroughly in the text. A *narrative* is a course of actual events about which we may have incomplete information. The situation calculus, unlike the event calculus, is not a narrative-based formalism. There is no inherent distinction in the situation calculus between actual and hypothetical events and actions, and the usual style in which situation calculus formulae are written does not facilitate the representation of incompletely specified sequences of events.

When we are dealing with an incompletely specified narrative, yet another form of default reasoning is usually required in order to get the expected consequences from a logical description, namely *event occurrence minimisation*. This form of minimisation captures the default assumption that the only events that occur that are relevant to the domain are the ones that are known to occur.

Without this assumption, very few useful conclusions can be drawn from a narrative description. Because without it, we can't rule out the possibility that between any two known events, a third, unknown event, might occur to undo the effects of the first, possibly affecting the preconditions of the second, and potentially diverting the course of history onto a completely different path from the one it would have taken.

1.12 Philosophical Reflections

A considerable philosophical literature on the subject of the frame problem has arisen. The thoughts of these writers often seem to be based on a rather impressionistic understanding of the original frame problem, and are of limited interest in this book.[20] But it seems appropriate to conclude this opening chapter with a brief review of the philosophical literature on the subject.

Dennett, who may have been responsible for the earliest reference to the frame problem in the philosophical literature [Dennett, 1978, pp. 125–126], asserts (in a much later essay) that the frame problem is,

> . . . a new, deep epistemological problem — accessible in principle but unnoticed by generations of philosophers — brought to light by the novel methods of AI, and still far from being solved. [Dennett, 1987]

Subsequent to Dennett's essay, the frame problem has been interpreted in numerous ways by philosophers.[21] There follows a collection of representative quotes. The first two are taken from the collection *The Robot's Dilemma: The Frame Problem in Artificial Intelligence* [Pylyshyn, 1987].[22]

> Instances of the frame problem are all of the form . . . given an enormous amount of stuff, and some task to be done using some of the stuff, what is the *relevant stuff* for the task. [Glymour, 1987]

> The frame problem is just [the problem of when to stop thinking] from an engineer's perspective. You want to make a device that is rational in the sense that its mechanisms of belief fixation are unencapsulated. But you also want the device you make to actually succeed in fixing a belief from time to time. [Fodor, 1987]

In an *unencapsulated* system, according to Fodor's use of the term, the search for evidence for a belief is not delimited arbitrarily (see Section 3 of the introduction). Later characterisations of the frame problem by philosophers have deviated even further from the original idea.

> [The frame problem is] the problem of second-guessing all the contingencies the programmer has not anticipated in symbolizing the knowledge he is attempting to symbolize. [Harnad, 1990]

The problem of induction as Hume viewed it was one of justifying some inferences about the future as opposed to others. The frame problem, likewise, is one of justifying some inferences about the future as opposed to others. The second problem is an instance of the first. [Fetzer, 1991]

Crockett [1994] conducts a useful survey of this literature, and attempts to extract a consensus, distinguishing the philosopher's "general" frame problem from the AI researcher's "specific" frame problem.

The general frame problem concerns how a "cognitive system" goes about updating its beliefs. . . . There is [no effective procedure] for determining which beliefs need updating and which do not [when the robot acts, or some part of its world changes] . . . which does not include examining every item in its "database". [Crockett, 1994, p. 91]

Crockett goes on to claim that "the attempt to find a principled way to solve the specific frame problem inexorably entangles one in the general frame problem" [Crockett, 1994, p. 93]. The present book testifies to the falsehood of this last claim, since it is precisely an attempt to find a principled way to solve the specific frame problem, and the attempt has been carried out without any obvious consideration of the so-called general frame problem.

However, I would like to engage the debate on one point. Fodor [1987] introduces the concept of a "fridgeon". Something is a *fridgeon* at a given time t if and only if it's a particle and Fodor's fridge is switched on at time t. The act of turning Fodor's fridge on or off apparently has dramatic consequences, if we take its effect on fridgeons into account. Countless billions of fluents change their values every time the fridge's state is changed.

How does the possibility of a fridgeon sit with my earlier crude characterisation of the common sense law of inertia, according to which inertia is normal and change is exceptional? Here's an example where a great deal changes. Does the common sense law of inertia prohibit the representation of the effect on fridgeons of turning Fodor's fridge on or off?

No, it doesn't. In fact, the example is very easily rendered in situation calculus with one effect axiom and one domain constraint. In the following representation, Fodor's example is modified very slightly, so that anything can be a fridgeon. The intended meaning of the predicate and function symbols should be obvious.

$$\text{Holds}(\text{Fridgeon}(x),s) \leftrightarrow \text{Holds}(\text{On},s)$$

$$\text{Holds(On,Result(Switch,s))} \leftrightarrow \neg \text{Holds(On,s)}$$

Any solution to the frame problem that can cope with domain constraints (such as those in Chapters 6, 7, 14 and 15) will be able to cope gracefully with this example.

As already pointed out in Section 1.9, the common sense law of inertia is best thought of as a representational device, rather than as a statement about the world. To think of it in terms of fluent counts is to adopt the second, faulty interpretation. Chiefly what this example reveals is the foolhardiness of any attempt to define the common sense law of inertia informally. The appropriate tool for arriving at a better understanding is mathematics.

Notes

1. McCarthy relates that he was reading a book on geometry at the time he coined the term "frame problem", and that he thought of the frame problem as analogous to that of choosing a co-ordinate frame.
2. I won't distinguish between actions and events in this book. The terms "action" and "event type" will be used interchangeably.
3. A charming, but etymologically incorrect, interpretation of the term "frame problem" appeals to an analogy with film animation. Very little changes from one *frame* to the next in an animated film.
4. Variables begin with lower-case letters and constants with upper-case letters. In displayed formulae, all variables are universally quantified with maximum scope unless otherwise indicated.
5. By a "domain" here, I mean a domain of application. This use of the word is independent of its use in formal logic to denote the set of objects in a model.
6. Σ also needs to include some axioms which guarantee that the blocks are distinct, that is to say $A \neq B \neq C \neq D$. At the moment, we only have one action type, but similar axioms ensuring that action types are distinct will also be required. Such "uniqueness-of-names" axioms are a common feature of formal descriptions of change, and will appear frequently in this book. We also need to be able to show, for example, that blocks are distinct from actions. In practice, this will be taken care of by using a many-sorted logic.
7. For brevity, I will often use the term "action" to mean action type.
8. The suggestions contained in Hayes's papers, as well as their drawbacks, are reviewed by Janlert [1987].
9. This temptation is perhaps more the product of wishful thinking than logical naivety. Later we will see how non-monotonicity can make wishes like this come true.

10. This assumes uniqueness-of-names axioms for action types, as mentioned in an earlier endnote.

11. There is a variety of ways in which explanation closure axioms can be written. I have employed a slightly different form from that first used by Haas.

12. This characterisation of elaboration tolerance assumes that we know how to quantify complexity. In the absence of a precise definition of "amount of information", the concept of elaboration tolerance relies on a certain amount of intuitive understanding.

13. A consequence of this criterion is that we expect the effort required to construct a theory from scratch to be proportional to the amount of information being represented. This is the "base case" of elaboration tolerance, where we imagine we're starting with an empty theory.

14. For the present, appending can be interpreted as conjoining. I use the vaguer term here to allow for a different interpretation later on.

15. Like Σ and Σ', Σ'' will have to include uniqueness-of-names axioms for blocks and action types. It will also need uniqueness-of-names axioms for colours so that we have, for example, Red$\neq$White.

16. I will adopt the same convention later on.

17. Both change and neutrality are violations of persistence.

18. I will drop the scare quotes from the word "monotonic" from now on when it is used in this context.

19. Some authors, such as Lin and Reiter [1994], use general purpose non-monotonic techniques to justify their monotonic formalisms, thus blurring the distinction even further.

20. Pat Hayes puts the matter less politely but more memorably: "Fodor doesn't know the frame problem from a bunch of bananas" [Hayes, 1987].

21. Of course, an AI researcher can also have a philosophical turn of mind. What distinguishes a philosopher from an AI researcher in this debate is the source of his or her salary. Philosophers are paid by university philosophy departments.

22. The philosophical debate continues in [Ford & Pylyshyn, 1996], which is a sequel to [Pylyshyn, 1987].

2 Logical Foundations

In this chapter, the formal foundations are laid for a non-monotonic solution to the frame problem, a solution that meets the criterion of elaboration tolerance. This chapter provides the logical background for the rest of the book. The reader is expected to be familiar with the basic material on the predicate calculus already, but some standard definitions are included here for completeness. The formalism of the situation calculus is then described, in more detail than in the previous chapter. Finally, McCarthy's circumscription is formally presented, and will be used as one of the main default reasoning formalisms throughout the book.

2.1 The Language of Predicate Calculus

The next few sections present the language and semantics of first- and second-order predicate calculus, beginning with the unsorted first-order case, moving on to the many-sorted first-order case, and finally presenting the many-sorted second-order case. The reader who is familiar with this material might prefer to skip these sections, and refer to them for reference only.

The well-formed formulae of a language of first-order predicate calculus with equality are defined as follows.

Preliminary Definitions. A *constant*, *function symbol*, or *predicate symbol* is any string of alphanumeric characters beginning with an upper-case letter. A *variable* is any string of alphanumeric characters beginning with a lower-case letter. A *non-logical symbol* is any variable, constant, function symbol, or predicate symbol. □

Each function symbol and predicate symbol has an associated arity.

Definition 2.1.1. The set of *terms* is defined as follows.

- A constant or variable is a term.

- If $\tau_1 \ldots \tau_n$ are terms and π is an n-ary function symbol then $\pi(\tau_1, \ldots, \tau_n)$ is a term. □

Definition 2.1.2. If $\tau_1 \ldots \tau_n$ are terms and ρ is an n-ary predicate symbol then $\rho(\tau_1, \ldots, \tau_n)$ is an *atom*. □

Definition 2.1.3. The *well-formed formulae* of first-order predicate calculus with equality are defined as follows.

- An atom is a well-formed formula.

- If τ_1 and τ_2 are terms, then $\tau_1 = \tau_2$ is a well-formed formula.

- If ϕ_1 and ϕ_2 are well-formed formulae, then so are $[\neg \phi_1]$, $[\phi_1 \wedge \phi_2]$, $[\phi_1 \vee \phi_2]$, $[\phi_1 \leftarrow \phi_2]$, $[\phi_1 \rightarrow \phi_2]$, and $[\phi_1 \leftrightarrow \phi_2]$.

- If ϕ is a well-formed formula and υ is a variable, then $[\forall \upsilon \phi]$ and $[\exists \upsilon \phi]$ are well-formed formulae.   □

I will usually abbreviate $\neg [\tau_1 = \tau_2]$ to $\tau_1 \neq \tau_2$. The logical connectives will be given their usual precedence. From highest to lowest, we have $\neg$ then $\wedge$ then $\vee$ then $\leftarrow$, $\rightarrow$ and $\leftrightarrow$, then the quantifiers $\forall$ and $\exists$. Parentheses may be omitted if the precedence rules render them unnecessary. Nested quantifiers will be simplified in the usual way. For example, $\forall x \forall y \forall z$ will be written $\forall x,y,z$. A variable is said to be *free* in a well-formed formula if it is not within the scope of any quantifier.

Definition 2.1.4. A *language* of first-order predicate calculus with equality is the set of all well-formed formulae of first-order predicate calculus with equality that can be constructed with a given set of non-logical symbols.   □

For notational convenience, I will sometimes introduce infix predicate symbols (for example, < or ≥) and infix function symbols (for example, + or *). In the special case of the comparative predicate symbols < and ≤, I will use standard abbreviations such as $\tau_1 \leq \tau_2 < \tau_3$ for $\tau_1 \leq \tau_2 \wedge \tau_2 < \tau_3$. Throughout the book, the symbol $\equiv_{def}$ will be reserved for equivalence by definition.

It's often convenient to speak of the language of a well-formed formula, which should be taken to mean the language whose only predicate symbols, function symbols, and constants are those mentioned in the formula.

The following is an example of a term.

$$\text{Result(Paint(x,Red,S0))}.$$

The following effect axiom from the previous chapter is an example of an atom and a well-formed formula.

$$\text{Holds(Colour(x,c),Result(Paint(x,c),s))}$$

The last chapter was, of course, full of examples of well-formed formulae. The universal frame axiom (F1) is another example.

$$\forall a,f,s \; [[\text{Holds(f,Result(a,s))} \leftrightarrow \text{Holds(f,s)}] \leftarrow \neg \text{Affects(a,f,s)}] \qquad \text{(F1)}$$

Universal quantifiers whose scope is an entire formula will normally be omitted. I will often abbreviate the terms "predicate symbol" and "function symbol" to just "predicate" and "function" respectively, where this doesn't lead to confusion. The term "well-formed formula" will usually be abbreviated to just "formula". The term "first-order predicate calculus with equality" will usually be abbreviated to "first-order predicate calculus" or just "predicate calculus".

2.2 The Semantics of Predicate Calculus

I will adopt a fairly standard Tarski-style semantics for predicate calculus. I will present first a semantics for unsorted predicate calculus, and then a semantics for the many-sorted version.

Let L be a language of first-order predicate calculus with equality.

Definition 2.2.1. An *interpretation* of L is a triple $\langle D,F,P \rangle$ where,

- D is a non-empty set of objects,

- F is a function that maps every constant symbol and every variable in L to an element of D, and that maps every n-ary function symbol in L to a function from D^n to D,[1] and

- P is a function that maps every n-ary predicate symbol in L to a subset of D^n. This set is known as the *extension* of the predicate.   □

I will use the following abbreviations. Let $M = \langle D,F,P \rangle$ be an interpretation.

- If ρ is a predicate symbol then $M[\![\rho]\!] = P(\rho)$.

- If τ is a constant then $M[\![\tau]\!] = F(\tau)$.

- If π is a function symbol then $M[\![\pi]\!] = F(\pi)$.

- If $\tau_1 \ldots \tau_n$ are terms and π is a function symbol then $M[\![\pi(\tau_1, \ldots, \tau_n)]\!] = M[\![\pi]\!] (M[\![\tau_1]\!], \ldots, M[\![\tau_n]\!])$.

Definition 2.2.2. The satisfaction relation $\Vdash$ between an interpretation M of L and a well-formed formula of L is defined as follows.

$M \Vdash \rho(\tau_1, \ldots, \tau_n)$ if $\langle M[\![\tau_1]\!], \ldots, M[\![\tau_n]\!] \rangle \in M[\![\rho]\!]$

$M \Vdash \tau_1 = \tau_2$ if $M[\![\tau_1]\!] = M[\![\tau_2]\!]$

$M \Vdash [\neg \phi]$ if $M \nVdash \phi$

$M \Vdash [\phi_1 \wedge \phi_2]$ if $M \Vdash \phi_1$ and $M \Vdash \phi_2$

$M \Vdash [\phi_1 \vee \phi_2]$ if $M \Vdash \phi_1$ or $M \Vdash \phi_2$

M ⊩ [φ₁ ← φ₂] if M ⊩ φ₂ implies M ⊩ φ₁

M ⊩ [φ₁ → φ₂] if M ⊩ φ₁ implies M ⊩ φ₂

M ⊩ [(φ₁ ↔ φ₂] if M ⊩ φ₁ if and only if M ⊩ φ₂

M ⊩ [∀ υ φ] if for all interpretations M' that agree with M except possibly in the interpretation of υ, M' ⊩ φ.

M ⊩ [∃ υ φ] if there is some interpretation M' that differs from M only in the interpretation of υ, such that M' ⊩ φ.

If M ⊩ φ then M is said to *satisfy* φ.   □

Definition 2.2.3. An interpretation M is a *model* of a formula φ if M ⊩ φ.   □

Definition 2.2.4. A formula φ is a *logical consequence* of a formula Σ (written Σ ⊨ φ) if for all models M of Σ, M ⊩ φ.   □

I will occasionally speak of the logical consequences of a set of well-formed formulae, by which is meant the logical consequences of the conjunction of the members of that set. Where the term "theory" is commonly used to denote a set of well-formed formulae closed under logical consequence, I will use the term to denote any set of well-formed formulae.

First-order predicate calculus is, of course, very well understood, and is the subject of a large body of theory. An elementary introduction is supplied by Lemmon [1965]. A more meta-theoretical introduction to logic is provided by Hamilton [1988]. For an introduction to the application of predicate calculus to artificial intelligence, see [Genesereth & Nilsson, 1987], and for its application to knowledge representation in particular, see [Davis, 1990].

As an example, consider the following trivial situation calculus formulae, whose intuitive meaning should be clear.

Holds(On,S0)

Holds(On,Result(Toggle,s)) ↔ ¬ Holds(On,s)

Let's call the conjunction of these formulae Σ. Besides the usual Holds predicate and Result function, the language of Σ includes the constants S0, On and Toggle. Consider any interpretation M = ⟨D,F,P⟩ of this language that meets the following criteria.

- D ⊇ {ONSIT,OFFSIT,TOGGLE}

- M⟦S0⟧ = ONSIT

- M⟦Toggle⟧ = TOGGLE

- ⟨M⟦On⟧,ONSIT⟩ ∈ M⟦Holds⟧

- ⟨M⟦On⟧,OFFSIT⟩ ∉ M⟦Holds⟧

- M⟦Result⟧ (TOGGLE,ONSIT) = OFFSIT

- M⟦Result⟧ (TOGGLE,OFFSIT) = ONSIT

We can verify by inspection that M is model of Σ. M also satisfies, for example,

$$Holds(On,Result(Toggle,Result(Toggle,S0))).$$

In fact, it should be clear that all models of Σ will be isomorphic to some model that meets the above criteria.[2] Therefore all models of Σ are also models of the above formula. So more generally we have,

$$\Sigma \vDash Holds(On,Result(Toggle,Result(Toggle,S0))).$$

2.3 Many-Sorted Predicate Calculus

Notice that any interpretation of Σ in the last section will have to interpret terms that, as far as the situation calculus is concerned, are intuitively meaningless, such as Result(On,On). Also, we need to provide axioms to rule out models with intuitively absurd consequences such as Toggle=On. For reasons such as this, it's common in the field of knowledge representation to use a *sorted* logic, in which, for example, actions and fluents can be assigned separate sorts.[3]

The well-formed formulae of a language of many-sorted first-order predicate calculus are the same as those for an unsorted language, except that,

- The language is associated with a finite number of sorts, and

- Each element of the language has an associated sort declaration, which all well-formed formulae must respect:

  - Each variable, constant symbol, and function symbol in the language has a corresponding sort, and

  - Each argument position of each predicate symbol and function symbol has a corresponding sort.

The semantics of many-sorted predicate calculus with equality is defined using sets indexed on sorts.

Definition 2.3.1. An Ω-*indexed set* S is a set, every member of which is associated with exactly one element of the set Ω (its *index*). I will write S_ω to denote the set of all $s \in S$ such that ω is the index of s.   □

Definition 2.3.2. Let L be a language of many-sorted first-order predicate calculus with equality. Let L have a set Ω of sorts, Ω-indexed sets C and V of constant symbols and variables respectively, an $\Omega^* \times \Omega$-indexed set F of function symbols, and an Ω^*-indexed set P of predicate symbols.[4] An *interpretation* of L is a triple $\langle D,F,P \rangle$ where,

- D is an Ω-indexed set of objects,

- F is a function mapping,

    - Every constant symbol in C_ω to D_ω,

    - Every variable in V_ω to D_ω, and

    - Every n-ary function symbol in $F_{\omega_1,...,\omega_n,\omega}$ to a function from $D_{\omega_1} \times ... \times D_{\omega_n}$ to D_ω, and

- P is a function mapping every n-ary predicate symbol in $P_{\omega_1,...,\omega_n}$ to a subset of $D_{\omega_1} \times ... \times D_{\omega_n}$.   □

The definitions of satisfaction and logical consequence are the same as for the unsorted case. However, with the new, more structured definition of an interpretation, the set of logical consequences of a formula can be smaller.

To see this, let's reconsider the example of the previous section. Let there be three sorts: situations (with variables s, s1, s2, etc.), fluents (f, f1, f2, etc.), and actions (a, a1, a2, etc.). Let Σ be the same conjunction of situation calculus formulae as before. Now it should be clear that some interpretations of Σ according to the old, unsorted definition are not interpretations at all according to the many-sorted definition. For example, consider any unsorted interpretation M $= \langle D,F,P \rangle$ of Σ that meets the following criteria.

- $D \supseteq \{ONSIT,OFFSIT\}$

- $M[\![S0]\!] = ONSIT$

- $M[\![Toggle]\!] = ONSIT$

- $\langle M[\![On]\!],ONSIT \rangle \in M[\![Holds]\!]$

- $\langle M[\![On]\!],OFFSIT \rangle \notin M[\![Holds]\!]$

- $M[\![Result]\!] (ONSIT,ONSIT) = OFFSIT$

- M⟦Result⟧ (ONSIT,OFFSIT) = ONSIT

This is the same list of criteria used in the example of the last section, except that the terms S0 and Toggle denote the same object in D. In other words S0=Toggle, which is intuitively absurd. According to the definitions for the unsorted case, this interpretation is also a model. Thus we have, according to the old definitions,

$$M \Vdash \text{Holds(On,Result(S0,Result(Toggle,Toggle)))}$$

which is quite meaningless.

However, according to the many-sorted semantics, M is not even an interpretation, let alone a model, since M⟦Toggle⟧ $\in$ D$_{\text{actions}}$ while M⟦S0⟧ $\in$ D$_{\text{situations}}$, and D$_{\text{actions}}$ is disjoint from D$_{\text{situations}}$. Furthermore, the formula,

$$\text{Holds(On,Result(S0,Result(Toggle,Toggle)))}$$

will no longer be well-formed if S0 and Toggle are assigned the correct sorts.

Before leaving this subject, it needs to be pointed out that adopting a many-sorted logic is not the only way to avoid counter-intuitive conclusions of this kind. The obvious way to do it with an unsorted logic is simply to introduce a special predicate for each kind of object. For the situation calculus, we could introduce the unary predicates Sit, Flu and Act. Then, every use of a quantifier $\forall$ x would be qualified with a condition of the form Sit(x), Flu(x) or Act(x). Finally, to get the same effect as the many-sorted version, we would then require axioms that ensured that these predicates were mutually exclusive. An example of such an axiom is,

$$\text{Sit(x)} \rightarrow \neg \text{Flu(x)} \wedge \neg \text{Act(x)}.$$

However, the option of a many-sorted logic allows formulae to be much more compactly written. Incidentally, if we were to confine our attentions to Herbrand interpretations, in which uniqueness-of-names is automatic, the absurd interpretation in the above example would not be legitimate. But it's easy to find similar examples with other kinds of absurd conclusion, which cannot be got rid of by this means.

2.4 Second-Order Predicate Calculus

Second-order predicate calculus, which will be required to define circumscription, generalises first-order predicate calculus by permitting quantification over predicates and functions. The language of second-order predicate calculus is basically that of first-order predicate calculus with the addition of predicate and function variables, which can appear with quantifiers. Function variables can be used in place of function symbols to construct terms, and predicate variables can be used in place of predicate symbols to construct atoms. The semantics is a straightforward generalisation of the first-order case.

Preliminary Definitions. A *function variable* or *predicate variable* is any string of alphanumeric characters beginning with a lower-case letter. □

Definition 2.4.1. The *terms* of second-order predicate calculus with equality are defined as follows.

- All the terms of first-order predicate calculus with equality are terms.

- If $\tau_1 \ldots \tau_n$ are terms and υ is an n-ary function variable then $\upsilon(\tau_1, \ldots, \tau_n)$ is a term. □

Each function symbol, predicate symbol, function variable and predicate variable has an associated arity. In addition, the language is associated with a finite number of sorts, and each element of the language has an associated sort declaration, which all well-formed formulae must respect:

- Each variable, constant symbol, function symbol, function variable and predicate variable in the language has a corresponding sort, and

- Each argument position of each function symbol, predicate symbol, function variable and predicate variable has a corresponding sort.

Definition 2.4.2. The *atoms* of second-order predicate calculus with equality are defined as follows.

- If $\tau_1 \ldots \tau_n$ are terms and ρ is an n-ary predicate symbol then $\rho(\tau_1, \ldots, \tau_n)$ is an atom.

- If $\tau_1 \ldots \tau_n$ are terms and υ is an n-ary predicate variable then $\upsilon(\tau_1, \ldots, \tau_n)$ is an atom. □

Definition 2.4.3. The *well-formed formulae* of second-order predicate calculus with equality are defined as follows.

- An atom is a well-formed formula.

- If τ_1 and τ_2 are terms, then $\tau_1 = \tau_2$ is a well-formed formula.

- If ϕ_1 and ϕ_2 are well-formed formulae, then so are $[\neg\ \phi_1]$, $[\phi_1 \wedge \phi_2]$, $[\phi_1 \vee \phi_2]$, $[\phi_1 \leftarrow \phi_2]$, $[\phi_1 \rightarrow \phi_2]$, and $[\phi_1 \leftrightarrow \phi_2]$.

- If ϕ is a well-formed formula and υ is a variable, then $[\forall \upsilon \phi]$ and $[\exists \upsilon \phi]$ are well-formed formulae.

- If ϕ is a well-formed formula and υ is a function variable or a predicate variable, then $[\forall \upsilon \phi]$ and $[\exists \upsilon \phi]$ are well-formed formulae. $\square$

Let L be a language of many-sorted second-order predicate calculus with equality.

Definition 2.4.4. Let L have a set Ω of sorts, Ω-indexed sets C and V of constant symbols and variables respectively, an $\Omega^* \times \Omega$-indexed sets F and U of function symbols and function variables respectively, and Ω^*-indexed sets P and W of predicate symbols and predicate variables respectively. An *interpretation* of L is a triple $\langle D,F,P \rangle$ where,

- D is an Ω-indexed set of objects,

- F is a function mapping,

  - Every constant symbol in C_ω to D_ω,

  - Every variable in V_ω to D_ω, and

  - Every n-ary function symbol in $F_{\omega_1,...,\omega_n,\omega}$ to a function from $D_{\omega_1} \times ... \times D_{\omega_n}$ to D_ω,

  - Every n-ary function variable in $U_{\omega_1,...,\omega_n,\omega}$ to a function from $D_{\omega_1} \times ... \times D_{\omega_n}$ to D_ω, and

- P is a function mapping,

  - Every n-ary predicate symbol in $P_{\omega_1,...,\omega_n}$ to a subset of $D_{\omega_1} \times ... \times D_{\omega_n}$, and

  - Every n-ary predicate variable in $W_{\omega_1,...,\omega_n}$ to a subset of $D_{\omega_1} \times ... \times D_{\omega_n}$, $\square$

The following abbreviations are adopted from Section 2.2. Let $M = \langle D,F,P \rangle$ be an interpretation.

- If ρ is a predicate symbol then $M[\![\rho]\!] = P(\rho)$.

- If τ is a constant then $M[\![\tau]\!] = F(\tau)$.

- If π is a function symbol then $M[\![\pi]\!] = F(\pi)$.

- If $\tau_1 \ldots \tau_n$ are terms and π is a function symbol then $M[\![\pi(\tau_1, \ldots, \tau_n)]\!] = M[\![\pi]\!]$ $(M[\![\tau_1]\!], \ldots, M[\![\tau_n]\!])$.

In addition, if υ is a predicate variable then let $M[\![\upsilon]\!] = P(\upsilon)$, and if υ is a function variable then let $M[\![\upsilon]\!] = F(\upsilon)$.

Definition 2.4.5. The satisfaction relation $\Vdash$ between an interpretation M of L and a well-formed formula of L is defined as follows.

$M \Vdash \rho(\tau_1, \ldots, \tau_n)$ where ρ is a predicate symbol if $\langle M[\![\tau_1]\!], \ldots, M[\![\tau_n]\!]\rangle \in M[\![\rho]\!]$

$M \Vdash \upsilon(\tau_1, \ldots, \tau_n)$ where υ is a predicate variable if $\langle M[\![\tau_1]\!], \ldots, M[\![\tau_n]\!]\rangle \in M[\![\upsilon]\!]$

$M \Vdash \tau_1 = \tau_2$ if $M[\![\tau_1]\!] = M[\![\tau_2]\!]$

$M \Vdash [\neg \phi]$ if $M \nVdash \phi$

$M \Vdash [\phi_1 \wedge \phi_2]$ if $M \Vdash \phi_1$ and $M \Vdash \phi_2$

$M \Vdash [\phi_1 \vee \phi_2]$ if $M \Vdash \phi_1$ or $M \Vdash \phi_2$

$M \Vdash [\phi_1 \leftarrow \phi_2]$ if $M \Vdash \phi_2$ implies $M \Vdash \phi_1$

$M \Vdash [\phi_1 \rightarrow \phi_2]$ if $M \Vdash \phi_1$ implies $M \Vdash \phi_2$

$M \Vdash [(\phi_1 \leftrightarrow \phi_2]$ if $M \Vdash \phi_1$ if and only if $M \Vdash \phi_2$

$M \Vdash [\forall \upsilon \phi]$ where υ is either a variable, a function variable or a predicate variable if for all interpretations M' that agree with M except possibly in the interpretation of υ, $M' \Vdash \phi$.

$M \Vdash [\exists \upsilon \phi]$ where υ is either a variable, a function variable or a predicate variable if there is some interpretation M' that differs from M only in the interpretation of υ, such that $M' \Vdash \phi$.

If $M \Vdash \phi$ then M is said to *satisfy* ϕ.   □

The definitions of a model and of logical consequence are inherited from Section 2.2.

2.5 The Ontology and Language of the Situation Calculus

The situation calculus, presented in [McCarthy & Hayes, 1969], has already been introduced informally in the first chapter.[5] My task here is to characterise it more formally. Although a great many papers have been written that are based on the situation calculus, it is rare to find a paper that sets out exactly what the situation calculus is. It's possible to regard it as nothing more than a particular ontology —

one that includes situations, fluents and actions. A stronger view would insist that it included certain functions and predicates, such as Result and Holds. Finally, it's possible to think of it as a certain style of formalisation using those functions and predicates, involving effect axioms and domain constraints expressed in a particular way.

I don't see any point in taking a stand on what the situation calculus is or isn't. The important thing, to avoid confusion in the field, is to be more or less in accord with common practice. However, I will define precisely how I will use situation calculus terminology throughout this book. Along the way I will try to point out alternative styles and ways of expressing the same thing.

Definition 2.5.1. A *language of the situation calculus* is a language of many-sorted first-order predicate calculus with equality, which includes,

- A sort for *situations*, with variables s, s1, s2, etc.,

- A sort for *fluents*, with variables f, f1, f2, etc.,

- A sort for *actions*, with variables a, a1, a2, etc.,

- A function Result from actions and situations to situations,[6]

- A predicate Holds whose arguments are a fluent and a situation. □

Intuitively, following McCarthy and Hayes [1969], we could think of a situation as "the complete state of the universe at an instant of time". However, we don't have to go so far as to commit ourselves to associating each situation with a unique instant of time. The same situation can obtain for longer than an instant, and can recur over and again. I will return to this issue shortly.

A fluent, according to [McCarthy & Hayes, 1969], is "a function whose domain is the space of situations". They distinguish various types of fluent. A *propositional fluent*, for example, is one that maps onto true or false. But throughout this book, I will use the logical device of *reification*, which McCarthy and Hayes did not use, and which leads to a slightly different, but ultimately equivalent, understanding of the nature of a fluent.

Suppose we want to represent the fact that it is raining in situation S0. One way to do this, using the notion of a propositional fluent above, is to write,

Raining(S0)

Here, following McCarthy and Hayes, the fluent Raining can be thought of as a function whose domain is the space of situations and whose range is {True,

False}. Strictly speaking, of course, it is a predicate whose argument is a situation. An alternative way of expressing the same fact is to write,

Holds(Raining,S0)

Here, the fluent Raining has been reified. Previously it was a predicate, and indeed its status is obviously close to that of a predicate. But in the second formula, it has been made into a concrete object. Objections can be raised to this manoeuvre on philosophical grounds (see [Galton, 1991], for instance), but it can be defended on pragmatic grounds. When fluents are reified, it's easy to write formulae that generalise over the set of all fluents (such as the universal frame axiom (F1)). Without reification, this would require second-order logic.

As well as propositional fluents, McCarthy and Hayes employed fluents for objects or quantities that change their values in different situations. Suppose the head chef in a restaurant is Fred in situation S0 and Mary in situation S1. Again, there is a reified and an unreified way to express these facts. Here's the unreified way.

HeadChef(S0,Fred)

HeadChef(S1,Mary)

To reify a formula such as this, let's introduce a function Value, which takes a situation as an argument. Then we can write,

Value(HeadChef,S0) = Fred

Value(HeadChef,S1) = Mary.

There is a small problem here. If we want to use a many-sorted logic, but we want Value to be a generic function, returning persons, blocks, colours, and so on depending on the context, then we have to alter the semantics we have chosen for sorts, which only allows a function to return objects of one sort.

However, another way out is not to introduce a Value function, but simply to stick with Holds and write,

Holds(HeadChef(Fred),S0)

Holds(HeadChef(Mary),S1).

This is the convention I will adopt from now on.

2.6 Situation Calculus Formulae

Next, we have definitions for the three classes of formulae most commonly found in the situation calculus literature: effect axioms, domain constraints, and observation sentences. There is considerable variation in the way these formulae are written in different papers, but their essence is the same. One popular technique, for example, is the introduction of special predicates, such as Causes, Precond, or Poss, so that effect axioms can be rendered more succinctly. We will see more of this technique later, but for now I will present these formulae in their sparest form.

Definition 2.6.1. An *effect axiom* is a formula of the form,

$$\forall s \, [Holds(\beta, Result(\alpha, s)) \leftarrow \Pi]$$

or of the form,

$$\forall s \, [Holds(\beta, Result(\alpha, s))]$$

or of the form,

$$\forall s \, [\neg \, Holds(\beta, Result(\alpha, s)) \leftarrow \Pi]$$

or of the form,

$$\forall s \, [\neg \, Holds(\beta, Result(\alpha, s))]$$

where Π is a formula in which every occurrence of a situation term is in a formula of the form $Holds(\beta_i, s)$ or $\neg \, Holds(\beta_i, s)$. ☐

Definition 2.6.2. A *domain constraint* is a formula of the form $\forall s \, \Pi$, where Π is a formula in which the every occurrence of a situation term is in a formula of the form $Holds(\beta_i, s)$ or $\neg \, Holds(\beta_i, s)$, and that contains at least one such occurrence. ☐

A collection of effect axioms and domain constraints is sometimes called a *domain theory* or *domain description*.

The previous chapter abounded with examples of effect axioms, which are formulae describing the direct effects of actions. For instance, we had,

$$Holds(Colour(x, White), Result(Bleach(x), s)).$$

As mentioned previously, domain constraints mean that actions can have ramifications beyond their direct effects, a phenomenon that we will encounter frequently, and that must be correctly handled by any solution to the frame problem. The only example of a domain constraint we have seen so far is the one about stacks of blocks.

$$\text{Holds(Stack(x,y,z),s)} \leftarrow \text{x} \neq \text{Table} \wedge \text{Holds(On(y,x),s)} \wedge \text{Holds(On(z,y),s)}$$

An interesting phenomenon is the possibility of *implied domain constraints*. An implied domain constraint is one that is a consequence of a collection of effect axioms, but that is not itself an axiom. For example, consider the following pair of effect axioms.

$$\text{Holds(F,Result(A,s))} \leftarrow \text{Holds(F1,s)}$$

$$\neg \text{Holds(F,Result(A,s))} \leftarrow \text{Holds(F2,s)}$$

The following domain constraint is a logical consequence of these two formulae.

$$\neg \text{[Holds(F1,s)} \wedge \text{Holds(F2,s)]}$$

Definition 2.6.3. An *observation sentence* is a formula in which every occurrence of Holds is of the form Holds(β,σ) or $\neg$ Holds(β,σ) where σ is a non-variable situation term, and which contains at least one such occurrence.   □

So far, the examples of observation sentences we have seen describe the situation S0. For example, in Chapter 1 we had,

$$\text{Holds(On(C,Table),S0).}$$

The definitions above are more liberal than these examples suggest. They allow for the involvement of new predicates, and for richer logical structure. To illustrate these features, we'll consider an electrical device controlled by a toggle switch. The switch toggles the status of the device: it turns the device on if it is off and off if it is on. This example is represented below, using an effect axiom that features the introduction of a new predicate Opposite, followed by an observation sentence constraining the situation S0 in a way that uses two existential quantifiers.

$$\text{Holds(Status(x),Result(Toggle,s))} \leftarrow \text{Holds(Status(y),s)} \wedge \text{Opposite(x,y)}$$

$$\exists x \text{ [Holds(Status(x),S0)} \wedge \neg \exists y \text{ [Holds(Status(y),S0)} \wedge \text{x} \neq \text{y]]}$$

The second of these formulae, which says that there is a unique status in the situation S0, if it were universally quantified over situations could serve instead as a domain constraint.

Formulae of these three sorts are often used to represent *temporal projection* problems in the literature. In a temporal projection problem, also called a *prediction* problem, a collection of effect axioms and domain constraints is conjoined to a collection of observation sentences about an *initial situation* (frequently called S0). The logical consequences of this conjunction (call it Σ) should tell us what fluents hold after any given sequence of actions. Such sequences are described using the Result function. For example, we might have a consequence like the following.

Σ ⊨ Holds(Colour(A,Red),Result(Paint(A,Red),Result(Paint(A,Blue),S0)))

Of course, to get the consequences we want, effect axioms, domain constraints and observation sentences are not enough. We also need a solution to the frame problem, which is what this book is all about. But for now, we are just concerned with what can be written using situation calculus formulae.

Effect axioms, domain constraints and observation sentences are not the only situation calculus formulae we can write. We have already seen frame axioms and explanation closure axioms. But plenty of other forms are possible.

Let's consider a slightly bizarre example, which I will use to illustrate some stylistically unorthodox uses of the situation calculus. This example concerns shooting a gun, and anticipates a whole genre of shooting examples that we will encounter shortly.[7]

- The two fluents we are interested in are Alive and Loaded.

- The gun has two chambers, and the fluent Loaded only holds if the chamber currently in front of the hammer has a bullet in it.

- The two actions we are interested in are Load and Shoot.

- The Load action loads a random chamber. If one chamber is loaded and the other is not, it loads the empty one. If both are loaded, it has no effect.

- The Shoot action makes Alive false if Loaded and possibly some other preconditions hold. Suppose we don't know what the other preconditions are.

- The Shoot action also puts the other chamber in front of the hammer.

An interesting feature of this example is that, starting with an empty gun, we don't know what the effect of a single Load action will be. The chamber with the bullet could be the one in front of the hammer, or it could be the other one. However, we do know that two Load actions in a row make Loaded true. So we can write,

Holds(Loaded,Result(Load,Result(Load,s))).

Similarly, we don't know what the outcome of a single Load followed by a single Shoot will be. And even though we know that the gun is loaded after two Loads, we cannot say what the outcome of two Loads followed by a Shoot will be, because we don't know the other preconditions of the Shoot action. But we can say for sure that the effect on Alive of a single Load followed by two Shoots will be the same as that of two Loads followed by a single Shoot. This we can express with the following formula.

Holds(Alive,Result(Shoot,Result(Shoot,Result(Load,s)))) ↔
Holds(Alive,Result(Shoot,Result(Load,Result(Load,s))))

As situation calculus formulae go, these two are very strange, especially the second one. The first is like a conventional effect axiom, except that it deals with a sequence of two actions instead of a single action. The second formula, though, is not like anything we've seen before. We can't write a conventional formula that conveys the same information, because any such formula would be too strong. But this formula, weak though it is, carries useful information, and might allow us to draw useful conclusions about certain sequences of actions.

2.7 Situations and the Result Function

The Result function effectively defines a *tree of situations*, as shown in Figure 2.1. Each path from the root of the tree to a given node corresponds to a hypothetical sequence of actions. The second formula above can be thought of as relating one hypothetical sequence of actions to another. In terms of the tree of situations, it relates one branch of the tree to another.

Of course, the semantics of the situation calculus is inherited from that of the predicate calculus. But this still leaves some room for interpretation at the intuitive level, as we will see in this section. Alternative views on the role of the tree of situations lead to different styles of using the situation calculus. So it's a good idea to be aware of the issues from the outset.

There are two ways to interpret the idea of a situation in the situation calculus, both compatible with the original proposal of McCarthy and Hayes, who define a situation as "the complete state of the universe at an instant of time" [McCarthy & Hayes, 1969].[8]

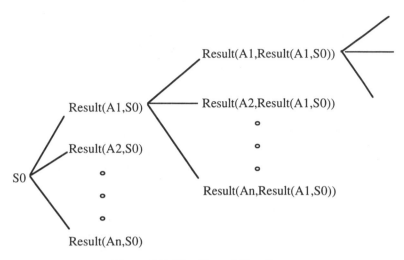

Figure 2.1: The Tree of Situations

On the one hand, we can think of a situation as essentially defined by the set of fluents that hold in it. According to this interpretation, we have the following axiom, which I call the *situation-state axiom*, since some authors reserve the term "state" for a set of fluents.

$$s1 = s2 \leftrightarrow \forall f\ [Holds(f,s1) \leftrightarrow Holds(f,s2)] \qquad (SS)$$

On the other hand, we can think of a situation as a unique node in the tree of situations defined by the Result function. According to this interpretation, we have the following axioms, which I call the *axioms of arboreality*, since they insist that the space of situations is tree-like.[9] Under this interpretation, a situation carries with it a record of the actions that led up to it.

$$Result(a1,s1) = Result(a2,s2) \rightarrow a1{=}a2 \wedge s1{=}s2 \qquad (Arb1)$$

$$S0 \neq Result(a,s) \qquad (Arb2)$$

Axioms (Arb1) and (Arb2) aren't, by themselves, sufficient to exclude models that include unwanted infinite chains, such as the one shown in Figure 2.2.

To exclude such infinite chains, we require a second-order axiom, such as the following induction axiom.[10] Fortunately, for most purposes, even when we want to interpret the space of situations as tree-like, an axiom like this is unnecessary.

$$\forall p\ [[p(S0) \wedge \forall a, s\ [p(s) \rightarrow p(Result(a,s))]] \rightarrow \forall s\ p(s)] \qquad (Ind)$$

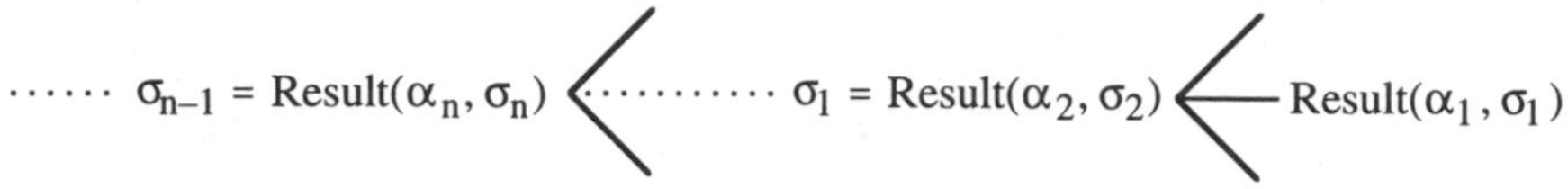

$$\cdots\cdots \; \sigma_{n-1} = \mathrm{Result}(\alpha_n, \sigma_n) \Longleftarrow \cdots\cdots\cdots \; \sigma_1 = \mathrm{Result}(\alpha_2, \sigma_2) \Longleftarrow \mathrm{Result}(\alpha_1, \sigma_1)$$

Figure 2.2: An Unwanted Infinite Chain

The situation-state axiom and the axioms of arboreality aren't inconsistent with each other. But the axioms of arboreality (especially given a uniqueness-of-names property for actions) do rule out certain formulae that are compatible with the first interpretation, such as,

$$\mathrm{Result}(\mathrm{Toggle},\mathrm{Result}(\mathrm{Toggle},s)) = s. \tag{2.7.1}$$

whose intended meaning is that toggling twice has no effect. The inclusion of any such formula introduces a cycle to the structure the Result function superimposes on the space of situations, making it a graph rather than a tree.

The situation calculus carries no inherent commitment to time. Time is easily introduced, but the two interpretations of situations and the Result function presented here lead to two alternative ways in which this can be done.

The axioms of arboreality arises from the implicit assumption that the Result function is essentially a temporal successor function. This leads naturally to the introduction of time as a fluent. We can write $\mathrm{Holds}(\mathrm{Time}(\tau),\sigma)$ to denote that the time is τ in σ. Obviously this would be incompatible with a formula like (2.7.1), but such formulae are ruled out by the axioms of arboreality anyway.

The situation-state axiom doesn't rule out the introduction of time as a fluent. But if we abandon the axioms of arboreality to allow formulae like (2.7.1), a formula that seems to make sense only in the context of the situation-state axiom, we need a different approach. Instead of associating a time point with each situation, we can associate a situation with each time point, by introducing a function State mapping time points to situations. I won't discuss this issue any further for now. In a later chapter on narratives, we will see how these proposals work out in more detail.

2.8   The Limitations of the Situation Calculus

What are the limitations of the situation calculus? This was the question posed by Gelfond, Lifschitz and Rabinov [1991] in response to a widespread feeling in the research community that the situation calculus was not expressive enough to be taken seriously as a formalism for representing change. Even McCarthy and

Hayes, authors of the first published paper to present the situation calculus, criticised its lack of expressivity.

> Consider the following example . . . Two people agree to meet again in a week. Then they part, and one goes to London, while the other flies to San Francisco. They both lead eventful lives, each independently of the other, and duly meet as arranged. In order to describe this using [situation calculus], we have to say what each of them is at [*sic*] just before and just after each noteworthy event involving the other, for each [situation] encompasses them both, being a state of the whole world. But this is clearly silly.
>
> There are other problems with the "situations" ontology (it is very hard to give a reasonable account of continuous processes, for example . . .), but this alone is enough to indicate that it is not a suitable foundation for a theory with any breadth. [Hayes, 1985a]

> The situation calculus . . . has important known limitations. The Result(a,s) formalism . . . has to be modified to handle continuous time. A quite different formalism is needed for expressing facts about concurrent events. The event calculus [of Kowalski and Sergot] is a candidate for meeting both these requirements. [McCarthy, 1988]

These two quotations touch on the three most frequently alleged drawbacks of the situation calculus.

- It cannot handle actions whose order of occurrence is unknown.

- It cannot handle concurrent actions.

- It cannot handle continuous change.

But each of these views is challenged by Gelfond, Lifschitz and Rabinov, who suggest extensions to standard situation calculus usage that enable the formalism to represent the phenomena mentioned.

Their suggestions were taken up and amplified by various authors, and with hindsight we can see that the limitations of the situation calculus are far less grave than was commonly believed. I won't go into these proposals here, since they will be dealt with in detail in later chapters. But I mention them now so that the reader is aware of their existence, and to counter the suspicion that the situation calculus is insufficiently expressive to be worthy of study.

2.9   Default Reasoning

As explained in Chapter 1, the naive deployment of situation calculus effect axioms leads to only a partial set of the logical consequences we would intuitively like. Effect axioms are only one half of the story. They describe what changes as the result of an action. To solve the frame problem, we need a parsimonious, flexible, and elaboration tolerant way to represent what does *not* change. With the appropriate formal foundations now laid, the rest of this chapter is devoted to presenting a first attempt at a non-monotonic solution to the frame problem.

Chapter 1 introduced the idea that we can view the task of solving the frame problem as the task of formalising the common sense law of inertia, part of which can be paraphrased as follows.

Normally, given any action (or event type) and any fluent, the action doesn't affect the fluent.

The key word here is "normally". What this sentence means is that it is exceptional for an action to change a fluent. Inertia is the default. This "law" is enshrined in the following recommendation which, to use McCarthy's term [1980], can be thought of as a "rule of conjecture" (as opposed to a rule of inference).

Assume an action does not change a given fluent unless there's reason to believe it does.

These two sentences embody an insight into how the frame problem might be solved that was present even in the seminal 1969 paper of McCarthy and Hayes.[11] If only we could append such a sentence to our situation calculus theory, the need for explicit frame axioms would be obviated. This basic idea was clarified in the early Seventies by Sandewall [1972]. But at that time, no formal apparatus for representing such sentences as these had been properly worked out.

The difficulty is that these sentences, like a great many that arise in knowledge representation and which have the character of *defaults* rather than straight facts, violate the monotonicity property of classical logic. Indeed, in the early Seventies, the monotonicity of classical logic was thought by many to rule it out as a medium for representing knowledge.

> In any logistic system, all the axioms are necessarily "permissive" —
> they all help to permit new inferences to be drawn. Each added
> axiom means more theorems; none can disappear.
>
> Because logicians are not concerned with systems that will later be
> enlarged, they can design axioms that only permit the conclusions
> they want. In [artificial intelligence] the situation is different. One
> has to learn . . . which kinds of deductions are not to be regarded
> seriously. [Minsky, 1975, p. 261]

As a consequence of sentiments such as these, the design of formal
frameworks for *default reasoning* was one of the major open issues in artificial
intelligence research in the mid to late Seventies. By 1980, the Artificial
Intelligence Journal was able to publish a special issue (in Volume 13) devoted to
progress in the area. Two of the formalisms presented there have stood the test of
time especially well, namely *default logic* [Reiter, 1980] and *circumscription*
[McCarthy, 1980].[12] Both of these formalisms have been applied to the frame
problem. The use of circumscription to address the frame problem is particularly
well understood, and the circumscriptive approach to default reasoning will be
the main one employed in this book.

Before moving on to a formal description of circumscription, I want to
mention two other formalisms for default reasoning that have been influential.
The first of these is *negation-as-failure*, with its accompanying completion
semantics, as used in logic programming [Clark, 1978]. I will be discussing the
application of logic programming techniques to the frame problem in some depth
later.[13] The second is Shoham's *model preference* framework [Shoham, 1988],
which has been used by Shoham and others to tackle the frame problem.
Shoham's framework, which came much later than any of the others mentioned
here, can be thought of as a generalisation of circumscription which, as we will
see shortly, is also based on an idea of model preference. I will say a little more
about Shoham's framework later, in the context of his work on the frame
problem.

2.10 Circumscription

Circumscription is a form of default reasoning due to John McCarthy. It was first
described informally in [McCarthy, 1977], and was presented formally in
[McCarthy, 1980]. As its name suggests, the basic idea of circumscription is to
limit the set of objects of which a predicate is true, a process which is known as
minimising the predicate. Circumscription augments standard first-order
predicate calculus with a second-order formula that does this. Before examining

this formula, let's look at an abstract example to get an intuitive idea of circumscription's effect. Let Σ be the conjunction of the following formulae.

$$P1(A)$$

$$P1(B)$$

$$P2(C)$$

Now, we obviously have $\Sigma \models P1(A)$. On the other hand, we don't have $\Sigma \models P1(C)$, and neither do we have $\Sigma \models \neg P1(C)$. Let the circumscription of Σ *minimising* the predicate P1 be denoted CIRC[Σ ; P1]. The effect of minimising P1 is to make P1 true of *only* those objects of which Σ forces it to be true, in other words to make P1 *false* for the rest. This gives us, for example, CIRC[Σ ; P1] $\models \neg P1(C)$, assuming A$\neq$C and B$\neq$C. More generally, we have,

$$CIRC[\Sigma ; P1] \models \forall x [P1(x) \leftrightarrow [x=A \vee x=B]].$$

In this case, the circumscription yields the *completion* of the predicate P1, an idea which we will be looking into later in the context of logic programming. The formal definition of circumscription is as follows.

First, some notation. Let ρ_1 and ρ_2 be predicates with arity n. Let $\overline{x}$ be a tuple of n distinct variables.

- $\rho_1 = \rho_2$ means $\forall \overline{x} [\rho_1(\overline{x}) \leftrightarrow \rho_2(\overline{x})]$

- $\rho_1 \leq \rho_2$ means $\forall \overline{x} [\rho_1(\overline{x}) \rightarrow \rho_2(\overline{x})]$

- $\rho_1 < \rho_2$ means $[\rho_1 \leq \rho_2] \wedge \neg [\rho_1 = \rho_2]$

Definition 2.10.1. Let ϕ be a formula that mentions the predicate symbol ρ. The *circumscription* of ϕ *minimising* ρ, written CIRC[ϕ ; ρ], is the second-order formula,

$$\phi \wedge \neg \exists q [\phi(q) \wedge q < \rho]$$

where $\phi(q)$ is the formula obtained by replacing all occurrences of ρ in ϕ by q. □

In other words, the circumscription of ϕ minimising ρ is ϕ itself plus the qualification that ρ has to be as small as ϕ will allow.

Since the circumscription is a formula of classical second-order logic, which is monotonic, what is the source of the non-monotonicity here? The non-monotonicity arises because whenever we conjoin a new formula to ϕ, we also conjoin a formula to $\phi(q)$, which is *inside* an existentially quantified part of the circumscription. Of course, if we were simply to conjoin the new formula to ϕ

without altering $\phi(q)$, we would preserve monotonicity. But the definition of circumscription means that to add a new fact is not simply a matter of conjoining it to the old theory.

Definition 2.10.1 is equivalent to,

$$\phi \wedge \forall q \, [[\phi(q) \wedge q \leq \rho] \rightarrow \rho \leq q].$$

This version is sometimes easier to use in proofs, as we'll now see.

Let's return to the simple example given at the beginning of this section, and confirm that the formal definition of circumscription gives the results we were aiming for.

Proposition 2.10.2. If Σ is $P1(A) \wedge P1(B) \wedge P2(C)$ then,

$$CIRC[\Sigma ; P1] \vDash \forall x \, [P1(x) \leftrightarrow [x=A \vee x=B]].$$

Proof. From the definition, we have $CIRC[\Sigma ; P1]$ is equivalent to,

$$\Sigma \wedge \forall q \, [[q(A) \wedge q(B) \wedge P2(C) \wedge q \leq P1] \rightarrow P1 \leq q].$$

Now consider $Q(x) \equiv_{def} [x=A \vee x=B]$. Clearly we have $Q(A)$ and $Q(B)$, and also $Q \leq P1$. So instantiating q to Q makes the left-hand-side of the implication true, allowing us to conclude the right-hand-side, giving $P1 \leq Q$. In other words,

$$\forall x \, [P1(x) \rightarrow [x=A \vee x=B]].$$

Conjoining this with Σ we get,

$$\forall x \, [P1(x) \leftrightarrow [x=A \vee x=B]]. \qquad \square$$

As with many proofs about circumscription, the trick here is to instantiate q so that it has the extension we expect P1 to have after the circumscription. We can then verify that it does indeed have that extension.

Circumscription can also be presented model theoretically. Many people find the model theoretic version easier to understand than the second-order presentation. It is certainly sometimes easier to prove properties of a circumscription by appealing to the model theory. The model theory of circumscription relies on the idea of a minimal model.

Definition 2.10.3. Let M_1 and M_2 be interpretations. M_1 is *as small as* M_2 *with respect to* a predicate ρ, written $M_1 \sqsubseteq_\rho M_2$, if

- M_1 and M_2 agree on the interpretation of everything except possibly ρ, and

- The extension of ρ in M_1 is a subset of its extension in M_2. $\qquad \square$

Definition 2.10.4. A model M_1 of a formula ϕ is *minimal with respect to* $\sqsubseteq_\rho$ if there is no model M_2 of ϕ such that $M_2 \sqsubseteq_\rho M_1$ and not $M_1 \sqsubseteq_\rho M_2$. $\square$

Two features of this preference relation among models are worth noting. Although they're entirely obvious from the definition, they are often a source of confusion for newcomers to circumscription.

- The comparison between models is based on set inclusion, and not on set cardinality. Although they may agree on the interpretation of everything else and the extension of ρ may have *fewer* members in M_1 than in M_2, it is not necessarily the case that $M_1 \sqsubseteq_\rho M_2$.

- As a consequence of this, it is not always the case that two models are comparable. In other words it is possible not to have $M_1 \sqsubseteq_\rho M_2$ and also not to have $M_2 \sqsubseteq_\rho M_1$.

Now we can show that minimal models are models of the circumscription.

Theorem 2.10.5. A model M of a formula ϕ is a model of the circumscription of ϕ minimising the predicate ρ if and only if M is minimal with respect to $\sqsubseteq_\rho$.

Proof. (If half) Let M be a model of ϕ that is minimal with respect to $\sqsubseteq_\rho$. Suppose M is not a model of the circumscription. Then there must be some q such that $\phi(q) \wedge q < \rho$ is satisfied in M. In that case we can construct a model M* that is identical to M, except that $M*[\![\rho]\!] = M[\![q]\!]$. Clearly $M* \sqsubseteq_\rho M$, although it's not the case that $M \sqsubseteq_\rho M*$. So M is not minimal, which is a contradiction.

(Only if half) Let M be a model of CIRC[ϕ ; ρ]. Suppose M is not minimal with respect to $\sqsubseteq_\rho$. Then there must be some model M* of ϕ such that $M*[\![\rho]\!] \subset M[\![\rho]\!]$.[14] In that case, since we can let $M[\![q]\!] = M*[\![\rho]\!]$, M does not satisfy $\neg \exists q$ [$\phi(q) \wedge q < \rho$] and is not therefore a model of the circumscription, which is a contradiction. $\square$

I labour this proof since it is uses a style of argument often employed in proofs about circumscription.

The choice of what to minimise in a circumscription is known as the *circumscription policy*. More complicated circumscription policies are permitted by the definitions in the next section. But one more definition is needed before we move on to these more expressive forms of circumscription. Whatever variant of circumscription we are using, it's convenient to define a notion of preference between models in terms of "as small as".

Definition 2.10.6. Let M_1 and M_2 be interpretations. M_1 is *preferable to* M_2 with respect to a circumscription policy if M_1 is as small as M_2 but M_2 is not as small as M_1 with respect to that policy. □

An interesting property of circumscription, as shown by Etherington, Mercer & Reiter [1985], is that not every circumscription of a consistent theory is itself consistent. In model theoretic terms, it's possible to have infinitely descending chains of ever more preferable models. Fortunately, we won't be encountering such theories in this book.

2.11 More Complicated Circumscription Policies

The definition of circumscription given in the last section only permits the simplest kind of circumscription policy, one in which a single predicate is minimised. Two generalisations of this definition, both described by McCarthy [1986], are required to make circumscription more usable: allowing predicates (and functions and constants) to vary, and minimising many predicates in parallel.

To motivate the need to allow predicates to vary, we'll examine one of the standard examples from the literature, namely the representation of the default rule that birds normally fly. Since this rule is a default, it has exceptions, such as penguins which, of course, don't fly even though they are birds. It's usual, in the literature, to have a single representative penguin, who is invariably called Tweety.

Default rules are usually represented in circumscription through the introduction of an *abnormality* predicate, which is minimised in the circumscription. For example, we can write Ab(x) to denote that x is abnormal in some respect. The default rule for this example then becomes,

$$\text{Flies}(x) \leftarrow \text{Bird}(x) \wedge \neg \text{Ab}(x). \qquad (2.11.1)$$

Ab will be minimised in the circumscription. The fact that penguins are exceptions to the rule is written,

$$\neg \text{Flies}(x) \leftarrow \text{Penguin}(x). \qquad (2.11.2)$$

The behaviour we want from our circumscription is the following. If we now add,

$$\text{Bird(Tweety)} \qquad (2.11.3)$$

then, in the absence of further information, by minimising Ab the circumscription should tell us that ¬ Ab(Tweety) and therefore Flies(Tweety). However, if we then add,

$$\text{Penguin(Tweety)} \qquad\qquad (2.11.4)$$

we expect this conclusion to go away, leaving us with the conclusion ¬ Flies(Tweety).

Unfortunately, this is not what we get simply by minimising Ab.

Let Σ be the conjunction of (2.11.1) to (2.11.3), which is the state of our knowledge before we learn that Tweety is a penguin. Obviously we don't have $\Sigma \models$ Flies(Tweety). But do we have CIRC[Σ ; Ab] $\models$ Flies(Tweety), as we would like? Unfortunately we don't, because it's easy to find a model of Σ in which Tweety does not fly, but which is minimal with respect to $\sqsubseteq_{Ab}$. This is because any reduction in the extension of Ab is paid for by an increase in the extension of Flies. To see this consider any model M_1 of Σ which meets the following criteria.

- $D \supseteq \{\text{TWEETY}\}$

- $M_1 [\![\text{Tweety}]\!] = \text{TWEETY}$

- $\text{TWEETY} \in M_1 [\![\text{Bird}]\!]$

- $\text{TWEETY} \notin M_1 [\![\text{Ab}]\!]$

- $\text{TWEETY} \in M_1 [\![\text{Flies}]\!]$

Now compare this with any model M_2 that is identical to M_1 except for the following.

- $\text{TWEETY} \in M_2 [\![\text{Ab}]\!]$

- $\text{TWEETY} \notin M_2 [\![\text{Flies}]\!]$

At first glance, we might think that $M_1 \sqsubseteq_{Ab} M_2$ since the extension of Ab is smaller in M_1 than M_2. But from the definition of $\sqsubseteq_{Ab}$, we neither have $M_2 \sqsubseteq_{Ab} M_1$ nor $M_1 \sqsubseteq_{Ab} M_2$ since M_1 and M_2 interpret Flies differently. This means that we don't have CIRC[Σ ; Ab] $\models$ Flies(Tweety), as required. We want a definition of circumscription that allows us to vary the extension of Flies in order to minimise Ab. (Predicates that are neither minimised nor allowed to vary are said to be *fixed*. In the simplest definition of circumscription, all predicates are fixed.)

Definition 2.11.5. Let ρ be a predicate symbol and σ^* be a tuple of n predicate, function or constant symbols. Let ϕ be a formula that mentions ρ and each symbol in σ^*. The *circumscription* of ϕ *minimising* ρ and *allowing* σ^* *to vary*, written CIRC[ϕ ; ρ ; $\sigma_1, \sigma_2, \ldots \sigma_n$], is the second-order formula,

$$\phi \wedge \neg \exists\, q, r^* \, [\phi(q \, ; r^*) \wedge q < \rho]$$

where r^* is a tuple of n predicate, function and constant variables, and where $\phi(q \, ; r^*)$ is the formula obtained by replacing all occurrences of ρ in ϕ by q and all occurrences of σ_i by r_i. $\qquad\square$

The model theoretic counterpart to this definition is straightforward.

Definition 2.11.6. Let M_1 and M_2 be interpretations. M_1 is *as small as* M_2 *with respect to* a predicate ρ *allowing* a tuple σ^* of predicate, function and constant symbols *to vary*, written $M_1 \sqsubseteq_{\rho;\sigma^*} M_2$, if

- M_1 and M_2 agree on the interpretation of everything except possibly ρ and/or zero or more members of σ^*, and

- The extension of ρ in M_1 is a subset of its extension in M_2. $\qquad\square$

The definition of minimality with respect to $\sqsubseteq_{\rho;\sigma^*}$ is what we would expect, yielding the counterpart to Theorem 2.10.5.

Theorem 2.11.7. A model M of a formula ϕ is a model of the circumscription of ϕ minimising the predicate ρ and allowing the tuple σ^* of predicate, function and constant symbols to vary if and only if M is minimal with respect to $\sqsubseteq_{\rho;\sigma^*}$.

Proof. This is the same *mutatis mutandis* as for Theorem 2.10.5. $\qquad\square$

If we now represent the birds example using a circumscription policy in which Flies and Penguin are allowed to vary, we get the result we were after. In other words, although we don't have CIRC[Σ ; Ab] $\models$ Flies(Tweety), we do have CIRC[Σ ; Ab ; Flies, Penguin] $\models$ Flies(Tweety). Re-examining the two models M_1 and M_2, we see that although we don't have $M_2 \sqsubseteq_{Ab} M_1$, we do have $M_2 \sqsubseteq_{Ab\,;\,Flies} M_1$.

Another natural and useful extension to the basic definition of circumscription allows policies in which more than one predicate is minimised.

First, we need to extend our notation. Let ρ^* be a tuple of predicates $\rho_1, \rho_2, \ldots \rho_n$ and let σ^* be a tuple of predicates $\sigma_1, \sigma_2, \ldots \sigma_n$, such that ρ_i and σ_i have the same arity.

- $\rho^* = \sigma^*$ means $\rho_i = \sigma_i$ for all $0 < i \le n$

- $\rho^* \le \sigma^*$ means $\rho_i \le \sigma_i$ for all $0 < i \le n$

- $\rho^* < \sigma^*$ means $[\rho^* \leq \sigma^*] \wedge \neg \, [\rho^* = \sigma^*]$

With this notation, the definition of a circumscription in which more than one predicate is minimised, known as *parallel circumscription*, is very similar to the single predicate case.

Definition 2.11.8. Let ρ^* be a tuple of n predicate symbols and σ^* be a tuple of m predicate, function and constant symbols. Let ϕ be a formula that mentions each symbol in ρ^* and σ^*. The *circumscription* of ϕ *minimising* ρ^* and *allowing* σ^* *to vary*, written CIRC$[\phi \; ; \rho_1, \rho_2, \ldots \rho_n \; ; \sigma_1, \sigma_2, \ldots \sigma_m]$, is the second-order formula,

$$\phi \wedge \neg \, \exists \; q^*, r^* \; [\phi(q^* \; ; r^*) \wedge q^* < \rho^*]$$

where q^* is a tuple of n predicate variables, r^* is a tuple of m predicate, function and constant variables, and where $\phi(q^* \; ; r^*)$ is the formula obtained by replacing all occurrences of ρ_i in ϕ by q_i and all occurrences of σ_i by r_i. $\qquad \square$

The model theory can be similarly extended.

Definition 2.11.9. Let M1 and M2 be interpretations. M1 is *as small as* M2 *with respect to* a tuple of predicate symbols ρ^* *allowing* a tuple σ^* of predicate, function and constant symbols *to vary*, written M1 $\sqsubseteq_{\rho^*;\sigma^*}$ M2, if

- M1 and M2 agree on the interpretation of everything except zero or more of the predicates in ρ^* and/or σ^*, and

- The extension of each ρ_i in M1 is a subset of its extension in M2. $\qquad \square$

Minimality with respect to the $\sqsubseteq_{\rho^*;\sigma^*}$ relation is defined in the obvious way. We then have the counterpart to Theorem 2.10.5 for the many predicate case.

Theorem 2.11.10. A model M of a formula ϕ is a model of the circumscription of ϕ minimising the tuple of predicates ρ^* and allowing a tuple of predicates, functions and constants σ^* to vary if and only if M is minimal with respect to $\sqsubseteq_{\rho^*;\sigma^*}$.

Proof. This is the same *mutatis mutandis* as for Theorem 2.10.5. $\qquad \square$

Other kinds of circumscription policy can also be defined, and we will encounter some of these along the way. Also, a number of well-known theorems about circumscription will be useful, and these will be presented at the appropriate time. A thorough overview of the theory of circumscription is given in [Lifschitz, 1994].

One of the things that makes circumscription so elegant is that it is a simple and natural extension of classical logic.[15] This means that it makes a clear separation between the classical aspects of a representation — those facts that are known to be true, and from which we can draw deductively valid inferences — and the non-monotonic aspects — default assumptions whose consequences we would be willing to give up in the face of contradicting evidence.

However, the naturalness of the definition of circumscription can be misleading. Constructing circumscription policies to solve particular representation problems is a tricky business, as early attempts to apply it to the frame problem demonstrated. These early attempts are the subject of the next chapter.

Notes

1. D^n is the set of all n-tuples of elements of D.

2. By "isomorphic" I mean the same modulo changes in the names of members of D.

3. The use of a sorted logic can also speed up search in theorem proving [Cohn, 1985].

4. $\Omega *$ is the set of all finite tuples of elements of Ω.

5. As pointed out in Chapter 1, the first appearance of the situation calculus was in McCarthy's unpublished 1963 memo, "Situations, Actions, and Causal Laws" [McCarthy, 1963].

6. Some authors prefer to write $Do(\sigma,\alpha)$ instead of $Result(\alpha,\sigma)$. This has the advantage that sequences of actions are written in the order in which the actions occur.

7. This genre originated with Hanks and McDermott [1987]. Their famous Yale shooting scenario has been the subject of numerous variations in the literature: the Stanford murder mystery, the Russian turkey shoot, the walking turkey shoot, to name but a few.

8. Furthermore, McCarthy has confirmed, in conversation, that both of these interpretations are compatible with his original intentions.

9. In effect, the axioms of arboreality are uniqueness-of-names axioms for situations.

10. The utility of this axiom is discussed in [Reiter, 1993].

11. The same insight can be expressed in many ways, each of which seems to reveal a different underlying conception of what is going on. Some appeal to the word "normally", other to the word "most", other to the word "assume" or to

phrases like "unless there's reason to believe otherwise". Somehow, when it comes to fomalisation, these differences disappear.

12. On the timescale of progress in logic, fifteen years is not very much. It remains to be seen whether any default reasoning formalism will truly stand the test of time. But I suspect that history will judge the development of these non-monotonic formalisms to be one of the most significant advances in logic this century.

13. Clark's completion semantics is not the only candidate semantics for negation-as-failure, and I will present others too.

14. Throughout this book, I use $\subset$ to denote strict subset, and reserve $\subseteq$ for non-strict subset.

15. McCarthy has remarked that circumscription would have been "entirely comprehensible to Hilbert and probably even to Frege" [McCarthy, 1996].

3 Towards a Non-Monotonic Solution

This chapter presents a first attempt to apply default reasoning techniques to formalise the common sense law of inertia, in order to solve the frame problem. While this attempt is on the right track, we will see that it is fundamentally flawed, for reasons first described by Hanks and McDermott using their well-known Yale shooting scenario. A number of formulations of the Yale shooting scenario are presented, illustrating some finer points in situation calculus style.

3.1 Formalising the Common Sense Law of Inertia

Recall that a number of authors, such as McCarthy and Hayes [1969] and Sandewall [1972], had the insight early on that the key to solving the frame problem was to formalise the common sense law of inertia, including the following default rule.

> *Normally, given any action (or event type) and any fluent, the action doesn't affect the fluent.*

At the time, this insight couldn't be made any more concrete. But with the advent of formal frameworks for default reasoning, such as circumscription, it became possible to formalise sentences such as this.

To see how to do this, let's re-examine the universal frame axiom we first encountered in Chapter 1.

$$[\text{Holds}(f,\text{Result}(a,s)) \leftrightarrow \text{Holds}(f,s)] \leftarrow \neg \text{Affects}(a,f,s) \qquad \text{(F1)}$$

This axiom says that the fluents that hold after an action takes place are the same as those that held beforehand, except for those the action affects. This, as you will remember, leaves us the tricky job of specifying exactly which fluents are not affected by exactly which actions, which is the essence of the frame problem.

If we simply replace the Affects predicate by an abnormality predicate, like that used in the birds example in the last chapter, we get the following.

$$[\text{Holds}(f,\text{Result}(a,s)) \leftrightarrow \text{Holds}(f,s)] \leftarrow \neg \text{Ab}(a,f,s) \qquad \text{(F2)}$$

This axiom can be read as saying, "It is abnormal for a given action to change a given fluent." In other words, it can be read as part of the common sense law of inertia. But if we want all the logical consequences this reading suggests, we have to treat the Ab predicate in the same way we treated it in the birds example. That is to say, we have to minimise it.

Suppose we are given a conjunction Σ of effect axioms, domain constraints and observation sentences. The obvious way to try to augment Σ with the common sense law of inertia is to conjoin it with (F2) and then circumscribe it, minimising Ab and allowing Holds to vary. In other words, we consider CIRC[Σ ∧ (F2) ; Ab ; Holds]. Holds must be allowed to vary for the same reason Flies was allowed to vary in the birds example: its extension in any model depends on the extension of the predicate being minimised. A similar circumscription policy was recommended by McCarthy [1986] to overcome the frame problem.

3.2 An Example that Works

As we will see shortly, this proposal doesn't work as well as we would expect. But first, let's see how it applies to an example for which it does work. Imagine two devices that can each be either on or off. The domain comprises two actions, one to toggle the state of each device. In the initial situation, both devices are on.

$$\text{Holds}(On1,S0) \tag{3.2.1}$$

$$\text{Holds}(On2,S0) \tag{3.2.2}$$

$$\text{Holds}(On1,\text{Result}(Toggle1,s)) \leftrightarrow \neg \, \text{Holds}(On1,s) \tag{3.2.3}$$

$$\text{Holds}(On2,\text{Result}(Toggle2,s)) \leftrightarrow \neg \, \text{Holds}(On2,s) \tag{3.2.4}$$

We also need some formulae to guarantee the uniqueness of the names of actions and fluents. A piece of notation due to Baker [1989] will be useful here. Suppose we are considering a language that includes the functions or constants f_1 to f_k. Then I will write UNA[$f_1, f_2, \ldots, f_k$] to abbreviate the conjunction of the formulae,

$$f_i(x_1, x_2, \ldots x_m) \neq f_j(y_1, y_2, \ldots, y_n)$$

for all $i < j < k$, and,

$$f_i(x_1, x_2, \ldots x_n) = f_i(y_1, y_2, \ldots, y_n) \rightarrow [x_1 = y_1 \wedge x_2 = y_2 \wedge \ldots \wedge x_n = y_n]$$

for all $i < k$. I will use this notation for uniqueness-of-names axioms from now on. For the present example, as is usual, we require uniqueness-of-names for situations, actions and fluents.

$$\text{UNA}[S0, \text{Result}] \tag{3.2.5}$$

$$\text{UNA}[On1, On2] \tag{3.2.6}$$

$$\text{UNA}[Toggle1, Toggle2] \tag{3.2.7}$$

These uniqueness-of-names axioms are not needed for the proof below, but without them we wouldn't be able to get useful results from the formalisation.

Now let Σ be the conjunction of (3.2.1) to (3.2.7), and consider CIRC[$\Sigma \wedge$ (F2) ; Ab ; Holds]. Intuitively, what we require from the circumscription here is the following consequence.

$$Ab(a,f,s) \rightarrow [a=Toggle1 \wedge f=On1] \vee [a=Toggle2 \wedge f=On2] \qquad [3.2.8]$$

We already have the if counterpart to this implication, namely,

$$Ab(a,f,s) \leftarrow [a=Toggle1 \wedge f=On1] \vee [a=Toggle2 \wedge f=On2]. \qquad [3.2.9]$$

This is a consequence of (3.2.3), (3.2.4), and (F2). With the only-if part, we will be able to use (F2) to infer that a device retains its state when it is not toggled. Of course, we could write the only-if formula down right away and include it directly in our formalisation. In this case, the task of determining this Ab formula is easy. But in a more complicated domain it might be very hard, which is why we want circumscription to do the job automatically, behind the scenes. To meet the criterion of elaboration tolerance, we expect our formal apparatus to solve the frame problem, not the human being who is writing the axioms.

Does the circumscription do its job properly, in this case? The proof of Proposition 3.2.10 below shows that it does.

Proposition 3.2.10. If Σ is the conjunction of (3.2.1) to (3.2.7) then,

$$\text{CIRC}[\Sigma \wedge (F2) ; Ab ; Holds] \models Ab(a,f,s) \leftrightarrow [a=Toggle1 \wedge f=On1] \vee \\ [a=Toggle2 \wedge f=On2].$$

Proof. Let ϕ be $\Sigma \wedge$ (F2). From Definition 2.11.8, CIRC[$\Sigma \wedge$ (F2) ; Ab ; Holds] is,

$$\phi \wedge \neg \exists\, q, r\, [\phi(q ; r) \wedge q < Ab]$$

where $\phi(q ; r)$ is the formula obtained by replacing every occurrence of Ab in ϕ by q and every occurrence of Holds by r. This is equivalent to,

$$\phi \wedge \forall\, q, r\, [[\phi(q ; r) \wedge q \leq Ab] \rightarrow Ab \leq q]. \qquad [3.2.11]$$

Now consider,

$$Q(a,f,s) \equiv_{def} [a=Toggle1 \wedge f=On1] \vee [a=Toggle2 \wedge f=On2].$$

If by instantiating q to Q in [3.2.11] we can make the left-hand-side of the implication true, we can conclude the right-hand-side, namely $Ab \leq Q$. Certainly we have $Q \leq Ab$, from [3.2.9]. Now we need to find some r such that $\phi(Q ; r)$ is true. Substituting Q for Ab in ϕ we get Σ conjoined to,

$$[\text{Holds}(f,\text{Result}(a,s)) \leftrightarrow \text{Holds}(f,s)] \leftarrow \quad\quad\quad [3.2.12]$$
$$\neg\, [[a=\text{Toggle1} \wedge f=\text{On1}] \vee [a=\text{Toggle2} \wedge f=\text{On2}]].$$

Now we need to find some r that, when substituted for Holds, makes $\Sigma \wedge$ [3.2.12] true, given ϕ. Consider the predicate R, defined below through an infinite disjunction.

$$R_0(f,s) \equiv_{\text{def}} s=\text{S0} \wedge [f=\text{On1} \vee f=\text{On2}]$$

$$R_{i+1}(f,s) \equiv_{\text{def}} \exists\, s'\, [s=\text{Result}(\text{Toggle1},s')] \wedge \neg\, R_i(\text{On1},s') \wedge f=\text{On1}] \vee$$
$$\exists\, s'\, [s=\text{Result}(\text{Toggle2},s')] \wedge \neg\, R_i(\text{On2},s') \wedge f=\text{On2}] \vee$$
$$\exists\, s'\, [s=\text{Result}(\text{Toggle1},s')] \wedge R_i(\text{On2},s') \wedge f=\text{On2}] \vee$$
$$\exists\, s'\, [s=\text{Result}(\text{Toggle2},s')] \wedge R_i(\text{On1},s') \wedge f=\text{On1}]$$

$$R(f,s) \equiv_{\text{def}} \bigvee_{i>0} R_i(f,s)$$

If we substitute R for Holds in $\Sigma \wedge$ [3.2.12], it's straightforward to verify that the formula follows from ϕ. We can now conclude the right-hand-side of [3.2.11], namely Ab $\leq$ Q. So we have,

$$\text{Ab}(a,f,s) \leftrightarrow [a=\text{Toggle1} \wedge f=\text{On1}] \vee [a=\text{Toggle2} \wedge f=\text{On2}]. \quad\quad \square$$

The proof of this proposition is tricky, because we have chosen to vary Holds. Since Holds takes a situation as an argument, we have to find an instantiation for r that ranges over the infinite number of situations it's possible to construct with the Result function.

3.3 The Hanks-McDermott Problem

The policy of minimising Ab while allowing Holds to vary is an obvious one, and it seems as if it should solve the frame problem. However, as Hanks and McDermott showed in 1986 [Hanks & McDermott, 1986],[1] this policy fails to generate the conclusions we require even with extremely straightforward examples. They distilled the essence of the difficulty into a single, simple example, the now famous Yale shooting scenario.[2]

In the Yale shooting scenario, someone is killed by a gunshot.[3] The formalisation comprises three actions — Load, Wait, and Shoot — and two fluents — Alive and Loaded. There are two effect axioms: the Load action puts a bullet in the gun, and the victim dies after a Shoot action so long as the gun is loaded at the time. There are no effect axioms about the Wait action, which is intended to have no effect on any fluent.

$$\text{Holds(Loaded,Result(Load,s))} \quad\quad\quad \text{(Y1)}$$

$$\neg\ \text{Holds(Alive,Result(Shoot,s))} \leftarrow \text{Holds(Loaded,s)} \quad\quad \text{(Y2)}$$

In addition, there are two observation sentences: the victim is alive in the initial situation, and the gun is unloaded.

$$\text{Holds(Alive,S0)} \quad\quad\quad \text{(Y3)}$$

$$\neg\ \text{Holds(Loaded,S0)} \quad\quad\quad \text{(Y4)}$$

Finally we have,

$$\text{UNA[Load, Wait, Shoot]} \quad\quad\quad \text{(Y5)}$$

$$\text{UNA[Alive, Loaded]} \quad\quad\quad \text{(Y6)}$$

$$\text{UNA[S0, Result].} \quad\quad\quad \text{(Y7)}$$

Now, Hanks and McDermott ask us to consider the situation that obtains after the sequence of actions: Load, Wait, Shoot — in other words the situation Result(Shoot,Result(Wait,Result(Load,S0))). What fluents hold in this situation, if we apply the circumscription policy of the previous section to these formulae?

Intuitively, what we intend here is for the gun to be loaded after the Load action, for it still to be Loaded after the Wait action, and, because the gun is still loaded, for the victim to die after the Shoot action. So, we expect the circumscription of (Y1) to (Y7) to have the consequence,

$$\neg\ \text{Holds(Alive,Result(Shoot,Result(Wait,Result(Load,S0))))} \quad\text{[3.3.1]}$$

Unfortunately, [3.3.1] does not follow from the circumscription.

Proposition 3.3.2. (The Hanks-McDermott Problem)[4] If Σ is the conjunction of (Y1) to (Y7) then,

$$\text{CIRC}[\Sigma \wedge \text{(F2)} \ ; \ \text{Ab} \ ; \ \text{Holds}] \not\models$$
$$\neg\ \text{Holds(Alive,Result(Shoot,Result(Wait,Result(Load,S0)))).}$$

Proof. Consider any model M of $\Sigma \wedge$ (F2) that meets the following criteria.

- M $\Vdash$ Holds(Loaded,Result(Load,S0))

- M $\Vdash \neg$ Holds(Loaded,Result(Wait,Result(Load,S0)))

- M $\Vdash$ Holds(Alive,Result(Shoot,Result(Wait,Result(Load,S0))))

It's easy to see that such models exist, and that they will all have the following properties.

- M ⊩ Ab(Load,Loaded,S0)

- M ⊩ Ab(Wait,Loaded,Result(Load,S0))

- M ⊩ ¬ Ab(Shoot,Alive,Result(Wait,Result(Load,S0)))

From this, we can see that some of those models will be minimal with respect to ⊑$_{Ab;Holds}$, because we cannot remove either of the above abnormalities and still have a model. Since in any of these models we have,

M ⊩ Holds(Alive,Result(Shoot,Result(Wait,Result(Load,S0))))

we also have,

CIRC[Σ ∧ (F2) ; Ab ; Holds] ⊭
¬ Holds(Alive,Result(Shoot,Result(Wait,Result(Load,S0)))).   □

This is one of the most important propositions in the book, so it's worth examining the proof closely. The essence of it is this. We have in mind a particular model (actually a class of models), which we expect the circumscription to supply. But, in addition to this *intended* model, in which the gun stays loaded through the Wait action and the victim dies, we find an *anomalous* model.[5] In the anomalous model, the gun is mysteriously unloaded by the Wait action, and the victim therefore survives.

The anomalous model has an abnormality that is absent in the intended model — the gun is unloaded by the Wait action. But because the gun is unloaded by the Wait action, the precondition of the Shoot action fails. And the victim's consequent survival means that the intended model has an abnormality that is absent in the anomalous model — the victim is dead after the Shoot action. It's as if we've traded one abnormality for another, and both models are minimal with respect to the extension of Ab.

When oscillating between model theoretic and proof theoretic arguments, as I have in the proofs of Propositions 3.2.10 and 3.3.2, it is easy convey the impression of sleight of hand. So it's instructive to consider the following question at this point. If we were to try to prove the negation of Proposition 3.3.2 using similar techniques to those in the proof of Proposition 3.2.10, where would the proof go wrong? Let's attempt the proof to see.

Let φ be Σ ∧ (F2). From Definition 2.11.8, CIRC[Σ ∧ (F2) ; Ab ; Holds] is,

$$\phi \wedge \neg \exists \, q, r \, [\phi(q ; r) \wedge q < Ab]$$

where φ(q ; r) is the formula obtained by replacing every occurrence of Ab in φ by q and every occurrence of Holds by r. This is equivalent to,

$$\phi \wedge \forall \, q, r \, [[\phi(q \, ; r) \wedge q \leq Ab] \rightarrow Ab \leq q]. \qquad [3.3.3]$$

Now let's try plugging in expressions for q and r that accord with the intended model. Consider,

$$Q(a,f,s) \equiv_{def} [a{=}Load \wedge f{=}Loaded] \vee$$
$$[a{=}Shoot \wedge f{=}Alive \wedge Holds(Loaded,s)].$$

If by instantiating q to Q in [3.3.3] we can make the left-hand-side of the implication true, we can conclude the right-hand-side, namely Ab ≤ Q. We have Q ≤ Ab, from (Y1), (Y2) and (F2). Now we need to find some r such that $\phi(Q \, ; r)$ is true. This is where we come unstuck. The source of the difficulty is the occurrence of the Holds predicate in the definition of Q.

When we substitute an expression for Holds in ϕ, we don't get rid of this residual Holds condition, because it is part of the definition of Q, which is itself being substituted for Ab. This Holds condition, which indicates that the truth of Ab(a,f,s) depends on what holds in s, prevents us from finding a suitable substitution for r. The proof of Proposition 3.2.10 relies on the fact that, in the domain of that proposition, the truth of Ab(a,f,s) does not depend on what holds in s. Of course, this will only be the case for very simple examples.

3.4 Variations on Hanks and McDermott's Theme

The problem uncovered by Hanks and McDermott wouldn't be very interesting if it only arose in a single obscure example. But the Yale shooting scenario is intended as a distillation of the essence of a universally applicable form of reasoning, namely the kind of default reasoning required to overcome the frame problem. So we shouldn't have to look far to find other examples that display similar phenomena. This section looks at a number of minor variations on the basic theme of the existence of anomalous models for intuitively plausible situation calculus formalisations, in which one abnormality is traded for another.

It's tempting to believe that the Hanks-McDermott problem only arises in the presence of actions with preconditions. It's the fact that the gun has to be loaded for the victim to die that provides the opportunity for the minimisation to go awry. But we can easily construct an example with no preconditions that manifests the same problem. Imagine a Blocks World in which the only action is to paint block x colour c, denoted Paint(x,c). (We need appropriate sorts for blocks and colours.)

$$Holds(Colour(x,c),Result(Paint(x,c),s)) \qquad (3.4.1)$$

$$\neg \, Holds(Colour(x,c_1),Result(Paint(x,c_2),s)) \leftarrow c_1{\neq}c_2 \qquad (3.4.2)$$

This action has no preconditions — it always succeeds. Now let's consider an initial situation S0 in which all blocks are red.

$$\text{Holds(Colour(x,c),S0)} \leftrightarrow \text{c=Red} \qquad (3.4.3)$$

The if-and-only-if form of this sentence ensures that blocks have only one colour in the initial situation.

Finally, we have the requisite uniqueness-of-names formulae.

$$\text{UNA[S0, Result]} \qquad (3.4.4)$$

$$\text{UNA[Paint]} \qquad (3.4.5)$$

$$\text{UNA[Colour]} \qquad (3.4.6)$$

We also need suitable uniqueness-of-names formulae for blocks and colours. Let's consider a domain with three colours, Red, Green, and Blue, and two blocks, A and B.

$$\text{UNA[Red, Green, Blue]} \qquad (3.4.7)$$

$$\text{UNA[A, B]} \qquad (3.4.8)$$

Although there are no preconditions in this example, we get intended and anomalous models, as in the Yale shooting scenario. Consider the situation,

$$\text{Result(Paint(B,Blue),Result(Paint(A,Green),S0)).}$$

What we require is for block B to retain its red colour while block A is painted green, then for it to become blue only when it is painted blue. Unfortunately, this does not follow from the circumscription.

Proposition 3.4.9. If Σ is the conjunction of (3.4.1) to (3.4.8) then,

$$\text{CIRC}[\Sigma \wedge (\text{F2}) \; ; \text{Ab} \; ; \text{Holds}] \not\models$$
$$\text{Holds(Colour(B,Red),Result(Paint(A,Green),S0)).}$$

Proof. Consider any model M of $\Sigma \wedge (\text{F2})$ that meets the following criteria.

- $\text{M} \Vdash \neg \text{Holds(Colour(B,Red),Result(Paint(A,Green),S0))}$

- $\text{M} \Vdash \text{Holds(Colour(B,Blue),Result(Paint(A,Green),S0))}$

- $\text{M} \Vdash \text{Holds(Colour(B,Blue),}$
  $\text{Result(Paint(B,Blue),Result(Paint(A,Green),S0)))}$

It's easy to see that such models exist, and that they will all have the following properties.

- M ⊩ Ab(Paint(A,Green),Colour(B,Blue),S0)

- M ⊩ Ab(Paint(A,Green),Colour(B,Red),S0)

- M ⊩ ¬ Ab(Paint(B,Blue),Colour(B,Blue),Result(Paint(A,Green),S0))

From this, we can see that some of those models will be minimal with respect to ⊑$_{Ab;Holds}$, because we cannot remove either of the above abnormalities and still have a model. Since in any of these models we have,

$$M ⊩ ¬ Holds(Colour(B,Red),Result(Paint(A,Green),S0))$$

we also have,

$$CIRC[Σ ∧ (F2) ; Ab ; Holds] ⊭$$
$$Holds(Colour(B,Red),Result(Paint(A,Green),S0)). \qquad □$$

In the class of anomalous models suggested by this proof, the Paint(A,Green) action mysteriously turns block B blue. This generates an extra abnormality. But the gain of this abnormality is offset against the loss of another abnormality later: when it comes to painting block B blue, we find that it's blue already, so the action has no effect.

As pointed out by Baker [1989], the formulation of the Yale shooting scenario in the previous section has another class of anomalous models, in which the victim mysteriously dies during the Wait action. As in the above example, these anomalous models don't exploit the presence of the precondition. They simply allow change to happen sooner than it has to. These models are characterised by the following properties.

- M ⊩ Holds(Loaded,Result(Load,S0))

- M ⊩ Holds(Loaded,Result(Wait,Result(Load,S0)))

- M ⊩ ¬ Holds(Alive,Result(Wait,Result(Load,S0)))

- M ⊩ Ab(Load,Loaded,S0)

- M ⊩ ¬ Ab(Wait,Loaded,Result(Load,S0))

- M ⊩ Ab(Wait,Alive,Result(Load,S0))

- M ⊩ ¬Ab(Shoot,Alive,Result(Wait,Result(Load,S0)))

In these models, the intended abnormality of the Shoot action with respect to Alive is traded for the abnormality of the earlier Wait action with respect to Alive. The victim is already dead when the shooting takes place, so the intended abnormality can be dropped. Inspired by this kind of anomalous model, it's possible to simplify the Yale shooting scenario even further, by omitting the Loaded precondition altogether, and still obtain anomalous models.

$$\neg \text{Holds(Alive,Result(Shoot,s))} \qquad (3.4.10)$$

$$\text{Holds(Alive,S0)} \qquad (3.4.11)$$

$$\text{UNA[S0, Result]} \qquad (3.4.12)$$

$$\text{UNA[Wait, Shoot]} \qquad (3.4.13)$$

Consider the situation Result(Shoot,Result(Wait,S0)) in the light of the above formulae. There's no avoiding the conclusion that the victim is dead after waiting then shooting. This follows directly from (3.4.10), even without circumscribing. But, after circumscription, we would like it to be a consequence of these formulae that the victim is still alive after the Wait action. It should be the Shoot action that kills them. Unfortunately, this does not follow.

Proposition 3.4.14. If Σ is the conjunction of (3.4.10) to (3.4.13) then,

$$\text{CIRC}[\Sigma \wedge (\text{F2}) ; \text{Ab} ; \text{Holds}] \not\vdash \text{Holds(Alive,Result(Wait,S0))}.$$

Proof. Consider any model M of $\Sigma \wedge (\text{F2})$ such that,

$$M \Vdash \neg \text{Holds(Alive,Result(Wait,S0))}$$

Any such M will have the following properties.

- $M \Vdash \text{Ab(Wait,Alive,S0)}$

- $M \Vdash \neg \text{Ab(Wait,Alive,Result(Wait,S0))}$

We cannot remove the above abnormality without introducing another one, so some of those models will be minimal with respect to $\sqsubseteq_{\text{Ab;Holds}}$. Since in any of these models we have,

$$M \Vdash \neg \text{Holds(Alive,Result(Wait,S0))}$$

we also have,

$$\text{CIRC}[\Sigma \wedge (\text{F2}) ; \text{Ab} ; \text{Holds}] \not\vdash \text{Holds(Alive,Result(Wait,S0))}. \qquad \square$$

In this sort of anomalous model, the victim dies inexplicably during the Wait action. Since the victim is already dead when the shooting takes place, this introduces no further abnormalities. The anomalous model has traded an abnormality during the Shoot action for one during the Wait action. Further anomalous models exist in which the victim doesn't even survive this long, but dies during the Load action.

3.5 Differences in Situation Calculus Style

Hanks and McDermott's original formalisation of the Yale shooting scenario used a slightly different situation calculus style to the one I have adopted. Represented in their style, the examples of the last section don't give rise to the anomalous models described. So it's instructive to examine their formulae in their original form. Here they are.

$$\text{Holds(Alive,S0)} \qquad \text{(HM1)}$$

$$\text{Holds(Loaded,Result(Load,s))} \qquad \text{(HM2)}$$

$$\text{Holds(Loaded,s)} \rightarrow \qquad \text{(HM3)}$$
$$[\text{Ab(Shoot,Alive,s)} \wedge \text{Holds(Dead,Result(Shoot,s))}]$$

$$[\text{Holds(f,s)} \wedge \neg \text{Ab(a,f,s)}] \rightarrow \text{Holds(f,Result(a,s))} \qquad \text{(HM4)}$$

Uniqueness of names formulae are also required. There are two differences between this formulation and that of Section 3.3. First, a different universal frame axiom is used. Instead of Axiom (F2), we have (HM4), which is equivalent to,

$$[\text{Holds(f,s)} \rightarrow \text{Holds(f,Result(a,s))}] \leftarrow \neg \text{Ab(a,f,s)}. \qquad [3.5.1]$$

In effect, [3.5.1] employs a one-way conditional in place of the biconditional in (F2). Second, the effect axiom (HM3) explicitly mentions an abnormality, while the analogous formula (Y2) does not.

What is the significance of these differences? Axiom (F2), with its biconditional, captures four kinds of default persistence.

- The forwards persistence of positive information. From $\text{Holds}(\beta,\sigma)$ we can deduce $\text{Holds}(\beta,\text{Result}(\alpha,\sigma))$.

- The backwards persistence of positive information. From $\text{Holds}(\beta,\text{Result}(\alpha,\sigma))$ we can deduce $\text{Holds}(\beta,\sigma)$.

- The forwards persistence of negative information. From $\neg \text{Holds}(\beta,\sigma)$ we can deduce $\neg \text{Holds}(\beta,\text{Result}(\alpha,\sigma))$.

- The backwards persistence of negative information. From $\neg \text{Holds}(\beta,\text{Result}(\alpha,\sigma))$ we can deduce $\neg \text{Holds}(\beta,\sigma)$.

The use of a one-way conditional in [3.5.1] means that we get only two of these types of persistence: positive information persists forwards, and negative information persists backwards. In the Yale shooting scenario, as formalised by Hanks and McDermott, only the forwards persistence of positive information is required. Indeed, they use the separate fluent Dead to denote that the victim is not alive, so that all information is effectively positive, while the formalisation of Section 3.4 uses the formula ¬ Holds(Alive,σ) to denote this.

The form of (HM4) has a further implication. An important feature of the situation calculus style used throughout this book is that the only mention of the Ab predicate is in (F2). If we have an effect axiom that tells us that action α changes fluent β in situation σ, then it follows from that axiom and (F2) that Ab(α,β,σ). There is no need to include this consequence explicitly in the effect axiom. With Axiom (HM4), abnormality is also automatically derivable in this way, but only for actions that change fluents from true to false, and not for those that change fluents from false to true.

The following question then arises, with respect to Hanks and McDermott's formalisation. Why does Ab(Shoot,Alive,s) appear in the consequent of (HM3), since this abnormality will be automatically derivable anyway? Observe that this abnormality is in fact only automatically derivable for situations in which Alive holds in s. So the only possible role for the Ab literal in (HM3) is to rule out anomalous models, like those described in the previous section, in which the victim dies during the Wait (or Load) action. The form of (HM3) prevents the abnormality of Shoot with respect to Alive to be traded for anything. In the presence of (HM3), Shoot is abnormal with respect to Alive, so long as Loaded holds, even if the victim is already dead.

Hanks and McDermott's original formalisation exhibits the phenomenon of anomalous models very nicely, which was its intended purpose. But as an example of knowledge representation it's open to criticism. In sum,

- The forwards persistence of negative information is not dealt with,

- Negative information is not represented as such, but is handled through the introduction of new fluents, and

- The occurrence of an Ab literal in an effect axiom serves no legitimate purpose.

Indeed, the formulation of Section 3.4 has been more popular in the literature. But whichever situation calculus style is adopted, the phenomenon of anomalous models — the Hanks-McDermott problem — arises anyway.

3.6 The Importance of the Hanks-McDermott Problem

The impact of the Hanks-McDermott problem[6] on the artificial intelligence community was considerable. Hanks and McDermott didn't just show that the difficulty arises with circumscription and the situation calculus. Their paper suggested that the problem was very deep.

> . . . circumscription is not the culprit here — Reiter's proof-theoretic default logic has the same problem. We can also express the same problem in McDermott's nonmonotonic logic and show that the theory has the same two fixed points [corresponding to the intended and anomalous models].

> Nor is the situation calculus to blame: in a previous paper we use a simplified version of McDermott's temporal logic and show that the same problem arises, again for all three default logics. . . . it appears that three default logics are inherently unable to represent the domain correctly. [Hanks & McDermott, 1986]

On this last point, Hanks and McDermott were simply wrong, as we will see later. With hindsight, we can see that they jumped to a false general conclusion from too few examples. But the implications for the role of logic in artificial intelligence, had they been right, would have been dire.

> . . . the claim implicit in the development of nonmonotonic logics — that a simple extension to classical logic would result in the power to express an important class of human nondeductive reasoning — is certainly called into question by our result. [Hanks & McDermott, 1986]

Recall that formal techniques for default reasoning were largely motivated by the objection that logic, with its monotonic consequence relation, couldn't serve as a foundation for artificial intelligence (see the quote by Minsky in Section 2.9). But there were two ways to take the Hanks-McDermott problem. To some, it sounded the death knell for logic in artificial intelligence. To others it offered a challenge.

Notes

1. Hanks and McDermott's result was first published in a prize-winning paper in the 1986 AAAI conference. But it was already sufficiently well known in the community for there to be papers in the same conference addressing the problem

they raised. An extended version of the paper was later published in the Artificial Intelligence Journal [Hanks & McDermott, 1987]. A related counter-example, due to Lifschitz, is reported in McCarthy's paper itself [1986].

2. The "Yale shooting scenario" is so-called because Hanks and McDermott were both at Yale University when they formulated it.

3. Researchers with unusually sensitive dispositions sometimes have difficulty coping with the violence of the Yale shooting scenario. These researchers manage to remain active by denying that the victim is human. They usually assume that it's a turkey instead. Hence the scenario is frequently referred to as the "Yale turkey shoot".

4. In fact, Hanks and McDermott's formalisation was slightly different from mine. In particular, they employed a universal frame axiom which featured a one-way implication in place of the biconditional in (F2). I will be discussing this difference later on.

5. In fact, there is a whole class of anomalous models. For convenience, I will often speak of *the* anomalous model, which can be taken to mean any arbitrary member of this class.

6. The ambiguous term "Yale shooting problem" is common in the literature. I prefer the term "Hanks-McDermott problem" for the task of solving the frame problem in such a way that anomalous models don't arise, and I reserve the term "Yale shooting scenario" for the example Hanks and McDermott used to illustrate their point, which has become a standard benchmark in the field.

4 Chronological Minimisation

This chapter presents one of the earliest proposals for solving the Hanks-McDemott problem, namely chronological minimisation. The idea behind chronological minimisation is to postpone change until as late as possible. On the way to presenting the technique, we see how the Hanks-McDermott problem arises in default logic, particular attention being given to the order in which defaults are applied. A new benchmark — the stolen car scenario — indicates that chronological minimisation, in its raw state, doesn't cope well with problems that involve reasoning backwards in time. Two techniques are sketched, namely occlusion and filtered preferential entailment, which have been developed to address this and other limitations.

4.1 The Yale Shooting Scenario in Default Logic

The Hanks-McDermott problem has been tackled, with varying degrees of success, in numerous ways. Every worthwhile attempt to solve the problem is based on some insight as to why the problem arises in the first place. To understand an attempted solution, we must be able to see through the fog of technical details to that insight. The aim of this section is to present the insight behind one of the most promising techniques for addressing the Hanks-McDermott problem, namely *chronological minimisation*.

In a nutshell, the idea is this. The Hanks-McDermott problem arises from a failure to respect the directionality of time. This failure is most dramatically highlighted when default logic [Reiter, 1980] is used to address the frame problem instead of circumscription. To see this, let's reformulate the Yale shooting scenario in terms of default logic. As we will see, the same problem arises with default logic as with circumscription. But default logic's more constructive proof-theory permits us to see things that aren't apparent with the circumscriptive formulation.

First, an overview of default logic. Where circumscription augments a classical first-order theory with a second-order "rule of conjecture", default logic augments it with a set of *default rules*. These are like the rules of inference ordinarily used in the proof theoretic presentation of a logic, except that they are defaults, which is to say they only apply when they don't give rise to contradiction. The resulting *default theory* will have a number of *extensions*. Here are the formal definitions.

Definition 4.1.1. A *default rule* has the form,

$$\frac{\phi_1(\overline{x}) : \phi_2(\overline{x})}{\phi_3(\overline{x})}$$

where $\overline{x}$ is a tuple of variables, and each $\phi_i(\overline{x})$ is a well-formed formula whose free variables are those in $\overline{x}$.   □

The intuitive meaning of such a rule is the following: if $\phi_1(\overline{x})$ is true and $\phi_2(\overline{x})$ is consistent then assume $\phi_3(\overline{x})$. If $\phi_2(\overline{x})$ is the same as $\phi_3(\overline{x})$ then the default rule is said to be a *normal default*. I will refer to the top part of a default rule as its *antecedent*, and the bottom part as its *consequent*.

Following Hanks and McDermott, the default rule with which we will try to address the frame problem is a normal default with an empty $\phi_1(\overline{x})$ part.

$$\frac{: \neg\, Ab(a,f,s)}{\neg\, Ab(a,f,s)}$$

In other words, assume $\neg\, Ab(a,f,s)$ where it is consistent to do so. The Ab predicate has the same meaning as in the circumscriptive attempt at the problem, and this default rule fulfils the same purpose as the minimisation of Ab in the circumscription.

Definition 4.1.2. A *default theory* is a pair $\langle\Delta,\Sigma\rangle$, where Δ is a set of default rules, and Σ is a sentence of first-order predicate calculus.[1]   □

Σ encapsulates certain knowledge of the domain, from which we can draw deductively valid inferences, while Δ represents our default knowledge, from which we draw defeasible conclusions. We will consider the default theory $\langle\Delta,\Sigma\rangle$ where,

$$\Delta = \left\{ \frac{: \neg\, Ab(a,f,s)}{\neg\, Ab(a,f,s)} \right\}$$

and Σ is the conjunction of (Y1) to (Y4) with (F2), taken from the last chapter. (Note that the uniqueness-of-names axioms (Y5) to (Y7) are not required here.) As a reminder, here are those formulae again.

$$Holds(Loaded,Result(Load,s)) \tag{Y1}$$

$$\neg\, Holds(Alive,Result(Shoot,s)) \leftarrow Holds(Loaded,s) \tag{Y2}$$

$$Holds(Alive,S0) \tag{Y3}$$

$$\neg\, Holds(Loaded,S0) \tag{Y4}$$

$$[\text{Holds(f,Result(a,s))} \leftrightarrow \text{Holds(f,s)}] \leftarrow \neg \, \text{Ab(a,f,s)} \qquad \text{(F2)}$$

It would now be natural to ask what follows from this default theory. But in terms of default logic, this is not quite the right question, because default logic doesn't have any inherent notion of logical consequence. Rather, given a default theory, it defines the notion of an "acceptable set of beliefs" or "extension", as we will see in the next section.

4.2 Generating Extensions in Default Logic

When we apply default logic's notion of an acceptable set of beliefs (an extension) to the above formulation of the Yale shooting scenario, we find that the definitions approve two such sets, corresponding closely to the intended and anomalous models we found using circumscription. On closer examination, we find that the anomalous extension results from applying the default rule backwards in time, while the intended extension results from applying it forwards. Here come the formal details.

In the following definition, where $\phi(\overline{x})$ denotes a formula whose free variables are those in $\overline{x}$, $\phi(\tau_1 \ldots \tau_n)$ denotes the same formula with each x_i replaced by τ_i.

Definition 4.2.1. A set of well-formed formulae is an *extension* of a default theory $\langle \Delta, \Sigma \rangle$ if it is a fixed point of the operator Γ, defined as follows. If S is a set of well-formed formulae with no free variables, then $\Gamma(S)$ is the smallest set such that,

- $\Sigma \subseteq \Gamma(S)$,

- If ϕ is a logical consequence of $\Gamma(S)$, then $\phi \in \Gamma(S)$, and

- If Δ includes the default rule,

$$\frac{\phi_1(\overline{x}) : \phi_2(\overline{x})}{\phi_3(\overline{x})}$$

and $\phi_1(\tau_1 \ldots \tau_n) \in \Gamma(S)$ and $\neg \, \phi_2(\tau_1 \ldots \tau_n) \notin \Gamma(S)$, then $\phi_3(\tau_1 \ldots \tau_n) \in \Gamma(S)$, where each τ_i is a non-variable term. □

Each extension of a default theory is supposed to represent an acceptable set of beliefs, given that theory. The definition looks a little tricky, but it suggests a fairly natural way to construct extensions: start with a set containing just Σ and its logical consequences, then repeatedly choose an applicable default, add its consequent, and form the corresponding deductive closure, until nothing more can be added.

More precisely, given a default theory $\langle \Delta, \Sigma \rangle$, we can construct extensions according to the recipe given below. This non-deterministic algorithm[2] isn't guaranteed to produce an extension, except under certain conditions. This is because there is no guarantee that additions to S will not invalidate the conditions that made the earlier application of a default rule possible. However, in the special case of normal defaults, this cannot happen. Fortunately, the only default rule in our example is a normal default, so we can proceed with impunity.

S' := {}
S := $\Sigma \cup$ logical consequences of Σ
Wnile S $\neq$ S'
   S' := S
   Choose any ϕ_1, ϕ_2, ϕ_3 and $\tau_1 \ldots \tau_n$

     such that $\dfrac{\phi_1(\overline{x}) : \phi_2(\overline{x})}{\phi_3(\overline{x})}$ in Δ

     and $\phi_1(\tau_1 \ldots \tau_n) \in$ S and $\neg \phi_2(\tau_1 \ldots \tau_n) \notin$ S
   S := S $\cup \phi_3(\tau_1 \ldots \tau_n)$
   S := S $\cup$ logical consequences of S
End While

Furthermore, in most interesting cases, the algorithm will not terminate, since the default rules will be applicable an infinite number of times. However, in such cases each intermediate S is a subset of some extension, so we can still use the algorithm to obtain useful information by executing the loop a finite number of times.

4.3 The Directionality of Time

Let's apply this algorithm to the default theory representing the Yale shooting scenario, in other words the default theory $\langle \Delta, \Sigma \rangle$ where,

$$\Delta = \left\{ \frac{: \neg \text{ Ab(a,f,s)}}{\neg \text{ Ab(a,f,s)}} \right\}$$

and Σ is the conjunction of (Y1) to (Y4) with (F2).

First we'll partially construct an intended extension. We start with the set S = $\Sigma \cup$ the logical consequences of Σ. Now we have a choice as to how we apply the default rule. Let's choose to add,

¬ Ab(Wait,Loaded,Result(Load,S0)).

The default rule permits this, since it is consistent with S. Next we add in the logical consequences of the new addition, which will include,

Holds(Loaded,Result(Wait,Result(Load,S0)))

from (F2), and therefore, from (Y2),

¬ Holds(Alive,Result(Shoot,Result(Wait,Result(Load,S0)))).

We would need to iterate the algorithm forever to obtain an extension, but we have already shown that extensions exist that include the above intended consequence. Now for anomalous extensions, which we get simply by making a different choice when we apply the default rule. Again we start with the set S = Σ ∪ the logical consequences of Σ. But this time, applying the default rules, let's choose to add,

¬ Ab(Shoot,Alive,Result(Wait,Result(Load,S0))).

This sentence is consistent with S, so the default rule permits its addition. Now we add in the logical consequences of this new addition, and we get, amongst other sentences,

¬ Holds(Loaded,Result(Wait,Result(Load,S0))).

We already had,

Holds(Loaded,Result(Load,S0))

and taken together, these two sentences give us,

Ab(Wait,Loaded,Result(Load,S0)).

This gives us the undesired consequence,

Holds(Alive,Result(Shoot,Result(Wait,Result(Load,S0)))).

So we have shown that default logic yields anomalous extensions for the Yale shooting scenario in just the same way that circumscription yields anomalous models.

Besides demonstrating that the Hanks-McDermott problem is not merely an artefact of circumscription, the exercise of showing how it arises with default logic offers an insight into why the difficulty arises, and suggests a way out. The intended extension arises when the default rule is applied in chronological order, in other words earliest abnormalities are considered first. The anomalous extension arises when the default rules is applied in reverse chronological order: later abnormalities are considered first.

To put it another way, the intended extension is the result of postponing change until as late as possible. So why not try to formalise the idea of postponing change until as late as possible, and build it into our framework for reasoning about action? This technique, known as *chronological minimisation*, was adopted by several authors, such as Kautz [1986], Lifschitz [1986], and Shoham [1986], as a way of overcoming the frame problem without running into the difficulties described by Hanks and McDermott.

4.4 Formalising Chronological Minimisation

How should we set about the task of formalising chronological minimisation? It's easy to see that default logic is not up to the job, because it doesn't permit the application of default rules to be prioritised in any way. Circumscription suffers from a similar problem. It doesn't allow us to declare that the minimisation of $Ab(\alpha,\beta,\sigma)$ should take precedence over the minimisation of $Ab(\alpha_1,\beta,Result(\alpha_2,\sigma))$. In short, we are obliged to modify our method of default reasoning.

One option is to start from scratch and code the idea of chronological minimisation into our default reasoning right from the start. This was the approach of Kautz [1986], and this is the approach I will adopt here. Of course, we will end up with a more flexible tool if we design a generic formalism for default reasoning with the requisite power and specialise it to solve the frame problem. This was the path followed by Lifschitz [1986] with prioritised circumscription, and Shoham [1986] with the idea of model preference. But just to see how chronological minimisation works, we can settle for a specialised definition.[3]

To begin with, let's adopt the axioms of arboreality (Arb1) and (Arb2) from Section 2.7.

$$Result(a1,s1) = Result(a2,s2) \rightarrow a1{=}a2 \land s1{=}s2 \qquad (Arb1)$$

$$S0 \neq Result(a,s) \qquad (Arb2)$$

These axioms ensure that situation terms can be ordered, a prerequisite for formalising a criterion of chronological minimisation in situation calculus.[4] A situation term σ_1 *precedes* a situation term $Result(\alpha,\sigma_2)$ if $\sigma_1{=}\sigma_2$ or if σ_1 precedes a situation term which itself precedes σ_2.

As usual, our theory will include effect axioms, domain constraints, and observation sentences, along with the frame axiom (F2) and the axiom of arboreality (Arb1). Now, we can formalise the conditions under which one model of such a theory is chronologically as small as another, by analogy with the model theoretic presentation of circumscription (see Section 2.10).

Definition 4.4.1. Let M_1 and M_2 be interpretations of a language of the situation calculus. M_1 is *chronologically as small as* M_2, written $M_1 \sqsubseteq_{chron} M_2$, if

- M_1 and M_2 agree on the interpretation of everything except possibly Ab and Holds, and

- For all situation terms σ_1, either

  - $\{\langle a,f \rangle \mid \langle a,f,M_1[\![\sigma_1]\!] \rangle \in M_1[\![Ab]\!]\} \subseteq \{\langle a,f \rangle \mid \langle a,f,M_2[\![\sigma_1]\!] \rangle \in M_2[\![Ab]\!]\}$, or

  - There is some situation term σ_2 that precedes σ_1 such that $\{\langle a,f \rangle \mid \langle a,f,M_1[\![\sigma_2]\!] \rangle \in M_1[\![Ab]\!]\} \subset \{\langle a,f \rangle \mid \langle a,f,M_2[\![\sigma_2]\!] \rangle \in M_2[\![Ab]\!]\}$. $\quad\square$

Let me clarify the second of these conditions. Whereas the flawed circumscription policy of the last chapter demands a blanket minimisation of Ab, the above definition minimises Ab bit by bit. The second condition of the definition treats each situation term separately. According to the flawed circumscription policy, M_1 is as small as M_2 only if the extension of Ab in M_1 is a subset of that in M_2. Chronological minimisation is more liberal. M_1 can be chronologically as small as M_2 even if there is some σ_1 for which M_2 beats M_1, in the sense that the Ab's extension is smaller in M_2 than in M_1 for σ_1. This is allowed so long as there is also a preceding σ_2 for which M_1 beats M_2. In other words, if M_1 beats M_2 for σ_2, then it doesn't matter whether or not it is beaten by M_2 for Result($\alpha_n, \ldots$ Result(α_1,σ_1) $\ldots$).

Chronologically minimal models are now defined in the obvious way, leading naturally to a corresponding definition of logical consequence.

Definition 4.4.2. A model M_1 of a formula ϕ is *chronologically minimal* if there is no model M_2 of ϕ such that $M_2 \sqsubseteq_{chron} M_1$ and not $M_1 \sqsubseteq_{chron} M_2$. $\quad\square$

Definition 4.4.3. Let Σ be the conjunction of a set of effect axioms, domain constraints, and observation sentences, along with Axioms (Arb1), (Arb2) and (F2). A formula ϕ is a *logical consequence* of the chronological minimisation of Σ (written $\Sigma \vDash_{chron} \phi$) if for all chronologically minimal models M of Σ, M $\Vdash \phi$.$\square$

A second-order axiom, like the circumscription axiom, can be written to capture this notion of minimisation proof-theoretically (see [Kautz, 1986] or [Lifschitz, 1986]), but I won't present it here because the model-theoretic characterisation is enough to see how chronological minimisation operates.

4.5   The Yale Shooting Scenario

Does chronological minimisation really overcome the Hanks-McDermott problem? Let's apply it to the Yale shooting scenario, and see how it fares. Unlike the flawed circumscription policy, we are expecting chronological minimisation to keep the intended model, but reject the anomalous model as non-minimal.

Proposition 4.5.1. If Σ is the conjunction of (Y1) to (Y6) with (Arb1), (Arb2) and (F2), then,

$$\Sigma \vDash_{chron} \neg\, Holds(Alive,Result(Shoot,Result(Wait,Result(Load,S0)))).$$

Proof. Suppose there exists a chronologically minimal model M of Σ such that,

$$M \Vdash Holds(Alive,Result(Shoot,Result(Wait,Result(Load,S0)))).$$

Any such M must have the following properties.

- M $\Vdash \neg$ Holds(Loaded,Result(Wait,Result(Load,S0)))

- M $\Vdash$ Holds(Loaded,Result(Load,S0))

- M $\Vdash$ Ab(Wait,Loaded,Result(Load,S0))

Now we can easily construct a model M' with the following properties.

- M' agrees with M on the interpretation of everything except possibly for,

    - The predicate Holds, and

    - The predicate Ab for the situation term Result(Load,S0) and situation terms preceded by Result(Load,S0).

- M' $\Vdash$ Holds(Loaded,Result(Wait,Result(Load,S0)))

- M' $\Vdash$ Holds(Loaded,Result(Load,S0))

- M' $\Vdash \neg$ Ab(Wait,Loaded,Result(Load,S0))

Obviously,

$$M' \Vdash \neg\, Holds(Alive,Result(Shoot,Result(Wait,Result(Load,S0)))).$$

Furthermore M' $\sqsubseteq_{chron}$ M but not M $\sqsubseteq_{chron}$ M', since the extension of Ab is smaller for Result(Load,S0) in M' than in M. Therefore M cannot be chronologically minimal, which is a contradiction. So all chronologically minimal models must have,

$\neg$ Holds(Alive,Result(Shoot,Result(Wait,Result(Load,S0)))).   □

So chronological minimisation rejects the anomalous model of the Yale shooting scenario, and permits the desired conclusion to be drawn. This is certainly progress. But the Yale shooting scenario is just one example. How do we know that the Hanks-McDermott problem, or something similar, won't arise with other examples? This is an important question, and we'll be returning to it later on. For the moment the question is irrelevant, because it isn't hard to find examples where chronological minimisation does indeed supply counter-intuitive conclusions. The best known of these is the *stolen car scenario*, due to Kautz [1986].

4.6 The Stolen Car Scenario

While the Yale shooting scenario was designed to test a formalism's aptitude for solving *prediction* (or *projection*) problems. In a prediction problem, we know what fluents hold in the initial situation, and we want to know what fluents hold after a sequence of actions. Prediction is reasoning forwards in time, from causes to effects.

Dealing with the stolen car scenario is best thought of as an *explanation* (or *postdiction*) problem. In an explanation problem, we know that certain fluents hold in situations other than the initial situation, and we want to know what led to those fluents holding. While prediction concerns reasoning forwards in time from causes to effects, explanation concerns reasoning backwards in time, from effects to possible causes. Chapter 17 will deal with explanation in some detail. For now, we're just concerned with the difficulty chronological minimisation has with problems like the stolen car scenario.

The task with the stolen car scenario is to model the reasoning involved in the following story. Suppose I park my car in the morning and go to work. According to my knowledge at lunch time, the common sense law of inertia should allow me to infer by default that the car is still where I left it. However, when I return to the car park in the evening I find that it has gone. Its disappearance requires an explanation. That is to say, we want to reason backwards in time to the (possible) causes of the car's disappearance. In this case, the only reasonable explanation for the car's disappearance is that it was stolen some time between morning and evening. So my previous conclusion that the car was still there at lunch time is open to question. The car may have been stolen any time after I parked it and before I observed that it was gone, so I cannot say anything about its whereabouts at lunch time.

As Kautz [1986] observed, the trouble with chronological minimisation is that, since it postpones change until as late as possible, it will yield the conclusion that the car was stolen immediately before my return to the car park in the evening. This is clearly too strong a conclusion. It may have been stolen then. But for all I know, it could have been stolen just after I parked it.

The stolen car scenario can be represented by just three sentences, following Baker [1989]. Instead of representing the interval between morning and evening explicitly, we will make do with two successive Wait actions. The only fluent is Stolen, representing that the car is not in the car park.

$$\neg \, \text{Holds(Stolen,S0)} \qquad\qquad \text{(SC1)}$$

$$\text{S2} = \text{Result(Wait,Result(Wait,S0))} \qquad\qquad \text{(SC2)}$$

$$\text{Holds(Stolen,S2)} \qquad\qquad \text{(SC3)}$$

This is, perhaps, not the best representation of the stolen car scenario, and we will return to the issue of representing explanation problems later. But it serves to illustrate the difficulty with chronological minimisation, which manifests itself here as the overly strong conclusion that the car disappeared during the second Wait. The car could equally well have disappeared during the first Wait, and we would like our formalisation of the common sense law of inertia to respect this possibility. Let's make this a little more precise.

Proposition 4.6.1. If Σ is the conjunction of (SC1) to (SC3) with (Arb1), (Arb2) and (F2), then,

$$\Sigma \vDash_{\text{chron}} \text{Ab(Wait,Stolen,Result(Wait,S0))} \wedge \neg \, \text{Ab(Wait,Stolen,S0)}.$$

Proof. From (SC1) to (SC3) and (F2), we can easily show that,

$$\text{Ab(Wait,Stolen,Result(Wait,S0))} \vee \text{Ab(Wait,Stolen,S0)}.$$

So we have three classes of models:

- Those in which we have both Ab(Wait,Stolen,Result(Wait,S0)) and Ab(Wait,Stolen,S0),

- Those in which we have just Ab(Wait,S0), and

- Those in which we have just Ab(Wait,Stolen,Result(Wait,S0)).

For every model M in the first two classes, there is a model M' in the third class such that M' $\sqsubseteq_{\text{chron}}$ M but not M $\sqsubseteq_{\text{chron}}$ M'. Therefore only models in the third class are chronologically minimal. $\qquad\square$

What we would like, instead, is to be able to show,

$$\Sigma \vdash_{\text{chron}} \text{Ab}(\text{Wait,Stolen,Result}(\text{Wait,S0})) \lor \text{Ab}(\text{Wait,Stolen,S0})$$

and also that there exist models M_1 and M_2 such that,

$$M_1 \Vdash \text{Ab}(\text{Wait,Stolen,Result}(\text{Wait,S0}))$$

and,

$$M_2 \Vdash \text{Ab}(\text{Wait,Stolen,S0}).$$

4.7 Improving Chronological Minimisation

Many of the shortcomings of chronological minimisation in its basic form have been addressed by Sandewall [1991], [1993], [1994]. Sandewall introduces two significant innovations: *filtered preferential entailment* and *occlusion*. Sandewall employs a narrative-based temporal logic rather than the situation calculus or the event calculus, but variants of these two ideas are applicable to both those formalisms, as we will see much later in the book.

The idea behind filtered preferential entailment is to separate (or filter) observation sentences from effect axioms in such a way that the minimisation required to overcome the frame problem is applied only to the latter sentences and not to the former. This manoeuvre implements an important principle which I will discuss at greater length in the next chapter, namely the *principle of separation*. Conforming to this principle ensures that the Hanks-McDermott problem cannot arise, since facts about what fluents hold at particular time points cannot interfere with the minimisation process. Sandewall's approach is related to *forced separation*, which will be discussed in Chapter 16.

Occlusion is a way of blocking the common sense law of inertia for certain fluents at certain times. In many examples, the effect of an action on a fluent is unknown. For example, consider the effect of dropping a glass, and suppose that the outcome of such an action is unknown: the glass might shatter or it might remain intact. Given that the glass is intact before it is dropped, the naive application of the common sense law of inertia would insist that it was still intact afterwards. Using occlusion, such examples can be dealt with. In addition, in [Sandewall, 1991], a combination of occlusion and filtered preferential entailment is used to tackle the stolen car scenario. The idea of occlusion is very similar to that of the Releases predicate, which will be discussed in Section 15.3.

Notes

1. In fact, Σ could be a sentence of any logic, but we'll stick to first-order predicate calculus here.

2. It isn't strictly speaking correct to refer to this as an algorithm since the set of logical consequences of S is not necessarily recursively enumerable.

3. My definition of chronological minimisation differs slightly from each of the accounts given by the three cited authors.

4. In particular examples, the axioms of arboreality are often subsumed by uniqueness-of-names axioms for situations. But it's worth presenting them separately here, to emphasise their special role in chronological minimisation.

5 Causal Minimisation

This chapter describes another approach to the Hanks-McDermott problem, namely causal minimisation. In causal minimisation, all change has to be caused by action. In the context of causal minimisation, an important idea is introduced, namely the principle of separation. This principle, which lies at the heart of causal minimisation, is also the basis of more robust solutions to be presented later. Causal minimisation is less robust than we might like, as it is incapable, in the form it takes in the present chapter, of representing certain phenomena, such as actions whose effects are context-dependent. Later in the book, we will se how a variant of causal minimisation can be applied to the event calculus to yield a more expressively flexible formalism.

5.1 Eliminating Spontaneous Change

Causal minimisation [Haugh, 1987], [Lifschitz, 1987] is another approach to the Hanks-McDermott problem. As I said at the beginning of the last chapter, any worthwhile proposal is based on some insight into the nature of the problem. Causal minimisation was inspired by the observation that in the anomalous model of the Yale shooting scenario there are changes that aren't caused by any action. The gun becomes unloaded spontaneously, for no reason.

Attempts to solve the Hanks-McDermott using chronological minimisation usually leave the style of representation untouched — in our case this is standard situation calculus — while altering the formalism for default reasoning. Causal minimisation, on the other hand, often employs a standard form of default reasoning, such as unmodified circumscription, while augmenting the representation. This augmentation takes the form of an extra predicate standing for a causal relationship. The new predicate is minimised instead of the Ab predicate in the traditional representation.

My presentation of causal minimisation follows closely that of Lifschitz [1987]. Two new predicates are introduced: Causes and Precond. The formula Causes(a,f,v) represents that action a causes fluent f to take on truth value v. A new sort for truth values is introduced, which has constants True and False. We have,

$$\text{True} \neq \text{False}. \tag{CM1}$$

As well as providing for a succinct substitute for the conventional effect axiom, the Precond predicate will enable us to solve the *qualification problem* [McCarthy, 1977]. McCarthy describes the qualification problem as follows.

. . . In order to fully represent the conditions for the successful performance of an action, an impractical and implausible number of qualifications would have to be included in the sentences expressing them. [McCarthy, 1980]

The formula Precond(f,v,a) represents that fluent f must have truth value v for action a to be effective. The qualification problem is addressed by minimising the Precond predicate. We have the following domain independent axioms.

$$[\text{Success(a,s)} \land \text{Causes(a,f,v)}] \rightarrow \qquad\qquad\qquad (\text{CM2})$$
$$[\text{Holds(f,Result(a,s))} \leftrightarrow v = \text{True}]$$

$$\neg \text{ Affects(a,f,s)} \rightarrow [\text{Holds(f,Result(a,s))} \leftrightarrow \text{Holds(f,s)}] \qquad (\text{CM3})$$

Axiom (CM3), which replaces the usual frame axiom (F2), insists that all change is caused by action. Success and Affects are not predicate symbols of the language, but are abbreviations defined as follows.

$$\text{Success(a,s)} \equiv_{\text{def}} \forall f\ [\text{Precond(f,v,a)} \rightarrow [\text{Holds(f,s)} \leftrightarrow v = \text{True}]]$$

$$\text{Affects(a,f,s)} \equiv_{\text{def}} \text{Success(a,s)} \land \exists\ v\ \text{Causes(a,f,v)}$$

Now, to represent a particular domain, in place of the effect axioms of the conventional representation, we have to list the effects of each action via the Causes predicate, and the preconditions of each action via the Precond predicate. I will call such sentences *causal axioms*. Observation sentences are written in the usual way.

5.2   The Yale Shooting Scenario

For the purposes of causal minimisation, the Yale shooting scenario is represented as follows. Axioms (YC1) to (YC5) are already familiar.

$$\text{Holds(Alive,S0)} \qquad\qquad\qquad (\text{YC1})$$

$$\neg\ \text{Holds(Loaded,S0)} \qquad\qquad\qquad (\text{YC2})$$

$$\text{UNA[Load, Wait, Shoot]} \qquad\qquad\qquad (\text{YC3})$$

$$\text{UNA[Alive, Loaded]} \qquad\qquad\qquad (\text{YC4})$$

$$\text{UNA[S0, Result]} \qquad\qquad\qquad (\text{YC5})$$

Causal axioms (YC6) to (YC8) are in place of the effect axioms (Y1) and (Y2) in the conventional representation.

$$\text{Causes(Load,Loaded,True)} \qquad \text{(YC6)}$$

$$\text{Causes(Shoot,Alive,False)} \qquad \text{(YC7)}$$

$$\text{Precond(Loaded,True,Shoot)} \qquad \text{(YC8)}$$

The circumscription policy to overcome the frame problem, for the Yale shooting scenario and for any other domain, is to minimise Causes in parallel with Precond, allowing Holds to vary. In other words, given the conjunction Σ of a set of observation sentences and causal axioms, we are interested in,

$$\text{CIRC}[\Sigma \ ; \ \text{Causes, Precond} \ ; \ \text{Holds}].$$

This leads us to the following proposition, which says that causal minimisation deals correctly with the Yale shooting scenario.

Proposition 5.2.1. If Σ is the conjunction of (YC1) to (YC8) with (CM1) to (CM3) then,

$$\text{CIRC}[\Sigma \ ; \ \text{Causes, Precond} \ ; \ \text{Holds}] \vDash$$
$$\neg \ \text{Holds(Alive,Result(Shoot,Result(Wait,Result(Load,S0)))).}$$

Proof. First, we show that all models of the circumscription satisfy the following sentences.

$$\text{Causes(a,f,v)} \leftrightarrow [a=\text{Load} \wedge f=\text{Loaded} \wedge v=\text{True}] \vee \qquad [5.2.2]$$
$$[a=\text{Shoot} \wedge f=\text{Alive} \wedge v=\text{False}]$$

$$\text{Precond(f,v,a)} \leftrightarrow [f=\text{Loaded} \wedge v=\text{True} \wedge a=\text{Shoot}] \qquad [5.2.3]$$

From (YC6) to (YC8), we see that all models have to satisfy the if halves of these sentences. It remains to demonstrate the only-if halves. Let's consider Causes first. Suppose M is a model of the circumscription that does not satisfy the only-if half of [5.2.2]. Now consider any model M' of Σ that meets the following criteria.

- M' agrees with M on the interpretation of everything except Causes and Holds

- M' $\Vdash$ [5.2.2]

- M' $\Vdash$ Holds(Alive,S0)

- M' $\Vdash \neg$ Holds(Loaded,S0)

- M' $\Vdash$ Holds(f,Result(a,s)) if and only if,

    - M' $\Vdash$ Holds(f,s) and M' $\Vdash \neg$ Affects(a,f,s), or

- M' ⊩ Causes(a,f,True) and M' ⊩ Success(a,s)

It's clear that such an M' exists, and that the extension of Causes in M' is a strict subset of that in M. So M' is as small as M with respect to the circumscription policy, but M is not as small as M'. So M is not a model of the circumscription, which is a contradiction. Therefore the only-if half of [5.2.2] must be satisfied by all models of the circumscription. The argument for [5.2.3] is analogous.

Given [5.2.2] and [5.2.3], we can use (CM2) and (CM3) to show,

Holds(Loaded,Result(Wait,Result(Load,S0)))

and therefore,

¬ Holds(Alive,Result(Shoot,Result(Wait,Result(Load,S0)))).   □

Note the important role played by the uniqueness-of-names axiom (YC5) in this proof. Without it, an appropriate M' would not exist for every M. Axiom (YC5) ensures that each situation term denotes a unique object in M. This means that there are no loops in the tree of situations, which guarantees the consistency of the recursive definition of Holds in M'.

As mentioned in the previous section, this formulation addresses the qualification problem as well as the frame problem. The minimisation of Precond effectively represents the assumption that the known preconditions of an action are the only preconditions of the action. The formulation is elaboration tolerant with respect to preconditions, since the incorporation of a new precondition for an action only requires the conjunction of a new Precond sentence.

However, there are other aspects to the qualification problem which aren't addressed by this approach. I won't be looking into the qualification problem in any more detail here. For further discussion, see [Lin & Reiter, 1994].

5.3 The Principles of Separation and Directionality

As I remarked at the beginning of the present discussion, causal minimisation is based on the idea of restricting change to that which is caused by action. In the anomalous model of the Yale shooting scenario that arises when circumscription is applied naively to the frame problem, there is a spontaneous change. But this observation only gives us insight into the way causal minimisation works at a very abstract level. On a more technical level, how does causal minimisation avoid the Hanks-McDermott problem?

Let's begin by considering exactly why there is no analogue of the anomalous model of the Yale shooting scenario for causal minimisation. Formally speaking, we have the following proposition.

Proposition 5.3.1. Let Σ be the conjunction of (YC1) to (YC8) with (CM1) to (CM3). Let M be any model of Σ such that M⊩ Causes(Wait,Loaded,False). Then M is not a model of CIRC[Σ ; Causes, Precond ; Holds].

Proof. The proposition is a corollary of [5.2.2], which was shown in the proof of Proposition 5.2.1. □

But what lies behind the proof of this proposition? In the anomalous model arising with the naive approach, the gun becomes unloaded during the Wait action. In other words, we have Ab(Wait,Loaded,Result(Load,S0)). In terms of causal predicates, an anomalous would have to have Causes(Wait,Loaded,False).

In the naive approach, the presence of the Wait abnormality obviates the need for Shoot to be abnormal with respect to Alive when a shooting takes place after a Wait. Naturally, circumscription will prefer models in which that abnormality is absent. Hence the anomalous model, and our inability to draw the intuitive conclusion that the victim dies.

But with causal minimisation, this trading of abnormalities is not possible. The analogue in causal minimisation of,

$$Ab(Shoot,Alive,Result(Wait,Result(Load,S0)))$$

is Causes(Shoot,Alive,False), which is an axiom. We can't get rid of it from our models, whatever else we add. This is a consequence of a very important principle, which I call the *principle of separation*. This is the key to causal minimisation, and to other approaches that will be presented later in the book.

The minimisation required to overcome the frame problem should not be dependent on the outcome of temporal projection.

With the naive approach, abnormalities are derived from effect axioms via the universal frame axiom. From the effect axiom,

$$\neg \text{ Holds(Alive,Result(Shoot,s))} \leftarrow \text{Holds(Loaded,s)}$$

and the universal frame axiom,

$$[\text{Holds(f,Result(a,s))} \leftrightarrow \text{Holds(f,s)}] \leftarrow \neg \text{ Ab(a,f,s)}$$

we derive the abnormality,

$$\text{Ab(Shoot,Alive,s)} \leftarrow \text{Holds(Loaded,s)}.$$

But whether we have Holds(Loaded,σ) for any given σ depends on what holds in σ, which in turn depends on the outcome of the very projection process for which we are trying to do the minimisation. Little wonder the whole process is unstable. Metaphorically speaking, the ground of Holds facts is constantly shifting beneath the feet of the minimisation process.

However, if the principle of separation is observed, this feedback loop is cut. The influence is only one way, from minimisation to temporal projection and not the other way round.

The claim that causal minimisation embodies the principle of separation is made more precise by the following theorem.

Theorem 5.3.2. Let Σ be the conjunction of (YC5) plus uniqueness-of-names axioms for fluents and actions plus (CM1) to (CM3) with a finite number of observation sentences of the form Holds(β,S0) or $\neg$ Holds(β,S0) where β is a fluent, and n Causes sentences,

$$\text{Causes}(\alpha_1,\beta_1,\upsilon_1) \dots \text{Causes}(\alpha_n,\beta_n,\upsilon_n)$$

where α_i is an action, β_i is a fluent and υ_i is a truth value, and m Precond sentences,

$$\text{Precond}(\beta_{n+1},\upsilon_{n+1},\alpha_{n+1}) \dots \text{Precond}(\beta_{n+m},\upsilon_{n+m},\alpha_{n+m}).$$

where β_i is a fluent and α_i is an action. Then,

$$\text{CIRC}[\Sigma \text{ ; Causes, Precond ; Holds}] \vDash \text{Causes(a,f,v)} \leftrightarrow$$
$$[a = \alpha_1 \wedge f = \beta_1 \wedge v = \upsilon_1] \vee \dots \vee [a = \alpha_n \wedge f = \beta_n \wedge v = \upsilon_n].$$

and,

$$\text{CIRC}[\Sigma \text{ ; Causes, Precond ; Holds}] \vDash \text{Precond(f,v,a)} \leftrightarrow$$
$$[f = \beta_{n+1} \wedge v = \upsilon_{n+1} \wedge a = \alpha_{n+1}] \vee \dots \vee$$
$$[f = \beta_{n+m} \wedge v = \upsilon_{n+m} \wedge a = \alpha_{n+m}].$$

Proof. The proof is a simple generalisation of the central part of the proof of Proposition 5.2.1. The Causes and Precond sentences in Σ ensure that all models of the circumscription will satisfy the if halves of the sentences in question. It remains to demonstrate the only-if halves. Let's consider Causes first. Suppose M is a model of the circumscription that does not satisfy,

$$\text{Causes(a,f,v)} \rightarrow \qquad\qquad\qquad [5.3.3]$$
$$[a = \alpha_1 \wedge f = \beta_1 \wedge v = \upsilon_1] \vee \dots \vee [a = \alpha_n \wedge f = \beta_n \wedge v = \upsilon_n].$$

Now consider any model M' of Σ that meets the following criteria.

- M' agrees with M on the interpretation of everything except Causes and Holds

- M' ⊩ Causes(a,f,v) ↔
  $$[f = \beta_1 \wedge v = \upsilon_1 \wedge a = \alpha_1] \vee \ldots \vee$$
  $$[f = \beta_n \wedge v = \upsilon_n \wedge a = \alpha_n]$$

- M' ⊩ Holds(β,S0) for each Holds(β,S0) in Σ

- M' ⊩ ¬ Holds(β,S0) for each ¬ Holds(β,S0) in Σ

- M' ⊩ Holds(f,Result(a,s)) if and only if,

    - M' ⊩ Holds(f,s) and M' ⊩ ¬ Affects(a,f,s), or

    - M' ⊩ Causes(a,f,True) and M' ⊩ Success(a,s)

It's clear that such an M' exists, and that the extension of Causes in M' is a strict subset of that in M. So M' is as small as M with respect to the circumscription policy, but M is not as small as M'. So M is not a model of the circumscription, which is a contradiction. Therefore the only-if half of [5.3.3] must be satisfied by all models of the circumscription. The argument for Precond is analogous. □

Causal minimisation illustrates another important principle, which I call the principle of directionality. According to this principle,

Information about a given time should be deductively independent from information about any later time.

In a theory that respects this principle, the potential feedback route from later to earlier times has been cut off. The principle can be expressed more precisely in the following way.

Let Σ be any formula of many-sorted first-order predicate calculus with equality whose language includes a sort of *temporal objects* which is interpreted as a temporally ordered structure, and a binary *temporal predicate* η, whose two arguments are a fluent and a temporal object respectively. Let σ1* be a (possibly partitioned)[1] tuple of predicate symbols and σ2* be a tuple of predicate, constant and function symbols, where the circumscription of Σ minimising σ1* and allowing σ2* to vary is designed to solve the frame problem.

Definition 5.3.4. Σ conforms to the *principle of directionality* if, for any fluent β and any temporal object τ,

CIRC[Σ ; σ1* ; σ2*] ⊨ η(β,τ) implies CIRC[TR[Σ] ; σ1* ; σ2*] ⊨ η(β,τ)

where TR[Σ] is Σ with every occurrence of $\rho(\overline{x})$ replaced by $\rho(\overline{x}) \wedge x_k < \tau$ where ρ is any predicate symbol whose k^{th} argument is a temporal object. $\square$

The function TR temporally restricts the theory Σ so that information about temporal objects at or later than τ is impotent. A very significant observation is that almost all the classes of formulae about which interesting theorems can be proved conform to the principle of directionality.

In standard situation calculus, the temporal objects are situations, and the temporal predicate is Holds. In versions of the situation calculus extended to deal with narratives, and in the event calculus, both of which we'll encounter later on, the temporal objects are time points and the temporal predicate is HoldsAt. For the principle of directionality to make sense in the context of unmodified situation calculus, situations have to interpreted as temporally ordered. Accordingly, the axioms of arboreality (Arb1) and (Arb2) need to be added to a theory before it can be determined whether or not it conforms to the principle.

Given these additional axioms, it can easily be verified that the conditions of Theorem 5.3.2 demand a theory that conforms to the principle of directionality. Indeed, the principle of directionality often seems to underpin the principle of separation, as it does here.

Significantly, as we saw in Section 4.6, chronological minimisation falls down when applied to theories that violate the principle,[2] specifically to those that include observation sentences for situations after S0 such as the stolen car scenario. In general, the correlation between theories that violate the principle of directionality and those that fail to yield intuitively correct results is very high. Methods for handling explanation problems and dealing with observation sentences without violating the principle of directionality will be presented in Chapter 17.

5.4 Actions with Context-Dependent Effects

Theorem 5.3.2, which complies with Lifschitz's appeal [1991] for theorems that apply to whole classes of examples rather than to single benchmark problems like the Yale shooting scenario, permits us to minimise Causes and Precond first, and to do temporal projection later via Axioms (CM2) and (CM3). (The minimisation results in the completion of the Causes and Precond predicates. The idea of completion crops up regularly throughout the book.) In effect, all that needs to be inferred about Causes and Precond is manifest in the causal axioms themselves. No deduction via other axioms is necessary.

Why can't we achieve the same effect with the Ab predicate? Why not simply supply Ab information directly and explicitly, in the form of sentences like causal axioms, instead of making it implicit in the effect axioms? We can't do this because Ab takes a situation as an argument. The crucial thing about Causes and Precond is that they do not have arguments, such as situations, whose properties are time-varying. This is how causal minimisation is able to observe the principle of separation.

This brings us to one of the limitations of causal minimisation. Because the Causes and Precond predicates are not indexed on situations, they are unable to represent certain kinds of knowledge. In particular, they are unable to represent actions with context-dependent effects, that is to say actions whose effects depend on the fluents that hold at the time the action is performed. For example, if I toggle a light switch, the light comes on if it's off at the time, but goes off if it's on. Similarly, if I add a weight to one side of a balance, the total weight on that side after the action depends on the total weight at the time the action was performed.

Let's attempt to formalise these two examples. The light switch example is already familiar from Chapter 2. It can be rendered with usual style effect axioms as follows.

$$\text{Holds(On,Result(Toggle,s))} \leftarrow \neg \text{Holds(On,s)}$$

$$\neg \text{Holds(On,Result(Toggle,s))} \leftarrow \text{Holds(On,s)}$$

We note that no corresponding set of Causes and Precond sentences is possible. However, by varying our knowledge representation a little, we can cope with this example. We can split the Toggle action into two: a SwitchOn action and a SwitchOff action. For these actions to be successful, they have to satisfy appropriate preconditions. In usual style effect axioms, we have,

$$\text{Holds(On,Result(SwitchOn,s))} \leftarrow \neg \text{Holds(On,s)}$$

$$\neg \text{Holds(On,Result(SwitchOff,s))} \leftarrow \text{Holds(On,s)}.$$

Corresponding causal axioms can easily be written.

$$\text{Causes(SwitchOn,On,True)}$$

$$\text{Causes(SwitchOff,On,False)}$$

$$\text{Precond(On,True,SwitchOn)}$$

$$\text{Precond(On,False,SwitchOff)}$$

But it should be obvious that this manoeuvre is a cheat. We have placed part of the burden of deciding what the effects of a given action are in a given situation on the supplier of the axioms. It's clear that these two actions really are one action, whose effects in any particular situation are exactly what we're expecting our formalisation to work out for us.

The example draws our attention to a useful distinction. Effect axioms written in the usual style blur the difference between *action preconditions*, which have to hold for an action to be successful and have any effect at all, and *fluent preconditions*, which are part of the context that defines the particular effect of the action.[3] In the light switch example, the light's status is really a fluent precondition, but for the purposes of causal minimisation, we can perform the ill-advised trick of disguising it as an action precondition.

With many examples, the trick of disguising fluent preconditions as action preconditions is not possible anyway. Take the example of adding weights to a balance. The domain includes a single action and a single fluent. The term Add(w) denotes the action of adding w units of weight to the balance. The fluent Weight(w) represents that the total weight on the balance is w units. I assume a suitable sort for w, and that the + operator is interpreted appropriately. Using effect axioms, we write,

$$Holds(Weight(w1),Result(Add(w2),s)) \leftarrow$$
$$Holds(Weight(w3),s) \wedge w1=w2+w3.$$

Clearly it's not possible to write corresponding causal axioms. Nor is it possible to disguise the fluent precondition involving the current weight on the balance as an action precondition. Neither the Precond nor the Causes predicate have access to the sort of information they would require to represent this example. The circumscriptive calculus of events which will be presented in Chapter 14 employs causal predicates that do have access to such information.

5.5 Causal Minimisation and Explanation

Its inability to represent context-dependent effects is not the only drawback of causal minimisation. Like chronological minimisation, causal minimisation has trouble with explanation problems.

Consider the representation of the stolen car scenario from the last chapter.

$$\neg\, Holds(Stolen,S0) \hspace{4cm} (SC1)$$

$$S2 = Result(Wait,Result(Wait,S0)) \hspace{2cm} (SC2)$$

$$Holds(Stolen,S2) \hspace{4cm} (SC3)$$

First of all, notice that these sentences violate the conditions that make Theorem 5.3.2 applicable (along with the principle of directionality). The observation sentence (SC3) refers to a situation other than S0, which means we cannot use Theorem 5.3.2 to complete the Causes and Precond predicates. (The completion process would yield predicates with empty extensions in this case.) To see why, we only have to observe that, from (SC1) to (SC3) and Axiom (CM3), we have,

$$\text{Affects(Wait,Stolen,S0)} \lor \text{Affects(Wait,Stolen,Result(Wait,S0))}.$$

From this and the definition of Affects, we have,

$$\exists \text{ v Causes(Wait,Stolen,v)} \land [\text{Success(Wait,S0)} \lor \text{Success(Wait,Result(Wait,S0))}]$$

which, when plugged into (CM2), taking account of (SC1) to (SC3), gives,

$$\text{Causes(Wait,Stolen,True)}.$$

This means that a Wait action *always* makes Stolen not hold, whatever the circumstances. This has the unfortunate consequence that if I recover my car, the next time I perform a Wait action, the car will be stolen again. We would prefer a disjunctive conclusion that picks out just the two Wait actions in question, perhaps by identifying the situations in which they occur. Lifschitz and Rabinov [1989] propose a way to overcome this problem based on the idea of *miracles* or unknown actions. I will be discussing their proposal, along with several others that can potentially help causal minimisation with this problem, in a special chapter on explanation.

Before leaving the topic of explanation, it's worth noting that there is at least one benchmark problem that causal minimisation gets right and which chronological minimisation gets wrong, namely the so-called Stanford murder mystery [Baker, 1989].[4] The Stanford murder mystery resembles the Yale shooting scenario, except that the status of the gun is unknown in the initial situation, but it is known that the victim is alive in the initial situation and dead after a Shoot action followed by a Wait action. The task is to explain the victim's death.

When this scenario is formalised in the obvious way, causal minimisation correctly yields the conclusion that gun was loaded in the initial situation, and that the victim died as a result of the shooting. Causal minimisation works in this case because, in contrast to the stolen car scenario, the explanation doesn't demand the introduction of any new effects of actions. Chronological minimisation, on the other hand, by postponing change until as late as possible, will insist that the victim dies as a result of the Wait action, since it comes *after* the Shoot action.

5.6 Ramifications and Causal Minimisation

The final issue I want to discuss in relation to causal minimisation is that of *domain constraints*, which is closely related to the *ramification problem* [Finger, 1987], [Ginsberg & Smith, 1987]. Recall that a domain constraint is a formula in which the variable s is universally quantified and the only occurrences of the Holds predicate are of the form Holds(β,s). Domain constraints express temporally invariant facts about the logical relationship between fluents. Here's a self-explanatory example.

$$\text{Holds(Alive,s)} \leftrightarrow \neg \text{Holds(Dead,s)} \qquad \text{(DC1)}$$

Suppose we augment the Yale shooting scenario with this formula. We would like to get the same conclusions as before, and in addition we would like the fluent Dead to track the negation of the fluent Alive. Naturally, as before, we would expect the victim to remain alive until the shooting, and only then to die. Unfortunately, with the addition of the domain constraint (DC1), we can no longer conclude that the victim survives the loading of the gun.

Here are the rest of the axioms. The only difference from the formulation of the Yale shooting scenario is in the uniqueness-of-names axiom (DC6).

$$\text{Holds(Alive,S0)} \qquad \text{(DC2)}$$

$$\neg \text{Holds(Loaded,S0)} \qquad \text{(DC3)}$$

$$\text{UNA[S0, Result]} \qquad \text{(DC4)}$$

$$\text{UNA[Load, Wait, Shoot]} \qquad \text{(DC5)}$$

$$\text{UNA[Alive, Loaded, Dead]} \qquad \text{(DC6)}$$

$$\text{Causes(Load,Loaded,True)} \qquad \text{(DC7)}$$

$$\text{Causes(Shoot,Alive,False)} \qquad \text{(DC8)}$$

$$\text{Precond(Loaded,True,Shoot)} \qquad \text{(DC9)}$$

Proposition 5.6.1. If Σ is the conjunction of (DC1) to (DC9) and (CM1) to (CM3) then,

CIRC[Σ ; Causes, Precond ; Holds] $\nvDash$ Holds(Alive,Result(Load,S0)).

Proof. First we note that the circumscription no longer entails,

Causes(a,f,v) ↔ [a=Load ∧ f=Loaded ∧ v=True] ∨
[a=Shoot ∧ f=Alive ∧ v=False].

since it would follow from this sentence that,

¬ [Holds(Alive,Result(Wait,Result(Load,S0))) ↔
Holds(Alive,Result(Shoot,Result(Wait,Result(Load,S0)))))]

which would yield Causes(Shoot,Dead,True) from (DC1), which is a contradiction. Therefore, in any model of the circumscription, the extension of Causes must contain at least three elements: one for ⟨Load, Loaded, True⟩, plus one for ⟨Shoot, Alive, False⟩, plus at least one more.

Now, it's straightforward to verify that a model M of Σ exists that meets the following criteria.

- M ⊩ Causes(a,f,v) ↔
    [a=Load ∧ f=Loaded ∧ v=True] ∨ [a=Shoot ∧ f=Alive ∧ v=False] ∨
    [a=Load ∧ f=Dead ∧ v=True] ∨ [a=Load ∧ f=Alive ∧ v=False]

- M ⊩ ¬ ∃ s [Holds(Alive,s) ∧ Holds(Loaded,s)]

The second criterion can be met because the victim has already died during the Load action. The absence of a situation in which Alive and Loaded both hold allows the extension of Causes to exclude ⟨Shoot, Alive, False⟩. It's clear that no model exists in which the extension of Causes is a strict subset of that in M, so M is a model of the circumscription. From the extension of Causes, Axiom (DC1), and Axiom (CM2), we can show that M ⊩ ¬ Holds(Alive,Result(Load,S0)). □

The point is that the addition of the domain constraint forces into existence some Causes facts that are not explicitly provided in the causal axioms. This gives circumscription a choice: there are several combinations of Causes facts which can be added to yield minimal models. Several of these are anomalous. Besides the model described in the above proof, for example, there is an equally anomalous model in which Wait unloads the gun, as in the anomalous model of the unmodified Yale shooting scenario. This obviates the need for any extra Causes facts about Dead, since the victim never dies.

There have been several proposals for extending causal minimisation to deal correctly with domain constraints. Lifschitz [1987] recommends partitioning the set of fluents into those that are *primitive* and those that are *derived*. Axiom (CM3) can be reformulated so that it only applies to primitive fluents. Following [Lifschitz, 1990], let's introduce a new predicate Frame, where Frame(f) represents that fluent f is a primitive fluent. Then we have,

$$[\text{Frame}(f) \wedge \neg \ \text{Affects}(a,f,s)] \rightarrow \qquad\qquad (\text{CM4})$$
$$[\text{Holds}(f,\text{Result}(a,s)) \leftrightarrow \text{Holds}(f,s)]$$

where Affects is defined as before.

Now, only primitive fluents are included in the "frame" to which the common sense law of inertia applies. These *frame fluents* are listed explicitly. For the Yale shooting scenario extended with the domain constraint (DC1), we require the following sentence.[5]

$$\text{Frame}(f) \leftrightarrow f=\text{Loaded} \vee f=\text{Alive} \qquad\qquad (\text{DC10})$$

Now the circumscription produces the desired result. For example, Proposition 5.6.1 no longer holds.

Proposition 5.6.2. If Σ is the conjunction of (DC1) to (DC10) with Axioms (CM1), (CM2), and (CM4), then,

$$\text{CIRC}[\Sigma \ ; \text{Causes}, \text{Precond} \ ; \text{Holds}] \vDash \text{Holds}(\text{Alive},\text{Result}(\text{Load},S0)).$$

Proof. It suffices to show that all models of the circumscription satisfy,

$$\text{Causes}(a,f,v) \leftrightarrow [a=\text{Load} \wedge f=\text{Loaded} \wedge v=\text{True}] \vee \qquad [5.6.3]$$
$$[a=\text{Shoot} \wedge f=\text{Alive} \wedge v=\text{False}].$$

The rest of the proof is the straightforward application of the axioms. To see that [5.6.3] holds, observe that, since we have $\neg$ Frame(Dead), we have $\neg$ Affects(a,Dead,s) for any a or s. So the presence of Axiom (DC1) does not have any bearing on the extension of Causes. Given this, the proof of [5.6.3] is the same here as in the proof of Proposition 5.2.1. $\qquad\qquad \square$

The ramification problem and actions with indirect effects will feature prominently in the rest of the book. Without the issue of ramifications, the frame problem would be a lot easier to solve.

Notes

1. Partitioned tuples of predicate symbols are relevant to prioritised circumscription, which hasn't been defined yet.
2. The formal definition of the principle needs to be adjusted slightly for chronological minimisation, which doesn't employ standard circumscription.
3. This distinction is due to Pednault [1988].
4. Baker himself didn't call the problem the Stanford murder mystery. The research community has adopted this name because Baker was a Ph.D. student at Stanford when he wrote his influential paper.

5. This sentence is a completed definition of Frame. Alternatively, the frame fluents can be specified by sentences of the form Frame(β), and circumscription can be used to complete the Frame predicate.

6 Introducing State-Based Minimisation

This chapter introduces state-based minimisation. Because it uses standard situation calculus and standard circumscription, state-based minimisation is, in a sense, very simple. But it's also hard to understand. The chapter motivates the basic components of the technique one at a time (using plenty of diagrams), showing how they work together to provide a solution. One of these components, namely the existence-of-situations axiom that guarantees the existence of a situation corresponding to every legitimate combination of fluents, requires further development for state-based minimisation to meet the criterion of expressive flexibility. This development is postponed to the next chapter.

6.1 Varying the Result Function

In 1989, Baker proposed a technique for solving the frame problem that is startling in its simplicity, which I call *state-based minimisation* [Baker, 1989], [Baker & Ginsberg, 1989], [Baker, 1991].[1] Unlike chronological minimisation, it doesn't require a new default reasoning formalism: it relies on standard circumscription. Unlike causal minimisation, it doesn't involve a new way of writing effect axioms: it works with standard situation calculus formulae. It simply requires the adoption of a few extra axioms, and a slight modification of the circumscription policy originally proposed by McCarthy [1986].

Furthermore, it supplies correct results for some problems where unmodified chronological or causal minimisation go wrong, including those involving domain constraints, and certain explanation problems. However, despite its simplicity, state-based minimisation is notoriously hard to understand. Or rather, it's hard to understand why state-based minimisation works when McCarthy's original proposal, which is so similar, fails.

State-based minimisation has two components. First, instead of varying the Holds predicate, as in McCarthy's original circumscription policy [1986], the Result function is varied. Second, an axiom is added that guarantees the existence of a situation for every legitimate combination of fluents. Let's look at the new circumscription policy first, using the Yale shooting scenario to motivate it.

In the anomalous model of the Yale shooting scenario, one abnormality is traded for another. At the cost of gaining Ab(Wait,Loaded,Result(Load,S0)), we have managed to shed Ab(Shoot,Alive,Result(Wait,Result(Load,S0))). This trade is possible because in the anomalous model Result(Wait,Result(Load,S0)) does not denote a situation in which Alive and Loaded hold.

However, Result(Load,S0) does denote a situation in which Alive and Loaded hold, and indeed every model satisfies Ab(Shoot,Alive,Result(Load,S0)), even the anomalous one. The Ab predicate seems to be sensitive to the particular Result term used to name a situation, in other words to particular sequences of actions. We can read this abnormality as follows: "Shoot is abnormal with respect to Alive in the situation you get if you start in S0 and then perform a Load action".

On reflection, this doesn't seem right at all. We really want to be able to read the abnormality as follows: "Shoot is abnormal with respect to Alive in any situation in which Alive and Loaded holds". Read this way, an abnormality holds regardless of what happens to be denoted by particular Result terms. Read the first way, whether or not an abnormality is present in a given model depends entirely on what happens to be denoted by particular Result terms.

Why is the Ab predicate sensitive to sequences of actions, and how can we render it sensitive to combinations of fluents instead? The answer is simple. In the circumscription, the Result function must be allowed to vary. Then the interpretation of Result terms is like a loose cog, detached from the mechanism of determining abnormalities.

Let's see how this works for the Yale shooting scenario. We'll use the usual axioms, first encountered in Chapter 3. Here they are once again, including the universal frame axiom (F2). Note the omission of Axiom (Y7), the uniqueness-of-names axiom for situations.

$$\text{Holds(Loaded,Result(Load,s))} \tag{Y1}$$

$$\neg\,\text{Holds(Alive,Result(Shoot,s))} \leftarrow \text{Holds(Loaded,s)} \tag{Y2}$$

$$\text{Holds(Alive,S0)} \tag{Y3}$$

$$\neg\,\text{Holds(Loaded,S0)} \tag{Y4}$$

$$\text{UNA[Load, Wait, Shoot]} \tag{Y5}$$

$$\text{UNA[Alive, Loaded]} \tag{Y6}$$

$$[\text{Holds(f,Result(a,s))} \leftrightarrow \text{Holds(f,s)}] \leftarrow \neg\,\text{Ab(a,f,s)} \tag{F2}$$

Let Σ be the conjunction of (Y1) to (Y6) with (F2). Now consider,

$$\text{CIRC}[\Sigma \,;\, \text{Ab} \,;\, \text{Result}].$$

Does this circumscription have the anomalous model familiar from Chapter 3, in which the Wait action mysteriously unloads the gun? Figure 6.1 depicts (a fragment of) the anomalous model. The bubbles are situations. The letters inside the bubbles indicate whether or not the fluents Alive and Loaded hold in the corresponding situation, according to the Holds predicate: A stands for Alive and

L stands for Loaded. A selection of pertinent Result terms appears in the bottom left-hand corner, and the lines emanating from them indicate the situations they denote. The box in the bottom right-hand corner displays the abnormalities demanded by the rest of the picture.

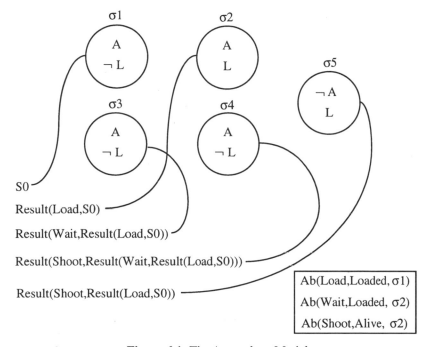

Figure 6.1: The Anomalous Model

Of course, this is still a model of Σ. The question is whether it is minimal with respect to the new circumscription policy, in which Result varies and Holds is fixed. The answer is no. It's not a model of the new circumscription policy. Figure 6.2 shows why. This figure shows a model that is preferable to that in Figure 6.1. In this model, the same collection of situations has been kept, but the denotations of a couple of Result terms have been changed. Pictorially, this means detaching the corresponding lines from their bubbles and re-attaching to other bubbles. The box of abnormalities responds by shrinking. It now contains a subset of the abnormalities in Figure 6.1. It's easy to see that no further manipulations of this sort can reduce the abnormalities any more, so this is a minimal model.[2] In this model, the gun stays loaded, and the victim dies.

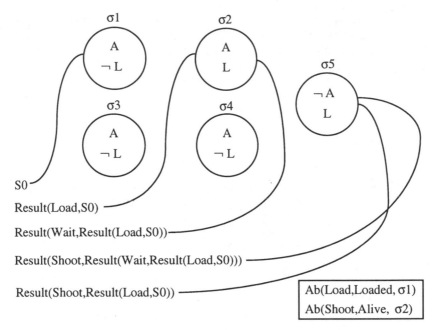

Figure 6.2: A Preferable Model Varying Result

If the pictorial equivalent of finding a preferable model with respect to the new circumscription policy is to move the lines emanating from Result terms (varying Result), the pictorial equivalent of finding a preferable model with respect to the old circumscription policy is to change the contents of the bubbles (varying Holds). Can we do this and produce a preferable model to that in Figure 6.1? We've already proved formally that this is impossible (Proposition 3.3.2). But Figure 6.3 shows it graphically, and highlights the difference between the two circumscription policies.

All we can do to try to ensure that the Wait action doesn't unload the gun is alter the contents of the bubbles. We can't move the lines around any more. Result(Wait,Result(Load,S0)) has to point to σ3, but we can make Alive and Loaded hold in σ3. Then, not Alive will hold in s4. But the effect of this is not to shrink the box of abnormalities, but rather to replace one abnormality with another. Ab(Load,Loaded,σ1) goes, but Ab(Shoot,Alive,σ3) comes in its place. Notice that this is a distinct abnormality from Ab(Shoot,Alive,σ2).

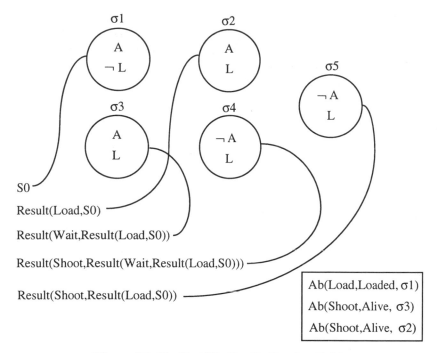

Figure 6.3: The Best We Can Do Varying Holds

So far so good. Varying Result seems to be a good idea. But just varying Result is not enough to overcome the Hanks-McDermott problem. The second component of state-based minimisation is an existence-of-situations axiom.

6.2 Adding an Existence-of-Situations Axiom

Although Figure 6.1 depicts a minimal model, and although this model is preferable to the usual anomalous model, CIRC[Σ ; Ab ; Result] has other anomalous models, which need to be eliminated. Figure 6.4 shows a model in which the Load action not only loads the gun, but also mysteriously kills the victim. As briefly mentioned in Chapter 3, anomalous models of CIRC[Σ ; Ab ; Holds] also exist that have this form.

The model in Figure 6.4 comprises just two situations: σ1 and σ2. So we know straight away that it is incomparable to the model in Figure 6.2. But is it minimal? The box in the bottom right-hand corner contains just two abnormalities, and it's easy to verify that moving the lines indicating the denotations of situation terms isn't going to reduce this box any further.

The difficulty here motivates the second innovation of state-based minimisation. The crucial difference between the anomalous model in Figure 6.4 and the expected model in Figure 6.2 is that the right combinations of fluents don't even exist in the anomalous model. There is no situation in which Alive and Loaded hold. If there were, there would have to be a corresponding abnormality. And, as already argued, this abnormality should be present in every model.

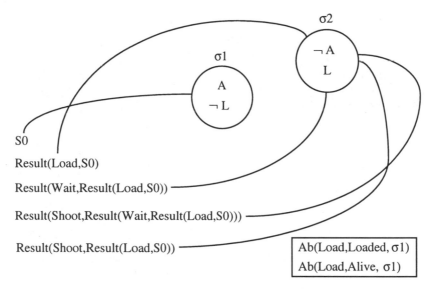

Figure 6.4: Another Anomalous Model

What we need is an axiom that guarantees the presence of every legitimate combination of fluents in every model, an *existence-of-situations axiom*. For the Yale shooting scenario, in addition to the usual axioms, we have the following existence-of-situations axiom.

$$\exists s \, [\text{Holds(Alive,s)} \wedge \text{Holds(Loaded,s)}] \wedge \qquad \text{(YB1)}$$
$$\exists s \, [\text{Holds(Alive,s)} \wedge \neg \, \text{Holds(Loaded,s)}] \wedge$$
$$\exists s \, [\neg \, \text{Holds(Alive,s)} \wedge \text{Holds(Loaded,s)}] \wedge$$
$$\exists s \, [\neg \, \text{Holds(Alive,s)} \wedge \neg \, \text{Holds(Loaded,s)}]$$

We're nearly home and dry now, at least as far as the Yale shooting scenario is concerned. Now let Σ be the conjunction of (Y1) to (Y6) plus (F2) and (YB1), and consider CIRC[Σ ; Ab ; Result]. The anomalous model in Figure 6.4 is ruled out by Axiom (YB1), because it doesn't include a situation in which Alive and

Loaded hold. And so long as there is such a situation, there must be a corresponding abnormality for Shoot with respect to Alive. The trade of abnormalities that made the model in Figure 6.4 possible is no longer on the cards.

There's more to be said about existence-of-situations axioms, not least because we don't want to have to write an axiom like (YB1) for a domain with a non-trivial number of fluents. But we haven't quite got the Yale shooting scenario right yet. There's one more piece of the jigsaw puzzle to put in place before we consider existence-of-situations axioms in more depth, namely the issue for domain closure.

6.3 The Need for Domain Closure Axioms

Believe it or not, CIRC[Σ ; Ab ; Result] still doesn't have all the logical consequences we are expecting. Yet again we find that there are anomalous models, this time due to the possible presence of nameless fluents. Figure 6.5 depicts one such model.

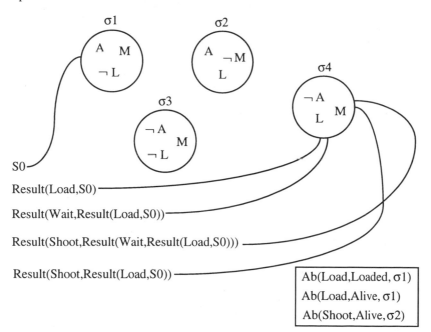

Figure 6.5: An Anomalous Model with a Nameless Fluent

This model resembles the one in Figure 6.4. The victim dies mysteriously during the Load action. But this time, as stipulated by the existence-of-situations axiom, there is a situation, namely σ2, in which Alive and Loaded hold. And there is a corresponding abnormality for the Shoot action with respect to Alive, an abnormality we can't get rid of by trading it for another.

So why can't we make Result(Load,S0) point to σ2, and get rid of the offending abnormality? The reason is that this will introduce two new abnormalities on the nameless fluent M (see Figure 6.6).

The trouble here is that the existence-of-situations axiom hasn't covered the nameless fluent. It has asserted the existence of situations with all four possible combinations of Alive and Loaded, but it hasn't guaranteed the existence of situations for all eight possible combinations of Alive, Loaded and M.

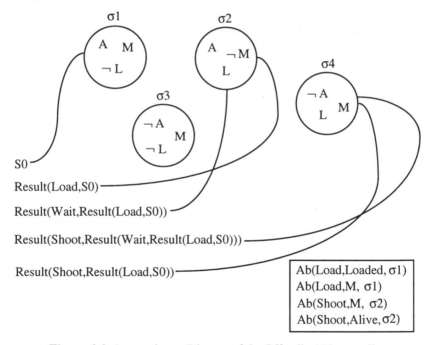

Figure 6.6: Attempting to Dispose of the Offending Abnormality

But the problem is easily remedied. We simply have to add a *domain closure axiom* for fluents.

$$f = \text{Alive} \lor f = \text{Loaded} \qquad \text{(YB2)}$$

If the only fluents are Alive and Loaded, there can't be any mysterious nameless fluents to bother us. The existence-of-situations axiom (YB1) covers all cases. At last we can prove the proposition we want to prove.

Proposition 6.3.1. If Σ is the conjunction of (Y1) to (Y6), with (YB1), (YB2), and Axiom (F2), then,

$$\text{CIRC}[\Sigma \; ; \text{Ab} \; ; \text{Result, S0}] \vDash$$
$$\neg \text{ Holds(Alive,Result(Shoot,Result(Wait,Result(Load,S0)))).}$$

Proof. First, we show that the circumscription satisfies the following sentence.

$$\text{Ab(a,f,s)} \leftrightarrow [[f = \text{Alive} \wedge a = \text{Shoot} \wedge \text{Holds(Alive,s)} \wedge \quad [6.3.2]$$
$$\text{Holds(Loaded,s)}] \vee [f = \text{Loaded} \wedge a = \text{Load} \wedge \neg \text{ Holds(Loaded,s)}]]$$

Let M be a model of the circumscription. There are twelve cases to consider, corresponding to the four possible combinations of the two fluents, Alive and Loaded, with the three actions Load, Wait and Shoot. For each of these cases, we ask which fluents persist and which do not. Fortunately all the cases are analogous, so we can focus on one. Let $\sigma 1$ be a situation in which Alive and Loaded hold, and consider the effect of the Shoot action in $\sigma 1$.

We know Ab(Shoot,Alive,$\sigma 1$) from (Y2). We want to show that $\neg$ Ab(Shoot,Loaded,$\sigma 1$). Suppose Ab(Shoot,Loaded,$\sigma 1$). Now let M' be a model that is identical to M except that M' satisfies $\neg$ Ab(Shoot,Loaded,$\sigma 1$), and M'⟦Result(Shoot,s1)⟧ = $\sigma 2$, where $\sigma 2$ is a situation in which Loaded holds but Alive doesn't. It's clear that M' exists because,

- Σ doesn't constrain what happens to the Loaded fluent when a Shoot action takes place in $\sigma 1$, and

- The existence-of-situations axiom (YB1) tells us that in every model a situation like $\sigma 2$ exists.

Clearly M' is smaller than M with respect to the circumscription policy, because it doesn't have Ab(Shoot,Loaded,$\sigma 1$). Since this contradicts the assumption that M is a model of the circumscription, we must have not Ab(Shoot,Loaded,$\sigma 1$).

As already mentioned, the other eleven cases are analogous, so we can show (6.3.1). From [6.3.2], it's easy to show classically that the proposition holds. □

Now, we have a solution to the frame problem that works for the Yale shooting scenario. But what's so special about it? It's taken a very intricate reasoning process to arrive at the right combination of axioms and circumscription policy. Let's take a step back, and examine the final product. We have the six original axioms describing the Yale shooting scenario (Y1) to (Y6). These axioms are unmodified, standard situation calculus, with no extra predicates introduced. We have added two extra axioms: one for existence-of-situations and one for domain closure. And we have made a minor modification to McCarthy's original circumscription policy: varying Result instead of Holds. We haven't had to introduce a new form of default reasoning, but have made do with standard circumscription.

So, even though the solution we've arrived at is subtle, it's also very simple. Furthermore, it turns out to be somewhat more robust than its predecessors. Shortly we'll see how it fares with explanation problems and with actions with ramifications. First though, we need to address the problem of having to write a complicated existence-of-situations axiom for each domain. This is the subject of the next section, and of much of the next chapter.

Before moving on to the topic of a universal existence-of-situations axiom, a few remarks are in order about the relationship between state-based minimisation, causal minimisation, and the principle of separation. Baker writes,

> It should be noted that, in a certain sense, our solution works for the same reason that causal minimisation does. Causal minimisation is not tempted to unload the gun because it is minimising the extent of the Causes predicate rather than actual changes in the world . . . Similarly, our solution minimises even those abnormality facts associated with situations that do not really happen. [Baker, 1991]

This point is crucial to a proper understanding of state-based minimisation. What it amounts to is this: state-based minimisation observes the principle of separation. Recall that the principle of separation is that the minimisation required to overcome the frame problem should not be dependent on the outcome of temporal projection (see Section 5.3). At least as far as simple projection problems are concerned (for example, where observation sentences only mention the initial situation), the minimisation of Ab does not depend in any way on the denotation of Result terms, in other words on the outcome of the projection process. Explanation problems are another matter. These are discussed briefly in the next chapter and in more depth in Chapter 17.

The advantage state-based minimisation confers over causal minimisation is that it has greater representational flexibility. It copes easily with domain constraints and context-dependent effects, both of which are a source of trouble for unmodified causal minimisation. Chapters 14 and 15 use a hybrid of causal and state-based minimisation to get the representational flexibility of the latter in the framework of a narrative-based formalism that uses causal predicates, namely the event calculus. There as here, the adoption of the state-based approach permits representational flexibility without sacrificing the principle of separation. The minimisation required to overcome the frame problem should not be dependent on the outcome of temporal projection.

6.4   A Universal Existence-of-Situations Axiom

As Baker points out [1991], Axiom (YB1) "violates the spirit of the nonmonotonic enterprise". If it forced us to write out by hand an axiom like (YB1) for each domain we were interested in, state-based minimisation would hardly constitute a very satisfactory solution to the frame problem.

Disregarding domain constraints for the moment, and disregarding the possibility of a domain with an infinite number of fluents, it's obvious that an existence-of-situations axiom like (YB1) will have 2^n conjuncts for a domain comprising n fluents. However, as we will see shortly, it's a straightforward task to write a general form of the axiom that will apply to any given domain. This axiom is easily compact enough to meet the criterion of representational parsimony.

The trouble starts when we admit domain constraints. Then, the task of writing a universal existence-of-situations axiom becomes much less straightforward. To see why, consider a domain with three fluents: Alive, Loaded, and Walking. Without domain constraints, we would need the following existence-of-situations axiom. (This formula is a consequence of the universal existence-of-situations axiom which I'll be talking about soon. I'm presenting it in its domain specific form here to highlight the issue of domain constraints.)

$$\exists s \, [Holds(Alive,s) \land Holds(Loaded,s) \land Holds(Walking,s)] \land \quad (6.4.1)$$
$$\exists s \, [Holds(Alive,s) \land \neg Holds(Loaded,s) \land Holds(Walking,s)] \land$$
$$\exists s \, [\neg Holds(Alive,s) \land Holds(Loaded,s) \land Holds(Walking,s)] \land$$
$$\exists s \, [\neg Holds(Alive,s) \land \neg Holds(Loaded,s) \land Holds(Walking,s)] \land$$
$$\exists s \, [Holds(Alive,s) \land Holds(Loaded,s) \land \neg Holds(Walking,s)] \land$$
$$\exists s \, [Holds(Alive,s) \land \neg Holds(Loaded,s) \land \neg Holds(Walking,s)] \land$$
$$\exists s \, [\neg Holds(Alive,s) \land Holds(Loaded,s) \land \neg Holds(Walking,s)] \land$$
$$\exists s \, [\neg Holds(Alive,s) \land \neg Holds(Loaded,s) \land \neg Holds(Walking,s)]$$

But suppose we have the domain constraint,[3]

$$Holds(Walking,s) \rightarrow Holds(Alive,s). \quad (W1)$$

Axioms (6.4.1) and (W1) contradict each other. Axiom (W1) tells us that there is no situation in which Walking holds and Alive does not hold. This directly contradicts the third and fourth lines of Axiom (6.4.1). We need a more liberal existence-of-situations axiom, one in which the offending two lines are "crossed out".

$$\exists s \; [\text{Holds(Alive,s)} \land \text{Holds(Loaded,s)} \land \text{Holds(Walking,s)}] \land \quad (6.4.2)$$
$$\exists s \; [\text{Holds(Alive,s)} \land \lnot \text{Holds(Loaded,s)} \land \text{Holds(Walking,s)}] \land$$
$$\exists s \; [\text{Holds(Alive,s)} \land \text{Holds(Loaded,s)} \land \lnot \text{Holds(Walking,s)}] \land$$
$$\exists s \; [\text{Holds(Alive,s)} \land \lnot \text{Holds(Loaded,s)} \land \lnot \text{Holds(Walking,s)}] \land$$
$$\exists s \; [\lnot \text{Holds(Alive,s)} \land \text{Holds(Loaded,s)} \land \lnot \text{Holds(Walking,s)}] \land$$
$$\exists s \; [\lnot \text{Holds(Alive,s)} \land \lnot \text{Holds(Loaded,s)} \land \lnot \text{Holds(Walking,s)}]$$

Axiom (6.4.2) fits the bill. But this axiom was easy to set down because the domain constraint (W1) is very simple. Suppose we had a large set of domain constraints expressing complicated logical relationships between fluents. Then the task would be very difficult. In the general case, to do it by hand is exactly as hard as doing propositional calculus theorem proving by hand. Naturally, we'll be expecting our universal existence-of-situations axiom to do the job for us, automatically. It must guarantee the existence of a situation for all possible combinations of fluents consistent with the domain constraints. And it must take these domain constraints into account behind the scenes.

The task of designing a universal existence-of-situations axiom is a tricky one. The whole issue is investigated in detail in the next chapter. With a universal existence-of-situations axiom in place, state-based minimisation can fulfil its promise, and be applied to wide range of different problems, including those involving ramifications and certain explanation problems.

Notes

1. The name "state-based minimisation" alludes to the temptation to think that the technique identifies a situation with the set of fluents that hold in it, in other words with a corresponding *state*. Although this is one way to understand the technique (emphasised in [Baker & Ginsberg, 1989]), this identification is not strictly speaking one of its features.
2. Or rather, this is a fragment of many minimal models. To display a whole model would require an infinite sheet of paper (or arbitrarily small writing).
3. This domain constraint is used in the "walking turkey shoot" benchmark problem.

7 Generalising State-Based Minimisation

The previous chapter introduced the basic idea of state-based minimisation, but suspended the problem of designing a universal existence-of-situations axiom. This problem has to be tackled before state-based minimisation can claim to be a satisfactory solution to the frame problem. Baker [1989], [1991] offers two formalisations of a universal existence-of-situations axiom. I'll present them both here. My presentation follows Baker's closely. The first formalisation uses first-order logic, but relies on the assumption that we are only interested in interpretations with a finite number of fluents. The second uses second-order logic, and works for any number of fluents. Using the universal existence-of-situations axiom, a number of benchmark projection and explanation problems are formalised.

7.1 Logical Prerequisites

Before moving on to the details of the two formalisations, two new pieces of logical machinery need to be introduced: hierarchies of sorts, and prioritised circumscription.

The first-order formalisation is based on the idea of a *generalised fluent*, which is a combination of fluents formed by the functions And and Neg. Generalised fluents are a *supersort* of the sort of fluents. In the definition of a language of many-sorted predicate calculus given in Chapter 2, each variable of the language was associated with exactly one sort. A simple generalisation of this idea permits sorts to be placed in a hierarchy. A hierarchically-sorted language is assumed to have an associated set of *primitive sorts*, which can be combined to form supersorts. The idea is conceptually straightforward, but for the record, here's a formal definition of an interpretation for such a language.

Definition 7.1.1. Let L be a language of hierarchically-sorted first-order predicate calculus with equality. Let L have a set Ω of primitive sorts. A sort in the language L is a subset of Ω. Let L have a set Ψ of sorts, Ψ-indexed sets C and V of constant symbols and variables respectively, an $\Psi^* \times \Psi$-indexed set F of function symbols, and an Ψ^*-indexed set P of predicate symbols. An *interpretation* of L is a triple $\langle D, F, P \rangle$ where,

- D is an Ω-indexed set of objects,

- F is a function mapping,

  - Every constant symbol in C_ψ to $\bigcup_{\omega \in \psi} D_\omega$,

  - Every variable in V_ψ to $\bigcup_{\omega \in \psi} D_\omega$, and

- Every n-ary function symbol in $F_{\psi_1,\ldots,\psi_n,\psi}$ to a function from $\bigcup_{\omega \in \psi_1} D_\omega \times \ldots \times \bigcup_{\omega \in \psi_n} D_\omega$ to $\bigcup_{\omega \in \psi} D_\omega$, and

- P is a function mapping every n-ary predicate symbol in $P_{\psi_1,\ldots,\psi_n}$ to a subset of $\bigcup_{\omega \in \psi_1} D_\omega \times \ldots \times \bigcup_{\omega \in \psi_n} D_\omega$ □

The second new piece of logical machinery I want to introduce here is *prioritised circumscription* [Lifschitz, 1985]. This is an important generalisation of the forms of circumscription defined in Sections 2.10 and 2.11. It will be required to represent universal existence-of-situations axioms, and it will come in handy in later chapters too.

The basic idea is straightforward. In default reasoning, it's common to have to represent multiple default assumptions. In circumscription, this is done by minimising more than one predicate at once. Sometimes these multiple defaults will conflict. Standard parallel circumscription is neutral about the outcome of such conflicts, yielding a different model for each possible resolution. Frequently though, we find that different defaults have different levels of importance. We may prefer to adopt default A, even if it's at the expense of default B. Prioritised circumscription facilitates this sort of ordering among defaults.

Before the formal presentation, let's make this more concrete with an example. This will be a variation of the birds and penguins example from Chapter 2. This time Tweety is going to be a bat instead of a penguin. The two (potentially) conflicting defaults are,

- Normally mammals don't fly, and

- Normally bats do fly.[1]

These are represented in the usual way, using abnormality predicates.

$$\neg \, Flies(x) \leftarrow Mammal(x) \wedge \neg \, AbMammal(x) \qquad (7.1.2)$$

$$Flies(x) \leftarrow Bat(x) \wedge \neg \, AbBat(x) \qquad (7.1.3)$$

The abnormality predicates AbMammal and AbBat will be minimised. We also know, of course, that bats are mammals. Finally, Tweety is a bat.

$$Mammal(x) \leftarrow Bat(x) \qquad (7.1.4)$$

$$Bat(Tweety) \qquad (7.1.5)$$

The question is whether or not Tweety can fly, according to these formulae. Let Σ be the conjunction of (7.1.2) to (7.1.5), and consider what follows from the circumscription CIRC[Σ ; AbMammal, AbBat ; Flies]. It should be clear that the circumscription will have two kinds of model: one in which AbBat(Tweety) and ¬ Flies(Tweety), and one in which AbMammal(Tweety) and Flies(Tweety). So the circumscription does not entail either Flies(Tweety) or ¬ Flies(Tweety).

This may be exactly what is required from the circumscription. But we might want to incorporate into our formalisation a preference for the second default, perhaps reflecting the fact that (abnormally) non-flying bats are more unusual than (abnormally) flying mammals.[2] In terms of circumscription, we would like to be able to impose an ordering on the predicates we are minimising corresponding to the prioritisation we require, and for our definition to supply us with consequences that reflect that prioritisation. In the bats and mammals example, we would like to prioritise the minimisation of AbBat over that of AbMammal. This is accomplished by the following definitions.

First, some notation. Let $\rho1^*$ be a tuple of n predicates, which is partitioned into disjoint tuples of predicates $\rho1^1, \rho1^2, \ldots \rho1^k$. Let $\rho2^*$ be a tuple of n predicates with the same arities as those in $\rho1^*$, which is partitioned into disjoint tuples of predicates $\rho2^1, \rho2^2, \ldots \rho2^k$ corresponding to the partitioning of $\rho1^*$. So $\rho1^i$ and $\rho2^i$ are tuples of the same number of predicates, having corresponding arities.

- $\rho1^* \leqslant \rho2^*$ means $\displaystyle\bigwedge_{i=1}^{k} \left[\bigwedge_{j=1}^{i-1} [\rho1^j = \rho2^j] \rightarrow [\rho1^i \leq \rho2^i] \right]$

- $\rho1^* < \rho2^*$ means $\rho1^* \leqslant \rho2^*$ and not $\rho1^* = \rho2^*$

Definition 7.1.6. Let ρ^* be a tuple of n predicate symbols, and σ^* be a tuple of m predicate, function and constant symbols. Let ρ^* be partitioned into disjoint tuples of predicates $\rho^1, \rho^2, \ldots \rho^k$. Let ϕ be a formula that mentions each symbol in ρ^* and σ^*. The *circumscription* of ϕ *minimising* each ρ^i at a *higher priority* than ρ^{i+1}, and *allowing* σ^* *to vary*, written CIRC$[\phi ; \rho^1 > \rho^2 > \ldots > \rho^k ; \sigma^*]$, is the second-order formula,

$$\phi \wedge \neg \exists\, q^*, r^*\, [\phi(q^* ; r^*) \wedge q^* < \rho^*]$$

where q^* is a tuple of n predicate variables, r^* is a tuple of m predicate, function and constant variables, and where $\phi(q^* ; r^*)$ is the formula obtained by replacing all occurrences of ρ_i in ϕ by q_i and all occurrences of σ_i by r_i, and where $<$ is defined according to the partitioning given above ☐

Now if we let Σ be the conjunction of (7.1.2) to (7.1.5), we have,

CIRC$[\Sigma ; \text{AbBat} > \text{AbMammal} ; \text{Flies}] \models \text{Flies(Tweety)}.$

Here's the model theoretic characterisation of prioritised circumscription. (It's interesting to compare this definition to that of "chronologically as small as" in Section 4.4. Chronological minimisation can be thought of as a kind of prioritised minimisation, with higher priority being given to minimising change at earlier times [Lifschitz, 1986].)

Definition 7.1.7. Let $\rho*$ be a tuple of n predicate symbols, and $\sigma*$ be a tuple of m predicate, function and constant symbols. Let $\rho*$ be partitioned into disjoint tuples of predicates $\rho^1, \rho^2, \ldots \rho^k$. Let M_1 and M_2 be interpretations. M_1 is *as small as* M_2 *with respect to the policy of minimising each ρ^i at a higher priority than ρ^{i+1}*, and *allowing $\sigma*$ to vary*, written $M_1 \sqsubseteq_{\rho^1 > \rho^2 > \ldots > \rho^k; \sigma*} M_2$, if

- M_1 and M_2 agree on the interpretation of everything except zero or more of the predicates in $\rho*$ and/or $\sigma*$, and

- There is some i such that for all j < i, the extension in M_1 of each predicate in ρ^j is equal to its extension in M_2, and the extension in M_1 of each predicate in ρ^i is a subset of its extension in M_2.   □

The notion of a minimal model is defined in the obvious way. Two theorems are of interest here, which I will state without proof. The first asserts the expected equivalence between the axiomatic and model theoretic characterisations of prioritised circumscription.

Theorem 7.1.8. Let $\rho*$ be a tuple of n predicate symbols, and $\sigma*$ be a tuple of m predicate, function and constant symbols. Let $\rho*$ be partitioned into disjoint tuples of predicates $\rho^1, \rho^2, \ldots \rho^k$. Let ϕ be a formula that mentions each symbol in $\rho*$ and $\sigma*$. A model M of ϕ is a model of CIRC[ϕ ; $\rho^1 > \rho^2 > \ldots > \rho^k$; $\sigma*$] if and only if M is minimal with respect to $\sqsubseteq_{\rho^1 > \rho^2 > \ldots > \rho^k; \sigma*}$.   □

The second theorem permits the reduction of a prioritised circumscription to a conjunction of parallel circumscriptions. A proof of (a generalisation of) this theorem can be found in [Lifschitz, 1994].

Theorem 7.1.9. Let $\rho*$ be a tuple of n predicate symbols, and $\sigma*$ be a tuple of m predicate, function and constant symbols. Let $\rho*$ be partitioned into disjoint tuples of predicates $\rho^1, \rho^2, \ldots \rho^k$. Let ϕ be a formula that mentions each symbol in $\rho*$ and $\sigma*$. Then,

$$\text{CIRC}[\phi \; ; \; \rho^1 > \rho^2 > \ldots > \rho^k \; ; \; \sigma*]$$

is equivalent to,

$$\text{CIRC}[\phi \; ; \; \rho^1 > \rho^2 > \ldots > \rho^{k-1} \; ; \; \rho^k \cup \sigma*] \wedge \text{CIRC}[\phi \; ; \; \rho^k \; ; \; \sigma*],$$

where $\rho^k \cup \sigma^*$ is obtained by appending ρ^k to σ^*. □

Obviously this theorem can be applied k times to reduce the prioritised circumscription of ρ^* to a conjunction of parallel circumscriptions.

We're now in a position to formalise a universal existence-of-situations axiom. I should emphasise that, although we require the extra logical apparatus defined in this section to do this, the claim that state-based minimisation employs standard, unmodified circumscription still holds in so far as prioritised circumscription is itself a standard technique.

7.2 First-Order Formalisations

The old sort of fluents now becomes a primitive sort, which I will call the *simple fluents*. In addition, there is a primitive sort of *compound fluents*. The sort of generalised fluents (with variables g, g1, g2, etc.) is the set comprising the simple and the compound fluents. The predicate Holds can now take a generalised fluents as an argument. (I will usually abbreviate "generalised fluent" to "fluent" from now on.) But the frame axiom (F2) will still quantify over simple fluents, so that the commonsense law of inertia doesn't apply to compound fluents.

As already mentioned, generalised fluents are built up using two new functions. The term And(g1,g2) denotes the fluent that holds when fluents g1 and g2 hold. The term Not(g) denotes the fluent that holds when g does not hold. We no longer have to write Holds(f,s) but can also write Holds(g,s), where g is a generalised fluent. We have the following axioms.

$$\text{Holds(And(g1,g2),s)} \leftrightarrow \text{Holds(g1,s)} \wedge \text{Holds(g2,s)} \qquad \text{(GF1)}$$

$$\text{Holds(Not(g),s)} \leftrightarrow \neg\, \text{Holds(g,s)} \qquad \text{(GF2)}$$

In essence, the universal existence-of-situations axiom we need, guaranteeing the presence in every model of a situation for each possible combination of fluents, is simply,

$$\text{Holds(g,Sit(g)).}$$

This axiom employs a Skolem function Sit in place of the existential quantifier we might expect. Unfortunately, this axiom isn't quite right. To begin with, it contradicts Axioms (GF1) and (GF2). To see this, just consider Sit(And(Alive,Not(Alive))). The proposed existence-of-situations axiom gives,

$$\text{Holds(And(Alive,Not(Alive)),S)}$$

where S is Sit(And(Alive,Not(Alive))). From Axiom (GF1), this yields,

$$\text{Holds(Alive,S)} \wedge \text{Holds(Not(Alive,S))}$$

which from Axiom (GF2) gives,

$$\text{Holds(Alive,S)} \wedge \neg \text{Holds(Alive,S)}.$$

But this isn't the only problem with the proposed axiom. It would also contradict any domain constraint, for reasons described in the last section. A convenient way to render the axiom consistent is simply to turn it into a default. We do this by introducing a new predicate AbSit. The formula AbSit(g) represents that g is an illegitimate combination of fluents. There can be no situation corresponding to such a combination. But for every legitimate combination, there must be a corresponding situation. We have,

$$\text{Holds(g,Sit(g))} \leftarrow \neg \text{AbSit(g)}. \qquad \text{(EoS1)}$$

To make this a default, the predicate AbSit needs to be minimised at a higher priority than Ab. The minimisation of AbSit in effect represents the default assumption that the known domain constraints are the only domain constraints. Why the prioritisation? If the two predicates were minimised at the same priority (or with the opposite prioritisation), it would be possible to reduce the extension of Ab for the price of an increase in the extension of AbSit. For example, the extension of AbSit could contain all the generalised fluents that include Alive and Loaded. This would take us back to the anomalous model illustrated in Figure 6.4. The whole idea was to pin down the situations that exist in each model prior to minimising the effects of actions.

Finally, we need some uniqueness-of-names axioms that take into account the new functions And, Not and Sit. If our domain includes a finite number of constants β_1 to β_n for simple fluents, we write,

$$\text{UNA[Sit]} \qquad \text{(EoS2)}$$

$$\text{UNA}[\beta_1, \ldots, \beta_n, \text{And, Not}]. \qquad \text{(EoS3)}$$

Without Axioms (EoS2) and (EoS3), it would be possible to construct an anomalous model either by equating two incompatible generalised fluents (if (EoS3) is missing) or by equating the corresponding situations for two incompatible generalised fluents (if (EoS2) is missing). This absolves the corresponding situations from the need to exist. Suppose we have a model that satisfies $\text{And(Not}(\beta_1),\beta_2)=\text{And}(\beta_1,\text{Not}(\beta_2))$ for two simple fluents β_1 and β_2. Then Axioms (GF1) and (GF2) yield,

$$\neg \exists s \ [\text{Holds(And(Not}(\beta_1),\beta_2),s)].$$

Since Axiom (EoS1) is (by necessity) a default, this doesn't lead to contradiction, but simply implies $AbSit(And(Not(\beta_1),\beta_2))$. The inclusion of Axioms (EoS2) and (EoS3) prevents this.

Axioms (GF1), (GF2) and (EoS1) to (EoS3) give us what we want, subject to one important restriction. They only work for domains with a finite number of fluents. This restriction can be enforced in one of two ways. Either we can legislate that we are only concerned with interpretations in which there is a finite number of fluents. Or, more satisfactorily, we can include a domain closure axiom: given a finite number of simple fluent constants $\beta_1, \ldots, \beta_n$, we write,

$$f = \beta_1 \vee \ldots \vee f = \beta_n. \tag{EoS4}$$

In the next section, I will discuss the need for this restriction in more detail, and propose a way to get around it, using second-order logic.

Now, given the conjunction Σ of a set of observation sentences that mention only the initial situation S0, effect axioms, and domain constraints, with Axioms (GF1), (GF2) and (EoS1) to (EoS4), we are interested in,

$$CIRC[\Sigma \; ; AbSit > Ab \; ; Holds, Result, S0].$$

One crucial difference between this formulation and the domain specific formulation of Section 6.3, apart from the prioritised minimisation of AbSit, is that Holds has been allowed vary. Allowing extra predicates to vary, since it permits models to be compared that couldn't be compared previously, only strengthens the circumscription: everything that follows from a circumscription in which a predicate ρ is held fixed still follows if ρ is allowed to vary. The reason for insisting that Holds is allowed to vary here is that the extension of Holds depends directly on that of AbSit. So if Holds were not allowed to vary, the minimisation of AbSit would be ineffectual.

Before moving on to some examples, I want to look at an alternative first-order formulation, which is similar to one I'll be using later when I come to present a circumscriptive event calculus. In the following formalisation, the sort of generalised fluents has been dispensed with, and a new sort for sets is introduced, with variables h, h1, h2, etc. There is no need for the And and Not functions, and no need for hierarchies of sorts.

$$h1 = h2 \leftrightarrow \forall f \, [In(f,h1) \leftrightarrow In(f,h2)] \tag{S1}$$

$$\forall \, h1,f1 \, \exists \, h2 \, \forall f2 \, [In(f2,h2) \leftrightarrow [In(f2,h1) \vee f2=f1]] \tag{S2}$$

$$\exists \, h \, \forall \, f \, [\neg \, In(f,h)] \tag{S3}$$

Axioms (S1) to (S3) in effect formalise a fragment of Zermelo-Fraenkel set theory,[3] with membership represented by the predicate In. The formula In(f,h) represents that fluent f is a member of the set h. Axiom (S1) says that set identity is determined by membership. Axiom (S2) says that any set can be combined with a fluent to give a new set. Axiom (S3) says that the empty set exists. Here's the new existence-of-situations axiom.

$$[Holds(f,Sit(h)) \leftrightarrow In(f,h)] \leftarrow \neg AbSit(h) \qquad (EoS5)$$

AbSit now takes a set as an argument instead of a generalised fluent. Uniqueness-of-names axiom for fluents and for the Sit function are required, for the same reason as before. This formalisation suffers from the same restriction to finitely many fluents as the first formalisation, so we also require a domain closure axiom. Given a finite number of fluent constants β_1 to β_n, we write,

$$UNA[Sit] \qquad (EoS6)$$

$$UNA[\beta_1, \ldots, \beta_n] \qquad (EoS7)$$

$$f = \beta_1 \vee \ldots \vee f = \beta_n. \qquad (EoS8)$$

The circumscription is just the same as before. Given the conjunction Σ of a set of observation sentences that mention only the initial situation S0, effect axioms, and domain constraints, with Axioms (S1) to (S3) and (EoS5) to (EoS8), we are interested in,

$$CIRC[\Sigma ; AbSit > Ab ; Holds, Result, S0].$$

Although their effect is the same, the two formulations differ in one important way. The set-theoretic formulation only guarantees the existence of a single situation for every legitimate combination of fluents. The formulation using And and Not, however, guarantees the existence of many situations for each such combination (assuming that there is more than one fluent in the domain). This is because any given combination of simple fluents corresponds to many different generalised fluents. For example, the generalised fluent $And(\beta_1,\beta_2)$ is logically distinct from the intuitively equivalent generalised fluent $And(\beta_2,\beta_1)$. Axiom (EoS1) ensures that a distinct situation exists for both generalised fluents.

7.3 Applying State-Based Minimisation

Of course, using the universal existence-of-situations axiom, we expect to obtain the right conclusions with the Yale shooting scenario, as before. The domain specific existence-of-situations axiom (YB1) is omitted. The axioms are otherwise the same, except for the uniqueness-of-names axiom (YB3).

$$\text{Holds(Loaded,Result(Load,s))} \tag{Y1}$$

$$\neg \text{ Holds(Alive,Result(Shoot,s))} \leftarrow \text{Holds(Loaded,s)} \tag{Y2}$$

$$\text{Holds(Alive,S0)} \tag{Y3}$$

$$\neg \text{ Holds(Loaded,S0)} \tag{Y4}$$

$$\text{UNA[Load, Wait, Shoot]} \tag{Y5}$$

$$f = \text{Alive} \vee f = \text{Loaded} \tag{YB2}$$

$$\text{UNA[Alive, Loaded, And, Not]} \tag{YB3}$$

Proposition 7.3.1. If Σ is the conjunction of (Y1) to (Y5) with (YB2) and (YB3), plus Axioms (GF1), (GF2), (EoS1), (EoS2) and (F2), then,

$$\text{CIRC}[\Sigma \text{ ; AbSit} > \text{Ab ; Holds, Result, S0}] \vDash$$
$$\neg \text{ Holds(Alive,Result(Shoot,Result(Wait,Result(Load,S0))))}.$$

Proof. From Theorem 7.1.9, we have,

$$\text{CIRC}[\Sigma \text{ ; AbSit} > \text{Ab ; Holds, Result, S0}]$$

is equivalent to,

$$\text{CIRC}[\Sigma \text{ ; AbSit ; Ab, Holds, Result, S0}] \wedge \text{CIRC}[\Sigma \text{ ; Ab ; Holds, Result, S0}].$$

We can show that the proposition follows from the second of these conjuncts using the same proof as for Proposition 6.3.1, given that [7.3.2] follows from the first conjunct. ([7.3.2] is identical to the domain specific existence-of-situations axiom (YB1).)

$$\exists s \text{ [Holds(Alive,s)} \wedge \text{Holds(Loaded,s)]} \wedge \tag{7.3.2}$$
$$\exists s \text{ [Holds(Alive,s)} \wedge \neg \text{Holds(Loaded,s)]} \wedge$$
$$\exists s \text{ [}\neg \text{Holds(Alive,s)} \wedge \text{Holds(Loaded,s)]} \wedge$$
$$\exists s \text{ [}\neg \text{Holds(Alive,s)} \wedge \neg \text{Holds(Loaded,s)]}.$$

To see that [7.3.2] follows from $\text{CIRC}[\Sigma \text{ ; AbSit ; Ab, Holds, Result, S0}]$, we first show that,

$$\text{CIRC}[\Sigma \text{ ; AbSit ; Ab, Holds, Result, S0}] \vDash \neg \exists \text{ g [AbSit(g)]}. \tag{7.3.3}$$

This follows because, given any model M of Σ, it's easy to construct a model M' that differs from M only in the way it interprets AbSit, Ab, Holds, Result and S0, and in which AbSit has an empty extension. Obviously any such M' will be minimal.

From [7.3.3] and (EoS1), we have Holds(γ,Sit(γ)), and therefore $\exists$ s [Holds(γ,s)], for each of the following generalised fluents.

$$\gamma = \text{And(Alive,Loaded)}$$

$$\gamma = \text{And(Alive,Not(Loaded))}$$

$$\gamma = \text{And(Not(Alive),Loaded)}$$

$$\gamma = \text{And(Not(Alive),Not(Loaded))}$$

[7.3.2] follows directly from this and Axioms (GF1) and (GF2).   □

So the new formulation works out well for the Yale shooting scenario. This time, though, we have a formalisation that carries over to more complicated problems as well. For example, the sort of domain constraint that scuppered causal minimisation is dealt with correctly by state-based minimisation. Consider what happens when we incorporate the domain constraint (D1).

$$\text{Holds(Alive,s)} \leftrightarrow \neg \text{Holds(Dead,s)} \tag{D1}$$

The universal existence-of-situations axiom adjusts smoothly and silently to the addition of this domain constraint. By forcing an increase in the extension of AbSit, the new domain constraint cuts out some of the situations that had to exist before. Recall that, with causal minimisation, the addition of (D1) meant that it was no longer possible to prove that the victim even survived the loading of the gun (see Section 5.6). State-based minimisation has no such difficulty.

The whole collection of axioms for the Yale shooting scenario extended with the "dead or alive" domain constraint is as follows.

$$\text{Holds(Loaded,Result(Load,s))} \tag{D2}$$

$$\neg \text{Holds(Alive,Result(Shoot,s))} \leftarrow \text{Holds(Loaded,s)} \tag{D3}$$

$$\text{Holds(Alive,S0)} \tag{D4}$$

$$\neg \text{Holds(Loaded,S0)} \tag{D5}$$

$$\text{UNA[Load, Wait, Shoot]} \tag{D6}$$

$$\text{UNA[Alive, Loaded, Dead, And, Not]} \tag{D7}$$

$$\text{f = Alive} \vee \text{f = Loaded} \vee \text{f = Dead} \tag{D8}$$

Proposition 7.3.4. If Σ is the conjunction of (D1) to (D8) with Axioms (GF1), (GF2), (EoS1), (EoS2) and (F2), then,

CIRC[Σ ; AbSit > Ab ; Holds, Result, S0] $\models$ Holds(Alive,Result(Load,S0)).

Proof. The proposition follows straightforwardly, using the same style of proof as in that of Proposition 7.3.1, if we can show the following,

$$\exists s \; [\text{Holds(Alive,s)} \wedge \text{Holds(Loaded,s)} \wedge \neg \, \text{Holds(Dead,s)}] \wedge$$
$$\exists s \; [\text{Holds(Alive,s)} \wedge \neg \, \text{Holds(Loaded,s)} \wedge \neg \, \text{Holds(Dead,s)}] \wedge$$
$$\exists s \; [\neg \, \text{Holds(Alive,s)} \wedge \text{Holds(Loaded,s)} \wedge \text{Holds(Dead,s)}] \wedge$$
$$\exists s \; [\neg \, \text{Holds(Alive,s)} \wedge \neg \, \text{Holds(Loaded,s)} \wedge \text{Holds(Dead,s)}].$$

This in turn follows from the fact that the circumscription entails,

$$\text{AbSit(g)} \leftrightarrow [\text{Holds(Alive,Sit(g))} \leftrightarrow \text{Holds(Dead,Sit(g))}]$$

which again can be shown using the same style of proof as in that of Proposition 7.3.1. $\qquad \Box$

The "walking turkey shoot" is another benchmark problem involving a domain constraint [Baker, 1991].[4] It's similar to the Yale shooting scenario, but instead of the "dead or alive" domain constraint (D1), we have,

$$\text{Holds(Walking,s)} \rightarrow \text{Holds(Alive,s)}. \qquad \text{(W1)}$$

The walking turkey shoot discourages us from thinking of fluents as partitioned *a priori* into those that are primitive (made to hold/not to hold directly by an action) and those that are derived (made to hold/not to hold indirectly, as a ramification of an action). Using (W1), we might conclude that Alive holds as a ramification of an action that makes Walking hold, but conclude that Walking no longer holds as a ramification of a later action that makes Alive not hold. So neither Alive nor Walking can be considered as primitive.[5]

In addition to (W1), the walking turkey shoot has the following axioms. These resemble those for the usual Yale shooting scenario, except that instead of asserting that the victim is alive in S0, (W4) asserts that the victim is walking in S0. Also, because we have a new fluent, Walking, we have correspondingly modified uniqueness-of-names and domain closure axioms (W7) and (W8).

$$\text{Holds(Loaded,Result(Load,s))} \qquad \text{(W2)}$$

$$\neg \, \text{Holds(Alive,Result(Shoot,s))} \leftarrow \text{Holds(Loaded,s)} \qquad \text{(W3)}$$

$$\text{Holds(Walking,S0)} \qquad \text{(W4)}$$

$$\neg \text{ Holds(Loaded,S0)} \tag{W5}$$

$$\text{UNA[Load, Wait, Shoot]} \tag{W6}$$

$$\text{UNA[Alive, Loaded, Walking, And, Not]} \tag{W7}$$

$$f = \text{Alive} \vee f = \text{Loaded} \vee f = \text{Walking} \tag{W8}$$

Proposition 7.3.5. If Σ is the conjunction of (W1) to (W8) with Axioms (GF1), (GF2), (EoS1), (EoS2) and (F2), then,

$$\text{CIRC}[\Sigma ; \text{AbSit} > \text{Ab} ; \text{Holds, Result, S0}] \vDash$$
$$\neg \text{ Holds(Walking,Result(Shoot,Result(Wait,Result(Load,S0))))}.$$

Proof. A proof in the same style as that of Proposition 7.3.4 is easily constructed. □

All in all, Baker's state-based minimisation seems to cope well with the indirect ramifications of actions, at least in so far as they can be captured by domain constraints. However, as several authors have emphasised, sometimes the indirect effects of an action are hard to capture using domain constraints, because of a one-way causal relationship that apparently obtains between the fluents affected by the action [Giunchiglia & Lifschitz, 1995], [Lin, 1995], [McCain & Turner, 1995].

The point is illustrated by the stuffy room scenario [Ginsberg & Smith, 1987], in which there are three fluents: Stuffy, which represents that the room is stuffy, and Blocked1 and Blocked2, which represent respectively that air vent one is blocked and that air vent two is blocked. There are two actions: Close1 and Close2, which respectively represent closing vent one and closing vent two. We have,

$$\text{Holds(Blocked1,Result(Close1,s))} \tag{SR1}$$

$$\text{Holds(Blocked2,Result(Close2,s))} \tag{SR2}$$

$$\text{UNA[Close1, Close2]} \tag{SR3}$$

$$\text{UNA[Blocked1, Blocked2, Stuffy, And, Not]} \tag{SR4}$$

$$f = \text{Blocked1} \vee f = \text{Blocked2} \vee f = \text{Stuffy} \tag{SR5}$$

We want to capture the constraint that if both vents are blocked, the room is stuffy. The natural way to do this seems to be with a domain constraint.

$$\text{Holds(Stuffy,s)} \leftrightarrow \text{Holds(Blocked1,s)} \wedge \text{Holds(Blocked2,s)} \tag{SR6}$$

Now suppose one of the vents is blocked in the initial situation, and the other is unblocked.

$$Holds(Blocked1,S0) \qquad (SR7)$$

$$\neg\ Holds(Blocked2,S0) \qquad (SR8)$$

Clearly we have,

$$\neg\ Holds(Stuffy,S0).$$

But what can we conclude about Result(Close2,S0)? It isn't hard to see that the domain constraint allows for two possibilities. Either closing vent two causes the room to become stuffy, or it causes vent one to become blocked.

Proposition 7.3.6. If Σ is the conjunction of (SR1) to (SR8) with Axioms (GF1), (GF2), (EoS1), (EoS2) and (F2), then,

$$CIRC[\Sigma\ ;\ AbSit > Ab\ ;\ Holds,\ Result,\ S0] \not\models Holds(Stuffy,Result(Close2,S0)).$$

Proof. A minimal model that satisfies $\neg$ Holds(Stuffy,Result(Close2,S0)) is easily constructed. □

This isn't the conclusion we might have hoped for. We would like to exclude the possibility that closing one vent causes the opening of the other. We would like to capture the fact that the Stuffy fluent is, in some sense, causally dependent on the other two fluents, and not the other way around.[6] In the walking turkey shoot and the "dead or alive" scenarios, the domain constraints were binary — they involved just two fluents. The stuffy room scenario introduces a *ternary* domain constraint.

One way to tackle the stuffy room example is to reject the use of domain constraints altogether. The outcomes of the Close1 and Close2 actions can be expressed directly using effect axioms.

$$Holds(Stuffy,Result(Close1,s)) \leftarrow Holds(Blocked2,s)$$

$$Holds(Stuffy,Result(Close2,s)) \leftarrow Holds(Blocked1,s)$$

While this approach is viable for simple domain constraints like (SR6), it soon breaks down when more fluents are involved, and when more complex collections of effect axioms are involved. Consider the following domain constraint.

$$Holds(\beta,s) \leftarrow Holds(\beta_1,s) \wedge Holds(\beta_2,s) \wedge \ldots \wedge Holds(\beta_n,s) \qquad (7.3.7)$$

where β and each β_i are fluent constants. Suppose that there are m_i effect axioms for the fluent β_i. Then the number of effect axioms required to take the place of (7.3.7), assuming that β is causally dependent on each β_i as in the stuffy room example, will be of the order of $\sum_{i=1}^{n} m_i$.

Even ignoring the question of how, in the general case, the right collection of effect axioms is to be derived from a collection of domain constraints if the latter are all that we know, it's clear that to confine ourselves to effect axioms is to abandon representational parsimony and elaboration tolerance. So a principled approach to the representation of the indirect effects of actions is required — one that preserves both representational parsimony and elaboration tolerance, but at the same time permits the representation of asymmetrical causal dependencies between fluents.

A number of proposals exist for dealing with this issue. One approach is to use Lifschitz's distinction between frame and non-frame fluents [Lifschitz, 1990] (see Section 5.6). By taking the Stuffy fluent out of the frame, and thus insulating it from the common sense law of inertia, the problem can be overcome. Other authors, such as those already cited, prefer an explicitly causal approach to the problem. In the circumscriptive event calculus that will be presented in Chapters 14 and 15, benchmarks like the stuffy room scenario are represented very naturally using a causal approach.

7.4 State-Based Minimisation and Explanation

Recall that causal minimisation dealt correctly with the Stanford murder mystery but not with the stolen car scenario (Section 5.5), and that chronological minimisation dealt incorrectly with both (Sections 4.6 and 5.5). Before revisiting the stolen car scenario, let's see how state-based minimisation fares with the Stanford murder mystery. Recall that the status of the gun is unknown in the initial situation, and the victim is alive in the initial situation and dead after a Shoot action followed by a Wait action.

$$\text{Holds(Alive,S0)} \tag{MM1}$$

$$\text{S2} = \text{Result(Wait,Result(Shoot,S0))} \tag{MM2}$$

$$\neg \, \text{Holds(Alive,S2)} \tag{MM3}$$

$$\neg \, \text{Holds(Alive,Result(Shoot,s))} \leftarrow \text{Holds(Loaded,s)} \tag{MM4}$$

$$\text{UNA[Wait, Shoot]} \tag{MM5}$$

$$UNA[Alive, Loaded, And, Not] \qquad (MM6)$$

$$f = Alive \lor f = Loaded \qquad (MM7)$$

The desired explanation is simply that the gun was loaded in S0, and that Ab(Wait,Alive,S0). Note that the Wait takes place after the Shoot, not before it as in the Yale shooting scenario. As Baker points out [1991], neither McCarthy's original circumscription policy, nor chronological minimisation, nor causal minimisation fare particularly well with this problem.[7] State-based minimisation, however, has no difficulty with it.

Proposition 7.4.1. If Σ is the conjunction of (MM1) to (MM7) with Axioms (GF1), (GF2), (EoS1), (EoS2) and (F2), then,

$$CIRC[\Sigma ; AbSit > Ab ; Holds, Result, S0, S2] \vDash$$
$$Holds(Loaded,S0) \land Ab(Shoot,Alive,S0).$$

Proof. From (MM1) to (MM3) and (F2), we have,

$$Ab(Shoot,Alive,S0) \lor Ab(Wait,Alive,Result(Shoot,S0)).$$

We need to show $\neg$ Ab(Wait,Alive,Result(Shoot,S0)). First, we observe that,

$$\exists s [Holds(Alive,s) \land Holds(Loaded,s)] \land \qquad [7.4.2]$$
$$\exists s [Holds(Alive,s) \land \neg Holds(Loaded,s)] \land$$
$$\exists s [\neg Holds(Alive,s) \land Holds(Loaded,s)] \land$$
$$\exists s [\neg Holds(Alive,s) \land \neg Holds(Loaded,s)].$$

This sentence was demonstrated, for a different theory, in the proof of Proposition 7.3.1 The proof here is essentially the same. Now consider any model M in which Ab(Wait,Alive,Result(Shoot,S0)). Because of [7.4.2], we have M $\Vdash$ Ab(Shoot,Alive,σ) for some σ such that Holds(Alive,σ) and Holds(Loaded,σ). This means that we can construct an M' that is the same as M except that,

- M' $[\![S0]\!] = \sigma$ and therefore Holds(Loaded,S0), and

- M' $\vDash \neg$ Ab(Wait,Alive,Result(Shoot,S0)).

M' is preferable to M according to the circumscription policy, so M cannot be a model of the circumscription. Therefore we have,

$$\neg Ab(Wait,Alive,Result(Shoot,S0))$$

and Ab(Shoot,Alive,S0). A similar argument is easily constructed to show that S0 must denote a situation in which Loaded holds. $\qquad \square$

As claimed by Baker [1989], state-based minimisation also yields the desired conclusions about the stolen car scenario. Here are the formulae for the stolen car scenario again, augmented with the requisite uniqueness-of-names and domain closure axioms.

$$\neg \text{Holds(Stolen,S0)} \qquad \text{(SCB1)}$$

$$\text{S2} = \text{Result(Wait,Result(Wait,S0))} \qquad \text{(SCB2)}$$

$$\text{Holds(Stolen,S2)} \qquad \text{(SCB3)}$$

$$\text{UNA[Stolen, And, Not]} \qquad \text{(SCB4)}$$

$$\text{f} = \text{Stolen} \qquad \text{(SCB5)}$$

We're hoping for the disjunctive conclusion that the car disappeared during one of the Wait actions. We don't want a stronger conclusion than this, in other words one that identifies a particular Wait action as the culprit.

Proposition 7.4.3. If Σ is the conjunction of (SCB1) to (SCB5) with Axioms (GF1), (GF2), (EoS1), (EoS2) and (F2), then,

$$\text{CIRC}[\Sigma \; ; \text{AbSit} > \text{Ab} \; ; \text{Holds, Result, S0, S2}] \models \text{Ab(Wait,Stolen,S0)} \lor \\ \text{Ab(Wait,Stolen,Result(Wait,S0))}$$

but,

$$\text{CIRC}[\Sigma \; ; \text{AbSit} > \text{Ab} \; ; \text{Holds, Result, S0, S2}] \not\models \text{Ab(Wait,Stolen,S0)}$$

and,

$$\text{CIRC}[\Sigma \; ; \text{AbSit} > \text{Ab} \; ; \text{Holds, Result, S0, S2}] \not\models \\ \text{Ab(Wait,Stolen,Result(Wait,S0))}.$$

Proof. From (SCB1) to (SCB3) and (F2), we have,

$$\text{Ab(Wait,Stolen,S0)} \lor \text{Ab(Wait,Stolen,Result(Wait,S0))}.$$

We also have,

$$\neg [\text{Ab(Wait,Stolen,S0)} \land \text{Ab(Wait,Stolen,Result(Wait,S0))}]$$

It's easy to see that we can construct models of Σ corresponding to either disjunct. In other words, we have models in which just Ab(Wait,Stolen,S0), and models in which just Ab(Wait,Stolen,Result(Wait,S0)). Neither kind of model is preferable to the other according to the circumscription policy, so the circumscription will also have models of both kinds.   □

So we seem to get the consequence we intuitively expect. However, it could be argued that the disjunctive conclusion we obtain doesn't really constitute an explanation at all. It simply says that one of the Wait actions must have been abnormal. From the frame axioms (F2), it can be seen that the abnormality of a Wait action is not sufficient to bring about a change in the value of Stolen. It's a necessary condition of such a change, not a sufficient one.

Furthermore, as Baker points out [1989], if the stolen car domain is augmented with more fluents, even state-based minimisation goes awry. Suppose we augment the stolen car domain with the fluent Alive, and add the following sentence.

$$\text{Holds(Alive,S0)} \qquad \text{(SCB6)}$$

Sadly, we cannot conclude from the circumscription that Alive persists through the Wait actions. This is because, with the stolen car scenario represented as above, the circumscription is forced to accommodate an abnormality that permits the disappearance of the car. Unlike abnormalities that are derived from effect axioms, circumscription has a free hand in deciding what this extra abnormality should be. For example, the circumscription has models in which Ab(Wait,Stolen,σ) such that $\neg$ Holds(Alive,σ). In these models, Alive cannot persist through the first Wait action.

Proposition 7.4.4. If Σ is the conjunction of (SCB1) to (SCB6) with Axioms (GF1), (GF2), (EoS1), (EoS2) and (F2), then,

CIRC[Σ ; AbSit > Ab ; Holds, Result, S0, S2] $\nvdash$ Holds(Alive,Result(Wait,S0)).

Proof. Consider any interpretation M that meets the following criteria.

- M $\Vdash$ Ab(Wait,Stolen,Result(Wait,S0))

- M $\Vdash$ Ab(Wait,Alive,S0)

- M $\Vdash \neg$ Holds(Alive,Result(Wait,S0))

It's clear that a model of this form can be constructed. Furthermore, a model of the circumscription can be constructed that has this form. To see this, note that it's impossible to get rid of the second abnormality without altering the denotation of Result(Wait,S0)), thus changing the first abnormality. $\square$

Fortunately, as shown in [Shanahan, 1993], this difficulty is just an artefact of the style of representation used in (SCB1) to (SCB3). An alternative style of representation for explanation problems is proposed in [Shanahan, 1993] that

gets around the problem. This will be presented in Chapter 17, which is devoted
to the topic of explanation.

Finally, state-based minimisation, even using the alternative style of
representation, does get into trouble with explanation problems involving non-
deterministic action, as shown by Kartha [1994]. There are a number of ways to
overcome this problem, including the use of an appropriate style of
representation for non-determinism, along with the adoption of an *abductive*
approach to explanation [Shanahan, 1989], [Shanahan, 1993], as opposed to the
deductive approach, which is the only one employed so far in this book. Again,
detailed discussion of this issue is postponed until Chapter 17.

7.5   A Second-Order Existence-of-Situations Axiom

Unlike the axiom used in the first attempt to capture the Yale shooting scenario
using state-based minimisation, the first-order formalisations of a universal
existence-of-situations axiom in Section 7.2 *are* in the "spirit of the non-
monotonic enterprise". They're concise, and they tolerate elaboration in the form
of new domain constraints. But they still have a certain restriction. They assume
that the domain comprises a finite number of fluents.[8] This confines our attention
to fairly uninteresting domains. For example, it excludes the possibility of a
fluent representing the value of a numerical quantity, such as the amount of
weight on a balance, or the height of a falling ball, or the number of people in a
building. All of these fluents have numerical arguments with an infinite number
of possible values.[9]

Why do we have this restriction? Whether we pick Axioms (GF1), (GF2),
(EoS1) and (EoS2), or Axioms (S1) to (S3) plus (EoS5) to (EoS8), we have the
same problem. They only guarantee the existence of situations that can be
constructed by combining other situations whose existence they guarantee. This
forever condemns their products to finitude.

But why do we need to guarantee the existence of situations corresponding to
infinite sets of fluents? Well, if we don't we run into the same kind of difficulty
we had in Section 6.3 when we tried to do without domain closure axioms. As
usual, the difficulty manifests itself in the form of anomalous models. There, the
trouble was with nameless fluents. Here the trouble is with infinite sets of fluents.

Figure 7.1 shows an anomalous model that is closely analogous to that in
Figure 6.5. There exists a situation for all possible finite combinations of fluents,
indicated by the bubble with the bold outline. (More about this bubble in a
moment.) But there is a crucial infinite combination of fluents for which no
corresponding situation exists, and consequently the victim mysteriously dies

during the Wait action. If we attempt to dispose of the offending abnormality by attaching Result(Wait,Result(Load,S0)) to σ2 instead of σ3, we simply find another abnormality popping up in its place, namely Ab(Wait,M_1,σ3).

The crucial combination of fluents for which no corresponding situation exists is one in which Alive, Loaded, and M_1, M_2, . . . all hold. If we want Alive to persist through the Wait action, we have to sacrifice the persistence of M_1. Of course, it's important that Σ excludes the crucial combination. So it's vital that a Σ exists that excludes this combination, but that satisfies the existence-of-situations axiom.

Let's assume we're dealing with the formalisation using generalised fluents. To see that such a Σ exists, it suffices to show that we can find a set of situations that satisfies the existence-of-situations axiom, but that excludes any given combination of the fluents.

In fact, we can go further. The following theorem shows that we can find a set of situations that satisfies the existence-of-situations axiom, but that excludes any given set of combinations of the fluents.

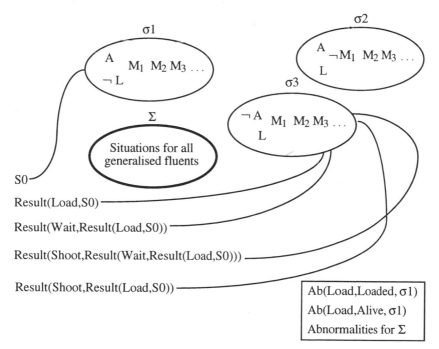

Figure 7.1: An Anomalous Model with Infinitely Many Fluents

Definition 7.5.1. A generalised fluent g *satisfies* a set F of fluents if,

- g is a simple fluent and g ∈ F, or

- g = Not(f) and f ∉ F, or

- g = And(g1,g2) and both g1 and g2 satisfy F.   □

Lemma 7.5.2. Let F be an infinite set of fluents. Let P be 2^F (the set of sets of fluents). Given any generalised fluent g, there exist infinitely many members of P that are satisfied by g.

Proof. There are infinitely many simple fluents in F not mentioned by g, and consequently infinitely many combinations of these. For each of these combinations there is a distinct member of P that is satisfied by g.   □

Lemma 7.5.3. Let F be an infinite set of fluents. Let P be 2^F. Given any generalised fluent g and any finite subset Q of P, there exists a member of P that is not in Q, that is satisfied by g.

Proof. From Lemma 7.5.2, there are infinitely many members of P that are satisfied by g. So Q, being finite, cannot contain all of them.   □

Theorem 7.5.4. Let F be an infinite set of fluents. Let P be 2^F. Given any finite subset Q of P, there exists a subset R of P that is disjoint from Q, and that satisfies all generalised fluents.

Proof. For any generalised fluent g, let s(g) be any member of P that is not in Q, that is satisfied by g. Lemma 7.5.3 tells us that some s(g) exists for every g. Let R be {f | ∃ g [f = s(g)]}.   □

From Theorem 7.5.4, it's easy to see that Σ exists in Figure 7.1 if we formalise existence-of-situations using generalised fluents. Theorem 7.5.4 guarantees the existence of a set of situations satisfying Axioms (GF1), (GF2) and (EoS1) that excludes any situation in which Alive, Loaded, and M_1, M_2, . . . all hold.

Σ also exists if we formalise existence-of-situations using sets instead. To see this, suppose we have infinitely many fluents, and imagine an interpretation in which there is a set corresponding to each finite subset of these fluents, but no infinite sets of fluents. Obviously satisfying Axioms (S1) and (S3) is no problem for such an interpretation. But it also satisfies Axiom (S2), because we can pick any set in the interpretation and add any fluent to it and we always get another set in the interpretation.

So, to summarise, the formalisations of the existence-of-situations axiom offered in the last section are inadequate for dealing with infinitely many fluents. Accordingly, Baker proposes an alternative, second-order formalisation. Here it is.

$$[\text{Holds}(f, \text{Sit}(p)) \leftrightarrow p(f)] \leftarrow \neg \text{AbSit}(p) \tag{EoS9}$$

The predicate AbSit and the function Sit now take a predicate as their argument, where they previously took a generalised fluent or a set. This predicate itself takes a single fluent as its argument. Since the predicate p in Axiom (EoS9) can have any extension, finite or infinite, the restriction to finite sets of fluents of first-order formalisations is overcome.

As usual, we need certain uniqueness-of-names axioms.

$$\text{UNA}[\text{Sit}] \tag{EoS10}$$

$$\text{UNA}[\beta_1, \ldots, \beta_n] \tag{EoS11}$$

The circumscription policy to overcome the frame problem is, as before, to minimise AbSit at a higher priority than Ab, and to allow Holds, Result, and S0 to vary. The circumscription is now third-order, which goes beyond any of the definitions of circumscription presented so far. As Baker says [1991], the required generalisation of circumscription is "entirely straightforward".

However, the fact that the formalisation is now third-order is a little disconcerting. Fortunately, the need for a third-order formalisation isn't inherent in state-based minimisation. The circumscriptive event calculus introduced in Chapter 14 employs a first-order analogue of the existence-of-situations axiom, but is immune to the problems with infinite sets of fluents described in this section.

As we would expect, it can be shown that the formulae describing the Yale shooting scenario yield the correct conclusions with the second-order existence-of-situations axiom. The axioms are familiar, except that we can now safely omit the domain closure axiom for fluents.

$$\text{Holds}(\text{Loaded}, \text{Result}(\text{Load}, s)) \tag{Y1}$$

$$\neg \text{Holds}(\text{Alive}, \text{Result}(\text{Shoot}, s)) \leftarrow \text{Holds}(\text{Loaded}, s) \tag{Y2}$$

$$\text{Holds}(\text{Alive}, \text{S0}) \tag{Y3}$$

$$\neg \text{Holds}(\text{Loaded}, \text{S0}) \tag{Y4}$$

$$\text{UNA}[\text{Load}, \text{Wait}, \text{Shoot}] \tag{Y5}$$

UNA[Alive, Loaded]   (Y6)

Proposition 7.5.5. If Σ is the conjunction of (Y1) to (Y6), plus Axioms (EoS9), (EoS10) and (F2), then,

$$CIRC[\Sigma ; AbSit > Ab ; Holds, Result, S0] \vDash$$
$$\neg\ Holds(Alive,Result(Shoot,Result(Wait,Result(Load,S0)))).$$

Proof. All we need to do is show,

$$\exists s\ [Holds(Alive,s) \wedge Holds(Loaded,s)] \wedge \qquad\qquad [7.5.6]$$
$$\exists s\ [Holds(Alive,s) \wedge \neg\ Holds(Loaded,s)] \wedge$$
$$\exists s\ [\neg\ Holds(Alive,s) \wedge Holds(Loaded,s)] \wedge$$
$$\exists s\ [\neg\ Holds(Alive,s) \wedge \neg\ Holds(Loaded,s)]$$

and then the proof reduces to that of Proposition 7.3.1. We can prove [7.5.6] in the same way that it was shown in the proof of Proposition 7.3.1, based on the easily demonstrated fact that,

$$CIRC[\Sigma ; AbSit ; Ab, Holds, Result, S0] \vDash \neg\ \exists\ p\ [AbSit(p)]. \qquad \Box$$

Corresponding propositions can be proved for each of the other benchmark problems described in Sections 7.3 and 7.4.

From now on, I will adopt this section's second-order existence-of-situations axiom whenever state-based minimisation is applied to the situation calculus.

7.6 General Theorems about State-Based Minimisation

Showing that a technique works for a string of benchmark problems is all very well. But, as many authors have pointed out [Lifschitz, 1991], [Lin & Shoham, 1991], [Sandewall, 1994], we ultimately want to be able to prove more general theorems, which demonstrate the applicability of the technique to a wide class of problems. Otherwise, we can never be sure that a new benchmark problem won't be invented that invalidates the technique.

Lifschitz [1991] has supplied such a theorem for state-based minimisation. What the theorem tells us is that, under suitable conditions, the minimisation of the predicates Ab and AbSit in state-based minimisation generates a completed form of those predicates.[10] That is to say, they reduce to manageable if-and-only-if formulae. In later chapters, we will encounter many instances of *separation theorems*, which play a similar role in simplifying apparently complicated circumscriptions.

Another general result about the range of applicability of state-based minimisation has been established by Kartha [1996]. Kartha shows that state-based minimisation yields the same results as a tailor-made *action description language*[11] for two overlapping classes of theories, namely those in which actions have only deterministic effects, and those that involve only temporal projection (and not explanation).

Notes

1. Exceptions might include injured bats.
2. This preference also illustrates the principle of *specificity*, which says, roughly, that higher priority should be given to defaults that concern more specific classes of objects. (This has never struck me as a very plausible principle, but discussion of the topic would be out of place here.)
3. For an introduction to Zermelo-Fraenkel set theory, see [Hamilton, 1988].
4. The walking turkey shoot is due to Matt Ginsberg, but was first described by Baker.
5. This way of formulating the domain constraint is open to criticism, because it masks the true causal relationship between Walking and Alive, which is that Alive is a precondition for any action that makes Walking hold. The general point about the primitive/derived distinction still holds, however.
6. Of course, we can easily imagine a computerised air flow system in which closing one vent does indeed cause the other to open. But that would be a different example.
7. The Wait action in the murder mystery exposes certain problems for these techniques, which is why it's included.
8. In Chapter 14, I will be employing three axioms very similar to (S1) to (S3) to write a first-order universal existence-of-situations axiom which doesn't suffer from this restriction.
9. For an example of a domain with uncountably many fluents, see [Shanahan, 1995a].
10. In addition, he deploys a Frame predicate to indicate those fluents which are subject to the common sense law of inertia, which is also minimised.
11. The idea of an action description language is presented in the next chapter.

8 Tailor-Made Techniques

The bulk of work presented in this book is based on a general purpose representational formalism — either predicate calculus or logic programming — augmented with a general purpose default reasoning mechanism — either circumscription or negation-as-failure. A number of authors have proposed solutions to the frame problem that, at least as a preliminary methodological step, forego general purpose representational techniques in favour of techniques specially tailored for reasoning about action. This chapter covers two bodies of work that have this flavour: the so-called monotonic solutions to the frame problem, and work based on the language $\mathcal{A}$.

In the monotonic approaches, the frame problem is overcome by the explicit representation of formulae that are logically equivalent to, but more compact than, the full set of frame axioms. However, as I've already argued in Chapter 1, when extended to deal with complex domains, these approaches have to specify formally how these formulae are to be generated from a given domain description. This specification in effect defines a non-monotonic consequence relation that is tailored for reasoning about action.

In the language $\mathcal{A}$, not only is the non-monotonic consequence relation tailored specifically for reasoning about action, but the language itself is specially designed for the representation of the effects of actions. Although the language $\mathcal{A}$ wasn't originally intended as a stand-alone formalism, both these approaches can be thought of as minimalist in the sense that they offer very spare solutions to the frame problem by eschewing the full power of more general purpose default reasoning techniques such as circumscription.

8.1 Explanation Closure Axioms

With admirable succinctness, Haas [1987] pointed out something that everybody working on the frame problem seemed not have noticed before, namely that situation calculus frame axioms can be replaced by axioms written in a different style that do the same job, but that are very much more compact.

Consider the usual axioms for the Yale shooting scenario.

$$\text{Holds(Loaded,Result(Load,s))} \qquad \text{(Y1)}$$

$$\neg \text{ Holds(Alive,Result(Shoot,s))} \leftarrow \text{Holds(Loaded,s)} \qquad \text{(Y2)}$$

$$\text{Holds(Alive,S0)} \qquad \text{(Y3)}$$

$$\neg \text{ Holds(Loaded,S0)} \qquad \text{(Y4)}$$

$$\text{UNA[Load, Wait, Shoot]} \qquad \text{(Y5)}$$

$$\text{UNA[Alive, Loaded]} \qquad \text{(Y6)}$$

The following is a suitable collection of frame axioms for this example.[1]

$$\text{Holds(Loaded,Result(Wait,s))} \leftarrow \text{Holds(Loaded,s)} \qquad \text{(YF1)}$$

$$\text{Holds(Alive,Result(Load,s))} \leftarrow \text{Holds(Alive,s)} \qquad \text{(YF2)}$$

$$\text{Holds(Alive,Result(Wait,s))} \leftarrow \text{Holds(Alive,s)} \qquad \text{(YF3)}$$

$$\text{Holds(Alive,Result(Shoot,s))} \leftarrow \text{Holds(Alive,s)} \wedge \qquad \text{(YF4)}$$
$$\neg \text{Holds(Loaded,s)}$$

$$\neg \text{Holds(Loaded,Result(Wait,s))} \leftarrow \neg \text{Holds(Loaded,s)} \qquad \text{(YF5)}$$

$$\neg \text{Holds(Loaded,Result(Shoot,s))} \leftarrow \neg \text{Holds(Loaded,s)} \qquad \text{(YF6)}$$

$$\neg \text{Holds(Alive,Result(Load,s))} \leftarrow \neg \text{Holds(Alive,s)} \qquad \text{(YF7)}$$

$$\neg \text{Holds(Alive,Result(Wait,s))} \leftarrow \neg \text{Holds(Alive,s)} \qquad \text{(YF8)}$$

$$\neg \text{Holds(Alive,Result(Shoot,s))} \leftarrow \neg \text{Holds(Alive,s)} \qquad \text{(YF9)}$$

From (Y1) to (Y6) plus (YF1) to (YF9), the conclusion,

$$\neg \text{Holds(Alive,Result(Shoot,Result(Wait,Result(Load,S0))))}$$

follows by classical deduction. Recall that the motivation for dispensing with explicit frame axioms is that their number increases rapidly with the complexity of the domain being represented. In a domain with n fluents and m actions, we require of the order of $n \times m$ frame axioms.

Now consider the following collection of formulae, which are intended as substitutes for (YF1) to (YF4).

$$\neg \text{[Holds(Loaded,s)} \wedge \neg \text{Holds(Loaded,Result(a,s))]} \qquad \text{(EY1)}$$

$$\text{[}\neg \text{Holds(Loaded,s)} \wedge \text{Holds(Loaded,Result(a,s))]} \rightarrow a = \text{Load} \qquad \text{(EY2)}$$

$$\text{[Holds(Alive,s)} \wedge \neg \text{Holds(Alive,Result(a,s))]} \rightarrow \qquad \text{(EY3)}$$
$$\text{[a = Shoot} \wedge \text{Holds(Loaded,s)]}$$

$$\neg \text{[}\neg \text{Holds(Alive,s)} \wedge \text{Holds(Alive,Result(a,s))]} \qquad \text{(EY4)}$$

Formulae in this style are called *explanation closure axioms* [Schubert, 1990], and were introduced by Haas [1987]. In general, we require a pair of explanation closure axioms for each fluent in the domain.

It's easy to show that this formulation of the Yale shooting scenario yields the consequence we expect for the victim. Let Σ be the conjunction of (Y1) to (Y6) with (EY1) and (EY4).

Proposition 8.1.1.

Σ ⊨ ¬ Holds(Alive,Result(Shoot,Result(Wait,Result(Load,S0)))).

Proof. From (Y1) we have,

Holds(Loaded,Result(Load,S0)).

From this and (EY1) we have,

Holds(Loaded,Result(Wait,Result(Load,S0))).

The proposition follows from this and (Y2).   □

Let's extend the Yale shooting domain slightly. Suppose that there are two ways to be killed. As well as a Shoot action, we have a Poison action, which always results in the victim's death. Then we have the following additional effect axiom.

¬ Holds(Alive,Result(Poison,s))

The explanation closure axiom (EY3) is now false, and must be replaced by the following.

[Holds(Alive,s) ∧ ¬ Holds(Alive,Result(a,s))] →
[a = Shoot ∧ Holds(Loaded,s)] ∨ [a = Poison]

Despite the addition of an extra fluent, the number of explanation closure axioms required for the extended domain is the same. Admittedly the replacement for (EY3) is larger, since the consequent of the implication has an extra disjunct. But the increase in complexity of the collection of explanation closure axioms is proportional to the increase in complexity of the collection of effect axioms. It should be easy to see that, using explanation closure axioms instead of frame axioms, this will be the case in general. This contrasts markedly with the rate of increase in the number of frame axioms required to capture a domain relative to the rate of increase in the complexity of the corresponding collection of effect axioms.

8.2 Ramifications and Explanation Closure

As Schubert demonstrates, the explanation closure approach can be applied to actions that have indirect effects (ramifications) through domain constraints [Schubert, 1990, Section 3]. For example, recall the formulation of the Yale shooting scenario extended with the fluent Dead, from the last chapter.[2]

$$\text{Holds(Alive,s)} \leftrightarrow \neg \text{Holds(Dead,s)} \qquad \text{(DE1)}$$

$$\text{Holds(Loaded,Result(Load,s))} \qquad \text{(DE2)}$$

$$\neg \text{Holds(Alive,Result(Shoot,s))} \leftarrow \text{Holds(Loaded,s)} \qquad \text{(DE3)}$$

$$\text{Holds(Alive,S0)} \qquad \text{(DE4)}$$

$$\neg \text{Holds(Loaded,S0)} \qquad \text{(DE5)}$$

$$\text{UNA[Load, Wait, Shoot]} \qquad \text{(DE6)}$$

$$\text{UNA[Alive, Loaded, Dead]} \qquad \text{(DE7)}$$

The requisite explanation closure axioms are (EY1) to (EY4), exactly as before. Note that the following explanation closure formula is a logical consequence of (DE1) and (EY3), so there's no need to include it explicitly.

$$[\neg \text{Holds(Dead,s)} \wedge \text{Holds(Dead,Result(a,s))}] \rightarrow$$
$$[a = \text{Shoot} \wedge \text{Holds(Loaded,s)}]$$

Accordingly, we get all the conclusions we would intuitively expect for this example. However, it's wishful thinking to expect domain constraints to be dealt with so straightforwardly in general. Consider the walking turkey shoot scenario introduced in the last chapter.

$$\text{Holds(Walking,s)} \rightarrow \text{Holds(Alive,s).} \qquad \text{(WE1)}$$

$$\text{Holds(Loaded,Result(Load,s))} \qquad \text{(WE2)}$$

$$\neg \text{Holds(Alive,Result(Shoot,s))} \leftarrow \text{Holds(Loaded,s)} \qquad \text{(WE3)}$$

$$\text{Holds(Walking,S0)} \qquad \text{(WE4)}$$

$$\neg \text{Holds(Loaded,S0)} \qquad \text{(WE5)}$$

$$\text{UNA[Load, Wait, Shoot]} \qquad \text{(WE6)}$$

$$\text{UNA[Alive, Loaded, Walking]} \qquad \text{(WE7)}$$

Let Σ be the conjunction of (WE1) to (WE7) with (EY1) to (EY4). As is easily verified, we have,

$\Sigma \vDash \neg$ Holds(Walking,Result(Shoot,Result(Wait,Result(Load,S0)))).

We get this conclusion without having to modify the explanation closure axioms (see [Schubert, 1994]).[3] However, we do *not* have,

$\Sigma \vDash$ Holds(Walking,Result(Load,S0)).

In other words, the Load action might have (mysteriously) curtailed the victim's walk. If we expect the Walking fluent to persist, we have to say so explicitly by adding a suitable explanation closure axiom.

$$[\text{Holds(Walking,s)} \wedge \neg \text{Holds(Walking,Result(a,s))}] \rightarrow$$
$$[a = \text{Shoot} \wedge \text{Holds(Loaded,s)}]$$

With the addition of this axiom, the victim continues walking until the Shoot action.

Using a non-monotonic approach, we expect the addition of a new domain constraint such as (WE1) to be a trivial exercise. The new domain constraint is conjoined to the old theory, and circumscription (or whichever default reasoning formalism we've chosen) deals automatically with persistence. Using explanation closure, the addition of a new domain constraint seems to require a lot more work, especially if it introduces a new fluent.

The extra effort apparently entailed by the explanation closure approach brings us to an important issue. Advocates of a monotonic approach to the frame problem come in two varieties, and their attitude to this extra workload is different.

- Some authors maintain that explanation closure axioms should be constructed individually, by hand, in just the same way that effect axioms are [Schubert, 1994].

- Some authors believe that the automatic derivation of explanation closure axioms is required for a true solution to the frame problem [Lin & Reiter, 1994].

Authors of the first variety would deny that any extra workload is involved in adding a domain constraint. The construction, by hand, of a pair of explanation closure axioms for each fluent is necessary anyway. The addition of domain constraints has no bearing on this task. According to members of this group, non-monotonic approaches that insist on persistence license conclusions that are far too strong anyway.[4] Non-change needs to be axiomatised in just the same way that change needs to be axiomatised. Using explanation closure axioms, this can be done fairly succinctly.

My reply to this argument is contained in Section 1.9. Non-monotonic approaches to the frame problem should be thought of as supplying a different underlying logical substrate to that supplied by classical, monotonic logic. In monotonic approaches, the underlying substrate is neutral with respect to persistence. In the absence of any information about change or persistence, monotonic approaches remain silent. In non-monotonic approaches, the underlying logical substrate is positive with respect to persistence. In the absence of any information to the contrary, non-monotonic approaches assume persistence.

The question to address in choosing between these approaches is this. Which underlying substrate is the most convenient one upon which to build a representation of the effects of action? In one case, persistence and change have to be made explicit against a background of neutrality. In the other case, neutrality and change have to be made explicit against a background of persistence.[5] The issue is which is the most suitable background. In Section 1.9, I argue that a background of persistence is the right choice, for the sake of both representational parsimony and elaboration tolerance.

The ambitions of the second kind of advocate of a monotonic approach are not dissimilar to those of researchers who prefer to follow the non-monotonic path. Both kinds of researcher would prefer to obviate the need to hand-code axioms for persistence. The alternative to hand-coding, for those who are attracted to the monotonic approach, is to automatically derive the required axioms for explanation closure. This is especially tricky in the presence of domain constraints, as we'll see later. As I argued in Section 1.10, when pushed to its limits in this way, the so-called monotonic approach to the frame problem resembles a non-monotonic approach with a tailor-made consequence relation.

8.3   Automatically Derived Frame Axioms

The automatic derivation of explanation closure axioms (or axioms subsuming the required explanation closure axioms) is one of the ultimate aims of the work of Reiter and Lin [Reiter, 1991], [Lin & Reiter, 1994]. Reiter's approach combines a technique due to Pednault [1989] with the work of Haas [1987] and Schubert [1990] described above. Let me begin by relaying Pednault's proposal.

Pednault presents a technique for automatically deriving frame axioms from situation calculus effect axioms. Let Σ be a conjunction of observation sentences and effect axioms.

Let the language of Σ be (temporarily) augmented with the nullary predicate symbols True and False, which will be defined by the following axioms.

$$\text{True} \qquad \qquad (T1)$$

$$\neg \, \text{False} \qquad \qquad (T2)$$

Next we assume a prior division of the condition part of every conditional effect axiom into two halves: one concerning action preconditions, and another concerning fluent preconditions. Recall that an action precondition has to hold for the action in question to be possible, while the a fluent precondition has to hold for an action to have a particular effect (see Section 5.4). Now, given Axioms (T1) and (T2), every effect axiom in Σ will either be equivalent to a *positive* effect axiom of the form,

$$\text{Holds}(\beta, \text{Result}(\alpha, s)) \leftarrow \Pi \wedge \Gamma$$

or to a *negative* effect axiom of the form,

$$\neg \, \text{Holds}(\beta, \text{Result}(\alpha, s)) \leftarrow \Pi \wedge \Phi$$

where Π represents a set of action preconditions, and Γ and Φ represent sets of fluent preconditions. Effect axioms that don't involve preconditions of one or either variety can still be expressed in this form, since Π, Γ and Φ can each be simply True.

Given Axioms (T1) and (T2), for each action α and fluent β in the language of Σ, the conjunction of all effect axioms for α and β in Σ is equivalent to a formula of the form,

$$\bigwedge_{i=1}^{n} [\text{Holds}(\beta, \text{Result}(\alpha, s)) \leftarrow \Pi \wedge \Gamma_i] \wedge$$
$$\bigwedge_{i=1}^{m} [\neg \, \text{Holds}(\beta, \text{Result}(\alpha, s)) \leftarrow \Pi \wedge \Phi_i]$$

where Π represents a set of action preconditions and each Γ_i and Φ_i represents a set of fluent preconditions. Note that this is still the case if Σ is lacking one or either kind of effect axiom for α and β, since Π, Γ_1 and Φ_1 can each be False, with $n = m = 1$.

This is logically equivalent to the formula,

$$[\text{Holds}(\beta,\text{Result}(\alpha,s)) \leftarrow \Pi \wedge \bigvee_{i=1}^{n} \Gamma_i] \wedge$$

$$[\neg\, \text{Holds}(\beta,\text{Result}(\alpha,s)) \leftarrow \Pi \wedge \bigvee_{i=1}^{m} \Phi_i].$$

Now we're in a position to specify the frame axioms required to complement the effect axioms in Σ. Given that the conjunction of all effect axioms for α and β in Σ is equivalent to the above formulae, the frame axioms we require are,

$$\text{Holds}(\beta,\text{Result}(\alpha,s)) \leftarrow \Pi \wedge \text{Holds}(\beta,s) \wedge \bigwedge_{i=1}^{n} \neg\, \Phi_i$$

and,

$$\neg\, \text{Holds}(\beta,\text{Result}(\alpha,s)) \leftarrow \Pi \wedge \neg\, \text{Holds}(\beta,s) \wedge \bigwedge_{i=1}^{n} \neg\, \Gamma_i.$$

These formulae can be simplified in the obvious way by eliminating the predicate symbols True and False wherever they appear. The language of the frame axioms is then identical to the language of Σ.

Let $\text{FA}(\Sigma)$ denote the conjunction of the required frame axioms for Σ, as defined above. The formula $\Sigma \wedge \text{FA}(\Sigma)$ should yield the logical consequences we would expect if we had written the frame axioms by hand.

Take the formulae representing the Yale shooting scenario, for example. Let Σ be the conjunction of (Y1) to (Y6) (see Section 8.1).

Proposition 8.3.1.

$\Sigma \wedge \text{FA}(\Sigma) \vDash \neg\, \text{Holds}(\text{Alive},\text{Result}(\text{Shoot},\text{Result}(\text{Wait},\text{Result}(\text{Load},\text{S0})))).$

Proof. Σ is logically equivalent to the conjunction of the following formulae, given Axioms (T1) and (T2).

$$[\text{Holds}(\text{Loaded},\text{Result}(\text{Load},s)) \leftarrow \text{True} \wedge \text{True}] \wedge$$
$$[\neg\, \text{Holds}(\text{Loaded},\text{Result}(\text{Load},s)) \leftarrow \text{False} \wedge \text{False}]$$

$$[\text{Holds}(\text{Alive},\text{Result}(\text{Load},s)) \leftarrow \text{False} \wedge \text{False}] \wedge$$
$$[\neg\, \text{Holds}(\text{Alive},\text{Result}(\text{Load},s)) \leftarrow \text{False} \wedge \text{False}]$$

$$[\text{Holds}(\text{Loaded},\text{Result}(\text{Wait},s)) \leftarrow \text{False} \wedge \text{False}] \wedge$$
$$[\neg\, \text{Holds}(\text{Loaded},\text{Result}(\text{Wait},s)) \leftarrow \text{False} \wedge \text{False}]$$

$$[\text{Holds}(\text{Alive},\text{Result}(\text{Wait},s)) \leftarrow \text{False} \wedge \text{False}] \wedge$$
$$[\neg\, \text{Holds}(\text{Alive},\text{Result}(\text{Wait},s)) \leftarrow \text{False} \wedge \text{False}]$$

[Holds(Loaded,Result(Load,s)) ← False ∧ False] ∧
[¬ Holds(Loaded,Result(Load,s)) ← False ∧ False]

[Holds(Alive,Result(Shoot,s)) ← False ∧ False] ∧
[¬ Holds(Alive,Result(Shoot,s)) ← True ∧ Holds(Loaded,s))].

From these, we get the following collection of (simplified) frame axioms.

Holds(Loaded,Result(Load,s)) ← Holds(Loaded,s)

Holds(Alive,Result(Load,s)) ← Holds(Alive,s)

¬ Holds(Alive,Result(Load,s)) ← ¬ Holds(Alive,s)

Holds(Loaded,Result(Wait,s)) ← Holds(Loaded,s)

¬ Holds(Loaded,Result(Wait,s)) ← ¬ Holds(Loaded,s)

Holds(Alive,Result(Wait,s)) ← Holds(Alive,s)

¬ Holds(Alive,Result(Wait,s)) ← ¬ Holds(Alive,s)

Holds(Loaded,Result(Shoot,s)) ← Holds(Loaded,s)

¬ Holds(Loaded,Result(Shoot,s)) ← ¬ Holds(Loaded,s)

Holds(Alive,Result(Shoot,s)) ← Holds(Alive,s) ∧ ¬ Holds(Loaded,s)

¬ Holds(Alive,Result(Shoot,s)) ← ¬ Holds(Alive,s)

From (Y1) we have,

Holds(Loaded,Result(Load,S0)).

From this and the fourth of the above frame axioms, we get,

Holds(Loaded,Result(Wait,Result(Load,S0))).

The proposition follows from this and (Y2). ☐

Note that FA(Σ) is a slightly larger and stronger collection of frame axioms than the hand-coded set in Section 8.1 ((YF1) to (YF9)). In particular, it entails that Loaded is unaffected by the Shoot action, a point on which the hand-coded frame axioms were neutral. What's the significance of this difference?

One way to think of Pednault's proposal is as embodying a strong completeness assumption about what is known about the effects of actions [Reiter, 1991]. It yields a correct set of frame axioms under this assumption. Alternatively, it can be thought of as incorporating an incautious approach to incomplete information. In the absence of information, inertia is always assumed. Finally, the interpretation I prefer is the same as the one I've advanced for the common sense law of inertia (which Pednault's proposal can be thought of as realising), namely that it supplies an underlying substrate of persistence, as an alternative to the underlying substrate of neutrality supplied by unadorned classical logic. The adornment, in this case, is the extra conjunct appended to Σ, namely $FA(\Sigma)$, whose inclusion is reminiscent of the way circumscription functions.

However, according to this last interpretation, there should be two ways to violate the implicit assumption of persistence: through an explicit description of change, and through an explicit description of neutrality. The second option seems to be missing here. How would it be possible, in Pednault's scheme, to be neutral about whether the gun remains loaded after a Shoot action, as is possible by hand-coding the frame axioms?

As Reiter points out [1991], neutrality can often be achieved through the introduction of an extra fluent. In this particular example, we can write,

$$\neg \, \text{Holds(Loaded,Result(Shoot,s))} \leftarrow \text{Holds(Bullets(1),s)}$$

and include effect axioms for the new fluent Bullets(n), which represents that the gun contains n bullets. The number of bullets in the gun in the initial situation may be unknown.

Similar remarks to these can be made in response to any argument against non-monotonic approaches that objects to the incautious nature of the inertia assumptions they make. In order to make the proposal work for actions with non-deterministic effects in general, however, more thought is required. As far as non-monotonic approaches are concerned, the work of Kartha and Lifschitz, whose Releases predicate facilitates the representation of such actions, is relevant here. Their suggestions will be pursued in Chapter 15.

8.4 Successor State Axioms

Reiter's work absorbs Pednault's idea of automatically derived frame axioms and reapplies it to Haas and Schubert style explanation closure axioms [Reiter, 1991]. Each axiom he derives combines all the effect axioms and explanation closure axioms for a given fluent into a single formula, known as a *successor state axiom*.[6]

Effect axioms, in Reiter's scheme, are written in a form that represents action preconditions more compactly, using a new predicate Poss. The formula

Poss(a,s) represents that action a is possible in situation s. Instead of writing positive effect axioms of the form,

$$\text{Holds}(\beta,\text{Result}(\alpha,s)) \leftarrow \Pi \wedge \Gamma$$

or negative effect axioms of the form,

$$\neg \, \text{Holds}(\beta,\text{Result}(\alpha,s)) \leftarrow \Pi \wedge \Phi$$

where Π represents a set of action preconditions, we now write, respectively,

$$\text{Holds}(\beta,\text{Result}(\alpha,s)) \leftarrow \text{Poss}(\alpha,s) \wedge \Gamma$$

and,

$$\neg \, \text{Holds}(\beta,\text{Result}(\alpha,s)) \leftarrow \text{Poss}(\alpha,s) \wedge \Phi.$$

In addition, one formula is required for Poss.

$$\text{Poss}(\alpha,s) \leftarrow \Pi$$

This minor amendment eliminates unnecessary repetitions of sets of action preconditions.

Suppose Σ is a conjunction of observation sentences and effect axioms are expressed in this way. Given Axioms (T1) and (T2), for each fluent β in the language of Σ, the conjunction of all positive effect axioms for β in Σ is equivalent to a *general* positive effect axiom of the form,

$$\text{Holds}(\beta,\text{Result}(a,s)) \leftarrow \text{Poss}(a,s) \wedge \bigvee_{i=1}^{n} [a = \alpha 1_i \wedge \Gamma_i] \qquad [8.4.1]$$

where each Γ_i represents a set of fluent preconditions.[7] Similarly, the conjunction of all negative effect axioms for β in Σ is equivalent to a *general* negative effect axiom of the form,

$$\neg \, \text{Holds}(\beta,\text{Result}(a,s)) \leftarrow \text{Poss}(a,s) \wedge \bigvee_{i=1}^{m} [a = \alpha 2_i \wedge \Phi_i] \qquad [8.4.2]$$

where each Φ_i represents a set of fluent preconditions.

Now, we can specify a full set of explanation closure axioms for Σ, by analogy to the way a full set of frame axioms was defined for a given domain description in the last section. We have,

$$[\text{Poss}(a,s) \wedge \text{Holds}(\beta,s) \wedge \neg \, \text{Holds}(\beta,\text{Result}(a,s)] \rightarrow \qquad [8.4.3]$$
$$\bigvee_{i=1}^{m} [a = \alpha 2_i \wedge \Phi_i]$$

and,

$$[\text{Poss}(a,s) \wedge \neg \, \text{Holds}(\beta,s) \wedge \text{Holds}(\beta,\text{Result}(a,s))] \rightarrow \qquad [8.4.4]$$

$$\bigvee_{i=1}^{n} \, [a = \alpha 1_i \wedge \Gamma_i].$$

Combining [8.4.1] to [8.4.4] yields the successor state axiom for the fluent β.

$$\text{Poss}(a,s) \rightarrow [\text{Holds}(\beta,\text{Result}(a,s)) \leftrightarrow \bigvee_{i=1}^{n} \, [a = \alpha 1_i \wedge \Gamma_i] \vee \qquad [8.4.5]$$

$$[\text{Holds}(\beta,s) \wedge \neg \, \bigvee_{i=1}^{m} \, [a = \alpha 2_i \wedge \Phi_i]]]$$

As with the automatically derived frame axioms of the last section, successor state axioms can be simplified by eliminating occurrences of True and False. Let SSA[Σ] denote the result of replacing the effect axioms in Σ by the conjunction of all the simplified successor state axioms obtained from Σ by the process described above.

Let Δ be Σ minus all effect axioms. If we have,

$$\Delta \vDash \neg \, \exists \, a,s \, [\text{Poss}(a,s) \wedge \bigvee_{i=1}^{n} \, [a = \alpha 1_i \wedge \Gamma_i] \wedge \bigvee_{i=1}^{m} \, [a = \alpha 2_i \wedge \Phi_i]]$$

then Δ entails that [8.4.5] is logically equivalent to the conjunction of [8.4.1] to [8.4.4] (see [Reiter, 1991]). One reason why this equivalence is not guaranteed without the above condition is that if the condition parts of both [8.4.1] and [8.4.2] are satisfied by Δ for some β, then Δ will be inconsistent with [8.4.1] and [8.4.2], even though the corresponding successor state axiom would be consistent with Δ. But the condition also rules out cases where Δ is consistent with [8.4.1] and [8.4.2], specifically when there are implied domain constraints (see Section 2.6).

Needless to say, the Yale shooting scenario can be expressed using effect axioms in the form required for the above process, and the successor state axioms obtained yield all the expected conclusions. For the sake of variety though, I'll illustrate the approach with a different example, lifted from Reiter's paper.

The example involves two fluents. The term Holding(x) represents that an agent is holding the object x, and the term Broken(x) represents that object x is broken. The agent can perform three actions. It can drop an object, blow an object up, or repair an object. These three actions are denoted respectively by the terms Drop(x), BlowUp(x), and Repair(x). Their effects are represented by the following formulae.

$$\text{Holds(Broken(x),Result(Drop(x),s))} \leftarrow \text{Poss(Drop(x),s)} \wedge \quad \text{(DBR1)}$$
$$\text{Fragile(x)}$$

$$\text{Holds(Broken(x),Result(BlowUp(x),s))} \leftarrow \text{Poss(BlowUp(x),s)} \quad \text{(DBR2)}$$

$$\neg \text{ Holds(Broken(x),Result(Repair(x),s))} \leftarrow \text{Poss(Repair(x),s)} \quad \text{(DBR3)}$$

$$\neg \text{ Holds(Holding(x),Result(Drop(x),s))} \leftarrow \text{Poss(Drop(x),s)} \quad \text{(DBR4)}$$

The action preconditions for the three actions are represented as follows. For simplicity, I'll assume that the BlowUp and Repair actions are always possible.

$$\text{Poss(Drop(x),s)} \leftarrow \text{Holds(Holding(x),s)} \quad \text{(DBR5)}$$

$$\text{Poss(BlowUp(x),s)} \quad \text{(DBR6)}$$

$$\text{Poss(Repair(x),s)} \quad \text{(DBR7)}$$

Finally, we have an observation sentence for the initial situation, along with the assertion that object A is fragile, and uniqueness-of-names axioms for actions and fluents.

$$\text{Holds(Holding(A),S0)} \quad \text{(DBR8)}$$

$$\text{Fragile(A)} \quad \text{(DBR9)}$$

$$\text{UNA[Holding, Broken]} \quad \text{(DBR10)}$$

$$\text{UNA[Drop, BlowUp, Repair]} \quad \text{(DBR11)}$$

Let Σ be the conjunction of (DBR1) to (DBR11).

Proposition 8.4.6.

$$\text{SSA}[\Sigma] \models \text{Holds(Broken(A),Result(BlowUp(A),}$$
$$\text{Result(Repair(A),Result(Drop(A),S0))))}.$$

Proof. The generalised positive effect axioms for the two fluents Holding and Broken are as follows.

$$\text{Holds(Holding(x),Result(a,s))} \leftarrow \text{Poss(a,s)} \wedge \text{False}$$

$$\text{Holds(Broken(x),Result(a,s))} \leftarrow \text{Poss(a,s)} \wedge [[a = \text{Drop(x)} \wedge \text{Fragile(x)}] \vee$$
$$[a = \text{BlowUp(x)} \wedge \text{True}]]$$

The generalised negative effect axioms are,

$$\neg \text{ Holds(Holding(x),Result(a,s))} \leftarrow \text{Poss(a,s)} \wedge [a = \text{Drop(x)} \wedge \text{True}]$$

$\neg$ Holds(Broken(x),Result(a,s)) $\leftarrow$ Poss(a,s) $\land$ [a = Repair(x) $\land$ True].

From these, we obtain the following (simplified) successor state axioms.

Poss(a,s) $\rightarrow$ [Holds(Holding(x),Result(a,s)) $\leftrightarrow$ [8.4.7]
Holds(Holding(x),s) $\land \neg$ [a = Drop(x)]

Poss(a,s) $\rightarrow$ [Holds(Broken(x),Result(a,s)) $\leftrightarrow$ [8.4.8]
[a = Drop(x) $\land$ Fragile(x)] $\lor$ [a = BlowUp(x)] $\lor$
[Holds(Broken(x),s) $\land \neg$ [a = Repair(x)]]]]

From (DBR5) and (DBR8), we have,

SSA[Σ] $\vDash$ Poss(Drop(A),S0).

From this, (DBR9), and [8.4.8], we get,

SSA[Σ] $\vDash$ Holds(Broken(A),Result(Drop(A),S0)).

Applying [8.4.8] again, given (DBR7), we get,

SSA[Σ] $\vDash \neg$ Holds(Broken(A),Result(Repair(A),Result(Drop(A),S0))).

The proposition follows from this, given (DBR6), by applying [8.4.8] again. $\square$

An equivalence result relating Pednault's and Reiter's approaches has been established by Kartha [1993], who compares them to each other, as well as to Baker's state-based minimisation (see Chapters 6 and 7), by defining a series of translations from the language $\mathcal{A}$ (see Section 8.6).

Before returning to the issue of domain constraints and ramifications, let's take a step back and review the motivation for the use of successor state axioms and the development of the SSA operator. In a sense, the SSA operator offers nothing over and above what is offered by the FA operator defined in the last section. If we push computational questions into the background and concentrate purely on the issue of formalisation (as is my policy throughout this book), then in both cases we achieve representational parsimony and elaboration tolerance.

Unlike circumscription, both the FA operator and the SSA operator directly yield first-order theories. Indeed, as both Pednault [1989] and Reiter [1991] emphasise for their respective approaches, the resulting first-order theories have elegant computational properties. At this level, the SSA operator has the advantage of producing a more succinct first-order final product than the FA operator. This advantage is inherited from the greater compactness of explanation closure axioms compared to frame axioms. However, as solutions to the frame problem conceived as a question of formalisation independent of computation, the two approaches are equally matched. It's no harder to write $\Sigma \wedge FA[\Sigma]$ than to write $SSA[\Sigma]$.

Both approaches are elaboration tolerant to the same extent as, and for the same reason as, circumscriptive approaches. All three approaches are non-monotonic, despite the fact that Reiter's work developed out of Schubert's strictly monotonic approach, in the following sense. If Σ is a collection of situation calculus formulae, and $CIRC[\Sigma]$ denotes the circumscription of Σ according to some policy designed to solve the frame problem, then *none* of the following properties hold.

$$\text{If } CIRC[\Sigma] \vDash \phi \text{ then } CIRC[\Sigma \wedge \psi] \vDash \phi$$

$$\text{If } \Sigma \wedge FA[\Sigma] \vDash \phi \text{ then } \Sigma \wedge \psi \wedge FA[\Sigma \wedge \psi] \vDash \phi$$

$$\text{If } SSA[\Sigma] \vDash \phi \text{ then } SSA[\Sigma \wedge \psi] \vDash \phi$$

In all three cases, additions to a domain description — new facts about actions or fluents — are gracefully absorbed with the minimum effort. All three solutions could be said to meet the first and third criteria for a good solution to the frame problem proposed in Section 1.6, namely representational parsimony and elaboration tolerance. But what about the second criterion, namely expressive flexibility? This question leads us back to the issue of domain constraints.

8.5 Ramifications and Successor State Axioms

Recognising that a satisfactory solution to the frame problem must have expressive flexibility, Lin and Reiter extended the successor state axiom approach to deal with domain constraints [Lin & Reiter, 1994]. Their approach is based on the observation that adding of a collection domain constraints to a collection of effect axioms is essentially the same as adding a collection of extra effect axioms. For example, suppose we add the following domain constraint to the effect axioms for the fragile object scenario above.

$$\text{Holds}(\text{Useless}(x),s) \leftrightarrow \text{Holds}(\text{Broken}(x),s)$$

Given (DBR1) to (DBR3), this has the same effect as adding the following extra effect axioms.

$$\text{Holds}(\text{Useless}(x),\text{Result}(\text{Drop}(x),s)) \leftarrow \text{Poss}(\text{Drop}(x),s) \wedge \text{Fragile}(x)$$

$$\text{Holds}(\text{Useless}(x),\text{Result}(\text{BlowUp}(x),s)) \leftarrow \text{Poss}(\text{BlowUp}(x),s)$$

$$\neg \text{Holds}(\text{Useless}(x),\text{Result}(\text{Repair}(x),s)) \leftarrow \text{Poss}(\text{Repair}(x),s)$$

From such an expanded set of effect axioms, successor state axioms can be constructed according to the definition given in the previous section.

$$Poss(a,s) \rightarrow [Holds(Useless(x),Result(a,s)) \leftrightarrow [a = Drop(x) \wedge Fragile(x)] \vee$$
$$[a = BlowUp(x)] \vee [Holds(Broken(x),s) \wedge \neg [a = Repair(x)]]]$$

Lin and Reiter supply a formal criterion for the correctness of a collection of successor state axioms with respect to a corresponding collection of domain constraints and effect axioms. This criterion appeals to a non-monotonic solution to the frame problem based on [Lin & Shoham, 1991].

Although Lin and Reiter supply a basic recipe for the generation of successor state axioms in the presence of domain constraints, this doesn't form the basis of a mechanical procedure. Based on Lin and Reiter's work, Pinto [1994] describes a procedure for generating successor state axioms in the presence of certain classes of domain constraints. However, he also shows that no general procedure can exist for generating successor state axioms in the presence of a collection of domain constraints, since there exist collections of domain constraints for which there is no corresponding collection of successor state axioms exists.

8.6   The Language *A*

Gelfond and Lifschitz introduced a very simple language, called *A*, for describing the effects of actions [Gelfond & Lifschitz, 1993].[8] In their own words, the purpose of introducing this language is as follows.

> A particular methodology for representing action can be formally described as a translation from *A*, or from a subset or superset of *A*, into a "target language", — for instance, into a language based on classical logic or on circumscription, or into a logic programming language. [Gelfond & Lifschitz, 1993]

An example of the sort of exercise Gelfond and Lifschitz have in mind is supplied by Kartha [1993], who translates *A* into three target languages, namely the formalisms of Pednault [1989] and Reiter [1991] presented in the first five sections of this chapter, and the formalism of Baker [1991] presented in Chapters 6 and 7. Similar projects have been carried out for various logic programming formalisms for representing action [Denecker & De Schreye, 1993], [Dung, 1993], [Thielscher, 1994].

The language *A* is defined as follows. It includes two non-empty, disjoint sets of symbols for fluents and actions. A *fluent expression* is a fluent possibly preceded by the symbol ¬. A *v-proposition* has the form,

$$\beta \textbf{ after } \alpha_1 ; \ldots ; \alpha_n$$

where β is a fluent expression, $n \geq 0$, and α_1 to α_n are actions. If $n = 0$, this is written,

$$\textbf{initially } \beta.$$

An *e-proposition* has the form,

$$\alpha \textbf{ causes } \beta \textbf{ if } \beta_1, \ldots, \beta_m$$

where α is an action, $m \geq 0$, and β and $\beta_1, \ldots, \beta_m$ are fluent expressions. If $m = 0$, this is written,

$$\alpha \textbf{ causes } \beta.$$

The well-formed formulae of $\mathcal{A}$ are the v-propositions and the e-propositions.

Using this simple language, a number of benchmark scenarios can be represented. For example, the Yale shooting scenario is represented as follows.

$$\text{Load } \textbf{causes } \text{Loaded}$$

$$\text{Shoot } \textbf{causes } \neg \text{ Alive } \textbf{if } \text{Loaded}$$

$$\textbf{initially } \text{Alive}$$

The semantics of the language is defined as follows.

Preliminary Definitions. A *state* is a set of fluents. A *transition function* is a mapping from actions and states to states. A *structure* is a pair $\langle \sigma_0, \Phi \rangle$, where σ_0 is a state, known as the *initial state*, and Φ is a transition function. □

Structures are analogous to interpretations.

Definition 8.6.1. The v-proposition,

$$\beta \textbf{ after } \alpha_1 ; \ldots ; \alpha_n$$

is *true* in a structure $\langle \sigma_0, \Phi \rangle$ if,

$$\beta \in \Phi(\alpha_n, \Phi(\alpha_{n-1}, \ldots, \Phi(\alpha_0, \sigma_0) \ldots))$$

and *false* otherwise. □

Let Σ be a set of well-formed formulae of $\mathcal{A}$.

Definition 8.6.2. A structure $\langle \sigma_0, \Phi \rangle$ is a *model* of Σ if every v-proposition in Σ is satisfied by $\langle \sigma_0, \Phi \rangle$, and for every action α, fluent β, and state σ,

- If Σ includes an e-proposition,

$$\alpha \text{ \textbf{causes} } \beta \text{ \textbf{if} } \beta_1, \ldots, \beta_m$$

then $\beta \in \Phi(\alpha,\sigma)$ if each of β_1 to β_m is in σ,

- If Σ includes an e-proposition,

$$\alpha \text{ \textbf{causes} } \neg \beta \text{ \textbf{if} } \beta_1, \ldots, \beta_n$$

then $\beta \notin \Phi(\alpha,\sigma)$ if each of β_1 to β_n is in σ,

- If Σ includes no e-proposition of either of the above forms, then $\beta \in \Phi(\alpha,\sigma)$ if and only if $\beta \in \sigma$. $\square$

Now we can define a notion of entailment. The definition only concerns v-propositions.

Definition 8.6.3. A v-proposition is *entailed* by Σ if it is true in every model of Σ. $\square$

It should be obvious from Definitions 8.6.2 and 8.6.3 that the consequence relation defined for $\mathcal{A}$ is non-monotonic, on account of the third condition attached to the definition of a model.

Let's see how the semantics language $\mathcal{A}$ copes with a simple example, namely the Yale shooting scenario. Let Σ be the formulae for the Yale shooting scenario given above, and let the domain of Σ include a Wait action.

Proposition 8.6.4. The v-proposition,

$$\neg \text{ Alive \textbf{after} Load ; Wait ; Shoot}$$

is entailed by Σ.

Proof. There are two models of Σ, corresponding to the two possible initial values of the Loaded fluent. These are $\langle\{\text{Loaded,Alive}\},\Phi\rangle$ and $\langle\{\text{Alive}\},\Phi\rangle$, where Φ is defined as follows.

$$\Phi(\text{Load}, \sigma) = \sigma \cup \{\text{Loaded}\}$$

$$\Phi(\text{Wait}, \sigma) = \sigma$$

$$\Phi(\text{Shoot}, \sigma) = \begin{cases} \{\beta \mid \beta \in \sigma \text{ and } \beta \neq \text{Alive}\} & \text{if Loaded} \in \sigma \\ \sigma \text{ otherwise} \end{cases}$$

It's easily verified that,

$$\text{Alive} \notin \Phi(\text{Shoot}, \Phi(\text{Wait}, \Phi(\text{Load}, \sigma_0)))$$

whether σ_0 is {Loaded,Alive} or {Alive}, from which the proposition follows. □

While $\mathcal{A}$ is adequate for representing certain very simple domains, its expressive power is extremely limited. In particular, it cannot represent,

- Fluents with arguments, such as Colour(x,c),

- Domain constraints, or actions with indirect effects,

- Narrative information,

- Concurrent action,

- Non-deterministic action, or

- Continuous change.

Many of these limitations have been overcome in subsequent work to extend the language. For example, Baral and Gelfond [1993] tackle the question of concurrent action, and Kartha and Lifschitz [1994] address various issues including ramifications and non-determinism. These improvements markedly widen the class of formalisms for which translations from $\mathcal{A}$ can be devised.

However, the language $\mathcal{A}$, and all of its variants, are inextricably tied to the ontology of the situation calculus. This makes it hard to see how it can fairly be used to evaluate or compare narrative-based formalisms like the event calculus, which will be presented in Chapters 12 to 15. However, an alternative action description language based on the ontology of the event calculus has been developed by Kakas and Miller [1997]. As we'll see in the next chapter, the situation calculus itself can be extended to deal with narrative information, and an analogously extended version of A might serve more universally the purpose for which the family of $\mathcal{A}$ languages was originally designed. The work of Baral, Gelfond and Provetti [1997] is a move in this direction.

Notes

1. This collection doesn't include the frame axiom,

$$\text{Holds(Loaded,Result(Shoot,s))} \leftarrow \text{Holds(Loaded,s)}$$

which we might have expected if we assumed (Y1) to (Y6) to be a complete description of the effects of actions. The explicit use of frame axioms gives us the option of leaving unwanted ones out.

2. There are some small differences. The domain closure axiom for fluents has been omitted. Such axioms are redundant here. Also the uniqueness-of-names axiom for fluents is simpler, since it doesn't have to account for And and Not.

3. Schubert extends the walking turkey example slightly and uses a different formalism, but his use of explanation closure axioms corresponds closely with that in the present discussion.

4. Loui [1987] presents a variety of examples that support this view.

5. There hasn't been much discussion so far of "making neutrality explicit". Section 15.3 introduces a predicate Releases for this purpose, following the work of Kartha and Lifschitz [1994].

6. Axioms similar to successor state axioms are also proposed by Elkan [1992], who introduces two new predicates, including a Causes predicate (see Chapter 5), for greater succinctness.

7. By convention, we'll say that $\bigvee_{i=1}^{n} \Psi$ for any expression Ψ is defined as False if n is 0.

8. An earlier version of their paper is [Gelfond & Lifschitz, 1992].

9 Narratives in the Situation Calculus

This chapter extends the situation calculus with the capacity to represent narratives. A *narrative* is a distinguished course of events about which we may have incomplete information. Unlike the event calculus, which is narrative-based, standard situation calculus doesn't have any facility for distinguishing particular sequences of events, or for representing the fact that a given event occurs or does not occur in such a sequence.

Two approaches to narratives are presented, both of which are modular, in the sense that they can be plugged in to a pre-existing solution to the frame problem without interfering with it. For each approach, corresponding *separation theorems* are proved, which guarantee this modularity. Along the way, some general purpose mathematical tools are developed for generating such separation theorems. Finally, an equivalence result for the two approaches is presented.

9.1 The Need for Narratives

Standard situation calculus is only capable of representing exactly specified sequences of hypothetical actions or events. Every possible sequence of events can be described by a corresponding Result term, and every Result term has the same status. It's not possible to distinguish a particular course of events, for example the actual course events, and reason about it. It's also not possible to incompletely specify a course of events, or to use default reasoning to fill in the gaps in such an incomplete specification.

Here's a motivating example. Before breakfast one morning, Mary checks her briefcase to make sure her lecture notes are inside, which indeed they are. She eats her breakfast, and then carries her briefcase to college. Mary knows that if she carries her briefcase from A to B then its contents will also be carried from A to B. So she concludes that, at the end of this sequence of events, her lecture notes are at college along with her briefcase. However, shortly after she sits down at her desk, her husband telephones to apologise for accidentally removing her notes from the briefcase before she left for work. With her new knowledge of her husband's actions, Mary can no longer conclude that her notes are at college.

Two forms of default reasoning feature in this story. To begin with, Mary employs a solution to the frame problem. She assumes that her breakfast, whatever other effects it may have, doesn't affect the whereabouts of the notes, and that they're still in her briefcase when she sets off for work. Second, at each stage in her reasoning, Mary assumes the events she knows about are the only relevant events that occur. She uses a form of default reasoning to fill in the gaps in her incomplete knowledge of the true course of events.

Distinguished sequences of events about which we may have incomplete information are called *narratives*. In this case, and in all of the examples we'll look at, the distinguished sequence of events in question is the course of events that actually takes place. Endowing the situation calculus with a basic ability to reason about narratives is fairly straightforward. There are two main approaches.

1. Adopt the axioms of arboreality (see Section 2.7). Identify one path through the tree of situations as the actual course of events. Introduce a narrative time line, such as the reals or the naturals. Associate a time point with each situation in the actual course of events, corresponding to the time when the situation starts. This is the approach taken by Pinto and Reiter [1993].

2. Introduce a narrative time line, such as the reals or the naturals. Associate a situation with each time point in the narrative time line. This is the approach taken in [Miller & Shanahan, 1994].

Although they adopt very different perspectives on the very nature of situations in the situation calculus, these two approaches ultimately turn out to give equivalent results, as shown at the end of the chapter. Shortly, we'll be looking at the two approaches in some detail. But one small difficulty has to be cleared up before Pinto and Reiter's approach can be made to work in combination with state-based minimisation. This difficulty is the subject of the next section.

9.2   Arboreality and Existence-of-Situations

In Pinto and Reiter's approach, we begin by adopting the axioms of arboreality.

$$\text{Result}(a1,s1) = \text{Result}(a2,s2) \rightarrow a1{=}a2 \wedge s1{=}s2 \qquad \text{(Arb1)}$$

$$S0 \neq \text{Result}(a,s) \qquad \text{(Arb2)}$$

Unfortunately these axioms disable all of the existence-of-situations axioms recommended in Chapter 7. A little work needs to be done to restore coherence when the axioms of arboreality are combined with state-based minimisation, as they will be in the next section.

Both arboreality and existence-of-situations are important concepts outside of the topic of narratives. So their compatibility is a pressing issue. On the other hand, neither of the approaches to narratives I'm going to present are dependent in any way on state-based minimisation. Indeed, Pinto and Reiter's own presentation of their work employs Reiter's monotonic approach to the frame problem [Reiter, 1991] (see Sections 8.4 and 8.5). In fact, both approaches can be used in combination with various solutions to the frame problem.

The difficulty I've been alluding to manifests itself slightly differently for different existence-of-situations axioms. For now, let's assume the second-order axiom from Section 7.5.

$$[\text{Holds}(f, \text{Sit}(p)) \leftrightarrow p(f)] \leftarrow \neg \text{AbSit}(p) \qquad \text{(EoS9)}$$

The Yale shooting scenario is represented using the familiar formulae (Y1) to (Y6) first encountered in Chapter 3. The problem is illustrated in Figure 9.1, which shows an anomalous model of the Yale shooting scenario. Notice that the existence-of-situations axiom is satisfied. There is a situation for each combination of the two fluents Alive and Loaded.

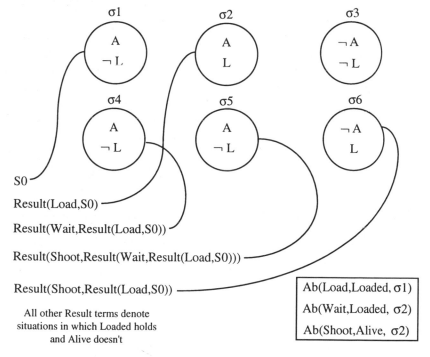

Figure 9.1: Arboreality Brings Back the Anomalous Model

With state-based minimisation, we expect to be able to eliminate this model by making Result(Wait,Result(Load,S0)) denote σ2, thus eliminating the unwanted abnormality without introducing any new ones. But in the presence of Axioms (Arb1) and (Arb2), we are forbidden from doing this, because

Result(Load,S0) already denotes σ2 and Result(Load,S0) cannot be equal to Result(Wait,Result(Load,S0)). The situation σ2 is the only situation in which Alive and Loaded hold, so there's nothing else to make Result(Wait,Result(Load,S0)) denote that would achieve the desired effect. The existence-of-situations axiom has insisted on the presence of one situation in which Alive and Loaded hold, but we need more than one.[1]

Exactly the same problem arises if we choose the first-order existence-of-situations axiom defined with sets (Axiom (EoS5) from Section 7.2). However, if we pick the first-order existence-of-situations axiom defined with generalised fluents (Axiom (EoS1) from Section 7.2), then the interpretation in Figure 9.1 is not a model of the circumscription. This is because there is more than one way to represent the same combination of fluents as a generalised fluent. For example, And(Alive,Loaded) and And(Loaded,Alive) denote distinct objects (because of uniqueness-of-names) but represent the same combination of fluents.

This means that, using generalised fluents to express existence-of-situations, *several* situations always exist for each legitimate combination of fluents. But this only solves the problem for domains with finitely many fluents. Recall that the prevalence of domains with infinitely many fluents was the main motivation for introducing a second-order existence-of-situations axiom (Section 7.5). To solve the problem properly, we need an existence-of-situations axiom that guarantees the existence of a situation for every legitimate combination of fluents for every sequence of actions in the tree of situations, even if there are infinitely many fluents. Here's an axiom that expresses this. It's basically a reformulation of the second-order existence-of-situations axiom (EoS9).

$$[\text{Holds}(f,\text{Sit}(p,s1)) \leftrightarrow p(f)] \leftarrow \neg\ \text{AbSit}(p) \wedge [s1 = S0 \vee s1 = \text{Result}(a,s2)]$$

The Skolem function Sit now takes two arguments. Every sequence of actions expressible as a Result term now has its own private collection of situations — one for every legitimate combination of fluents — from which the circumscription can choose its denotation. The initial situation, which is also varied in the circumscription, has such a collection too.

A small simplification of this axiom is possible. The set of situations denoted by Result terms can always be placed in one-to-one correspondence with some infinite set (possibly the naturals, possibly the reals). This means the same set of situations augmented with the initial situation can be placed in one-to-one correspondence with the same infinite set. So we can guarantee a suitably large space of situations without mentioning S0. Here's the axiom.

$$[\text{Holds}(f,\text{Sit}(p,\text{Result}(a,s))) \leftrightarrow p(f)] \leftarrow \neg\ \text{AbSit}(p) \qquad \text{(EoS12)}$$

A uniqueness-of-names axiom for Sit will be required, as usual.

$$UNA[Sit] \qquad\qquad (EoS13)$$

With an infinite set of action names, the same argument can be used, via a one-to-one correspondence with the reals instead of the naturals, to show that this axiom is still adequate.

Modulo the substitution of (EoS12) for (EoS9), we're interested in the same circumscription as before. Similar modifications can be made to the other two forms of existence-of-situations axiom.

Since all of these modified existence-of-situations axioms guarantee the existence of more situations than the old versions, all the examples that worked with the old axioms will still go through with the new ones.

However, Axiom (EoS12) does seem rather ugly. While it can be argued that the idea of existence-of-situations has some intuitive basis — in the realm of possibility, there should be a situation for every legitimate combination of fluents — the need for the expanded space of situations supplied by Axiom (EoS12) seems to be purely an artefact of certain arbitrary properties of the formalism. Nevertheless, using Axiom (EoS12), Pinto and Reiter's approach to narratives can be reconciled with Baker's solution to the frame problem.

Before leaving the subject, it's worth noting that the additional inclusion of the induction axiom (Ind) (see Section 2.7) disables state-based minimisation altogether, as I will now show.

Suppose we adopt the axioms of arboreality (Arb1) and (Arb2), along with the following induction axiom.

$$\forall p \; [[p(S0) \land \forall a, s \; [p(s) \to p(Result(a,s))]] \to \forall s \; p(s)]. \qquad (Ind)$$

From Axiom (Ind), we can derive the following domain closure property.

$$s1 = S0 \lor \exists s2 \; [s1 = Result(a,s2)] \qquad\qquad [9.2.1]$$

So the space of situations is isomorphic to the tree of situations induced by the recursive application of the Result function to the initial situation. I'll call this property of the space of situations *strict arboreality*.

Now consider the addition of Axiom (EoS12). This axiom (along with Axiom (EoS13)) guarantees the existence of a situation corresponding to every legitimate combination of values for the fluents in the domain. Unfortunately, [9.2.1] tells us that each of these situations is either S0 or Result(a,s) for some a and s. To put it another way, [9.2.1] entails that it's possible to squeeze whatever space of situations is forced to exist by (EoS12) into the tree of situations.

This in turn forces the existence of a collection of actions that can transform the initial situation into one in which any given combination of fluents hold. If there are finitely many fluents, the smallest such collection would be a single action that cycled around the possible fluent combinations. If there are infinitely many fluents in the domain the implications are stranger still. Let,

- F be the set of fluents,

- A be the set of actions,

- S_P be the space of situations, according to the existence-of-situations axiom, and

- S_T be the tree of situations according to the axioms of arboreality.

Suppose there are no domain constraints, so that the extension of AbSit is empty. So the set of all legitimate combinations of fluents is 2^F. Then we have,

- $S_T = F \times A$, and

- $S_P = S_T \times 2^F$, from (EoS12).

But from [9.2.1], we also have $S_T = S_P$. From this it can be seen that A must be at least as large as 2^F. So if the set of fluents is finite, the set of actions can be finite. But if the set of fluents is the same size as $\mathbb{N}$, then the set of actions must be at least as large as $\mathbb{R}$. So the addition of Axiom (EoS12) forces the existence of a vast mass of extraneous foliage in the tree of situations. This conclusion still holds in the presence of domain constraints, so long as the AbSit condition doesn't rule out so many combinations of fluents that only countably many are left.

As an example, consider a set of actions that meets the following condition: for each situation σ in S_T, A includes a distinct action α for each combination C of fluents in 2^F, such that C holds in Result(α,σ). Using a set of actions such as this, an interpretation can be defined that satisfies induction over trees, the axioms of arboreality, and the existence-of-situations axiom (EoS12). Unfortunately, such interpretations are more than merely bizarre. One of their obvious properties is that they rule out the addition of a domain closure axiom for actions. But more significantly, they disable state-based minimisation altogether.

To see this, recall that the idea behind state-based minimisation is that models with unwanted abnormalities can be transformed into circumscriptively preferable models without those abnormalities by altering the denotation of one or more Result terms. A suitable space of situations is guaranteed to exist from which the required denotation can be drawn. But in any interpretation that satisfies induction over trees, the axioms of arboreality, and the existence-of-situations axiom (EoS12), every situation in this space is already tied down to a Result term. Since each Result term denotes a unique situation, unwanted abnormalities cannot be eliminated just by altering the denotations of Result terms. The requisite situation has to be plucked out of the extraneous foliage induced by the existence-of-situations axiom. This will affect the extension of the Ab predicate, and this in turn will make the new model incomparable to the old one as far as circumscription is concerned.

For present purposes, we have no option but to abandon (Ind), which is sad considering the importance attached to it by some authors [Reiter, 1993]. A more restrictive form of (Ind) that has more pleasing properties might be possible, but the issue is tangential here.

9.3 Associating a Time with Each Actual Situation

The first step in Pinto and Reiter's approach to narratives is the adoption of the axioms of arboreality. The second step is to introduce a new predicate Actual. The formula Actual(s) represents that the situation s is part of the narrative of actual events we are interested in. The following axioms ensure that Actual picks out a path through the tree of situations defined by the axioms of arboreality.[2]

$$\text{Actual(S0)} \qquad \text{(PR1)}$$

$$\text{Actual(Result(a,s))} \rightarrow \text{Actual(s)} \qquad \text{(PR2)}$$

$$[\text{Actual(Result(a1,s))} \land \text{Actual(Result(a2,s))}] \rightarrow a1 = a2 \qquad \text{(PR3)}$$

$$\text{Actual(s1)} \rightarrow s1 = S0 \lor \exists\, a,s2\, [s1 = \text{Result(a,s2)}] \qquad \text{(PR4)}$$

Now we introduce a narrative time line. We have a sort for time points (with variables t, t1, t2, etc.), and the infix predicates $<$ and $\leq$. We will only consider interpretations in which this sort is interpreted by the reals, and in which the $<$ and $\leq$ predicates are interpreted correspondingly.[3] A standard set of constant symbols standing for real valued time points will also be assumed (0, 1, 2, 3.5, 4.5, etc.). The formula Start(s,t) represents that the situation s starts at time t. Now we have,

$$\text{Actual(s)} \leftrightarrow \exists\, t\, [\text{Start(s,t)}] \qquad \text{(PR5)}$$

$$[\text{Start(s,t1)} \land \text{Start(s,t2)}] \rightarrow t1 = t2 \qquad \text{(PR6)}$$

$$[\text{Start(s,t1)} \land \text{Start(Result(a,s),t2)}] \rightarrow t1 < t2 \qquad \text{(PR7)}$$

$$\text{Start(S0,0).} \hspace{4cm} \text{(PR8)}$$

Finally, narratives are described via the Initially and Happens predicates, while conclusions about narratives are expressed using the HoldsAt predicate. The formula Initially(f) represents that fluent f is true in the initial situation, the formula Happens(a,t) represents that an event of type a occurs at time t, and the formula HoldsAt(f,t) represents that fluent f holds at time t. These predicates are defined as follows.

$$\text{Initially(f)} \leftrightarrow \text{Holds(f,S0)} \hspace{3cm} \text{(PR9)}$$

$$\text{Happens(a,t)} \leftrightarrow \exists \text{ s [Actual(Result(a,s))} \wedge \text{Start(Result(a,s),t)]} \hspace{0.5cm} \text{(PR10)}$$

$$\text{HoldsAt(f,t)} \leftrightarrow \exists \text{ s [Holds(f,s)} \wedge \text{Start(s,t1)} \wedge \text{t1} < \text{t} \wedge \hspace{1cm} \text{(PR11)}$$
$$[\neg \exists \text{ a [Actual(Result(a,s))]} \vee$$
$$\exists \text{ a,t2 [Start(Result(a,s),t2)} \wedge \text{t} \leq \text{t2]]]}$$

Axiom (PR10) relates event occurrences to actual situations via the Result function. Axiom (PR11) says that fluent f holds at time t if and only if f holds in some actual situation that starts before t and that, if it ends at all, ends after t.

Definition 9.3.1. A *simple narrative description* is a conjunction of finitely many formulae of the form Initially(β) or Happens(α,τ), where β is a fluent, α is an action or event type and τ is a time point. $\hspace{1cm} \square$

Definition 9.3.2. A simple narrative description is *linear* if it doesn't contain any two formulae of the form Happens($\alpha 1,\tau$) and Happens($\alpha 2,\tau$), where $\alpha 1 \neq \alpha 2$. $\hspace{0.3cm} \square$

More complicated narrative descriptions are possible, in which the exact times of the events are unknown. For the moment, we're only concerned with simple narrative descriptions. Furthermore, all events are assumed to be instantaneous. There are two ways to deal with events with duration. The first, employed in [Miller & Shanahan, 1994] is to make Happens into a three argument predicate, with one argument for the start of an event and another for the end. Then the problem of partially overlapping actions has to be dealt with. Alternatively, we can preserve the two argument form of Happens, and simply decompose events with duration into two sub-events corresponding to the start and end of the larger event. I will assume the latter approach here and throughout the book.

We're now in a position to supply a simple narrative description of the briefcase example. Suppose Mary eats her breakfast at 8:00 and goes to work at 9:00. Assume that the domain includes the actions Eat, which denotes the act of eating breakfast, and TakeCase, which denotes the act of carrying the briefcase to work. The following collection of formulae represents the state of Mary's knowledge before the telephone call from her husband.

$$\text{Initially(InCase)} \qquad \text{(BN1)}$$

$$\neg \text{ Initially(AtWork)} \qquad \text{(BN2)}$$

$$\text{Happens(Eat,8)} \qquad \text{(BN3)}$$

$$\text{Happens(TakeCase,9)} \qquad \text{(BN4)}$$

One more ingredient is required before a description like this can be useful. The predicate Happens needs to be minimised. Without *event occurrence minimisation*, we would have models in which spurious events occur, disrupting the course of the narrative. These models have to be eliminated so that temporal projection generates the required results.

Let's adopt state-based minimisation to overcome the frame problem. Let Σ be the conjunction of,

- A linear simple narrative description,

- A collection of effect axioms and domain constraints,

- Axioms (Arb1) and (Arb2),

- Axioms (PR1) to (PR11),

- Axioms (EoS12), (EoS13) and (F2), and

- Uniqueness-of-names axioms for actions and fluents.

    Then we are interested in,

    CIRC[Σ ; AbSit > Happens, Ab ; HoldsAt, Actual, Start, Holds, Result, S0]

which I'll denote CIRC$_{PR}$[Σ].[4]

Why do we need to use circumscription here at all? Why not simply write out a complete definition of Happens of the following form?

$$\text{Happens(a,t)} \leftrightarrow [[a = \text{Eat} \wedge t = 8] \vee [a = \text{TakeCase} \wedge t = 9]]$$

The reason is that it may not be clear what a completed definition of the Happens predicate should look like. This example is simple. But here are two kinds of knowledge about event occurrences which would make the task much harder.

- Events whose exact time of occurrence is unknown. We cannot easily construct a complete Happens definition in the presence of a sentence expressing the fact that an event occurred some time between two time points, or sentences expressing a partial ordering among a number of events.

- Logical dependencies among event occurrences. Our knowledge of the domain can include sentences expressing the fact that if an event of a certain type occurs at a given time (I set my alarm), then an event of another type occurs at a later time (my alarm goes off). It can also include constraints forbidding the occurrence of certain events.

The circumscription relieves us of the burden of working out by hand what the completed definition of the Happens predicate is under such circumstances. As I've said before, we expect our formal apparatus to solve the frame problem, not the human being who is writing the axioms. The same applies to event occurrence minimisation.

Event occurrence minimisation can be thought of as formalising one aspect of the common sense law of inertia, and accordingly can be thought of as a necessary component of any solution to the frame problem. If the common sense law of inertia says that "inertia is normal and change is exceptional", then in addition to the default rule that it is exceptional for a given action to affect a given fluent, our formalisation needs to capture the default rule that event occurrences are exceptional (see Section 1.9).

9.4   Two Theorems of Circumscription

We can now use narrative descriptions to draw useful conclusions. But before working through the briefcase example properly, I want to present a couple of theorems of circumscription which will be extremely useful in proving propositions about complicated circumscriptions.

The Hanks-McDermott problem serves to illustrate how fragile circumscription can be. Now that we've augmented state-based minimisation with a number of extra axioms, and introduced a new form of minimisation, how do we know that the circumscription still yields correct conclusions?

This section starts to answer this question through the presentation of two very powerful results that aid in the development of a whole class of other theorems that I call *separation theorems*. A separation theorem allows a complicated circumscription to be broken up into simpler parts. For example, we can use a separation theorem to show that the essential properties of state-based minimisation are preserved when it is augmented with event occurrence minimisation. Separation theorems reflect the *modularity* of a class of theories. The simple parts into which a complicated theory can be broken up can be thought of as independent modules, and the information flow between them is regulated in an easily comprehensible way.

The results in this section are not separation theorems in themselves, but rather facilitate the construction of separation theorems. They do this by setting out certain conditions under which the models of a simple circumscription can be extended to form models of a more complicated circumscription. To enable this, we need to be able to combine two languages, and to be able to combine two models of different languages.

Definition 9.4.1. If S1 is an Ω1-indexed set and S2 is an Ω2-indexed set, then S1 $\cup$ S2 is *well defined* if for all x such that x $\in$ S1 and x $\in$ S2, the index of x in S1 is the same as its index in S2. □

Let L1 be a language of many-sorted first-order predicate calculus with equality, with a set Ω1 of sorts, Ω1-indexed sets C1 and V1 of constant symbols and variables respectively, an Ω1* $\times$ Ω1-indexed set F1 of function symbols, and an Ω1*-indexed set P1 of predicate symbols. Let L2 be a language of many-sorted first-order predicate calculus with equality, with a set Ω2 of sorts, Ω2-indexed sets C2 and V2 of constant symbols and variables respectively, an Ω2* $\times$ Ω2-indexed set F2 of function symbols, and an Ω2*-indexed set P2 of predicate symbols.

Definition 9.4.2. L1 and L2 are *disjoint* if each of C1 and C2, F1 and F2, and P1 and P2 are disjoint respectively. □

Definition 9.4.3. L1 and L2 are *compatible* if V1 $\cup$ V2 is well-defined. □

Definition 9.4.4. If L1 and L2 are disjoint and compatible, then the language L1+L2 comprises the set Ω3 = Ω1 $\cup$ Ω2 of sorts, Ω3-indexed sets C1 $\cup$ C2 and V1 $\cup$ V2 of constant symbols and variables respectively, an Ω3* $\times$ Ω3-indexed set F1 $\cup$ F2 of function symbols, and an Ω3*-indexed set P1 $\cup$ P2 of predicate symbols. □

Let L1 and L2 be disjoint and compatible languages of many-sorted first-order predicate calculus.

Definition 9.4.5. If M1 = $\langle$D,F1,P1$\rangle$ and M2 = $\langle$D,F2,P2$\rangle$ are interpretations of L1 and L2 respectively, then M1+M2 is defined as follows.

- For all predicate symbols ρ in L1, M1+M2$[\![\rho]\!]$ = M1$[\![\rho]\!]$.

- For all predicate symbols ρ in L2, M1+M2$\llbracket\rho\rrbracket$ = M2$\llbracket\rho\rrbracket$.

- For all constants τ in L1, M1+M2$\llbracket\tau\rrbracket$ = M1$\llbracket\tau\rrbracket$.

- For all constants τ in L2, M1+M2$\llbracket\tau\rrbracket$ = M2$\llbracket\tau\rrbracket$.

- For all function symbols π in L1, M1+M2$\llbracket\pi\rrbracket$ = M1$\llbracket\pi\rrbracket$.

- For all function symbols π in L2, M1+M2$\llbracket\pi\rrbracket$ = M2$\llbracket\pi\rrbracket$. $\square$

Here's the first result. This theorem facilitates the construction of separation theorems that allow us to lift parts of a circumscribed formula outside the circumscription, thus rendering the remaining circumscribed portion more manageable.

Let Σ be a formula of L1 and Δ be a formula of L1+L2. Let ρ^* be a tuple of predicate symbols from L1, and let σ^* be a tuple of predicate, function and constant symbols from L1+L2 that includes every predicate, function and constant symbol in L2.

Theorem 9.4.6. If there exists a mapping F from interpretations of L1 to interpretations of L2 such that, for any interpretation M of L1 that satisfies Σ, M+F(M) is a model of Δ, then,

$$\text{CIRC}[\Sigma \wedge \Delta ; \rho^* ; \sigma^*]$$

is equivalent to,

$$\text{CIRC}[\Sigma ; \rho^* ; \sigma^*] \wedge \Delta.$$

Proof. First we show that CIRC$[\Sigma \wedge \Delta ; \rho^* ; \sigma^*]$ entails CIRC$[\Sigma ; \rho^* ; \sigma^*] \wedge \Delta$. To do this, we show that all models of CIRC$[\Sigma \wedge \Delta ; \rho^* ; \sigma^*]$ have the form M1+M2, where M1 is a model of CIRC$[\Sigma ; \rho^* ; \sigma^*]$ and M2 interprets only L2.

Consider any model M of CIRC$[\Sigma \wedge \Delta ; \rho^* ; \sigma^*]$. This is expressible in the form M1+M2 where M1 interprets only L1 and M2 interprets only L2. We need to show that M1 is a model of CIRC$[\Sigma ; \rho^* ; \sigma^*]$. Clearly M1 is a model of Σ, because M1+M2 is a model of Σ, and M2 interprets nothing mentioned in Σ. So we have to show that M1 is minimal with respect to ρ^* with σ^* allowed to vary. Suppose it's not. Then there's a model M1' of Σ that is smaller than M1 with respect to this policy. But if M1' is a model of Σ, then M1'+F(M1') must be a model of $\Sigma \wedge \Delta$. Furthermore, M1'+F(M1') must be smaller than M1+M2 with respect to ρ^* with σ^* allowed to vary. To see this, consider the following.

- M1'+F(M1') and M1+M2 agree on the interpretation of everything except ρ^* and σ^*. This must be the case because M1 and M2' must agree in this way, and everything interpreted by M2 and F(M1') is in σ^*.

- The extension of some ρ_i in M1'+F(M1') is smaller than its extension in M1+M2. This must be the case because the extension of some ρ_i in M1' is smaller than its extension in M1, and neither F(M1') nor M2 interpret anything in ρ^*.

Therefore M1+M2 cannot be a model of CIRC[$\Sigma \wedge \Delta$; ρ^* ; σ^*], which is a contradiction.

So we've shown that CIRC[$\Sigma \wedge \Delta$; ρ^* ; σ^*] entails CIRC[Σ ; ρ^* ; σ^*] $\wedge \Delta$. Now it remains to show the converse, namely that CIRC[Σ ; ρ^* ; σ^*] $\wedge \Delta$ entails CIRC[$\Sigma \wedge \Delta$; ρ^* ; σ^*]. Take any model M of CIRC[Σ ; ρ^* ; σ^*] $\wedge \Delta$. Obviously M is a model of $\Sigma \wedge \Delta$. Furthermore, M must be a minimal model with respect to ρ^* with σ^* allowed to vary, since it's a minimal model of Σ. $\qquad\square$

The basic idea behind this theorem is this. Large and complicated circumscriptive theories, if they're well constructed, often exhibit a natural modularity. Different components of the theory deal with different aspects of the problem, and the interaction between these modules is minimal. Theorem 9.4.6 facilitates the exploitation of this kind of modularity. In this particular case, the modularity arises because the flow of information between Σ and Δ is unidirectional. Σ informs Δ, but not the other way around.

The second result is along the same lines, but assists in the development of theorems that allow a circumscription in which two tuples of predicates are minimised to be split into two separate circumscriptions. In addition to the split in the tuple of minimised predicates, the formula being circumscribed is split into two. The resulting pair of circumscriptions is, of course, much easier to reason about than the original monolithic circumscription.

Let $\rho 1^*$ and $\rho 2^*$ be tuples of predicate symbols from L1 and L2 respectively. Let $\sigma 1^*$ be a tuple of predicate, function and constant symbols from L1. Let $\sigma 2^*$ be a tuple comprising every predicate, function and constant symbol in L2 not in $\rho 2^*$.

Theorem 9.4.7. If there exists a mapping G from interpretations of L1 to interpretations of L2 such that, for any interpretation M of L1 that satisfies Σ, M+G(M) is a model of CIRC[Δ ; $\rho 2^*$; $\sigma 2^*$], then,

$$\text{CIRC}[\Sigma \wedge \Delta\ ;\ \rho 1^*, \rho 2^*\ ;\ \sigma 1^*, \sigma 2^*]$$

is equivalent to,

$$\text{CIRC}[\Sigma ; \rho1^* ; \sigma1^*] \wedge \text{CIRC}[\Delta ; \rho2^* ; \sigma2^*].$$

Proof. The proof is along the same lines as that of Theorem 9.4.6. First we show that CIRC[$\Sigma \wedge \Delta$; $\rho1^*$, $\rho2^*$; $\sigma1^*$, $\sigma2^*$] entails CIRC[Σ ; $\rho1^*$; $\sigma1^*$] $\wedge$ CIRC[Δ ; $\rho2^*$; $\sigma2^*$]. To do this, we show that all models of CIRC[$\Sigma \wedge \Delta$; $\rho1^*$, $\rho2^*$; $\sigma1^*$, $\sigma2^*$] have the form M1+M2, where M1 is a model of CIRC[Σ ; $\rho1^*$; $\sigma1^*$], and M1+M2 is a model of CIRC[Δ ; $\rho2^*$; $\sigma2^*$].

Consider any model M of CIRC[$\Sigma \wedge \Delta$; $\rho1^*$, $\rho2^*$; $\sigma1^*$, $\sigma2^*$]. This is expressible in the form M1+M2 where M1 interprets only L1 and M2 interprets only L2. We need to show that M1 is a model of CIRC[Σ ; $\rho1^*$; $\sigma1^*$] and that M1+M2 is a model of CIRC[Δ ; $\rho2^*$; $\sigma2^*$]. First we show that M1 is a model of CIRC[Σ ; $\rho1^*$; $\sigma1^*$].

Clearly M1 is a model of Σ, because M1+M2 is a model of Σ, and M2 interprets nothing mentioned in Σ. So we have to show that M1 is minimal with respect to $\rho1^*$ with $\sigma1^*$ allowed to vary. Suppose it's not. Then there's a model M1' of Σ that is smaller than M1 with respect to this policy. But if M1' is a model of Σ, then M1'+G(M1') must be a model of $\Sigma \wedge \Delta$. Furthermore, M1'+G(M1') must be smaller than M1+M2 with respect to $\rho1^*$ with $\sigma1^*$ and $\sigma2^*$ allowed to vary. To see this, consider the following.

- M1'+F(M1') and M1+M2 agree on the interpretation of everything except $\rho1^*$, $\sigma1^*$, and $\sigma2^*$. This must be the case because M1 and M2' must agree in this way, and everything interpreted by M2 and G(M1') is in $\sigma2^*$.

- The extension of some $\rho1_i$ in M1'+G(M1') is smaller than its extension in M1+M2. This must be the case because the extension of some $\rho1_i$ in M1' is smaller than its extension in M1, and neither G(M1') nor M2 interpret anything in $\rho1^*$.

Therefore M1+M2 cannot be a model of CIRC[$\Sigma \wedge \Delta$; $\rho1^*$, $\rho2^*$; $\sigma1^*$, $\sigma2^*$], which is a contradiction.

Next we have to show that M1+M2 is a model of CIRC[Δ ; $\rho2^*$; $\sigma2^*$]. Suppose M1+M2 is not minimal with respect to $\rho2^*$ with $\sigma2^*$ allowed to vary. Then M1+G(M1), which is minimal with respect to that policy, must be smaller than M1+M2, since M1+G(M1) agrees with M1+M2 on the interpretation of everything except L2, and both $\rho2^*$ and $\sigma2^*$ are contained in L2. Therefore M1+M2 can't be a model of CIRC[$\Sigma \wedge \Delta$; $\rho1^*$, $\rho2^*$; $\sigma1^*$, $\sigma2^*$], which once again is a contradiction.

So we've shown that CIRC[$\Sigma \wedge \Delta$; $\rho1^*$, $\rho2^*$; $\sigma1^*$, $\sigma2^*$] entails CIRC[Σ ; $\rho1^*$; $\sigma1^*$] $\wedge$ CIRC[Δ ; $\rho2^*$; $\sigma2^*$]. Now it remains to show the converse, namely that CIRC[Σ ; $\rho1^*$; $\sigma1^*$] $\wedge$ CIRC[Δ ; $\rho2^*$; $\sigma2^*$] entails CIRC[$\Sigma \wedge \Delta$; $\rho1^*$, $\rho2^*$; $\sigma1^*$, $\sigma2^*$]. Take any model M of CIRC[Σ ; $\rho1^*$; $\sigma1^*$] $\wedge$ CIRC[Δ ; $\rho2^*$; $\sigma2^*$]. Obviously M is a model of $\Sigma \wedge \Delta$. Furthermore, M must be a minimal model with respect to $\rho1^*$ and $\rho2^*$ with $\sigma1^*$ and $\sigma2^*$ allowed to vary, since it's a minimal model of Σ with respect to $\rho1^*$ and a minimal model of Δ with respect to $\rho2^*$, and $\rho1^*$ and $\rho2^*$ are disjoint. □

In the next section, the two results just presented will be used to develop a separation theorem for the approach to representing narratives described in the previous section. In subsequent sections and chapters, this section's results will be further exploited to develop other separation theorems.

9.5 Two Separation Theorems for Narratives

The methodology for using the results of the last section is as follows. First, a class of theories is defined syntactically, in terms of two classes of formulae, one for Σ and one for Δ, such that the language of Σ excludes certain parts of the language of Δ. Then, a separation theorem is developed that enables Σ and Δ to be isolated from each other, through the construction of suitable mappings F and G, as defined in the statements of Theorems 9.4.6 and 9.4.7.

The first separation theorem presented here permits the parts of a situation calculus theory that deal with the effects of actions to be isolated, as far as circumscription is concerned, from the parts that deal with narrative information.

Let Σ be the conjunction of,

- A collection of effect axioms and domain constraints not mentioning the predicates HoldsAt, Actual, Start, Happens, and Initially, or the constant S0,

- Axiom (Arb1),

- Axioms (EoS12), (EoS13) and (F2), and

- Uniqueness-of-names axioms for actions and fluents.

Note that the effects of actions are described in exactly the way we are accustomed to. The ability to deal with narratives is built on top of standard situation calculus in a modular way.

Let Δ be the conjunction of,

- A linear simple narrative description,

- Axiom (Arb2),

- Axioms (PR1) to (PR11), and

- Uniqueness-of-names axioms for actions and fluents.

Let L1 be the language of Σ. Let L1+L2 be the language of Δ. Note that L2 includes the predicates HoldsAt, Actual, Start, Happens, and Initially, and the constant S0.

Theorem 9.5.1. $\text{CIRC}_{PR}[\Sigma \wedge \Delta]$ is equivalent to,

$$\text{CIRC}[\Sigma \; ; \text{AbSit} > \text{Ab} \; ; \text{Holds, Result}] \wedge$$
$$\text{CIRC}[\Delta \; ; \text{Happens} \; ; \text{HoldsAt, Actual, Start, S0}].$$

Proof. From Theorem 7.1.9, $\text{CIRC}_{PR}[\Sigma \wedge \Delta]$ is equivalent to,

$$\text{CIRC}[\Sigma \wedge \Delta \; ; \text{AbSit} \; ; \qquad\qquad\qquad\qquad [9.5.2]$$
$$\text{Happens, Ab, HoldsAt, Actual, Start, Holds, Result, S0}] \wedge$$
$$\text{CIRC}[\Sigma \wedge \Delta \; ; \text{Happens, Ab} \; ; \text{HoldsAt, Actual, Start, Holds, Result, S0}].$$

Consider the second of these conjuncts first. From Theorem 9.4.7, this is equivalent to,

$$\text{CIRC}[\Sigma \; ; \text{Ab} \; ; \text{Holds, Result}] \wedge$$
$$\text{CIRC}[\Delta \; ; \text{Happens} \; ; \text{HoldsAt, Actual, Start, S0}]$$

if we can find a mapping G from interpretations of L1 to interpretations of L2 such that, for any interpretation M of L1 that satisfies Σ, M+G(M) is a model of,

$$\text{CIRC}[\Delta \; ; \text{Happens} \; ; \text{HoldsAt, Actual, Start, S0}].$$

Consider any interpretation M of L1 that satisfies Σ. In the presence of the uniqueness-of-names axioms for fluents and actions, we can confine our attention to models in which fluent names and action names are interpreted as themselves. If the simple narrative description in Δ is equivalent to,

$$\bigwedge_{i=1}^{n} [\text{Initially}(\beta_i)] \wedge \bigwedge_{i=1}^{m} [\text{Happens}(\alpha_i, \tau_i)]$$

where $\tau_i < \tau_{i+1}$, then let G(M) be defined as follows.

- $G(M)[\![\text{S0}]\!]$ = any σ such that $\sigma \neq M[\![\text{Result}(\alpha, \sigma')]\!]$ for any α and σ', and $M[\![\text{Holds}]\!](\beta, \sigma)$ if and only if $\beta = \beta_i$ for some i, $0 < i \leq n$

- $G(M)[\![\text{Initially}]\!] = \{\beta_i \mid 0 < i \leq n\}$

- $G(M)[\![Happens]\!] = \{\langle \alpha_i, \tau_i \rangle \mid 0 < i \leq m\}$

- $G(M)[\![Actual]\!] =$
  $\{M[\![S0]\!], M[\![Result(\alpha_1, S0)]\!], \ldots,$
  $\quad M[\![Result(\alpha_m, \ldots Result(\alpha_1, S0) \ldots)]\!]\}$

- $G(M)[\![Start]\!] =$
  $\{\langle M[\![S0]\!], 0 \rangle, \langle M[\![Result(\alpha_1, S0)]\!], \tau_1 \rangle, \ldots,$
  $\quad \langle M[\![Result(\alpha_m, \ldots Result(\alpha_1, S0) \ldots)]\!], \tau_m \rangle\}$

- $G(M)[\![HoldsAt]\!] =$
  $\{\langle \beta_i, \tau \rangle \mid 0 \leq \tau < \tau_1 \text{ and } 0 < i \leq n\} \cup$
  $\{\langle \beta, \tau \rangle \mid \tau_i \leq \tau < \tau_{i+1} \text{ and } M \Vdash Holds(\beta, Result(\alpha_i, \ldots Result(\alpha_1, S0) \ldots))$
  $\quad \text{for some } i, 1 < i < m\} \cup$
  $\{\langle \beta, \tau \rangle \mid \tau > \tau_m \text{ and } M \Vdash Holds(\beta, Result(\alpha_m, \ldots Result(\alpha_1, S0) \ldots))\}$

It can easily be verified that M+G(M) is a model of Δ, and that it's minimal with respect to Happens.

Now let's return to [9.5.2] and consider the first conjunct. Using the same G as above, Theorem 9.4.6 can be applied to show that this conjunct is equivalent to,

$$\Delta \wedge CIRC[\Sigma ; AbSit ;$$
$$Happens, Ab, HoldsAt, Actual, Start, Holds, Result, S0].$$

which can be simplified to,

$$\Delta \wedge CIRC[\Sigma ; AbSit ; Ab, Holds, Result]$$

since Σ doesn't mention Happens, HoldsAt, Actual, Start, or S0. So the overall circumscription is equivalent to,

$$CIRC[\Sigma ; Ab ; Holds, Result] \wedge$$
$$CIRC[\Delta ; Happens ; HoldsAt, Actual, Start, S0] \wedge$$
$$\Delta \wedge CIRC[\Sigma ; AbSit ; Ab, Holds, Result]$$

which simplifies to,

$$CIRC[\Sigma ; Ab ; Holds, Result] \wedge CIRC[\Sigma ; AbSit ; Ab, Holds, Result] \wedge$$
$$CIRC[\Delta ; Happens ; HoldsAt, Actual, Start, S0]$$

which, from Theorem 7.1.9, is equivalent to,

$$CIRC[\Sigma ; AbSit > Ab ; Holds, Result] \wedge$$
$$CIRC[\Delta ; Happens ; HoldsAt, Actual, Start, S0]. \qquad \square$$

Here's another useful separation theorem. This one allows Axioms (PR1) to (PR11) to be lifted out of the circumscription of a narrative description. It can often be applied after Theorem 9.5.1.

Let Δ_N be the conjunction of a linear simple narrative description and the uniqueness-of-names axioms for fluents and actions. Let Δ_{PR} be the conjunction of Axiom (Arb2) with Axioms (PR1) to (PR11), and the uniqueness-of-names axioms for fluents and actions.

Let L1 be the language of Δ_N and L1+L2 be the language of Δ_{PR}. Note that L2 includes the predicates HoldsAt, Actual, and Start, and the constant S0.

Theorem 9.5.3. The circumscription

$$\text{CIRC}[\Delta_N \wedge \Delta_{PR} ; \text{Happens} ; \text{HoldsAt, Actual, Start, S0}]$$

is equivalent to,

$$\text{CIRC}[\Delta_N ; \text{Happens}] \wedge \Delta_{PR}.$$

Proof. From Theorem 9.4.6,

$$\text{CIRC}[\Delta_N \wedge \Delta_{PR} ; \text{Happens} ; \text{HoldsAt, Actual, Start, S0}]$$

is equivalent to,

$$\text{CIRC}[\Delta_N ; \text{Happens} ; \text{HoldsAt, Actual, Start, S0}] \wedge \Delta_{PR}$$

if there exists a mapping F from interpretations of L1 to interpretations of L2 such that, for any interpretation M of L1 that satisfies Δ_N, M+F(M) is a model of Δ_{PR}. Since Δ doesn't mention any of the predicates being varied in this circumscription, it can be simplified to,

$$\text{CIRC}[\Delta_N ; \text{Happens}] \wedge \Delta_{PR}.$$

So it remains to show that F exists. Consider any interpretation M of L1 that satisfies Δ_N. In the presence of the uniqueness-of-names axioms for fluents and actions, we can confine our attention to models in which fluent names and action names are interpreted as themselves. If the simple narrative description in Δ_N is equivalent to,

$$\bigwedge_{i=1}^{n} [\text{Initially}(\beta_i)] \wedge \bigwedge_{i=1}^{m} [\text{Happens}(\alpha_i, \tau_i)]$$

where $\tau_i < \tau_{i+1}$, then let F(M) be defined as follows.

- F(M)$\llbracket \sigma \rrbracket = \sigma$ if σ is a situation term

- $F(M)[\![Actual]\!] =$
  $\{M[\![S0]\!], F(M)[\![Result(\alpha_1,S0)]\!], \ldots,$
  $\qquad F(M)[\![Result(\alpha_m, \ldots Result(\alpha_1,S0) \ldots)]\!]\}$

- $F(M)[\![Start]\!] =$
  $\{\langle F(M)[\![S0]\!],0\rangle, \langle F(M)[\![Result(\alpha_1,S0)]\!],\tau_1\rangle, \ldots,$
  $\qquad \langle F(M)[\![Result(\alpha_m, \ldots Result(\alpha_1,S0) \ldots)]\!],\tau_m\rangle\}$

- $F(M)[\![HoldsAt]\!] = \{\langle \beta_i,\tau\rangle \mid 0 \le \tau < \tau_1 \text{ and } 0 < i \le n\}$

- $F(M)[\![Holds]\!] = \{\langle \beta_i, F(M)[\![S0]\!]\rangle \mid 0 < i \le n\}$

It can easily be verified that $M+F(M)$ is a model of Δ_{PR}.   □

After the application of this theorem, $CIRC[\Delta_N ; Happens]$ yields a simple completion for Happens.

Note that the conditions of both the above separation theorems forbid the inclusion of HoldsAt sentences in the theory being circumscribed. The inclusion of such sentences would violate the principle of directionality, and would make useful separation theorems very hard to prove.

Let's return to the example of the briefcase narrative, both to illustrate the use of these separation theorems, and as an example of the approach to narratives that associates an actual situation with each time point. Recall that the linear simple narrative description for this example is the following.

$$Initially(InCase) \qquad\qquad (BN1)$$

$$\neg\, Initially(AtWork) \qquad\qquad (BN2)$$

$$Happens(Eat,8) \qquad\qquad (BN3)$$

$$Happens(TakeCase,9) \qquad\qquad (BN4)$$

In addition, we have Mary's knowledge of the effects of actions. Besides the TakeCase and Eat actions, there is a Remove action, which is the act of taking the notes out of the briefcase. Two fluents are involved: InCase denotes that the notes are in the briefcase, and AtWork denotes that the notes are at work.

$$Holds(AtWork,Result(TakeCase,s)) \leftarrow Holds(InCase,s) \qquad (BN5)$$

$$\neg\, Holds(InCase,Result(Remove,s)) \qquad\qquad (BN6)$$

$$UNA[Eat, TakeCase, Remove] \qquad\qquad (BN7)$$

$$UNA[AtWork, InCase] \qquad\qquad (BN8)$$

Ignorant of her husband's actions, Mary concludes that her notes are at work at 10:00.

Proposition 9.5.4. Let Σ be the conjunction of (BN5) to (BN8) with Axioms (Arb1), (EoS12), (EoS13) and (F2). Let Δ be the conjunction of (BN1) to (BN4) with (BN7) and (BN8), Axiom (Arb2), and Axioms (PR1) to (PR11). Then,

$$\text{CIRC}_{\text{PR}}[\Sigma \wedge \Delta] \vDash \text{HoldsAt(AtWork,10)}.$$

Proof. From Theorem 9.5.1, the circumscription is equivalent to,

$$\text{CIRC}[\Sigma \, ; \, \text{AbSit} > \text{Ab} \, ; \, \text{Holds, Result}] \wedge$$
$$\text{CIRC}[\Delta \, ; \, \text{Happens} \, ; \, \text{HoldsAt, Actual, Start, S0}].$$

The first conjunct entails,

$$\neg \, \exists \, p \, [\text{AbSit(p)}] \qquad\qquad [9.5.5]$$

$$\text{Ab(a,f,s)} \leftrightarrow [a = \text{TakeCase} \wedge f = \text{AtWork} \wedge \qquad [9.5.6]$$
$$\neg \, \text{Holds(AtWork,s)} \wedge \text{Holds(InCase,s)}] \vee$$
$$[a = \text{Remove} \wedge f = \text{InCase} \wedge \text{Holds(InCase,s)}]].$$

The proof of this proceeds along familiar lines for such proofs, as found in that of Proposition 6.3.1, for example. The second conjunct entails,

$$\text{Happens(a,t)} \leftrightarrow [a = \text{Eat} \wedge t = 8] \vee [a = \text{TakeCase} \wedge t = 9]. \qquad [9.5.7]$$

This can be demonstrated by using Theorem 9.5.3 to split Δ into Δ_N and Δ_{PR} so that Axioms (PR1) to (PR11) can be lifted out of the circumscription, leaving just the narrative description to be circumscribed. From [9.5.7] and (PR10), we have,

$$\exists \, s \, [\text{Actual(Result(a,s))} \wedge \text{Start(Result(a,s),t)}] \leftrightarrow$$
$$[[a = \text{Eat} \wedge t = 8] \vee [a = \text{TakeCase} \wedge t = 9]].$$

From this, what we know about S0 (Axioms (PR1) and (PR8)), and Axiom (PR4), we have,

$$[\text{Actual(s1)} \wedge \text{Start(s1,t)}] \rightarrow [s1 = \text{S0} \wedge t = 0] \vee \qquad [9.5.8]$$
$$\exists \, s2 \, [s1 = \text{Result(Eat,s2)} \wedge t = 8] \vee$$
$$\exists \, s2 \, [s1 = \text{Result(TakeCase,s2)} \wedge t = 9].$$

From [9.5.8], and given the demands on the structure of Actual imposed by Axioms (PR1) to (PR7), we get,

$$\text{Actual(S0)} \wedge \text{Start(S0,0)}$$

$$\text{Actual(Result(Eat,S0))} \wedge \text{Start(Result(Eat,S0),8)}$$

$$\text{Actual(Result(TakeCase,Result(Eat,S0)))} \land$$
$$\text{Start(Result(TakeCase,Result(Eat,S0)),9)}.$$

These three are the only actual situations.[5] From this, given what we know about the initial situation, plus (BN5), [9.5.6], Axiom (F2), and Axiom (PR11), we can show HoldsAt(AtWork,10). □

When she learns that her husband removed the notes from her briefcase (at 8:30, say), Mary can revise her knowledge of the narrative simply by conjoining an appropriate formula representing this new event occurrence. Her previous (defeasible) conclusion that her notes are at work is reversed.[6]

$$\text{Happens(Remove,8.5)} \qquad\qquad \text{(BN9)}$$

Proposition 9.5.9. If Σ is the conjunction of (BN1) to (BN9) with Axioms (Arb1) and (Arb2), Axioms (PR1) to (PR11), and Axioms (EoS12), (EoS13) and (F2), then,

$$\text{CIRC}_{\text{PR}}[\Sigma] \vDash \neg \text{ HoldsAt(AtWork,10)}.$$

Proof. A proof in the same style as that of Proposition 9.5.4 is easily constructed. The main difference is that instead of [9.5.8], we have,

$$[\text{Actual(s1)} \land \text{Start(s1,t)}] \leftrightarrow [\text{s1} = \text{S0} \land \text{t} = 0] \lor$$
$$\exists \text{ s2 } [\text{s1} = \text{Result(Eat,s2)} \land \text{t} = 8] \lor$$
$$\exists \text{ s2 } [\text{s1} = \text{Result(Remove,s2)} \land \text{t} = 8.5]$$
$$\exists \text{ s2 } [\text{s1} = \text{Result(TakeCase,s2)} \land \text{t} = 9] \qquad\qquad □$$

9.6 Associating a Situation with Each Time Point

An alternative approach to the problem of augmenting the situation calculus with the ability to handle narratives is presented in [Miller & Shanahan, 1994]. The starting point of this approach is the narrative time line itself. Then, rather than associating a time point with each distinguished actual situation, a situation is associated with each time point. There is no inherent commitment to a tree-structured space of situations, so the axioms of arboreality can be omitted, and the more pleasing existence-of-situations axiom (EoS9) can be used instead of (EoS12).

The narrative time line is introduced in the same way as in the last section. We have a sort for time points interpreted by the reals, and the predicates < and ≤. The Initially and Happens predicates are preserved from the last section, so narratives are described in exactly the same way. The main innovation is the introduction of a new function State. The term State(t) denotes the situation that pertains at time t. We have the following axioms.

$$\text{Initially}(f) \leftrightarrow \text{Holds}(f,\text{State}(0)) \qquad \text{(MS1)}$$

$$\text{State}(t1) = \text{State}(0) \leftarrow \neg \exists \, a,t2 \, [\text{Happens}(a,t2) \wedge t2 < t1] \qquad \text{(MS2)}$$

$$\text{State}(t1) = \text{Result}(a1,\text{State}(t2)) \leftarrow [\text{Happens}(a1,t2) \wedge t2 < t1 \wedge \qquad \text{(MS3)}$$
$$\neg \exists \, a2,t3 \, [\text{Happens}(a2,t3) \wedge t2 < t3 < t1]]$$

The first axiom relates what initially holds to the state at time 0. Axiom (MS2) extends this state to cover all time points up to the first event. Axiom (MS3) maps each time point after the first event onto a situation expressed in terms of the Result function.

The HoldsAt predicate is defined in the following way.

$$\text{HoldsAt}(f,t) \leftrightarrow \text{Holds}(f,\text{State}(t)) \qquad \text{(MS4)}$$

Let's tackle the frame problem with state-based minimisation again. As before, the Happens predicate needs to be minimised, this time allowing State to vary since the denotation of State, which is what we're interested in, depends on Happens.

Let Σ be the conjunction of,

- A linear simple narrative description,

- A collection of effect axioms and domain constraints,

- Axioms (MS1) to (MS4),

- Axioms (EoS9), (EoS10) and (F2), and

- Uniqueness-of-names axioms for actions and fluents.

Then we are interested in,

$$\text{CIRC}[\Sigma \, ; \, \text{AbSit} > \text{Happens}, \text{Ab} \, ; \, \text{State}, \text{HoldsAt}, \text{Holds}, \text{Result}]$$

which I'll denote $\text{CIRC}_{\text{MS}}[\Sigma]$.

A separation theorem for this approach to narratives can be proved that permits the same separation of concerns as Theorem 9.5.1: for the purposes of circumscription, the part of the theory that deals with narratives can be isolated from that which deals with the effects of action.

Let Σ be the conjunction of,

- A collection of effect axioms and domain constraints not mentioning the predicate HoldsAt or the function State,

- Axioms (EoS9), (EoS10) and (F2), and

- Uniqueness-of-names axioms for actions and fluents.

  Let Δ be the conjunction of,

- A linear simple narrative description,

- Axioms (MS1) to (MS4), and

- Uniqueness-of-names axioms for actions and fluents.

  Let L1 be the language of Σ. Let L1+L2 be the language of Δ.

Theorem 9.6.1. $\mathrm{CIRC_{MS}}[\Sigma \wedge \Delta]$ is equivalent to,

$$\mathrm{CIRC}[\Sigma \; ; \; \mathrm{AbSit} > \mathrm{Ab} \; ; \; \mathrm{Holds, Result}] \; \wedge$$
$$\mathrm{CIRC}[\Delta \; ; \; \mathrm{Happens} \; ; \; \mathrm{State, HoldsAt}].$$

Proof. From Theorem 7.1.9, $\mathrm{CIRC_{MS}}[\Sigma \wedge \Delta]$ is equivalent to,

$$\mathrm{CIRC}[\Sigma \wedge \Delta \; ; \; \mathrm{AbSit} \; ; \qquad\qquad\qquad [9.6.2]$$
$$\mathrm{Happens, Ab, State, HoldsAt, Holds, Result}] \; \wedge$$
$$\mathrm{CIRC}[\Sigma \wedge \Delta \; ; \; \mathrm{Happens, Ab} \; ; \; \mathrm{State, HoldsAt, Holds, Result}].$$

Consider the second of these conjuncts first. From Theorem 9.4.7, this is equivalent to,

$$\mathrm{CIRC}[\Sigma \; ; \; \mathrm{Ab} \; ; \; \mathrm{Holds, Result}] \wedge \mathrm{CIRC}[\Delta \; ; \; \mathrm{Happens} \; ; \; \mathrm{State, HoldsAt}]$$

if we can find a mapping G from interpretations of L1 to interpretations of L2 such that, for any interpretation M of L1 that satisfies Σ, M+G(M) is a model of,

$$\mathrm{CIRC}[\Delta \; ; \; \mathrm{Happens} \; ; \; \mathrm{State, HoldsAt}].$$

Consider any interpretation M of L1 that satisfies Σ. In the presence of the uniqueness-of-names axioms for fluents and actions, we can confine our attention to models in which fluent names and action names are interpreted as themselves. If the simple narrative description in Δ is equivalent to,

$$\bigwedge_{i=1}^{n} [\mathrm{Initially}(\beta_i)] \wedge \bigwedge_{i=1}^{m} [\mathrm{Happens}(\alpha_i, \tau_i)]$$

where $\tau_i < \tau_{i+1}$, then let G(M) be defined as follows.

- $G(M)[\![Initially]\!] = \{ \beta_i \mid 0 < i \leq n \}$

- $G(M)[\![Happens]\!] = \{ \langle \alpha_i, \tau_i \rangle \mid 0 < i \leq m \}$

- $G(M)[\![State]\!](0) = $ any σ such that $M[\![Holds]\!](\beta, \sigma)$ if and only if $\beta = \beta_i$ for some i, $0 < i \leq n$

- $G(M)[\![State]\!](\tau) = G(M)[\![State]\!](0)$ if $0 \leq \tau \leq \tau_1$

- $G(M)[\![State]\!](\tau) = M[\![Result(\alpha_i, \ldots Result(\alpha_1, S0) \ldots)]\!]$ if $\tau_i < \tau \leq \tau_{i+1}$ for some i, $1 \leq i < m$

- $G(M)[\![State]\!](\tau) = M[\![Result(\alpha_m, \ldots Result(\alpha_1, S0) \ldots)]\!]$ if $\tau > \tau_m$

- $G(M)[\![HoldsAt]\!] =$
  $\{ \langle \beta_i, \tau \rangle \mid 0 \leq \tau < \tau_1 \text{ and } 0 < i \leq n \} \cup$
  $\{ \langle \beta, \tau \rangle \mid \tau_i < \tau \leq \tau_{i+1} \text{ and } M \Vdash Holds(\beta, Result(\alpha_i, \ldots Result(\alpha_1, S0) \ldots))$
         for some i, $1 < i < m \} \cup$
  $\{ \langle \beta, \tau \rangle \mid \tau > \tau_m \text{ and } M \Vdash Holds(\beta, Result(\alpha_m, \ldots Result(\alpha_1, S0) \ldots)) \}$

It can easily be verified that M+G(M) is a model of Δ, and that it's minimal with respect to Happens. The rest of the proof is straightforward, and follows the same argument as the analogous part of the proof of Theorem 9.5.1.   □

A second separation theorem for this approach can be proved, which is the dual of Theorem 9.5.3. It permits Axioms (MS1) to (MS4) to be lifted out of the circumscription of a narrative description.

Let Δ_N be the conjunction of a linear simple narrative description and the uniqueness-of-names axioms for fluents and actions. Let Δ_{MS} be the conjunction of Axioms (MS1) to (MS4) with the uniqueness-of-names axioms for fluents and actions.

Let L1 be the language of Δ_N and L1+L2 be the language of Δ_{MS}. Note that L2 includes the predicate HoldsAt and the function State.

Theorem 9.6.3. The circumscription

$$CIRC[\Delta_N \wedge \Delta_{MS} \,; Happens \,; State, HoldsAt]$$

is equivalent to,

$$CIRC[\Delta_N \,; Happens] \wedge \Delta_{MS}.$$

Proof. From Theorem 9.4.6,

$$CIRC[\Delta_N \wedge \Delta_{MS} \,; Happens \,; State, HoldsAt]$$

is equivalent to,

$$\text{CIRC}[\Delta_N \text{ ; Happens ; State, HoldsAt}] \wedge \Delta_{MS}$$

if there exists a mapping F from interpretations of L1 to interpretations of L2 such that, for any interpretation M of L1 that satisfies Δ_N, M+F(M) is a model of Δ_{MS}. Since Δ_N doesn't mention any of the predicates being varied in this circumscription, it can be simplified to,

$$\text{CIRC}[\Delta_N \text{ ; Happens}] \wedge \Delta_{MS}.$$

So it remains to show that F exists. Consider any interpretation M of L1 that satisfies Δ_N. In the presence of the uniqueness-of-names axioms for fluents and actions, we can confine our attention to models in which fluent names and action names are interpreted as themselves. If the simple narrative description in Δ_N is equivalent to,

$$\bigwedge_{i=1}^{n} [\text{Initially}(\beta_i)] \wedge \bigwedge_{i=1}^{m} [\text{Happens}(\alpha_i, \tau_i)]$$

where $\tau_i < \tau_{i+1}$, then let F(M) be defined as follows.

- F(M)$[\![\sigma]\!]$ = σ if σ is a Result term

- F(M)$[\![\text{State}]\!]$(0) = any σ such that $\sigma \neq$ F(M)$[\![\sigma']\!]$ for any Result term σ'

- F(M)$[\![\text{State}]\!](\tau)$ = F(M)$[\![\text{State}]\!]$(0) if $0 \leq \tau \leq \tau_1$

- F(M)$[\![\text{State}]\!](\tau)$ = F(M)$[\![\text{Result}(\alpha_i, \ldots \text{Result}(\alpha_1, S0) \ldots)]\!]$ if $\tau_i < \tau \leq \tau_{i+1}$ for some i, $1 \leq i < m$

- F(M)$[\![\text{State}]\!](\tau)$ = F(M)$[\![\text{Result}(\alpha_m, \ldots \text{Result}(\alpha_1, S0) \ldots)]\!]$ if $\tau > \tau_m$

- F(M)$[\![\text{HoldsAt}]\!]$ = $\{ \langle \beta_i, \tau \rangle \mid 0 \leq \tau < \tau_1 \text{ and } 0 < i \leq n \}$

- F(M)$[\![\text{Holds}]\!]$ = $\{ \langle \beta_i, \text{F(M)}[\![\text{State}(0)]\!] \rangle \mid 0 < i \leq n \}$

It can easily be verified that M+F(M) is a model of Δ_{MS}.   □

As with the corresponding separation theorems in the last section, the conditions for the separation theorems presented here forbid the inclusion of observation sentences in the theory being circumscribed. As usual, the inclusion of such sentences would violate the principle of directionality, giving rise to the usual problems attendant on such violations.

9.7 Comparing the Approaches

Does the approach of associating a situation with each actual time point yield the results we require? Let's see how this new approach to narratives fares with the briefcase example. To represent the narrative, we use exactly the same formulae as before.

$$\text{Initially(InCase)} \qquad\qquad \text{(BN1)}$$

$$\neg \text{ Initially(AtWork)} \qquad\qquad \text{(BN2)}$$

$$\text{Happens(Eat,8)} \qquad\qquad \text{(BN3)}$$

$$\text{Happens(TakeCase,9)} \qquad\qquad \text{(BN4)}$$

The effects of actions are also expressed in the same way.

$$\text{Holds(AtWork,Result(TakeCase,s))} \leftarrow \text{Holds(InCase,s)} \qquad \text{(BN5)}$$

$$\neg \text{ Holds(InCase,Result(Remove,s))} \qquad\qquad \text{(BN6)}$$

$$\text{UNA[Eat, TakeCase, Remove]} \qquad\qquad \text{(BN7)}$$

$$\text{UNA[AtWork, InCase]} \qquad\qquad \text{(BN8)}$$

And as we would expect, Mary can draw the same conclusion as before.

Proposition 9.7.1. Let Σ be the conjunction of (BN5) to (BN8) with Axioms (EoS9), (EoS10) and (F2). Let Δ be the conjunction of (BN1) to (BN4) with (BN7) and (BN8), and Axioms (MS1) to (MS4). Then,

$$\text{CIRC}_{MS}[\Sigma \wedge \Delta] \models \text{HoldsAt(AtWork,10)}.$$

Proof. From Theorem 9.6.1, the circumscription is equivalent to,

$$\text{CIRC}[\Sigma \text{ ; AbSit} > \text{Ab ; Holds, Result]} \wedge$$
$$\text{CIRC}[\Delta \text{ ; Happens ; State, HoldsAt]}.$$

As in the proof of Proposition 9.5.4, the first conjunct yields,

$$\text{Ab(a,f,s)} \leftrightarrow [\text{a = TakeCase} \wedge \text{f = AtWork} \wedge \qquad\qquad [9.7.2]$$
$$\neg \text{ Holds(AtWork,s)} \wedge \text{Holds(InCase,s)]} \vee$$
$$[\text{a = Remove} \wedge \text{f = InCase} \wedge \text{Holds(InCase,s)]]}$$

and, using Theorem 9.6.3, we can show that the second conjunct yields,

$$\text{Happens(a,t)} \leftrightarrow [\text{a = Eat} \wedge \text{t = 8]} \vee [\text{a = TakeCase} \wedge \text{t = 9]}. \qquad [9.7.3]$$

From [9.7.3] and (MS1) to (MS3), we have,

State(10) = Result(TakeCase,Result(Eat,State(0)))

which, using what we know about the initial situation, plus [9.7.2], Axiom (F2), and (BN5), yields,

Holds(AtWork,State(10))

from which the proposition follows directly using Axiom (MS4). □

The effect of adding (BN9) is also what we would expect.

Happens(Remove,8.5)   (BN9)

Proposition 9.7.4. If Σ is the conjunction of (BN1) to (BN9) with Axioms (MS1) to (MS4), and Axioms (EoS9), (EoS10) and (F2), then,

$$\text{CIRC}_{\text{MS}}[\Sigma] \models \neg \, \text{HoldsAt(AtWork,10)}.$$

Proof. The proof is a straightforward variation of that of Proposition 9.7.1. □

So the approach of associating a situation with each time point yields the same answers for the briefcase example as the approach of associating a time point with each actual situation. But can we say anything stronger, anything more general, about the relationship between the two approaches?

In fact, a theorem can be proved that says that the two approaches are equivalent, in the sense that they yield exactly the same HoldsAt consequences for a given linear simple narrative description, and a given domain theory. The theorem depends on an idea that's been central in this chapter, and that will also feature prominently in later chapters, namely the separation of concerns made possible by theories that are modular.

In the present case, the modules in question are those illustrated in Figure 9.2. The flow of information is from left to right. There is a module for the domain theory, a module for the narrative description, a module for the axioms of state-based minimisation, and a module for the axioms that link narrative descriptions to domain theories. The last of these modules comes in two varieties, one corresponding each approach to narrative information described in this chapter. The following theorem tells us that either variety can be plugged in to get the same results.

Let Σ be the conjunction of,

• A collection of effect axioms and domain constraints not mentioning the predicates HoldsAt, Actual, Start, Happens, and Initially, the function State, or the constant S0,

- Axiom (Arb1),

- Axioms (EoS12), (EoS13) and (F2), and

- Uniqueness-of-names axioms for actions and fluents.

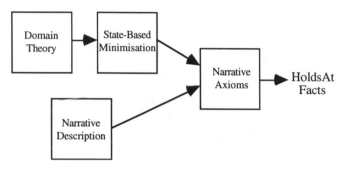

Figure 9.2: Modularity

Let Δ_N be the conjunction of a linear simple narrative description and the uniqueness-of-names axioms for fluents and actions. Let Δ_{PR} be the conjunction of Axiom (Arb2) with Axioms (PR1) to (PR11), and the uniqueness-of-names axioms for fluents and actions. Let Δ_{MS} be the conjunction of Axioms (MS1) to (MS4) with the uniqueness-of-names axioms for fluents and actions.

Theorem 9.7.5. For any fluent β and time point τ,

$$\text{CIRC}_{PR}[\Sigma \wedge \Delta_N \wedge \Delta_{PR}] \vDash \text{HoldsAt}(\beta,\tau)$$

if and only if,

$$\text{CIRC}_{MS}[\Sigma \wedge \Delta_N \wedge \Delta_{MS}] \vDash \text{HoldsAt}(\beta,\tau).$$

Proof. The proof of this theorem is lengthy, and is presented in Appendix A.   □

Notes

1. A similar difficulty is raised by Kartha [1994] in the context of non-deterministic action.

2. Axiom (PR1) is in fact redundant, because it follows from Axioms (PR5) and (PR8) below.

3. I will be making several assumptions like this in the rest of the book. The legitimacy of these manoeuvres depends on our ability, in principle, to fill the resulting gap between axioms and model theory to our satisfaction. For example,

a second-order axiomatisation of the naturals is straightforwardly written down. Based on this, the < predicate for the reals can be axiomatised, via their construction using the method of Dedekind cuts, which is described in many standard text books on set theory or real analysis. From the point of view of computation, the existence of well understood numerical algorithms and the possibility of procedural attachment is a source of comfort.

4. In fact, the position of Happens in this prioritisation is irrelevant for temporal projection problems.

5. For more detail of this part of the derivation, consult the proof of Lemma A.1 in Appendix A.

6. Note that Mary hasn't observed this directly. The point here is to assimilate a new event occurrence. It might turn out that Mary's five year old daughter put the notes back again while playing.

10 Incomplete Narratives and Concurrent Actions

This chapter builds on the work of the last chapter in two ways. First, incomplete narratives, specifically narratives with events whose exact order of occurrence is unknown, are discussed. This leads to a discussion of the danger of over-zealous event occurrence minimisation. A method is sketched for avoiding too much event occurrence minimisation based on the idea of identifying distinct narratives with *contexts*, and making event occurrence minimisation context-sensitive.

The second aim of this chapter is to augment the situation calculus with the ability to represent concurrent actions. One of the criticisms commonly levelled at the situation calculus in the past was its inability to deal with concurrency. A way to do this was outlined by Gelfond, Lifschitz and Rabinov [1991], and explored in detail by [Lin & Shoham, 1992]. Their technique is presented here. A key issue is how to handle concurrent actions whose effects are either cancelling or cumulative. Finally, the capacity to represent concurrent action is combined with the previous chapter's techniques for representing narratives.

10.1 Over-Zealous Event Occurrence Minimisation

Both approaches to representing narratives presented in the last chapter facilitate the description of events whose exact order of occurrence is unknown. Consider this extreme example, described by Hayes [1985a]. Two people meet, then go their separate ways, then meet again in a fortnight's time. During that fortnight, they each participate in many events. There are two parallel narratives, and the events in one narrative are quite independent of those in the other. Within each narrative, we know how the events are ordered. But the relative orderings of events across narratives is unknown. How do we describe the situation that obtains when they meet again, using the situation calculus?

As Hayes points out, it would be very tedious to try to describe this situation using the situation calculus Result function, because of the incompleteness of our information about the relative orderings of events across the two narratives. We would have to use a large disjunction, with one disjunct for each possible interleaving of events. However, with the addition of the Happens predicate, this example becomes relatively straightforward. Suppose there are n events in the first narrative and m in the second, and we know that all events happen before some time τ. Then the following sentences (in which time variables tl_1, $t2_1$, etc. are existentially quantified with maximum scope) are adequate.[1]

$$[\text{Happens}(Al_1, tl_1) \wedge \text{Happens}(Al_2, tl_2) \wedge \ldots \wedge \text{Happens}(Al_n, tl_n) \wedge$$
$$tl_1 < tl_2 \wedge tl_2 < tl_3 \wedge \ldots \wedge tl_{n-1} < tl_n \wedge tl_n < \tau]$$

$$[Happens(A2_1,t2_1) \wedge Happens(A2_2,t2_2) \wedge \ldots \wedge Happens(A2_m,t2_m) \wedge$$
$$t2_1 < t2_2 \wedge t2_2 < t2_3 \wedge \ldots \wedge t2_{m-1} < t2_m \wedge t2_m < \tau]$$

Let's consider a variation of this example. Suppose Mary is in London and Joe is in New York. At 8:00, Mary telephones Joe and wakes him up. At 8:05 the call finishes, and both Mary and Joe get back to whatever they were doing before. During the day, Mary takes part in many events, and she knows more or less what those events are. It's quite appropriate for Mary to assume that no relevant events occur in her part of the world except the ones she knows about. When she puts her notes in her case she wants to be able to assume they will stay there. On the other hand, she hasn't a clue what Joe is doing. Despite this, the blanket minimisation of Happens will insist that, because Mary doesn't know what Joe is doing, she must assume he's doing nothing, and is therefore still awake at 12 noon, at 7pm, and so on. In fact, in the absence of further information, she will be able to conclude that Joe remains awake for the rest of the week, and so on into the future.

In Section 1.9, I suggested that non-monotonic techniques like circumscription could be thought of as supplying a logical substrate in which persistence is the default and in which change and neutrality have to be made explicit. This is in contrast to unadorned classical (monotonic) logic, where the underlying logical substrate is neutral, and persistence and change have to be made explicit. The possibility of over-zealous event-occurrence minimisation (which Georgeff [1987] calls the problem of "overcommitment") entails the need for a mechanism for making explicit declarations of neutrality where even occurrences are concerned.

Let's introduce a little more detail into the parallel London and New York narratives. As before, Mary knows what's going on in London, but has at best a sketchy picture of what's happening in New York. Suppose Mary is stacking blocks in London and Joe is stacking blocks in New York.[2] Mary knows all the events that take place that are relevant to her block stacking. Suppose we have the following.

Happens(Move(A,B),10)

Happens(Move(C,A),20)

And suppose we want to conclude from this that Holds(On(A,B),State(30)), using a standard Blocks World theory about moving blocks, and some solution to the frame problem (such as state-based minimisation) to ensure that moving C doesn't affect A. Also, we need to minimise Happens, representing the assumption that Mary knows all the events that are relevant to her, to eliminate the possibility that A gets moved between 20 and 30 by another event.

How do we ensure that the latter minimisation doesn't also allow Mary to conclude that nothing happens in New York? Suppose blocks A, B, and C are in London and that blocks D, E, and F are in New York. Mary might know that Holds(On(D,E),State(10)). But she doesn't know what stacking events are taking place in New York, so she doesn't want to conclude that ¬ Happens(Move(D,F),11). But minimising Happens will allow this conclusion to be drawn, forcing her to conclude that D stays on E forever, even though Joe is busy moving blocks around in New York.

The way to avoid the over-zealous minimisation of event occurrences is,

- To recognise that Mary's and Joe's activities constitute separate narratives, and

- To minimise the occurrence of events only within those narratives for which we want to assume complete knowledge, permitting neutrality about event occurrences in the rest.

But how do we go about this? A first attempt at a solution assumes that geographical separation corresponds to narrative separation [Miller & Shanahan, 1994]. Let's look at this attempt briefly. In this solution, the term Location(a) denotes the geographical location of an event of type a. A new predicate Happens* is introduced for events that are part of a narrative for which complete knowledge is assumed. In this particular example, knowledge of the London narrative is assumed to be complete, while knowledge of the New York narrative is not. We have,

$$[\text{Happens}(a,t) \wedge \text{Location}(a) = \text{London}] \rightarrow \text{Happens}^*(a,t). \qquad (G1)$$

Now instead of minimising Happens, we will minimise Happens*. This has the effect of minimising the set of events that happen in London. In other words, it minimises the set of e's and t's such that Happens(e,t) ∧ Location(e) = London. But we still need another axiom that says that actions only affect fluents in the same geographical locations as themselves. Assuming that Location(f) denotes the location of fluent f, we have,

$$\text{Location}(e) = \text{Location}(f) \leftarrow \neg [\text{Holds}(f,\text{Result}(e,s)) \leftrightarrow \text{Holds}(f,s)]. \quad (G2)$$

To see how this works, let's consider the two block stacking narratives again. Further extending the application of the Location function, we have,

$$\text{Location}(\text{Move}(x,y)) = c \leftarrow [\text{Location}(x) = c \wedge \text{Location}(y) = c]$$

Location(On(x,y)) = c ← [Location(x) = c ∧ Location(y) = c]

Location(A) = Location(B) = Location(C) = London

Location(D) = Location(E) = Location(F) = NewYork.

We also need uniqueness-of-names axioms for locations, blocks, actions and fluents. Now from the minimisation of Happens* and Axiom (G1), we can show,

[Happens(e,t) ∧ Location(e) = London] → [[e = Move(A,B) ∧ t = 10] ∨
[e = Move(C,A) ∧ t = 20]].

From this we can conclude, using Axiom (G2), that whatever happens in New York does not affect what holds in London. In particular, given the frame axiom (F2) and the minimisation of Ab, we can show that,

¬ [Happens(e,t) ∧ 10 < t ≤ 30 ∧ Ab(e,On(A,B),State(t))]

which in turn gives, from Axioms (F1) and (N1),

Holds(On(A,B),State(30)).

We can draw this conclusion, although we don't know the sequence of events between time 10 and time 30, because we do know all the events between those times that can affect the relevant fluent. This is one conclusion we wanted for Mary. We also wanted her to be unable to conclude anything about what was happening in New York. Recall that Mary knew that a Move(D,E) action took place at time 10. But, as we require, we *cannot* show from the minimisation of Happens* that,

[Happens(e,t) ∧ Location(e) = NewYork] → [e = Move(D,E) ∧ t = 10]

which means that, as required, there are models in which we have, for example,

Happens(e,t) ∧ Location(e) = NewYork ∧ e = Move(D,F) ∧ t = 11.

10.2   Context-Sensitive Event Occurrence Minimisation

So far so good. The proposed solution works for this example. But the solution is nowhere near as general as we would like. To begin with, the identification of geographical separation with narrative separation is obviously naive. Suppose, for example, that the narratives we are interested in are telephone calls, rather than block stackings. Mary and Jane could be in adjacent rooms in London talking respectively to Joe and Fred in adjacent rooms in New York. But the events in Mary and Joe's conversation comprise one narrative and those in Jane and Fred's a different narrative.[3]

Furthermore, there are plenty of events going on at the atomic level which are in the same geographical location as Mary which she knows nothing about, and which she doesn't need to know anything about in order to reason about her block stacking. Similarly, there may be things happening just outside the window not significantly further away than the blocks she is stacking, which she doesn't need to know about to reason correctly about the blocks (leaves blowing, people walking along the street, and so on).

What we would like to capture somehow is the idea that a narrative has to encompass all the events that are relevant to a particular set of fluents, that is to say, all those events that affect those fluents. A natural starting point is to think of each narrative as a different context, in the sense of McCarthy [1993]. In the present example, the New York narrative is one context — certain things are true in that context, and certain actions and fluents are part of that context — and the London narrative is a separate context, with its own fluents, actions and true formulae. Then minimisation of event occurrences becomes context-sensitive. We will want to assume complete knowledge about certain contexts, but not about others.

The same event could be a part of many different narratives, and correspondingly same facts can be true in many different contexts. The 1989 earthquake in San Francisco, for example, certainly affected many people's otherwise independent lives. Furthermore, separate narratives can intersect briefly, as would happen if Joe telephoned Mary from New York and interrupted her block stacking. This event becomes part of both narratives.

The temporary intersection of otherwise separate narratives is potentially the source of a serious difficulty in correctly formalising the context-sensitive minimisation of event occurrences, because we cannot say in advance which events need to be included in any given context. This is reminiscent of the difficulty of finding a solution to the frame problem that can deal with ramifications. In effect, we would like an axiom that enshrines the following principle.

- Any event that, if it were included in a given context, would affect one or more fluents in that context, should be included in that context. And every other event should be excluded.

Here's an attempt to get what we want. The basic ideas about context are adopted from [McCarthy, 1993], although McCarthy's original intention was to apply them to a somewhat different problem, namely that of the lack of "generality" of formal theories in AI. Because nested contexts are not used, no special semantic machinery, such as that described in [Buvač & Mason, 1993], is required. Standard first-order predicate calculus model theory is enough. A new sort for contexts is introduced, with variables c, c1, c2, etc. The term Value(c,x) denotes the value of object x in context c. The formula In(c,x) represents that object x is part of context c, and the formula Ist(c,p) denotes that p is true in context c. First, we have a contextualised version of Axiom (MS3).

$$\text{Value(c,State(t1))} = \text{Result(a1,Value(c,State(t2)))} \leftarrow \qquad \text{(NC1)}$$
$$[\text{Ist(c,Happens(a1,t2))} \wedge t2 < t1 \wedge$$
$$\neg \exists \, a2,t3 \, [\text{Ist(c,Happens(a2,t3))} \wedge t2 < t3 < t1]]$$

To cope with the initial situation, we have contextualised versions of Axioms (MS1) and (MS2). The predicate Initially has been reified in order to make it context dependent.

$$\text{Ist(c,Initially(f))} \leftrightarrow \text{Holds(f,Value(c,State(0)))} \qquad \text{(NC2)}$$

$$\text{Value(c,State(t1))} = \text{Value(c,State(0))} \leftarrow \qquad \text{(NC3)}$$
$$\neg \exists \, a,t2 \, [\text{Ist(c,Happens(a,t2))} \wedge t2 < t1]$$

Now we no longer expect conclusions about what holds at a given time, in other words conclusions of the form Holds(f,State(t)). Instead we expect contextualised conclusions of the form Holds(f,Value(c,State(t))). A fluent that holds in one context may be undefined in another.

Narratives will be described as in the decontextualised version, in terms of Initially and Happens. But in addition, the fluents in the domain can be assigned to any number of contexts using the predicate In. Let's consider Mary's and Joe's narratives again. As well as Happens and Initially facts, the narrative description will incorporate In facts, such as the following. The context of Mary's narrative is called "Mary".

$$\text{In(c,On(x,y))} \leftarrow \text{In(c,x)} \wedge \text{In(c,y)}$$

$$\text{In(Mary,A)}$$

$$\text{In(Mary,B)}$$

$$\text{In(Mary,C)}$$

In will be minimised at a lower priority than Ab.[4] Then, axioms are required that link decontextualised Initially and Happens facts to contexts, so that Axioms (NC1) to (NC3) will apply to them.

$$\text{Ist(c,Happens(a,t))} \leftarrow \exists \text{ f,s [Ab(a,f,s)} \wedge \text{Happens(a,t)} \wedge \text{In(c,f)]} \quad \text{(NC4)}$$

$$\text{Ist(c,Initially(f))} \leftarrow \text{[Initially(f)} \wedge \text{In(c,f)]} \quad \text{(NC5)}$$

Instead of minimising Happens, we want to minimise the events that occur in each context that can affect fluents in that context. This is done by minimising the predicate Happens*, which is constrained by the following axiom.

$$\text{Happens*(c,a,t)} \leftarrow \exists \text{ f,s [Ist(c,Happens(a,t))} \wedge \quad \text{(NC6)}$$
$$\text{Ab(a,f,s)} \wedge \text{In(c,f)]}$$

Happens* is minimised at a lower priority than both Ab and In, and Ist is allowed to vary. In effect, Axioms (NC4) and (NC6) serve the same role as Axioms (G1) and (G2) in the naive attempt to get more selective minimisation presented in Section 10.1.

10.3 A Worked Example of Narratives as Contexts

To see how the above logical machinery works, I will now work through an example of two separate block stacking narratives. Let's assume that Joe and Mary are in adjacent rooms, rather than distant cities. In Room 1, Mary is stacking blocks A, B, and C. At the same time in Room 2, Joe is stacking blocks D, E, and F. Mary knows nothing of what Joe is doing.

The fluents known to be involved in the two contexts are as follows.

$$\text{In(c,On(x,y))} \leftarrow \text{In(c,x)} \wedge \text{In(c,y)}$$

$$\text{In(c,Clear(x))} \leftarrow \text{In(c,x)}$$

$$\text{In(Mary,A)}$$

$$\text{In(Mary,B)}$$

$$\text{In(Mary,C)}$$

$$\text{In(Joe,D)}$$

$$\text{In(Joe,E)}$$

$$\text{In(Joe,F)}$$

For the initial situation, we have,

$$\text{Initially(On(A,C))}$$

$$\text{Initially(On(C,Table))}$$

Initially(On(B,Table))

Initially(Clear(A))

Initially(Clear(B))

Initially(Clear(Table))

Initially(On(D,E)).

Mary's actions are as follows.

Happens(Move(A,B),10)

Happens(Move(C,A),20)

The following is the Blocks World theory we will use.

Holds(On(x,y),Result(Move(x,y),s)) ← [Holds(Clear(x),s) ∧   (B1)
        Holds(Clear(y),s)]

¬ Holds(On(x,z),Result(Move(x,y),s)) ← [Holds(Clear(x),s) ∧   (B2)
        Holds(Clear(y),s) ∧ y≠z]

Holds(Clear(z),Result(Move(x,y),s)) ← [Holds(Clear(x),s) ∧   (B3)
        Holds(Clear(y),s) ∧ Holds(On(x,z),s) ∧ y ≠ z ∧ x ≠ y]

¬ Holds(Clear(y),Result(Move(x,y),s)) ← [Holds(Clear(x),s) ∧   (B4)
        Holds(Clear(y),s) ∧ y ≠ Table]

Now we can show from the Blocks World theory and (F2) that,

Ab(Move(x,y),On(x,z),s)) ← [Holds(Clear(x),s) ∧ Holds(Clear(y),s) ∧
        Holds(On(x,z),s) ∧ z≠y]

which gives, from (NC6) and what we know about the contexts in this domain,

Ist(c,Happens(Move(x,y),t)) ← ∃ s [Holds(Clear(x),s) ∧
        Holds(Clear(y),s) ∧ Holds(On(x,z),s) ∧ z≠y ∧
        Happens(Move(x,y),t) ∧ In(x,c) ∧ In(y,c)].

Our chosen existence-of-situations axiom ensures that, for any x, y, and z,

z ≠ y → ∃ s [Holds(Clear(x),s) ∧ Holds(Clear(y),s) ∧ Holds(On(x,z),s)]

and therefore,

Ist(c,Happens(Move(x,y),t)) ← [Happens(Move(x,y),t) ∧
        In(x,c) ∧ In(y,c)].

This gives, as we might expect,

$$Ist(Mary,Happens(Move(A,B),10))$$

$$Ist(Mary,Happens(Move(C,A),20))$$

and consequently,

$$Happens*(Mary,Move(A,B),10)$$

$$Happens*(Mary,Move(C,A),20).$$

Then, through the minimisation of Ab and of Happens*, we have,

$$[Ist(Mary,Happens(a,t)) \wedge \exists f,s [Ab(a,f,s) \wedge In(Mary,f)]] \leftrightarrow$$
$$[[a = Move(A,B) \wedge t = 10] \vee [a = Move(C,A) \wedge t = 20]].$$

Now we can show, using (NC1) to (NC3), the Blocks World axioms, and (F2), that Holds(On(A,B),Value(Mary,State(30))), which is the desired result. However, although we have Initially(On(D,E)), and whatever actions of Joe's on blocks D, E, and F we described, we would not be able to conclude anything of the form Holds(On(x,y),Value(Mary,State(t))) where x and y were D, E, or F. Similarly, we cannot conclude Holds(On(A,B),Value(Joe,State(30))).

If we want to include information about one narrative explicitly in another, we can using the Ist predicate. For example, if Mary learns that D was on E in the initial situations, we can add,

$$Ist(Mary, Initially(On(D,E))).$$

However, this will not allow any further conclusions to be drawn from within the context of Mary's narrative about D, E or F. We can't show, for example, that Holds(On(D,E),Value(Mary,State(5))), although we can show that Holds(On(D,E),Value(Joe,State(5))). This is because the minimisation of Happens* only rules out models with extra events in Mary's narrative that affect fluents included in the context of her narrative. It cannot rule out the possibility of extra events that affect fluents outside the context of her narrative. If we wanted to, of course, we could always include D, E, and F in Mary's context.

The solution to the over-zealous minimisation of event occurrences presented here isn't entirely satisfactory, because it presupposes that the set of fluents included in a context is closed with respect to causal relevance. For example, suppose the context of Joe's narrative includes the fluent LightOn, denoting that the light in his office is on. Joe can switch the light on and off via a Toggle action. Imagine a situation in which the light is broken, but Joe doesn't know that it's broken. The Toggle action has no effect under these circumstances. So there is a fluent, which we can call Broken, which affects the outcome of Joe's Toggle actions, but whose value is unknown to Joe.

The formal apparatus of Section 10.2 conflates two uses of the idea of context in a way that prevents us from dealing correctly with examples such as this. A more complete solution would separate an agent's epistemic context — what he or she knows — from a fluent's causal context — the set of fluents that are causally relevant to it. The fluents that are causally relevant in a context are those on which the outcome of events in that context depend.

10.4 Concurrent Actions in the Situation Calculus

One of the criticisms most frequently levelled at the situation calculus before the publication of Gelfond, Lifschitz and Rabinov's paper "What Are the Limitations of the situation calculus?" [1991] was that it couldn't handle concurrent action. Gelfond, Lifschitz and Rabinov sketched a way of doing this in their paper. A slightly different technique was later presented by Lin and Shoham [1992], in somewhat greater detail.

Before either of these publications, an approach to concurrent action was outlined by Schubert [1990, Section 5]. But Schubert's pioneering attempt neglected two features of domains with concurrent action must be attended to in any such extension of the situation calculus, namely concurrent actions whose effects are cumulative, and concurrent actions whose effects cancel each other out.

As an example of two action whose effects are cumulative, consider the act of lifting a heavy object with the left hand and the act of lifting the same object with the right hand. Now suppose that neither action has any effect if performed separately (because the object is too heavy), yet the object is lifted off the ground if the two actions are performed simultaneously.[5]

As an example of two cancelling actions, consider the act of lifting the left side of a bowl of soup and the act of lifting the right side of the same bowl of soup [Gelfond, Lifschitz & Rabinov, 1991]. Performed separately, either of these lifting actions results in the soup being spilled. But if the bowl is lifted on both sides at once, the soup is not spilled.

This section offers techniques for coping with examples such as these within the framework of situation calculus. While Gelfond, Lifschitz and Rabinov's approach is tailored for causal minimisation, and relies on the Causes predicate (see Chapter 5), my presentation is closer to that of Lin and Shoham, since their effect axioms resemble standard situation calculus more closely. Unlike Lin and Shoham, who are concerned to integrate their approach to concurrent action with their own attempt at the frame problem [Lin & Shoham, 1991], my focus is on integrating it with state-based minimisation.

A new sort for *compound actions* is introduced (with variables g, g1, g2, etc.). I will use the term *simple action* to denote what was previously called just an action. The Result function and the Ab predicate now take compound actions as arguments instead of simple actions. The frame axiom (F2) becomes,

$$[Holds(f,Result(g,s)) \leftrightarrow Holds(f,s)] \leftarrow \neg Ab(g,f,s). \tag{F3}$$

Concurrent actions are introduced into the language of situation calculus through a new infix function. The term a & g denotes a compound action that has the same effect as the concurrent performance of the simple action a and the compound action g. Following Lin and Shoham, the term In(a,g) represents that the compound action g includes the simple action a.[6]

$$g1 = g2 \leftrightarrow \forall a \, [In(a,g1) \leftrightarrow In(a,g2)] \tag{GA1}$$

$$In(a2,a1 \, \& \, g1) \leftrightarrow [In(a2,g1) \lor a2 = a1] \tag{GA2}$$

$$[In(a,g) \leftrightarrow a = g] \leftarrow \forall a1,a2 \, [g \neq a1 \, \& \, a2] \tag{GA3}$$

Following both Gelfond, Lifschitz and Rabinov, and Lin and Shoham, a second new predicate is required to cope with cancelling effects. The formula Cancels(g,a,s) represents that the normal effects of action a are cancelled by the components of g if a and g are performed concurrently in situation s.

Now, wherever we previously wrote an effect axiom of the form,

$$\forall s \, [Holds(\beta,Result(\alpha,s)) \leftarrow \Pi]$$

we instead write a *concurrent effect axiom* of the form,

$$\forall s \, [Holds(\beta,Result(\gamma,s)) \leftarrow In(\alpha,\gamma) \land \neg Cancels(\gamma,\alpha,s) \land \Pi].$$

This style of effect axiom ensures that compound actions inherit the effects of their component primitive actions. But this inheritance needs to be made a default. Accordingly, the predicate Cancels is minimised [Lin & Shoham, 1992]. This minimisation must be done at a higher priority than the minimisation of Ab. Otherwise, the circumscription would be free to decrease the extension of Ab at the expense of an increase in the extension of Cancels.

Facts about cancellation are given explicitly.

Definition 10.4.1. A *cancellation axiom* is a formula of the form,

$$Cancels(\gamma,\alpha,s) \text{ if } \Pi$$

where Π is a formula in which every occurrence of a situation term is in a formula of the form Holds(β,s).   □

Let Σ be the conjunction of,

- A collection of concurrent effect axioms and domain constraints,

- A collection of cancellation axioms,

- A collection of observation sentences about the initial situation,

- Axioms (GA1) to (GA3),

- Axioms (EoS9), (EoS10) and (F3), and

- Uniqueness-of-names axioms for actions and fluents.

We're interested in,

CIRC[Σ ; AbSit > Cancels > Ab ; Holds, Result, S0].

Once again, the question arises of how genuine the need is for default reasoning here. An explicitly completed definition of Cancels could have been provided. And once again, the answer is that, although we're only going to consider examples with simple cancellation axioms here, we want to permit more complicated formulae describing what cancels what. Completed definitions of such formulae are much harder to construct.

Let's see how the apparatus described can be used to tackle the soup bowl example from the beginning of the section. There are two actions in the domain. The terms LiftLeft and LiftRight represent the action of lifting the left side of the soup bowl and lifting the right side of the soup bowl. The fluent OnTable holds when the bowl is on the table and the fluent Spilled holds when the soup is on the table but not in the bowl. We have the following concurrent effect axioms.

$$\text{Holds(Spilled,Result(g,s))} \leftarrow \text{In(LiftLeft,g)} \land \qquad \text{(LB1)}$$
$$\neg \text{Cancels(g,LiftLeft,s)}$$

$$\text{Holds(Spilled,Result(g,s))} \leftarrow \text{In(LiftRight,g)} \land \qquad \text{(LB2)}$$
$$\neg \text{Cancels(g,LiftRight,s)}$$

$$\neg \text{Holds(OnTable,Result(g,s))} \leftarrow \text{In(LiftRight,g)} \land \qquad \text{(LB3)}$$
$$\text{In(LiftLeft,g)} \land \neg \text{Cancels(g,LiftLeft \& LiftRight,s)}$$

And we have the following cancellation axioms.

$$\text{Cancels(g,LiftLeft,s)} \leftarrow \text{In(LiftRight,g)} \qquad \text{(LB4)}$$

$$\text{Cancels(g,LiftRight,s)} \leftarrow \text{In(LiftLeft,g)} \qquad \text{(LB5)}$$

As usual, we need some uniqueness-of-names axioms.

$$\text{UNA[LiftLeft,LiftRight]} \qquad \text{(LB6)}$$

$$\text{UNA[OnTable,Spilled]} \qquad \text{(LB7)}$$

In the initial situation, the soup bowl is on the table, and the soup is not spilled.

$$\text{Holds(OnTable,S0)} \qquad \text{(LB8)}$$

$$\neg \text{Holds(Spilled,S0)} \qquad \text{(LB9)}$$

Proposition 10.4.2. If Σ is the conjunction of (LB1) to (LB9) with Axioms (GA1) to (GA3), and Axioms (EoS9), (EoS10) and (F3), then,

$$\text{CIRC}[\Sigma ; \text{AbSit} > \text{Cancels} > \text{Ab} ; \text{Holds, Result, S0}] \vDash$$
$$\text{Holds(Spilled,Result(LiftLeft,S0))} \wedge$$
$$\text{Holds(Spilled,Result(LiftRight,S0))} \wedge$$
$$\text{Holds(OnTable,Result(LiftLeft,S0))} \wedge$$
$$\text{Holds(OnTable,Result(LiftRight,S0))} \wedge$$
$$\neg \text{Holds(Spilled,Result(LiftLeft \& LiftRight,S0))} \wedge$$
$$\neg \text{Holds(OnTable,Result(LiftLeft \& LiftRight,S0))}.$$

Proof. The minimisation of AbSit yields,

$$\neg \exists p \, [\text{AbSit(p)}] \qquad [10.4.3]$$

giving us the expected space of situations via Axiom (EoS9). The minimisation of Cancels yields,

$$\text{Cancels(g,a,s)} \leftrightarrow [a = \text{LiftLeft} \wedge \text{In(LiftRight,g)}] \vee \qquad [10.4.4]$$
$$[a = \text{LiftRight} \wedge \text{In(LiftLeft,g)}].$$

Because of [10.4.3] and [10.4.4], the minimisation of Ab yields,

$$\text{Ab(g,f,s)} \leftrightarrow [g = \text{LiftLeft} \wedge f = \text{Spilled} \wedge \neg \text{Holds(Spilled,s)}] \vee \quad [10.4.5]$$
$$[g = \text{LiftRight} \wedge f = \text{Spilled} \wedge \neg \text{Holds(Spilled,s)}] \vee$$
$$[g = \text{LiftLeft} \& \text{LiftRight} \wedge f = \text{OnTable} \wedge \text{Holds(OnTable,s)}]$$

The proof of [10.4.5], despite the modified form of the effect axioms, is analogous to other proofs involving state-based minimisation (such as that of Proposition 6.3.1). From [10.4.5] the proposition follows classically in a straightforward way. □

This proposition demonstrates all the capabilities of the approach. The lifting actions have both cumulative and cancelling effects. All that remains now is to integrate either the apparatus of this section with an approach to narratives, and we'll have a formalism that meets two of the most common criticisms of situation calculus, namely that it can't cope with concurrent action, and that it can't cope with events whose exact order of occurrence is unknown.

10.5 Narratives with Concurrent Actions

In this section, I'll show how to combine the previous section's techniques for representing concurrent action with the two approaches to narratives presented earlier in the chapter. The mechanism is the same for either approach. The basic idea, which comes from [Miller & Shanahan, 1994], is to collect together all simultaneous event occurrences into one maximal compound action term. Then, a new predicate Happens† is introduced, which takes the same arguments as Happens, but which only applies to these maximal action terms. Finally, the axioms that link narrative descriptions to effect axioms are modified to use Happens† instead of Happens.

The new predicate Happens† is defined as follows.

$$\text{Happens†}(g,t) \leftrightarrow \forall a \, [\text{Happens}(a,t) \leftrightarrow \text{In}(a,g)] \qquad \text{(CN)}$$

Happens† picks out the set of all actions that occur concurrently at time t. Now, whichever axioms we're using to endow the situation calculus with the ability to represent narratives they have to be modified so that they mention Happens† wherever they previously mentioned Happens. For example, Axioms (MS1) to (MS4) from Section 9.4 of the last chapter become,

$$\text{Initially}(f) \leftrightarrow \text{Holds}(f,\text{State}(0)) \qquad \text{(CMS1)}$$

$$\text{State}(t1) = \text{State}(0) \leftarrow \neg \, \exists \, a,t2 \, [\text{Happens†}(a,t2) \wedge t2 < t] \qquad \text{(CMS2)}$$

$$\text{State}(t1) = \text{Result}(a1,\text{State}(t2)) \leftarrow [\text{Happens†}(a1,t2) \wedge \qquad \text{(CMS3)}$$
$$t2 < t1 \wedge \neg \, \exists \, a2,t3 \, [\text{Happens†}(a2,t3) \wedge t2 < t3 < t1]]$$

$$\text{HoldsAt}(f,t) \leftrightarrow \text{Holds}(f,\text{State}(t)). \qquad \text{(CMS4)}$$

The required circumscription policy combines that of Section 9.4 for narratives and that of Section 10.4 for concurrent action. Happens† must be allowed to vary, since it depends on Happens. Let Σ be the conjunction of,

- A simple narrative description,

- A collection of effect axioms and domain constraints,

- A collection of cancellation axioms,

- Axiom (CN),

- Axioms (CMS1) to (CMS4),

- Axioms (GA1) to (GA3),

- Axioms (EoS9), (EoS10) and (F3), and

- Uniqueness-of-names axioms for actions and fluents.

  We're interested in,

$$\text{CIRC}[\Sigma \; ; \text{Happens, AbSit} > \text{Cancels} > \text{Ab} ;$$
$$\text{Happens}\dagger, \text{State, HoldsAt, Holds, Result}].$$

Using this apparatus, we can take the soup bowl example and render it as a narrative. Axioms (LB1) to (LB7) are imported from the previous section. Initially, the bowl is on the table and the soup isn't spilled. At time 10, the bowl is lifted on both sides simultaneously.

$$\text{Initially(OnTable)} \qquad\qquad \text{(LBN1)}$$

$$\neg \, \text{Initially(Spilled)} \qquad\qquad \text{(LBN2)}$$

$$\text{Happens(LiftLeft,10)} \qquad\qquad \text{(LBN3)}$$

$$\text{Happens(LiftRight,10)} \qquad\qquad \text{(LBN4)}$$

Now we can show that the soup bowl is off the table at time 11.

Proposition 10.5.1. If Σ is the conjunction of (LBN1) to (LBN4) with (LB1) to (LB7), (CN), (CMS1) to (CMS4), (GA1) to (GA3), (Eos11) and (F3), then,

$$\text{CIRC}[\Sigma \; ; \text{Happens, AbSit} > \text{Cancels} > \text{Ab} ;$$
$$\text{Happens}\dagger, \text{State, HoldsAt, Holds, Result, S0]} \models \neg \, \text{HoldsAt(OnTable,11)}.$$

Proof. The circumscription yields,

$$\text{Happens(a,t)} \leftrightarrow [t = 10 \wedge [a = \text{LiftLeft} \vee a = \text{LiftRight}]].$$

From this, Axiom (CN), and Axioms (GA1) to (GA3), we have,

$$\text{Happens}\dagger(g,t) \leftrightarrow [t = 10 \wedge [\text{In(a,g)} \leftrightarrow [a = \text{LiftLeft} \vee a = \text{LiftRight}]]].$$

From this and Axioms (CMS1) to (CMS3), we obtain,

$$\text{State(11)} = \text{Result(LiftLeft \& LiftRight,State(0))} \qquad [10.5.2]$$

The circumscription also yields,

$$\neg \text{ Holds(OnTable,Result(LiftLeft \& LiftRight,State(0))).} \qquad [10.5.3]$$

The proof of this the same as the proof of Proposition 10.4.2, but taking State(0) in place of S0. The proposition follows directly from [10.5.2], [10.5.3], and Axiom (CMS4). □

Obviously we can show that the soup is not spilled at time 11 in the same way.

As mentioned at the beginning of this section, the method I've described for combining the ability to represent concurrent action with the ability to represent narratives is applicable to both of this chapter's approaches to narratives. To use Pinto and Reiter's approach (see Section 9.3 of the last chapter) we need to replace Axiom (PR10) by,

$$\text{Happens}\dagger(g,t) \leftrightarrow \exists s \text{ [Actual (Result(g,s))} \wedge \text{Start(Result(g,s),t)].} \quad \text{(CPR)}$$

Then we simply have to replace Axioms (CMS1) to (CMS4) by Axioms (PR1) to (PR9) plus Axiom (CPR) and Axiom (PR11). We also need to include the axioms of arboreality. In other words, if Σ is the conjunction of,

- A simple narrative description,

- A collection of effect axioms and domain constraints,

- A collection of cancellation axioms,

- Axioms (CN),

- Axioms (Arb1) and (Arb2),

- Axioms (PR1) to (PR9), Axiom (CPR), and Axiom (PR11),

- Axioms (GA1) to (GA3),

- Axioms (EoS12), (EoS13) and (F3), and

- Uniqueness-of-names axioms for actions and fluents

then we're interested in,

$$\text{CIRC[}\Sigma \text{ ; Happens, AbSit > Cancels > Ab ;}$$
$$\text{Happens}\dagger, \text{HoldsAt, Actual, Start, Holds, Result, S0].}$$

Notes

1. A similar sentence can be used to deal with Sandewall's ferryboat connection scenario [Sandewall, 1991]. In this scenario, a passenger arrives at a ferry terminal some time between 22:55 and 23:05. The ferry leaves at 23:01. If the passenger is on board at 23:01, he gets to his destination. Otherwise he doesn't. Not knowing his exact arrival time at the terminal, we would expect a representation of this scenario to permit models in which both possibilities occur.

2. This example is adapted from one due to McCarthy.

3. Note that the narratives in question here are not the stories that Mary, Jane, Joe and Fred are telling each other, but are the sequences of events that comprise the speech acts in their conversations.

4. This minimisation is for convenience and is not intended to reflect any law of common sense.

5. I'll use the terms "concurrent" and "simultaneous" interchangeably.

6. The symbol "In" and the variables g, g1, etc. were used in Chapter 7 for a different purpose. I'm recycling them here.

11 The Foundations of Logic Programming

The preceding ten chapters relate the history of attempts to solve the frame problem using full first-order predicate calculus augmented with circumscription in the framework of the situation calculus. This chapter and the next tell the story of a parallel research programme, also started in the Sixties, namely that of logic programming. Substantial cross-fertilisation between these two research programmes didn't occur until the late Eighties. This chapter offers a basic introduction to logic programming and negation-as-failure. Negation-as-failure is of particular interest here, because it's a form of default reasoning, and can be used as the basis of an attempt to solve the frame problem.

11.1 The Basis of Logic Programming

The basic idea of logic programming, due largely to Bob Kowalski, is very simple. Certain kinds of logical formulae, in particular the *Horn clause* subset of predicate calculus, have elegant computational properties. In fact, under the right circumstances, theorem proving with Horn clauses can be regarded as computation. This leads to the possibility of a *logic program* — a mathematical object that can be read both *declaratively*, as a representation of facts about the world, and *procedurally*, as a program to be executed [Kowalski, 1974].[1] Following some historical remarks, this section and the next define the basic concepts of logic programming. A more detailed review of this material is to be found in [Lloyd, 1987].

The roots of logic programming are to be found in Alan Robinson's work in the Sixties on the *resolution* rule of inference [Robinson, 1965]. Resolution, which is defined for the *clausal* subset of first-order predicate calculus, is particularly easy to automate. Robinson's results were refined by several researchers, and this line of work culminated, from the point of view of logic programming, in SLD-resolution, which was first described by Kowalski [1974]. The acronym stands for "SL-resolution for Definite clauses".[2] SL-resolution is due to Kowalski and Keuhner [1971], and the acronym stands for "Linear resolution with Selection function".

The definition of SLD-resolution is still non-deterministic. For it to be machine executable, it has to be further restricted. The application of such a restricted form of SLD-resolution to the definite clause subset of predicate calculus yields a logic programming system, as embodied in the programming language PROLOG (PROgramming in LOGic) [Colmerauer, *et al.*, 1973].

Here are formal definitions of some of these concepts.

Definition 11.1.1. A *clause* is a formula of the following form.

$$\phi_1 \vee \phi_2 \vee \ldots \vee \phi_n \vee \neg\, \phi_{n+1} \vee \neg\, \phi_{n+2} \vee \ldots \vee \neg\, \phi_m$$

where $n \geq 0$, $m \geq 0$, and each ϕ_i is an atom.   □

A clause of this form is equivalently written,

$$\phi_1 \vee \phi_2 \vee \ldots \vee \phi_n \leftarrow \phi_{n+1} \wedge \phi_{n+2} \wedge \ldots \wedge \phi_m.$$

This is the syntax I'll use from now on.

Definition 11.1.2. A *Horn clause* is a clause in which at most one atom is positive.   □

Definition 11.1.3. A *definite clause* is a Horn clause in which exactly one atom is positive, written as,

$$\phi_1 \leftarrow \phi_2 \wedge \phi_3 \wedge \ldots \wedge \phi_n$$ □

If $n = 1$, then the "$\leftarrow$" can be omitted when the clause is written. It's usual to refer to ϕ_1 as the clause's *head*, and to $\phi_2 \wedge \phi_3 \wedge \ldots \wedge \phi_n$ as the clause's *body*. If ϕ_1 is $\rho(\tau_1, \ldots, \tau_m)$, then the clause is said to be a clause *for* the predicate symbol ρ.

Definition 11.1.4. A *goal clause* is a Horn clause in which no atoms are positive, written as,

$$\leftarrow \phi_1 \wedge \phi_2 \wedge \ldots \wedge \phi_n$$ □

The following are self-explanatory examples of definite clauses.

$$\text{Mortal}(x) \leftarrow \text{Human}(x)$$

$$\text{Human}(\text{Socrates})$$

$$\text{Holds}(\text{On}(x,y),\text{Result}(\text{Move}(x,y),s)) \leftarrow \text{Holds}(\text{Clear}(x),s) \wedge \text{Holds}(\text{Clear}(y),s)$$

The following is a goal clause.

$$\leftarrow \text{Mortal}(\text{Socrates})$$

Definition 11.1.5. The *empty clause* is a clause in which there are no atoms.   □

The conjunction of a set of definite clauses is a *logic program*. Given a logic program, we're interested in deriving the negation of a given goal clause. This is done by constructing a *refutation* of the goal clause using SLD-resolution. The refutation takes the form of a derivation of the empty clause from the goal clause. The details will be presented shortly. But first we need to be clear about the semantics of logic programs.

All Horn clauses, with the exception of the empty clause, are well-formed formulae of first-order predicate calculus. Accordingly, Horn clauses inherit their semantics from that of predicate calculus, where the empty clause is defined not to be satisfied by any interpretation. However, in logic programming, it's convenient to confine our attention to *Herbrand interpretations*, which are defined as follows.

Definition 11.1.6. A *ground term* is a term that doesn't contain any variables. □

Definition 11.1.7. The *Herbrand universe* of a language L of predicate calculus is the set of ground terms in L. □

Definition 11.1.8. A *Herbrand interpretation* of a language L of predicate calculus is an interpretation ⟨D,F,P⟩, where D is the Herbrand universe of L. □

Definition 11.1.9. A Herbrand interpretation of a formula ϕ of predicate calculus is a *Herbrand model* of ϕ if it is a model of ϕ. □

In a Herbrand interpretation, all terms are interpreted as themselves, and there are no objects in the domain that are not denoted by some term. In other words, uniqueness-of-names axioms and domain closure axioms are implicitly satisfied. The restriction to Herbrand interpretations is justified by the following theorem.

Let Σ be the conjunction of a set of definite clauses, and let ϕ be a formula of the form $\phi_1 \wedge \phi_2 \wedge \ldots \wedge \phi_n$ where each ϕ_i is an atom.

Theorem 11.1.10. $\Sigma \vDash \phi$ if and only if $M \Vdash \phi$ for all Herbrand models M of Σ.

Proof. Consider any model M1 of Σ. Let M2 be the Herbrand interpretation defined as follows.

- $M2[\![\tau]\!] = \tau$ for all terms τ

- $M2[\![\rho]\!] = \{\langle \tau_1, \ldots, \tau_m \rangle \mid M1[\![\langle \tau_1, \ldots, \tau_m \rangle]\!] \in M1[\![\rho]\!]\}$ for all m-ary predicates ρ

It's easy to verify that, since Σ comprises only definite clauses, and since M1 is a model of Σ, M2 must also be a model of Σ. Now it's clear that, for any atom $\rho(\tau_1, \ldots, \tau_m)$, $M2 \Vdash \rho(\tau_1, \ldots, \tau_m)$ if and only if $M1 \Vdash \rho(\tau_1, \ldots, \tau_m)$. So if $\rho(\tau_1, \ldots, \tau_m)$ is satisfied by all Herbrand models of Σ, it must be satisfied by all models of Σ. The converse is obviously true □

Without loss of information, a Herbrand interpretation can be identified with the set of atoms it satisfies. This permits us to speak of the intersection of two Herbrand interpretations, and leads to the following theorem.

Theorem 11.1.11. The intersection of all Herbrand models of Σ is itself a Herbrand model of Σ, called the *least Herbrand model*.

Proof. The theorem follows from the fact that, given any two Herbrand models M1 and M2 of a definite clause ψ, the intersection of those two models is also a model of ψ. To see that the intersection of M1 and M2 satisfies ψ, there are two cases to consider. Either M1 and M2 both satisfy the body of ψ or one of them doesn't. If they both do, then they also both satisfy the head, so both head and body will be satisfied by the intersection, which will therefore satisfy ψ. If either of M1 or M2 doesn't satisfy the body, then the head will not be satisfied in the intersection, which will therefore satisfy ψ.   □

An obvious corollary of this is that Σ has a model (the least Herbrand model), and is therefore consistent. The following theorem, which extends Theorem 11.1.10, is another corollary.

Theorem 11.1.12. $\Sigma \models \phi$ if and only if the least Herbrand model of Σ satisfies φ.

Proof. The theorem follows from the definition of the least Herbrand model.   □

It's common (but not compulsory) to regard the least Herbrand model as the meaning of a logic program.

It's very important to see that Theorems 11.1.10 to 11.1.12 rely on Σ being a set of definite clauses. Consider, for example, the following formulae.

$$\exists \, x \, P(x) \hspace{4cm} (11.1.13)$$

$$Q(A) \hspace{4cm} (11.1.14)$$

Let Δ be the conjunction of (11.1.13) and (11.1.14). Note that (11.1.13) is not a definite clause, and nor can it be equivalently rewritten as a definite clause. The only Herbrand model of Δ is {Q(A), P(A)}. So P(A) is satisfied in all Herbrand models of Δ. But P(A) is clearly not satisfied in all models of Δ.

This example illustrates the fundamental trade-off inherent in logic programming. By restricting ourselves to a subset of predicate calculus, we gain computational tractability (in the informal sense of the phrase) along with a degree of semantic clarity, but at the expense of expressive power. This loss of expressive power is made up for with a whole bag of representational tricks familiar to any logic programmer (see [Kowalski, 1979]). For this example, a Skolem constant can be introduced in place of the existential quantifier. Other representational difficulties are harder to deal with.

11.2 SLD-Resolution

The SLD-resolution rule of inference, which (suitably augmented) allows a set of definite clauses to be read as a program as well as a declarative representation, relies on the idea of *unification*, which is defined as follows.

Definition 11.2.1. A *substitution* is a finite set of the form $\{\upsilon_1/\tau_1, \ldots, \upsilon_n/\tau_n\}$, where each υ_i is a distinct variable and each τ_i is a term distinct from υ_i. □

Definition 11.2.2. If τ is a term and θ is a substitution, then $\tau\theta$ is the result of replacing every υ_i in τ where $\upsilon_i/\tau_i \in \theta$ with τ_i. Similarly, if ϕ is a finite conjunction of atoms then $\phi\theta$ is the result of replacing every υ_i in ϕ where $\upsilon_i/\tau_i \in \theta$ with τ_i. □

Definition 11.2.3. The substitution θ is a *unifier* for two atoms $\phi1$ and $\phi2$ if $\phi1\theta$ is identical to $\phi2\theta$. If such a unifier exists, then $\phi1$ and $\phi2$ are said to be *unifiable*. □

For example, the substitution $\{x/B, y/A\}$ is a unifier for the two atoms $P(x,A)$ and $P(B,y)$. It's also a unifier for the two atoms $P(x,A)$ and $P(y,y)$. On the other hand, the atoms $P(x,A)$ and $Q(y,B)$ are not unifiable.

Definition 11.2.4. A unifier $\theta1$ for two atoms $\phi1$ and $\phi2$ is a *most general unifier* for $\phi1$ and $\phi2$ if for every unifier $\theta2$ of $\phi1$ and $\phi2$ there exists a substitution $\theta3$ such that $\phi1\theta1\theta3$ is identical to $\phi1\theta2$. □

For example, the substitution $\{x/B, y/A\}$ is a unifier for the two atoms $P(x,A)$ and $P(y,y)$, but it's not a most general unifier. To see this, let $\theta1$ be $\{x/B, y/A\}$, and consider $\theta2$ be $\{y/A, x/y\}$. $\theta2$ is a unifier for the two atoms. We have $P(x,A)\theta1 = P(B,A)$ and $P(x,A)\theta2 = P(y,A)$. Clearly there's no substitution $\theta3$ such that $P(B,A)\theta3 = P(y,A)$. The substitution $\{y/A, x/y\}$, on the other hand, is a most general unifier.

An algorithm that computes a most general unifier for two given atoms is easily designed (see [Lloyd, 1987] for details). Such an algorithm is required if we want to automate the application of the SLD-resolution rule of inference, which is defined as follows.

Definition 11.2.5. A clause $\phi1$ is a *variant* of a clause $\phi2$ if there exist substitutions $\theta1$ and $\theta2$ such that $\phi1\theta1$ is identical to $\phi2$ and $\phi2\theta2$ is identical to $\phi1$. □

A variant of a clause is essentially the same clause with some of its variables renamed.

Definition 11.2.5. The goal clause

$$\leftarrow \phi_1\theta \wedge \ldots \wedge \phi_{k-1}\theta \wedge \psi_2\theta \wedge \ldots \wedge \psi_m\theta \wedge \phi_{k+1}\theta \wedge \ldots \wedge \phi_n\theta$$

is a *resolvent* of the goal clause $\leftarrow \phi_1 \wedge \phi_2 \wedge \ldots \wedge \phi_n$ with the definite clause $\psi_1 \leftarrow \psi_2 \wedge \psi_3 \wedge \ldots \wedge \psi_m$ using the substitution θ if θ is a most general unifier for ϕ_k and ψ_1.   □

Definition 11.2.6. Let Σ be the conjunction of a set of definite clauses, and let Γ_0 be a goal clause. An *SLD-refutation* of Γ_0 from Σ is a finite sequence of goal clauses Γ_0 to Γ_n and a sequence of substitutions θ_1 to θ_n, where Γ_n is the empty clause and each Γ_{i+1} is a resolvent of Γ_i with a variant of a clause in Σ using the substitution θ_{i+1}.   □

The task of showing that a formula of the form,

$$\phi_1 \wedge \phi_2 \wedge \ldots \wedge \phi_m$$

follows from Σ is now the search for an SLD-refutation of the goal clause,

$$\leftarrow \phi_1 \wedge \phi_2 \wedge \ldots \wedge \phi_m$$

from Σ.

For example, let Σ be the conjunction of the following definite clauses, which represent a certain perspective on the human condition.

$$\text{Unhappy}(x) \leftarrow \text{Mortal}(x) \wedge \text{Unenlightened}(x) \qquad \text{(HC1)}$$

$$\text{Mortal}(x) \leftarrow \text{Human}(x) \qquad \text{(HC2)}$$

$$\text{Human}(\text{Socrates}) \qquad \text{(HC3)}$$

$$\text{Unenlightened}(\text{Socrates}) \qquad \text{(HC4)}$$

Figure 11.1 depicts an SLD-refutation of the goal clause $\leftarrow \text{Unhappy}(\text{Socrates})$ from Σ, which also represents a proof of the formula Unhappy(Socrates). The empty clause is represented by a box. The selected atom in each goal clause is underlined.

This form of resolution is *linear* in the sense that each resolvent is obtained by resolving a definite clause with the last goal clause in the sequence. The underlined atom in each goal clause is the one that has been selected to resolve against.

In the example above, the original goal clause contains no variables. If the goal clause does contain variables, then an invaluable by-product of an SLD-refutation is the set of substitutions it generates.

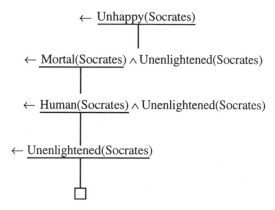

Figure 11.1: An SLD-Refutation

Definition 11.2.7. If $\theta 1 = \{\upsilon 1_1/\tau 1_1, \ldots, \upsilon 1_n/\tau 1_n\}$ and $\theta 2 = \{\upsilon 2_1/\tau 2_1, \ldots, \upsilon 2_m/\tau 2_m\}$ are substitutions, then the *composition* $\theta 1 \theta 2$ of $\theta 1$ and $\theta 2$ is the substitution $\theta 3 - \theta 4$, where $\theta 3$ is,

$$\{\upsilon 1_1/\tau 1_1 \theta 2, \ldots, \upsilon 1_n/\tau 1_n \theta 2\} \cup \theta 2$$

and $\theta 4$ is the set of all $\upsilon 1_i/\tau 1_i \theta 2$ such that $\upsilon 1_i = \tau 1_i \theta 2$ and all $\upsilon 2_j/\tau 2_j$ such that $\upsilon 2_j \in \{\upsilon 1_1, \ldots, \upsilon 1_n\}$. $\qquad\square$

Definition 11.2.8. Let Σ be the conjunction of a set of definite clauses, and let Γ be a goal clause. The set of all υ/τ such that υ is mentioned in Γ and $\upsilon/\tau \in \theta_1 \ldots \theta_n$, where θ_1 to θ_n is the sequence of substitutions in an SLD-refutation of Γ from Σ, is an *answer substitution* for Γ from Σ. $\qquad\square$

Figure 11.2 depicts another SLD-refutation from the definite clauses (HC1) to (HC4). This time, the original goal clause contains a variable. The answer substitution generated is {x/Socrates}. For readability, a different syntax for substitutions is used in figures.

The following soundness and completeness results for SLD-resolution underpin its utility. For proofs I appeal to Lloyd [1987]. Both results, in the form in which they appear here, mentioning answer substitutions, are due to Clark [1979].

Let Σ be the conjunction of a set of definite clauses. Let $\Gamma = \leftarrow \phi_1 \wedge \ldots \wedge \phi_n$ be a goal clause.

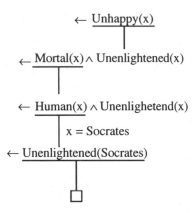

Figure 11.2: Another SLD-Refutation

Theorem 11.2.9. (Soundness of SLD-resolution) If there exists an SLD-refutation for Γ from Σ with answer substitution θ then,

$$\Sigma \models \phi_1\theta \wedge \phi_2\theta \wedge \ldots \wedge \phi_n\theta.$$

Proof. See [Lloyd, 1987, p. 43].   □

Theorem 11.2.10. (Completeness of SLD-resolution) If

$$\Sigma \models \phi_1\theta1 \wedge \phi_2\theta1 \wedge \ldots \wedge \phi_n\theta1$$

where $\theta1$ is a substitution, then there exists a substitution $\theta2$ and an SLD-refutation for Γ from Σ with answer substitution $\theta3$ such that $\phi_i\theta1 = \phi_i\theta3\theta2$ for each ϕ_i.

Proof. See [Lloyd, 1987, pp. 47–49].   □

Notice that Theorems 11.2.9 and 11.2.10 are not exact converses. Theorem 11.2.10 takes the form it has because an SLD-refutation always generates the most general answer substitution possible. In other words, it doesn't instantiate a variable unless it has to.

11.3   A Logic Programming System

Theorems 11.2.9 and 11.2.10 allow us to concentrate on a very narrow class of proofs when we're dealing exclusively with definite clauses. We know we can confine our attention to SLD-refutations, but we still don't know how to find such an SLD-refutation for a given goal clause from a given set of definite clauses. In particular, when attempting to construct an SLD-refutation, we're confronted with two choices at each resolution step.

- Which atom in a goal clause should be selected to resolve against?

- Which definite clause should be chosen to resolve with?

Before we have a fully automated theorem proving system, and before we're entitled to give definite clauses a dual reading as both declarative representations and programs, we have to automate these choices. First, let's consider the question of which atom in a goal clause to select for resolution.

Definition 11.3.1. A *selection function* is a function from a conjunction of atoms to one of the atoms in the conjunction (the *selected* atom). □

Let Σ be the conjunction of a set of definite clauses. Let $\Gamma = \leftarrow \phi_1 \wedge \ldots \wedge \phi_n$ be a goal clause.

Theorem 11.3.2. For any selection function F, if

$$\Sigma \vDash \phi_1\theta1 \wedge \phi_2\theta1 \wedge \ldots \wedge \phi_n\theta1$$

where $\theta1$ is a substitution, then there exists a substitution $\theta2$ and an SLD-refutation for Γ from Σ using the selection function F with answer substitution $\theta3$ such that $\phi_i\theta1 = \phi_i\theta3\theta2$ for each ϕ_i.

Proof. See [Lloyd, 1987, pp. 49–52]. □

Theorem 11.3.2 means that we can adopt any selection function we want in our attempt to fully automate SLD-resolution. We could even select atoms to resolve with at random. However, some sort of orderly regime for selecting atoms is desirable. An obvious possibility is always to select the leftmost or the rightmost atom.

Finally, we come to the issue of choosing the definite clause in Σ to resolve against. From the perspective of an omniscient God, this choice would always be clear. Given the goal clause Γ, an omniscient God can always choose a clause that He knows will lead ultimately to a refutation of Γ. For God, constructing a refutation for Γ doesn't involve any search.

A computer, on the other hand, has to search for a refutation. There's no way to know, in advance, whether the choice to resolve against a particular definite clause will lead ultimately to the derivation of the empty clause, or whether it will lead to the derivation of a goal clause containing an atom that is not unifiable with the head of any definite clause in Σ. Accordingly, the complete automation of SLD-resolution requires a *search strategy* as well as a selection function.

The programming language PROLOG [Colmerauer, *et al.*, 1973] augments SLD-resolution in the following three ways to yield a fully automated SLD-resolution theorem proving system.

* The *leftmost* atom in a goal clause is always chosen to resolve against.

* Definite clauses are tried in *top-to-bottom* (left to right) order, and a *depth-first* search strategy is employed.

* For efficiency reasons, the unification algorithm omits the *occurs check*. This means that it permits the unification of terms such as $f(x,x)$ and $f(y,g(y))$. Such terms are not strictly unifiable according to the definition, as they yield substitutions involving infinite terms.

Roughly speaking, the depth-first search strategy is implemented in the following way. When a goal clause is derived whose leftmost atom cannot be unified with an untried definite clause in Σ, the system backtracks to the most recent choice point, and tries the next definite clause down in Σ. The details don't concern us here.

Let's return to the example of Socrates' predicament. The example is augmented slightly to include the Buddha who, though human, is enlightened.

$$\text{Unhappy}(x) \leftarrow \text{Mortal}(x) \wedge \text{Unenlightened}(x) \qquad \text{(HCB1)}$$

$$\text{Mortal}(x) \leftarrow \text{Human}(x) \qquad \text{(HCB2)}$$

$$\text{Human(Buddha)} \qquad \text{(HCB3)}$$

$$\text{Human(Socrates)} \qquad \text{(HCB4)}$$

$$\text{Unenlightened(Socrates)} \qquad \text{(HCB5)}$$

Let Σ be the conjunction of (HCB1) to (HCB5), and let Γ be the goal clause,

$$\leftarrow \text{Unhappy}(x).$$

The task of finding an SLD-refutation for Γ from Σ using a "leftmost-first" selection function demands a search. The *search space* for this task is depicted as a tree in Figure 11.3. Unsuccessful partial refutations are terminated with the word "FAIL".

PROLOG's search strategy would be to visit the nodes of this tree in depth-first order. A depth-first search strategy is efficient in terms of both time and space. But a theorem prover that employs a depth-first strategy isn't guaranteed to find an SLD-refutation for a given goal even if one exists, because it can get lost in an infinite branch of the search space. A breadth-first search, on the other hand, is guaranteed to find an SLD-refutation if one exists.

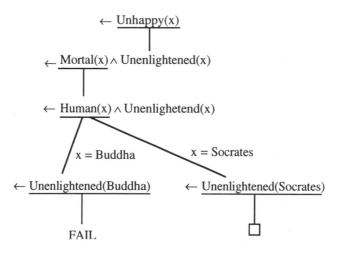

Figure 11.3: A Search Space

There is, of course, no SLD-refutation for the goal clause ← Unhappy(Buddha) from Σ. Does this mean that we can conclude that the Buddha is happy? We don't have Σ ⊨ ¬ Unhappy(Buddha). But recall that the meaning of a logic program is often taken to be its least Herbrand model. And we do have M ⊩ ¬ Unhappy(Buddha), where M is the least Herbrand model of Σ. Theorem 11.2.9 only guarantees the soundness of SLD-resolution with respect to conjunctions of atoms. Here's an example of a formula that the theorem is neutral about, and we find that classical model semantics and Herbrand model semantics disagree about it.

This disagreement stems from the fact that Herbrand model semantics embodies a *closed world assumption* [Reiter, 1978]. The whole issue of the representation of negative information, and the adoption of such assumptions, is extremely important, and will be discussed at length in the context of negation-as-failure. Negation-as-failure, being a form of default reasoning, is the main reason for embarking on a discussion of logic programming in the first place. Without it, logic programs would only be of limited interest in addressing the frame problem.

All the components of a *logic programming system* have now been described. A set of definite clauses Σ can now be interpreted as a program [Kowalski, 1974].

- The program is *invoked* by submitting a goal clause Γ to the system.

- Program *execution* is the process of finding an SLD-refutation for Γ from Σ using a leftmost-first selection function and a depth first search strategy.

- Each definite clause $\phi \leftarrow \phi_1 \wedge \ldots \wedge \phi_n$ in Σ is interpreted as a *procedure* whose body is the *sequence* of *procedure calls* $\phi_1; \ldots; \phi_n$.

  Traditional programming constructs are straightforwardly duplicated.

- A *conditional statement* can be represented via many definite clauses for the same predicate.

- A *loop* can be represented as a recursive procedure.

- A *data structure* can be represented as a term.

For example, the following logic program appends two lists together. It illustrates all three of the above features. The term Nil denotes the empty list, and the term Cons(x,l) denotes the list whose head is x and whose tail is l.

$$\text{Append(Nil,l,l)}$$

$$\text{Append(Cons(x,l1),l2,Cons(x,l3))} \leftarrow \text{Append(l1,l2,l3)}$$

This logic program corresponds, more or less, to the following algorithm, in which the functions Head and Tail have their usual meanings as list decomposition operators.

Procedure Append(l1,l2,l3)
    If l1 = Nil
    Then l3 := l2
    Else
        l4 := Append(Tail(l1),l2)
        l3 := Cons(Head(l1,l4))
    End If
End Append

If we invoke the logic program with the goal clause,

$$\leftarrow \text{Append(Cons(A,Cons(B,Nil)),Cons(C,Nil),l)}$$

then the theorem prover performs the computation shown in Figure 11.4, which yields an answer substitution that simplifies to l = Cons(A,Cons(B,Cons(C,Nil))).

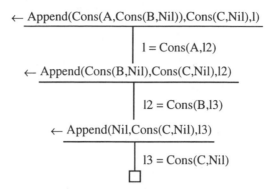

Figure 11.4: Executing the Append Program

With the setting up of a correspondence between definite clauses and computation, it becomes a straightforward matter to establish that every computable function can be computed by a set of definite clauses using SLD-resolution (see [Lloyd, 1987, pp. 52–55]). A related consequence of this correspondence is the following *semi-decidability* result. Given the conjunction of a set of definite clauses Σ and a conjunction of atoms ϕ, there is no algorithm that can determine in finite time whether an SLD-refutation of $\leftarrow \phi$ from Σ exists. On the other hand, there are algorithms that are guaranteed to find an SLD-refutation of $\leftarrow \phi$ from Σ in finite time if such a refutation does exist. An algorithm that conducts a breadth-first search of the search space generated by a leftmost-first selection function, choosing definite clauses in top-to-bottom order, is an example.

There are many introductory texts on PROLOG programming, such as [Clocksin & Mellish, 1987], and there's a wealth of literature on logic programming techniques, many of which were first discussed at length in Bob Kowalski's classic text, *Logic for Problem Solving* [1979]. Kowalski's book also incorporates a whole chapter on planning with the situation calculus. Curiously, although his treatment of the topic draws on negation-as-failure, the technique is not used to address the frame problem. As I've already mentioned, negation-as-failure is what makes logic programming really interesting from the point of view of solving the frame problem. But before presenting negation-as-failure and its application to reasoning about action, I want to examine the question of how far we can get in representing the effects of actions in logic programming without it.

11.4   Logic Programming and the Situation Calculus

Many of logic programming's ideas were anticipated in a seminal paper by Green [1969]. Furthermore, Green's paper applied these ideas specifically to the problem of reasoning about action using the situation calculus. By focusing on the definite clause subset of predicate calculus, Green was able to represent the effects of action using the situation calculus, and then to apply resolution-based theorem proving techniques to automatically generate plans.[3]

Unfortunately, as Green acknowledged, his work suffered from a serious drawback, namely the frame problem. With only the logic programming technology described so far in this chapter, we're in much the same position as Green in 1969. A more satisfactory treatment of the frame problem from a logic programming point of view awaits the development of negation-as-failure, which I'll be describing in the next section. But as a preliminary step towards the application of logic programming techniques to reasoning about action, we can adopt the approach Green was forced to adopt, and write explicit frame axioms.

Let's return to the Blocks World example from Chapter 1. Unlike Green but like Kowalski [1979, Chapter 6], I'll use a reified form of the situation calculus, employing the Holds predicate in the usual way. The two fluents are On(x,y) representing that block x is on location y, and Clear(x), which represents that location x doesn't have anything on it. The following definite clauses represent the initial situation S0, which is depicted in Figure 11.5. This figure also depicts the situation that's expected to result from moving A onto D.

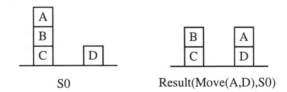

SO   Result(Move(A,D),S0)

Figure 11.5: Two Blocks World Situations

Holds(On(C,Table),S0)	(BW1)
Holds(On(B,C),S0)	(BW2)
Holds(On(A,B),S0)	(BW3)
Holds(On(D,Table),S0)	(BW4)
Holds(Clear(A),S0)	(BW5)

$$\text{Holds(Clear(D),S0)} \qquad \text{(BW6)}$$

$$\text{Holds(Clear(Table),S0)} \qquad \text{(BW7)}$$

The following two definite clauses capture the effects of the action Move(x,y).

$$\text{Holds(On(x,y),Result(Move(x,y),s))} \leftarrow \text{Holds(Clear(x),s)} \wedge \qquad \text{(BW8)}$$
$$\text{Holds(Clear(y),s)} \wedge \text{Diff(x,y)} \wedge \text{Diff(x,Table)}$$

$$\text{Holds(Clear(z),Result(Move(x,y),s))} \leftarrow \text{Holds(Clear(x),s)} \wedge \qquad \text{(BW9)}$$
$$\text{Holds(Clear(y),s)} \wedge \text{Holds(On(x,z),s)} \wedge \text{Diff(x,z)} \wedge \text{Diff(x,y)}$$

The formula Diff(x,y) represents that x and y are not equal. Unfortunately, we're obliged to write out each Diff fact as a separate definite clause. With five objects (A, B, C, D, and Table), twenty clauses are required. Here's a selection of four of them.

$$\text{Diff(A,B)}$$

$$\text{Diff(A,C)}$$

$$\text{Diff(D,Table)}$$

$$\text{Diff(Table,C)}$$

This isn't necessary in any real logic programming system, of course, in which a suitable inequality predicate will be built-in, and these clauses will be implicit.

Finally, we need some frame axioms. It's assumed that, if an action's precondition fails, then it has no effect. The first group is for the fluent On.

$$\text{Holds(On(x1,y1),Result(Move(x2,y2),s))} \leftarrow \qquad \text{(BW10)}$$
$$\text{Holds(On(x1,y1),s)} \wedge \text{Diff(x1,x2)}$$

$$\text{Holds(On(x1,y),Result(Move(x1,z),s))} \leftarrow \qquad \text{(BW11)}$$
$$\text{Holds(On(x1,y),s)} \wedge \text{Holds(On(x2,z),s)}$$

$$\text{Holds(On(x1,y),Result(Move(x1,z),s))} \leftarrow \qquad \text{(BW12)}$$
$$\text{Holds(On(x1,y),s)} \wedge \text{Holds(On(x2,x1),s)}$$

A second group is needed for the fluent Clear.

$$\text{Holds(Clear(x),Result(Move(y,z),s))} \leftarrow \qquad \text{(BW13)}$$
$$\text{Holds(Clear(x),s)} \wedge \text{Diff(x,z)}$$

$$\text{Holds(Clear(x),Result(Move(y,x),s))} \leftarrow \qquad \text{(BW14)}$$
$$\text{Holds(Clear(x),s)} \wedge \text{Holds(On(z,y),s)}$$

Figure 11.6 shows the search space for the goal clause,

$$\leftarrow \text{Holds(On(x,y),Result(Move(A,D),S0))}.$$

given the above logic program.

Two failing branches on the right-hand-side of the tree are not shown in full. Four SLD-refutations are found, with the answer substitutions $\{x/A, y/D\}$, $\{x/C, y/Table\}$, $\{x/B, y/C\}$, and $\{x/D, y/Table\}$. This exactly captures the scene depicted in the right-hand-side of Figure 11.5, which is what we require.

The same logic program can be used to find plans. To find a plan to get from the initial situation S0 to a desired situation in which fluents β_1 to β_n hold, we present the goal clause,

$$\leftarrow \text{Holds}(\beta_1,s) \wedge \text{Holds}(\beta_2,s) \wedge \ldots \wedge \text{Holds}(\beta_n,s).$$

Answer substitutions will have the form,

$$\{s/\text{Result}(\alpha_1 \ldots \text{Result}(\alpha_m,S0) \ldots)\}.$$

The sequence of actions α_m to α_1 is a plan to achieve the desired goal.

11.5 Negation as Failure

The Blocks World in the last section is trivial. It comprises just two fluents and one action. Accordingly, the number of frame axioms we had to write was manageable. This would not be the case if we were trying to represent a non-trivial domain, a significant fragment of naive physics, for example. With logic programming, as with full first-order predicate calculus, we need a solution to the frame problem, preferably a formalisation of the common sense law of inertia using some form of default reasoning.

Remarkably, logic programming systems were built that incorporated a simple, but surprisingly flexible, form of default reasoning as long ago as the early Seventies. The form of default reasoning in question is the *negation-as-failure* rule, which is due to Keith Clark [1978].[4] The basic idea is very straightforward. The negation-as-failure rule says that the negation of an atom ϕ can be inferred if no SLD-refutation of $\leftarrow \phi$ can be found. (A similar rule was employed in the MICROPLANNER system [Sussman & Winograd, 1970].) This rule paves the way for going beyond the expressiveness of definite clauses, and admitting clauses whose bodies include negated atoms. SLD-resolution can be correspondingly extended to incorporate the negation-as-failure rule, and the result is known as *SLDNF-resolution*.

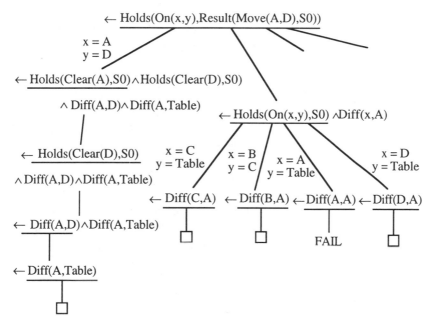

Figure 11.6: A Situation Calculus Search Space

The ramifications of this deceptively simple manoeuvre are considerable. While negation-as-failure is procedurally innocuous, semantically speaking it's a pit of snakes. A large class of formulae can be given a perfectly adequate semantics via their *completion* [Clark, 1978], which will be presented shortly. But enough cases are not dealt with satisfactorily by the semantics of completion for a large number of papers to have been written suggesting alternative semantics for negation-as-failure. Some of these will be reviewed in due course.

To begin with, it's helpful to define formally the kind of tree that constitutes the search space of SLD-refutations for a goal clause. Let Γ_0 be a goal clause and let Σ be the conjunction of a set of definite clauses.

Definition 11.5.1. An *SLD-tree* for Γ_0 from Σ using selection function F is a tree, each of whose nodes is a goal clause, defined as follows.

- The root node of the tree is Γ_0.

- If Γ is a node in the tree then, for each definite clause φ in Σ whose head unifies with F(Γ), that node has a child that is a resolvent of Γ with a variant of φ.   □

Consider the following example, which represents a very different perspective on the human condition from the example involving Socrates and the Buddha.

$$\text{Happy(x)} \leftarrow \text{Rich(x)} \wedge \text{Famous(x)}$$

$$\text{Rich(John)}$$

$$\text{Rich(Mary)}$$

$$\text{Famous(Fred)}$$

Let Σ be the conjunction of these clauses. Figure 11.7 depicts the SLD-tree for the goal ← Happy(x) from Σ using the usual leftmost-first selection function.

The tree in Figure 11.7 is known as a *finitely failed* SLD-tree, because each leaf in the tree is a non-empty goal. Given the completeness of SLD-resolution (Theorem 11.2.10), the existence of this tree tells us that $\Sigma \not\models \exists \, x \, \text{Happy(x)}$. This does not, of course, license the conclusion that $\Sigma \models \neg \, \exists \, x \, \text{Happy(x)}$. However, the negation-as-failure rule does license this conclusion. Negation-as-failure permits conclusions to be drawn that are not logical consequences according to classical predicate calculus semantics.

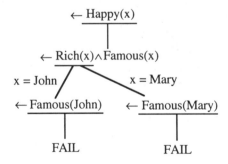

Figure 11.7: A Finitely Failed SLD-Tree

However, it's interesting to note that $\neg \, \exists \, x \, \text{Happy(x)}$ is satisfied by the least Herbrand model of Σ. As pointed out previously, the least Herbrand model of a logic program is commonly regarded as its intended meaning. Drawing a negative conclusion like this can be justified by appealing to the *closed world assumption* (CWA) [Reiter, 1978]. According to the CWA, if φ is not a logical consequence of a theory, we can conclude $\neg\, \phi$ from that theory. The CWA presupposes that all the information required to draw positive conclusions is present in a theory. In the context of clauses with negations in their bodies, the CWA allows us to draw contradictory conclusions, but the negation-as-failure rule can be thought of as extending the CWA to cater for such clauses.

The definition of SLDNF-resolution, which combines SLD-resolution with the negation-as-failure rule, is based on finitely failed trees like the one in Figure 11.7. But in Figure 11.7, only definite clauses were featured. Negation-as-failure derives its real usefulness from the fact that it allows negated atoms in the bodies of clauses. This complicates the required definition of a finitely failed tree, as we'll see shortly.

Because negation-as-failure is so different from classical negation, it seems inappropriate to represent it with the symbol "$\neg$", so in what follows I'll use "not" instead. The generalised definitions of a definite clause and a goal clause are as follows.

Definition 11.5.2. A *literal* has the form ϕ or not ϕ, where ϕ is an atom. If it has the form ϕ, then it's called a *positive* literal, and if it has the form not ϕ, then it's called a negative literal. $\qquad\square$

Definition 11.5.3. A *general clause* has the form,

$$\phi_1 \leftarrow \phi_2 \wedge \phi_3 \wedge \ldots \wedge \phi_n$$

where ϕ_1 is an atom and each ϕ_i such that $i > 1$ is a literal. $\qquad\square$

The following conventions are inherited from definite clauses. If $n = 1$, then the "$\leftarrow$" is omitted when a general clause is written. The atom ϕ_1 is the clause's *head*, and the conjunction $\phi_2 \wedge \phi_3 \wedge \ldots \wedge \phi_n$ is the clause's *body*. If ϕ_1 is $\rho(\tau_1, \ldots, \tau_m)$, then the clause is said to be a clause *for* the predicate symbol ρ.

Definition 11.5.4. A *general goal* has the form,

$$\leftarrow \phi_1 \wedge \phi_2 \wedge \ldots \wedge \phi_n$$

where each ϕ_i is a literal. $\qquad\square$

I've been using the term "logic program" loosely up to now to denote a collection of definite clauses. Now I'll pin the term down precisely.

Definition 11.5.5. A *logic program* is the conjunction of a finite set of general clauses. $\qquad\square$

All definite clauses are general clauses. The following is an example of a general clause that is not a definite clause.

$$\text{Unhappy}(x) \leftarrow \text{Mortal}(x) \wedge \text{not Enlightened}(x)$$

Several definitions that previously applied to definite clauses and goal clauses are now extended in obvious ways to encompass general clauses and general goals.

Definition 11.5.6. If ϕ is a finite conjunction of literals and θ is a substitution, then $\phi\theta$ is the result of replacing every υ_i in ϕ where $\upsilon_i/\tau_i \in \theta$ with τ_i. $\qquad\square$

Definition 11.5.7. A general clause $\phi 1$ is a *variant* of a general clause $\phi 2$ if there exist substitutions $\theta 1$ and $\theta 2$ such that $\phi 1\theta 1$ is identical to $\phi 2$ and $\phi 2\theta 2$ is identical to $\phi 1$. $\qquad\square$

Definition 11.5.8. A *selection function* is a function from a conjunction of literals to one of the literals in the conjunction (the *selected* literal). $\qquad\square$

Definition 11.5.9. The general goal

$$\leftarrow \phi_1\theta \wedge \ldots \wedge \phi_{k-1}\theta \wedge \psi_2\theta \wedge \ldots \wedge \psi_m\theta \wedge \phi_{k+1}\theta \wedge \ldots \wedge \phi_n\theta$$

is a *resolvent* of the general goal $\leftarrow \phi_1 \wedge \phi_2 \wedge \ldots \wedge \phi_n$ with the general clause $\psi_1 \leftarrow \psi_2 \wedge \psi_3 \wedge \ldots \wedge \psi_m$ using the substitution θ if θ is a most general unifier for ϕ_k and ψ_1. $\qquad\square$

A finitely failed SLDNF-tree is defined recursively as follows. Let Γ_0 be a general goal and let Σ be a logic program.

Definition 11.5.10. A *finitely failed SLDNF-tree* for Γ_0 from Σ using selection function F is a finite tree, each of whose nodes is a general goal, defined as follows.

- The root node of the tree is Γ_0.

- No node in the tree is the empty clause.

- If Γ is a node in the tree and $F(\Gamma)$ is positive then, for each clause ϕ in Σ whose head unifies with $F(\Gamma)$, that node has a child that is a resolvent of Γ with a variant of ϕ.

- If $\Gamma = \phi_1 \wedge \ldots \wedge \phi_n$ is a node in the tree and $F(\Gamma) = $ not ϕ_k contains no variables then,

- If there exists a finitely failed SLDNF-tree for ϕ_k from Σ using selection function F, then that node has the child

$$\phi_1 \wedge \cdots \phi_{k-1} \wedge \phi_{k+1} \wedge \cdots \wedge \phi_n$$

- Otherwise the node has no children. □

Notice that the definition only applies to selection functions that select literals containing no variables. Selection functions that are guaranteed to do this are known as *safe*. Clearly every finitely failed SLD-tree is a finitely failed SLDNF-tree. But the latter takes account of the possibility of general goals that include negated atoms. Now we can define the SLDNF counterpart of an SLD-refutation.

Definition 11.5.11. An *SLDNF-refutation* for Γ_0 from Σ using selection function F is a finite sequence of general goals Γ_0 to Γ_n and a sequence of substitutions θ_1 to θ_n, where Γ_n is the empty clause and each Γ_{i+1} is obtained from Γ_i in the following way.

- If $F(\Gamma_i)$ is positive then Γ_{i+1} is a resolvent of Γ_i with a variant of a clause in Σ using the substitution θ_{i+1}.

- If $F(\Gamma_i)$ is negative then there exists a finitely failed SLDNF-tree for Γ_i from Σ using selection function F, and θ_{i+1} is the empty set. □

As an example, consider the following modified version of the Socrates example from Section 11.3.

$$\text{Unhappy}(x) \leftarrow \text{Mortal}(x) \wedge \text{not Enlightened}(x) \qquad \text{(HCN1)}$$

$$\text{Mortal}(x) \leftarrow \text{Human}(x) \qquad \text{(HCN2)}$$

$$\text{Human}(\text{Buddha}) \qquad \text{(HCN3)}$$

$$\text{Human}(\text{Socrates}) \qquad \text{(HCN4)}$$

$$\text{Enlightened}(\text{Buddha}) \qquad \text{(HCN5)}$$

Clause (HCB1) has been replaced by (HCN1) in which, instead of Unenlightened(x), we write not Enlightened(x). Let Σ be the conjunction of (HCN1) to (HCN5). Figure 11.8 shows the search space for SLDNF-refutations for the general goal $\leftarrow$ Unhappy(x) from Σ using a leftmost first selection function. This is the search space that would be explored, in a depth-first fashion, by PROLOG, which incorporates negation-as-failure. The search for a finitely failed SLDNF-tree that results when a negative literal is encountered is depicted as an encapsulated search space just below the literal.

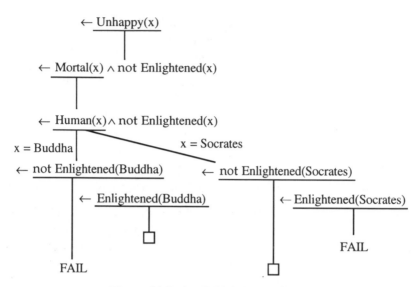

Figure 11.8: An SLDNF Search Space

The definition of an answer substitution is modified in the obvious way.

Definition 11.5.12. Let Σ be the conjunction of a set of general clauses, and let Γ be a general goal. The set of all υ/τ such that υ is mentioned in Γ and $\upsilon/\tau \in \theta_1 \ldots$. θ_n, where θ_1 to θ_n is the sequence of substitutions in an SLDNF-refutation of Γ from Σ, is an *answer substitution* for Γ from Σ.   □

As can be seen from Figure 11.8, there is an SLDNF-refutation for the goal ← Unhappy(x), which yields the answer substitution {x/Socrates}. It should be clear from the tree that if we were to add Enlightened(Socrates) to Σ, there would be no such SLDNF-refutation. In this sense, negation-as-failure is non-monotonic, and provides a form of default reasoning.

But what does the existence of an SLDNF-refutation really mean? Intuitively, by adopting the negation-as-failure rule, we are admitting Unhappy(Socrates) as a logical consequence of Σ. But if we let Σ' be the result of replacing the not symbol in Σ by "¬", then we have $\Sigma' \not\models$ Unhappy(Socrates). What then is the meaning of Σ if Unhappy(Socrates) is supposed to follow from it? This is the question addressed in the next section.

11.6   The Semantics of Negation-as-Failure

Inferences permitted by the CWA are justified by the assumption that a theory includes all the information that's required to draw positive conclusions.

Accordingly, if the positive conclusion ϕ cannot be drawn from a theory, the CWA licenses the conclusion $\neg\,\phi$. As already mentioned, the negation-as-failure rule can be thought of as extending the CWA, and is based on a similar assumption. According to this assumption, if I write,

$$P(x) \leftarrow Q(x) \wedge R(x)$$

and I don't write any further clauses for P, then it's assumed that this clause says everything that needs to be said about P. In other words, it's implicit that,

$$P(x) \rightarrow Q(x) \wedge R(x).$$

Similarly, if I write,

$$Q(A)$$

$$Q(B)$$

and I don't write any more clauses for Q, then it's implicit that,

$$Q(x) \rightarrow [x = A \vee x = B].$$

The result of augmenting a collection Σ of clauses with these implicit only-if formulae is known as the *completion* of Σ [Clark, 1978]. Through the completion, we can attempt to provide a model-theoretic characterisation of a logic program that matches the proof-theoretic (and computational) characterisation supplied by SLDNF-resolution. Here's the formal definition. Let Σ be a logic program.

Definition 11.6.1. Suppose there are k general clauses in Σ for the n-ary predicate symbol ρ. If $k > 0$, the *predicate completion* of ρ in Σ is the formula,

$$\rho(x_1, \ldots, x_n) \leftrightarrow \Pi_1 \vee \ldots \vee \Pi_k$$

where each Π_i has the form,

$$\exists\, y_1, \ldots, y_d\, [x_1 = \tau_1 \wedge \ldots \wedge x_n = \tau_n \wedge \psi_1 \wedge \ldots \wedge \psi_m]$$

where the ith general clause in Σ for ρ is of the form,

$$\rho(\tau_1, \ldots, \tau_n) \leftarrow \phi_1 \wedge \ldots \wedge \phi_m$$

such that ψ_k is ϕ_k with any occurrences of not replaced by "$\neg$", and y_1 to y_d are the variables mentioned in this clause.

If $k = 0$, the *predicate completion* of ρ in Σ is the formula,

$$\neg\,\rho(x_1, \ldots, x_n) \qquad\qquad \square$$

Definition 11.6.2. The *completion* of Σ, denoted COMP[Σ], is the conjunction of the predicate completions of all predicate symbols mentioned in Σ with the following uniqueness-of-names axiom.

$$\text{UNA}[\pi_1, \ldots, \pi_n]$$

where π_1 to π_n are all the function symbols and constants mentioned in Σ.   □

The definition of the completion of a predicate is syntactically sensitive in a way in which circumscription is not. Logically equivalent first-order theories have logically equivalent circumscriptions. The first-order predicate calculus theory,

$$P(x) \leftarrow \neg Q(x)$$

$$Q(A)$$

is logically equivalent to,

$$Q(x) \leftarrow \neg P(x)$$

$$Q(A).$$

So the circumscriptions of these two theories according to any given policy yields the same results. However, the completion of the logic program,

$$P(x) \leftarrow \text{not } Q(x)$$

$$Q(A)$$

is not equivalent to the completion of,

$$Q(x) \leftarrow \text{not } P(x)$$

$$Q(A).$$

However, the *products* of completion inherit their semantics from that of first-order predicate calculus with equality.[5] For example, let Σ be the set of general clauses (HCN1) to (HCN5) from the previous section. Then COMP[Σ] is the conjunction of the following formulae.

$$\text{Unhappy}(x_1) \leftrightarrow \exists x \, [x_1 = x \wedge \text{Mortal}(x) \wedge \neg \text{Enlightened}(x)]$$

$$\text{Mortal}(x_1) \leftrightarrow \exists x \, [x_1 = x \wedge \text{Human}(x)]$$

$$\text{Human}(x_1) \leftrightarrow [x_1 = \text{Socrates}] \vee [x_1 = \text{Buddha}]$$

$$\text{Enlightened}(x_1) \leftrightarrow x_1 = \text{Buddha}$$

UNA[Socrates, Buddha]

Its easy to see that COMP[Σ] $\models$ Unhappy(Socrates). Of course, if we now add Enlightened(Socrates) to Σ, this conclusion no longer follows. In other words, COMP[$\Sigma \wedge$ Enlightened(Socrates)] $\not\models$ Unhappy(Socrates).

For this example at least, the completion agrees with SLDNF-resolution. But how watertight is this correspondence? The soundness of SLDNF-resolution with respect to the completion isn't a problem, and was first proved by Clark [1978]. Let Σ be a logic program. Let $\Gamma = \leftarrow \phi_1 \wedge \ldots \wedge \phi_n$ be a general goal.

Theorem 11.6.3. (Soundness of SLDNF-resolution) If there exists an SLDNF-refutation for Γ from Σ with answer substitution θ then,

$$\text{COMP}[\Sigma] \models \psi_1\theta \wedge \psi_2\theta \wedge \ldots \wedge \psi_n\theta$$

where ψ_i is ϕ_i with any occurrences of not replaced by "$\neg$".

Proof. See [Clark, 1978].[6] $\square$

A satisfactory completeness result has turned out to be altogether more elusive. Completeness results for certain classes of logic programs have been obtained, but there are many problematic cases (see [Lloyd 1987, pp. 95–99]). One such class is the *hierarchical* logic programs.

Definition 11.6.4. A *level mapping* for the logic program Σ is a mapping from the set of predicate symbols mentioned in Σ to the natural numbers. The value yielded by this mapping is known as a predicate's *level*. $\square$

Definition 11.6.5. A logic program Σ is *hierarchical* if a level mapping for Σ exists such that for every general clause $\rho(\tau_1, \ldots, \tau_n) \leftarrow \Pi$ in Σ, the level of every predicate symbol mentioned in Π is less than the level of ρ. $\square$

Theorem 11.6.6. Let Σ be a hierarchical logic program. Let ϕ be a conjunction of atoms and negated atoms. Let θ be a substitution such that,

- For every variable υ in ϕ, there is a τ such that $\upsilon/\tau \in \theta$, and

- For all $\upsilon/\tau \in \theta$, τ is a ground term.

If $\Sigma \models \phi\theta$ then there exists an SLDNF-refutation for Γ from Σ with answer substitution θ.

Proof. See [Lloyd, 1987, pp. 99–100]. $\square$

The logic program comprising clauses (HC1) to (HC5) is hierarchical. Unfortunately though, the class of hierarchical logic programs excludes all logic programs with recursion, so the result is of limited utility.

The lack of a comprehensive completeness result isn't the only problem with completion semantics. Another difficulty is the fact that the completion of a logic program is often inconsistent.[7] A simple example of a logic program with an inconsistent completion is the following.

$$P(x) \leftarrow not\, P(x)$$

$$Q(A)$$

The second clause is included so that the Herbrand universe of the program is non-empty. The corresponding completion is the conjunction of the following formulae.

$$P(x_1) \leftrightarrow \exists\, x\, [x_1 = x \wedge \neg\, P(x)]$$

$$Q(x_1) \leftrightarrow x_1 = A$$

We only have to consider $P(A)$ to see that this is inconsistent.

Fortunately, it's possible to isolate large classes of useful logic programs that have consistent completions. One such class is that of *stratified* logic programs, which generalises that of hierarchical programs.

Definition 11.6.7. A logic program Σ is *stratified* if a level mapping for Σ exists such that for every general clause $\rho(\tau_1, \ldots, \tau_n) \leftarrow \Pi$ in Σ, the level of every predicate symbol mentioned in a positive literal in Π is less than or equal to the level of ρ, and the level of every predicate symbol mentioned in a negative literal in Π is strictly less than the level of ρ. ☐

Less formally, a stratified logic program is one that doesn't contain any recursion that goes through a negation. Thus, the following logic program, which is not hierarchical, *is* stratified.

$$P(x) \leftarrow P(x)$$

But the following one is not.

$$P(x) \leftarrow not\, P(x)$$

The following result is due to Apt, Blair and Walker [1987].

Theorem 11.6.8. Every stratified logic program has a consistent completion.

Proof. See [Apt, Blair & Walker, 1987]. ☐

The class of stratified logic programs is subsumed by the class of *call consistent* logic programs, which also have consistent completions [Kunen, 1989].

Definition 11.6.9. A *dependency graph* for a logic program Σ is a directed graph with signed edges that meets the following criteria.

- There is a node in the graph for each predicate symbol occurring in Σ,

- There is a positive (negative) edge from $\rho 1$ to $\rho 2$ if and only if Σ includes a general clause whose head mentions $\rho 1$ and whose body includes a positive (negative) literal mentioning $\rho 2$. $\qquad\square$

Definition 11.6.10. A logic program is *call consistent* if its dependency graph contains no cycles with an odd number of negative edges. $\qquad\square$

In other words, a call consistent program is one that doesn't contain any recursion that goes through an odd number of negations.

Theorem 11.6.11. Every call consistent logic program has a consistent completion.

Proof. See [Kunen, 1989]. $\qquad\square$

Although the class of call consistent programs covers a large proportion of the interesting logic programs, it still leaves a residue of pathological cases, whose completions are in *terra incognito*. This includes many potentially useful and interesting logic programs, whose completions have to be shown to be consistent individually.

For example, the following non-stratified logic program is a possible representation of the Nixon diamond [Reiter & Criscuolo, 1981]. This problem involves two defaults: typically Quakers are pacifists, and typically republicans are not pacifists. These defaults come into conflict when we consider Nixon, who is both a Quaker and a republican.

$$\text{Dove}(x) \leftarrow \text{Quaker}(x) \wedge \text{not Hawk}(x)$$

$$\text{Hawk}(x) \leftarrow \text{Republican}(x) \wedge \text{not Dove}(x)$$

$$\text{Quaker(Nixon)}$$

$$\text{Republican(Nixon)}$$

There is no SLDNF-refutation either for Dove(Nixon) or for not Dove(Nixon). However, if we add Quaker(John) to this logic program, then SLDNF-resolution licenses the conclusions not Hawk(John) and Dove(John).

The drawbacks of completion semantics have led numerous researchers to formulate alternative semantics for negation-as-failure. A comprehensive survey of these is given in [Apt & Bol, 1994]. A review of approaches based on abduction is given in [Kakas, Kowalski & Toni, 1993]. For present purposes, however, the completion semantics is adequate.

There is a close relationship between circumscription and completion, as shown by Reiter [1982] and Lifschitz [1985], and discussed in [Lifschitz, 1994]. Lifschitz's results will be presented in a later chapter.

Notes

1. It should be emphasised that the *idea* of logic programming isn't tied to Horn clauses. But Horn clauses are by far the best-known examples of objects which can be given this dual reading.
2. In fact, SLD-resolution is not strictly speaking a form of SL resolution, since it is more liberal in the selection functions it allows.
3. Ray Reiter once remarked to me (in jest, I think) that there have only been five good ideas in the whole of AI. Green's application of theorem proving techniques to problem solving with the situation calculus was one of them. Unfortunately I've forgotten the other four.
4. A favourite joke in the logic programming community concerns the apocryphal science journalist who, reporting on work at Imperial College, wrote that "Kowalski described Clark's work on negation as failure".
5. Where I've elected to deal with equality semantically, in Clark's original formulation, a more complicated collection of equality axioms was provided.
6. Lloyd [1987] offers a proof of the same result based on a more "constructive" definition of an SLDNF-refutation.
7. Similarly, a consistent theory of first-order predicate calculus can have an inconsistent circumscription [Etherington, Mercer & Reiter, 1985]. With circumscription these pathological cases are easy to avoid.

12 Logic Programs for Reasoning about Action

Logic programs can be used to represent the effects of actions in various ways. One approach, which was sketched in the last chapter, is to import the ontology of the situation calculus, and to represent situation calculus effect axioms as logic program clauses. This approach is explored further in this chapter, using negation-as-failure as a means of overcoming the frame problem. This chapter also introduces an alternative to the situation calculus that was developed in the logic programming community, namely Kowalski and Sergot's event calculus [1986].

Unlike the situation calculus, the event calculus is a narrative-based formalism. But, as in the logic programming version of the Situation calculus, the event calculus uses negation-as-failure to address the frame problem. The event calculus presented in this chapter is Kowalski and Sergot's original version. In the next chapter, this will be simplified and extended, while staying within the context of logic programming. A circumscriptive version of the simplified and extended version follows in Chapters 14 and 15.

12.1 Negation-as-Failure and the Situation Calculus

We're now in a position to advance on the work of Green [1969] and Kowalski [1979, Chapter 6], and attempt to express the common sense law of inertia in logic programming terms, using negation-as-failure.[1] Let's re-examine the Blocks World problem studied in Section 11.4 of the last chapter. The initial situation is captured by the following general clauses from the last chapter.

$$Holds(On(C,Table),S0) \qquad (BW1)$$

$$Holds(On(B,C),S0) \qquad (BW2)$$

$$Holds(On(A,B),S0) \qquad (BW3)$$

$$Holds(On(D,Table),S0) \qquad (BW4)$$

$$Holds(Clear(A),S0) \qquad (BW5)$$

$$Holds(Clear(D),S0) \qquad (BW6)$$

$$Holds(Clear(Table),S0) \qquad (BW7)$$

The two required effect axioms are also preserved.

$$Holds(On(x,y),Result(Move(x,y),s)) \leftarrow Holds(Clear(x),s) \land \qquad (BW8)$$
$$Holds(Clear(y),s) \land Diff(x,y) \land Diff(x,Table)$$

Holds(Clear(z),Result(Move(x,y),s)) ← Holds(Clear(x),s) ∧   (BW9)
Holds(Clear(y),s) ∧ Holds(On(x,z),s) ∧ Diff(x,z) ∧ Diff(x,y)

In the last chapter, the extension of the predicate Diff had to be enumerated explicitly. Using negation-as-failure, this isn't necessary. Instead, we simply write,

Diff(x,y) ← not Eq(x,y)

Eq(x,x).

But the most interesting use of negation-as-failure is to replace the explicit frame axioms (BN10) and (BN11) used in the last chapter by a formulation of the common sense law of inertia. We do this by writing the following universal frame axiom.

Holds(f,Result(a,s)) ← Holds(f,s) ∧ not Affects(a,f,s)   (F4)

The use of negation-as-failure in the body of this clause has the effect of making it a default. There are important differences between this and the universal frame axiom (F2) familiar from our study of circumscriptive approaches. One such difference is that we need to present explicit clauses for the Affects predicate, while the corresponding Ab predicate in (F2) requires no further axioms defining it. In particular, for this example we require,

Affects(Move(x,y),On(x,z),s) ← Holds(Clear(x),s) ∧   (BWN1)
Holds(Clear(y),s) ∧ Diff(x,y) ∧ Diff(x,Table)

Affects(Move(x,y),Clear(z),s) ← Holds(Clear(x),s) ∧   (BWN2)
Holds(Clear(y),s) ∧ Holds(On(x,z),s) ∧ Diff(x,z) ∧ Diff(x,y).

At first glance, it may seem as if the adoption of a universal frame axiom with negation-as-failure hasn't got us very far. We need just as many clauses to represent this problem as before. But there are two main improvements. First, these Affects clauses can easily be generated mechanically from the effect axioms, since they have the same bodies. Second, and more importantly, we only require as many Affects axioms as there are effect axioms. This contrasts favourably with the (roughly) n × m frame axioms required for a domain with n fluents and m actions. This contrast isn't highlighted by the current example because of its simplicity.

Figure 12.1 shows part of the search space explored by this logic program for the general goal ← Holds(On(x,y),Result(Move(A,D),S0). In some places, several resolution steps have been collapsed into one.

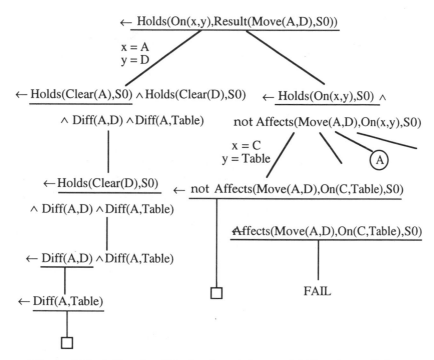

Figure 12.1: A Situation Calculus Search Space with Negation-as-Failure

There are four SLDNF-refutations contained in the tree, with the answer substitutions we would expect, namely {x/A, y/D}, {x/C, y/Table}, {x/B, y/C}, {x/D, y/Table}. The SLDNF-refutations yielding the first and second of these answer substitutions are shown in detail. The failing branch of the tree indicated by the letter A is expanded in Figure 12.2.

Comparing Figures 12.1 and 12.2 with Figure 11.6, it's apparent that there's a computational cost associated with the adoption of a universal frame axiom with negation-as-failure. This can be alleviated by the judicious use of a lemma storage technique to avoid the duplication of work. But a more pressing need in the context of this book is to evaluate this attempt at the frame problem from a logical and representational point of view.

12.2 Situation Calculus Semantic Issues

From Theorem 11.6.3 (the soundness of SLDNF-resolution), we know that the answer substitutions generated by the situation calculus logic program of the previous section are correct with respect to the completion of that logic program.

But it can easily be verified that the program is neither stratified nor call consistent, since Holds is expressed in terms of not Affects, which itself is expressed in terms of Holds. So the question arises of the consistency of its completion.

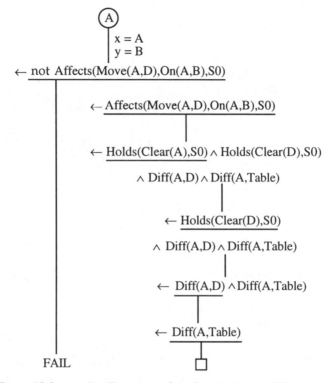

Figure 12.2: Another Fragment of the Search Space of Figure 12.1

In the light of the Hanks-McDermott problem, we should be especially wary of semantic difficulties, such as inconsistent completions. Indeed, it's natural to suspect that the Hanks-McDermott problem will arise in some form or another with the logic programming approach to reasoning about action. If it doesn't arise, it's equally natural to enquire how it's been avoided.

The completion of the Holds predicate in the conjunction of clauses (BW1) to (BW9) with (F4) is equivalent to,

$$\text{Holds}(f,S0) \leftrightarrow f = \text{On}(C,\text{Table}) \lor f = \text{On}(B,C) \lor f = \text{On}(A,B) \lor$$
$$f = \text{On}(D,\text{Table}) \lor f = \text{Clear}(A) \lor f = \text{Clear}(D) \lor f = \text{Clear}(\text{Table})$$

Holds(f,Result(a,s)) ↔ [f = On(x,y) ∧ a = Move(x,y) ∧ Holds(Clear(x),s) ∧
Holds(Clear(y),s) ∧ Diff(x,y) ∧ Diff(x,Table)] ∨
[f = Clear(z) ∧ a = Move(x,y) ∧ Holds(Clear(x),s) ∧
Holds(Clear(y),s) ∧ Holds(On(x,z),s) ∧ Diff(x,z) ∧ Diff(x,y)] ∨
[Holds(f,s) ∧ ¬ Affects(a,f,s)].

The second of these completions is strongly reminiscent of Reiter's successor state axioms (see Section 8.4).

It should be clear, without presenting a model, that this is consistent. The reason is that the recursion is well-founded. The consistency of this particular logic program is a corollary of the following more general theorem.

Definition 12.2.1. A *situation calculus program* is the conjunction of,

• A finite set of general clauses (*observation sentences*) of the form,

$$\text{Holds}(\beta, S0)$$

• A finite set of general clauses (*effect axioms*) of the form,

$$\text{Holds}(\beta_1, \text{Result}(\alpha, s)) \leftarrow \Pi$$

where Π doesn't mention the Affects predicate and every occurrence of the Holds predicate in Π is of the form Holds(β_2,s),

• A finite set of Affects clauses of the form,

$$\text{Affects}(\alpha, \beta_1, s) \leftarrow \Pi$$

where Π doesn't mention the Affects predicate and every occurrence of the Holds predicate in Π is of the form Holds(β_2,s),

• The universal frame axiom (F4), and

• A finite set of general clauses (*background sentences*) not mentioning the predicates Holds or Affects. □

The background sentences might include, for example, the clauses defining Diff.

Theorem 12.2.2. Let Σ be a situation calculus program including a set of background sentences Δ. If Δ has a consistent completion then so does Σ.

Proof. Let L be the language of Δ. (L doesn't include the predicates Holds or Affects.) Let M1 be an interpretation of L that satisfies COMP[Δ]. Let Σ' be Σ

with all occurrences of not replaced by "¬". Let N_i be an interpretation of Holds defined as follows for all $i \in \mathbb{N}$.

- $N_0[\![Holds]\!] = \{\langle M1[\![\beta]\!], M1[\![S0]\!]\rangle \mid Holds(\beta,S0) \text{ is in } \Sigma'\}$

- $N_{i+1}[\![Holds]\!] =$
  $\{\langle M1[\![\beta]\!], M1[\![Result(\alpha,\sigma)]\!]\rangle \mid$
  $\quad Holds(\beta,Result(\alpha,s)) \leftarrow \Pi \text{ is in } \Sigma' \text{ and } M1+N_i \Vdash \Pi(\sigma)\}$
  where $\Pi(\sigma)$ is Π with every occurrence of s replaced by σ

Let M2 be defined as follows.

- $M2[\![Holds]\!] = \bigcup_{i \in \mathbb{N}} N_i[\![Holds]\!]$

- $M2[\![Affects]\!] =$
  $\{\langle M1[\![\alpha]\!], M1[\![\beta]\!], M1[\![\sigma]\!]\rangle \mid$
  $\quad Affects(\alpha,\beta,s) \leftarrow \Pi \text{ is in } \Sigma' \text{ and } M1+M2 \Vdash \Pi(\sigma)\}$
  where $\Pi(\sigma)$ is Π with every occurrence of s replaced by σ

It can easily be verified that M1+M2 is a model of COMP[Σ].   □

As pointed out by Evans [1989], the Yale shooting scenario can be represented as a logic program. Interestingly, logic programming representations of the Yale shooting scenario tend to resemble Hanks and McDermott's original formulation (see Section 3.6) more closely than the formulation we've been using throughout the book.

$$Holds(Loaded,Result(Load,s)) \qquad \text{(YP1)}$$

$$Affects(Shoot,Alive,s) \leftarrow Holds(Loaded,s) \qquad \text{(YP2)}$$

$$Holds(Alive,S0) \qquad \text{(YP3)}$$

Let Σ be the conjunction of (YP1) to (YP3) with (F4).

Proposition 12.2.3. There is an SLDNF-refutation for the general goal,

$$\leftarrow \text{not } Holds(Alive,Result(Shoot,Result(Wait,Result(Load,S0))))$$

from the situation calculus program Σ.

Proof. See Figure 12.3.   □

A corollary of Proposition 12.2.3 and Theorem 11.6.3 (the soundness of SLDNF-resolution) is that,

COMP[Σ] ⊨ ¬ Holds(Alive,Result(Shoot,Result(Wait,Result(Load,S0)))).

Other expected consequences of the Yale shooting scenario can also be obtained from Σ. For example, there are SLDNF-refutations for the following general goals.

← Holds(Alive,Result(Wait,Result(Load,S0)))

← Holds(Loaded,Result(Wait,Result(Load,S0)))

Furthermore, since Σ is a situation calculus program, Theorem 12.2.2 tells us that COMP[Σ] is consistent.

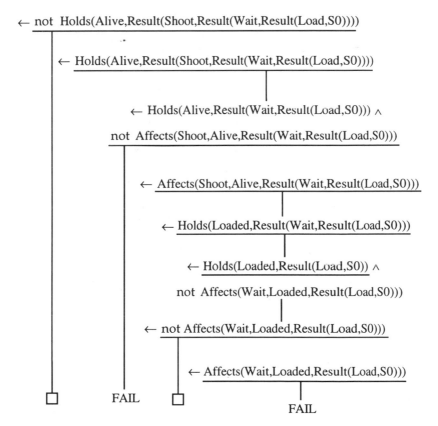

Figure 12.3: The Proof of Proposition 12.2.3

As we might expect, the conditions on Theorem 12.2.2 demand conformity to the principle of directionality (see Section 5.3).[2]

12.3   Knowledge Representation Issues

So negation-as-failure apparently avoids the Hanks-McDermott problem. How exactly is this achieved without resorting to causal, chronological, or state-based minimisation?

The answer lies in the way we're forced to represent negative information in a logic program. Negation-as-failure, by definition, doesn't distinguish between what is unknown and what is not true. Accordingly, negative information is simply represented by the absence of positive information. In the full predicate calculus representation of the Yale shooting scenario, we write,

$$\neg \text{Holds(Loaded,S0)}.$$

In the corresponding logic program, we simply omit any clauses referring to Loaded in S0, and negation-as-failure does the rest. Of course, if we didn't know whether Loaded held or not in S0, we wouldn't be able to represent this in the obvious way. (Although Miller has shown how this can be done in a logic programming context by introducing a Neg function for representing the negations of fluents [Miller, 1995a], [Miller, 1995b, Chapter 7]. Similar issues are tackled in [Denecker, *et al.*, 1992] using abduction.)

Similarly, in the full predicate calculus version we write,

$$\neg \text{Holds(Alive,Result(Shoot,s))} \leftarrow \text{Holds(Loaded,s)}.$$

In the logic programming version, we omit this formula. On the other hand, we do have to include a clause for Affects that blocks the persistence of Alive through a Shoot action performed in a situation in which Loaded holds. With negation-as-failure, blocking the persistence of a fluent has the same effect as making it not hold. We have no way of simply "releasing" a fluent from persistence. In other words, there's no way to represent ignorance of the effect of an action on a fluent.

The universal frame axiom itself is represented differently in a situation calculus program from its usual representation in full predicate calculus. Instead of,

$$[\text{Holds(f,Result(a,s))} \leftrightarrow \text{Holds(f,s)}] \leftarrow \neg \text{Ab(a,f,s)} \qquad \text{(F2)}$$

we have,

$$\text{Holds(f,Result(a,s))} \leftarrow \text{Holds(f,s)} \wedge \text{not Affects(a,f,s)}. \qquad \text{(F4)}$$

This is a crucial difference between the two formalisations. Where the biconditional in (F2) caters for both the forwards and backwards persistence of both positive and negative information, (F4) only caters explicitly for the forwards persistence of positive information. Negative information also persists forwards in the logic programming version, but by default: if negation-as-failure licenses the conclusion not Holds(f,s) for some fluent f and situation s then, in the absence of any effect axioms to the contrary, it will license the conclusion not Holds(f,Result(a,s)) for any action a.

The absence of the biconditional in (F4) also forces us to represent Affects information explicitly. Axiom (F2) yields abnormalities automatically from effect axioms.

Furthermore, because the contrapositive of (F4), namely,

not [Holds(f,s) ∧ not Affects(a,f,s)] ← not Holds(f,Result(a,s))

which is equivalent to,

not Holds(f,s) ← not Holds(f,Result(a,s)) ∧ not Affects(a,f,s)

does *not* follow, as it would if not were interpreted as classical negation, we don't have the backwards persistence of negative information. In fact, as Evans [1989] has shown by comparing two very similar logic programming representations of the Yale shooting scenario, negation-as-failure avoids the Hanks-McDermott problem by blocking contrapositives. In the following two logic programs, ¬ Holds(Alive,s) is represented as Holds(Dead,s) and ¬ Holds(Loaded,s) is represented as Holds(Unloaded,s).

Affects(Load,Unloaded,s)	(YPE1)
Holds(Dead,Result(Shoot,s)) ← not Holds(Unloaded,s)	(YPE2)
Affects(Shoot,Alive,s) ← Holds(Loaded,s)	(YPE3)
Holds(Alive,S0)	(YPE4)
Holds(Unloaded,S0)	(YPE5)

It can easily be confirmed that this program yields the expected conclusion, namely,

Holds(Dead,Result(Shoot,Result(Wait,Result(Load,S0))))

while the opposite conclusion, namely,

Holds(Alive,Result(Shoot,Result(Wait,Result(Load,S0))))

is obtained from the following program, which is identical except that the contrapositive form of Axiom (YPE3) is used.

$$\text{Affects(Load,Unloaded,s)} \qquad\qquad \text{(YPA1)}$$

$$\text{Holds(Dead,Result(Shoot,s))} \leftarrow \text{not Holds(Unloaded,s)} \qquad \text{(YPA2)}$$

$$\text{Holds(Unloaded,s)} \leftarrow \text{not Affects(Shoot,Alive,s)} \qquad \text{(YPA3)}$$

$$\text{Holds(Alive,S0)} \qquad\qquad \text{(YPA4)}$$

$$\text{Holds(Unloaded,S0)} \qquad\qquad \text{(YPA5)}$$

Similarly, by blocking the contrapositive of (F4), negation-as-failure can be thought of as encoding a form of chronological minimisation. In a sense, it's always the last negation in a chain of SLDNF-resolution steps that has the highest priority, and each step that involves resolving against (F4) is a step backwards in time. If the contrapositive form of (F4) were not blocked, the direction of inference would not have to reflect the direction of time in this way. A similar effect is achieved by Morris [1988] using Reiter's default logic.

To make this clear, consider the following two logic programs that would be logically equivalent if the negations were interpreted classically.

Program One	Program Two
$P(x) \leftarrow \text{not } Q(x)$	$R(x) \leftarrow \text{not } Q(x)$
$Q(x) \leftarrow \text{not } R(x)$	$Q(x) \leftarrow \text{not } P(x)$

The program on the right is obtained by taking the contrapositives of the clauses in the program on the left. The completions of the two programs are equivalent to the following.

Completion of Program One	Completion of Program Two
$P(x) \leftrightarrow \neg\, Q(x)$	$R(x) \leftrightarrow \neg\, Q(x)$
$Q(x) \leftrightarrow \neg\, R(x)$	$Q(x) \leftrightarrow \neg\, P(x)$
$\neg\, \exists\, x\, R(x)$	$\neg\, \exists\, x\, P(x)$

So $\neg\, P(A)$ and $R(A)$ are consequences of the completion of Program One, while $\neg\, R(A)$ and $P(A)$ are consequences of the completion of Program Two. The two programs can be thought of as encoding different priorities between two defaults. In both cases, it's the last negation in an SLDNF-refutation that gets highest priority. Furthermore, it's in the nature of negation-as-failure to *insist* on such a prioritisation. Because it blocks the contrapositive, a general clause cannot represent an "honest" implication instead of a default.

To summarise, negation-as-failure offers a simple solution to the frame problem that avoids the Hanks-McDermott problem, but at the expense of the expressive power we find in full first-order predicate calculus augmented with circumscription. For example, we have difficulty representing,

- Honest implication, in which the contrapositive holds, and

- Ignorance about whether something is true or false. (But see [Miller, 1995a], [Miller, 1995b, Chapter 7], and [Denecker, *et al.*, 1992].)

This is in addition to the limitations imposed by the restriction to general clauses that, for example, makes disjunction hard to represent.

Before leaving the topic of the situation calculus, a few remarks on the subject of ramifications are in order. The limitations of general clauses don't preclude the representation of certain domain constraints, although this topic has been largely neglected in the logic programming literature. However, care must be taken to ensure that the addition of domain constraints to a situation calculus program doesn't render its completion inconsistent. Intuitively, the completion will still be consistent if the fluents in the program are "stratified" (see Definition 11.6.7, but substitute "fluent" for "predicate"), and the heads of effect axioms only ever mention fluents at the lowest level of the stratification. Similar remarks apply to domain constraints in the context of the event calculus, which I will now present.

12.4 Introducing the Event Calculus

The situation calculus isn't the only formalism that can be used to represent the effects of action via logic programming. We've already seen, in Chapter 9, that standard situation calculus needs to be extended to cope with the representation of narratives, where a narrative is a distinguished course of events about which we may have incomplete information.[3] This section introduces the event calculus which, unlike the situation calculus, is a narrative-based formalism for reasoning about action. The event calculus will dominate the rest of the book.

The event calculus was first introduced by Kowalski and Sergot [1986]. Like the situation calculus, different variants of the formalism abound, and no clear definition of the event calculus exists. I'll be presenting several versions, beginning here with a logic programming version that resembles Kowalski and Sergot's original fairly closely.

In Kowalski and Sergot's event calculus, which I will henceforth call the *original* event calculus, the term After(e,f) is introduced to stand for a *period* of time initiated by the event e, during which the fluent f holds.[4] Similarly, the term

Before(e,f) stands for a period of time terminated by event e during which fluent f holds. The event e is an event *occurrence*, that is to say an event *token*, not an event type. In other words, e has a unique time of occurrence associated with it. The formula Holds(p) represents that p's fluent holds from the start to the end of p. Later versions of the event calculus dispensed with periods altogether.

The effects of events are described using the two predicates Initiates and Terminates, which are common to all variants of the event calculus. In the original version, we have,

$$\text{Holds(After(e,f))} \leftarrow \text{Initiates(e,f)} \qquad \text{(KS1)}$$

$$\text{Holds(Before(e,f))} \leftarrow \text{Terminates(e,f)}. \qquad \text{(KS2)}$$

In addition, the formulae Start(p,e) and End(p,e) represent respectively that the period e begins with the event e and that the period p ends with the event e. These predicates are constrained by the following axioms.

$$\text{Start(After(e,f),e)} \qquad \text{(KS3)}$$

$$\text{End(Before(e,f),e)} \qquad \text{(KS4)}$$

$$\text{Start(Before(e2,f),e1)} \leftarrow \text{Eq(After(e1,f),Before(e2,f))} \qquad \text{(KS5)}$$

$$\text{End(After(e1,f),e2)} \leftarrow \text{Eq(After(e1,f),Before(e2,f))} \qquad \text{(KS6)}$$

The formula Eq(p1,p2) represents that periods p1 and p2 are the same. We have,

$$\text{Eq(After(e1,f),Before(e2,f))} \leftarrow \text{Holds(After(e1,f))} \land \qquad \text{(KS7)}$$
$$\text{Holds(Before(e2,f))} \land \text{Time(e1,t1)} \land \text{Time(e2,t2)} \land$$
$$t1 < t2 \land \text{not Broken(t1,f,t2)}$$

$$\text{Broken(t1,f1,t3)} \leftarrow \text{Holds(After(e,f2))} \land \text{Incompatible(f1,f2)} \land \qquad \text{(KS8)}$$
$$\text{Time(e,t2)} \land t1 < t2 \land t2 < t3$$

$$\text{Broken(t1,f1,t3)} \leftarrow \text{Holds(Before(e,f2))} \land \text{Incompatible(f1,f2)} \land \qquad \text{(KS9)}$$
$$\text{Time(e,t2)} \land t1 < t2 \land t2 < t3.$$

The formula Broken(t1,f,t2) represents that the fluent f ceases to hold between times t1 and t2. The formula Incompatible(f1,f2) represents that the fluents f1 and f2 cannot hold at the same time. For example, f1 may represent the negation of f2. Clauses for Incompatible are part of the domain description. The formula Time(e,t) represents that event e occurs at time t.[5]

The intended meaning of the formula t1 < t2, where t1 and t2 are time points, is obvious. However, it isn't obvious how this intended meaning is to be realised in a logic program. Fortunately, this matter needn't detain us for very long, since it's peripheral to our main theme. Computationally speaking, of course, there's no problem, since every computer is endowed with floating point and integer comparison operations. For a formal account of the semantics of arithmetic constraints in the context of logic programming, see [Jaffar & Lassez, 1987].

As we'll see shortly, the frame problem is overcome through the use of negation-as-failure in Axiom (KS7), which supplies a form a default persistence and can be thought of as embodying the common sense law of inertia.

Finally, the formula HoldsAt(f,t) represents that fluent f holds at time t, and is constrained by the following axioms. The formula In(t,p) represents that time point falls within period p.

$$\text{HoldsAt(f,t)} \leftarrow \text{Holds(After(e,f))} \wedge \text{In(t,After(e,f))} \qquad \text{(KS10)}$$

$$\text{HoldsAt(f,t)} \leftarrow \text{Holds(Before(e,f))} \wedge \text{In(t,Before(e,f))} \qquad \text{(KS11)}$$

$$\text{In(t,p)} \leftarrow \text{Start(p,e1)} \wedge \text{End(p,e2)} \wedge \text{Time(e1,t1)} \wedge \qquad \text{(KS12)}$$
$$\text{Time(e2,t2)} \wedge t1 < t \wedge t < t2$$

$$\text{In(t,p)} \leftarrow \text{Start(p,e1)} \wedge \text{not End(p,e2)} \wedge \text{Time(e1,t1)} \wedge t1 < t \qquad \text{(KS13)}$$

$$\text{In(t,p)} \leftarrow \text{End(p,e1)} \wedge \text{not Start(p,e2)} \wedge \text{Time(e1,t1)} \wedge t < t1 \qquad \text{(KS14)}$$

Axioms (KS13) accounts for the case when a period has no known end, in which case the period is assumed to go on forever, in accordance with the idea of minimising event occurrences (see Chapters 9 and 10). Axiom (KS14) caters for the symmetrical case when a period has no known beginning.[6]

12.5 Applying the Original Event Calculus

The axioms of the last section can be applied to the same class of problems as the narrative situation calculus presented in Chapter 9. Given a description of the effects of events (actions) and narrative description, the axioms supply conclusions of the form HoldsAt(f,t). However, the representational differences between the two formalisms are considerable.

The differences begin with the way that the effects of events are described. Instead of situation calculus style effect axioms, the event calculus has Initiates, Terminates and Incompatible clauses. Kowalski and Sergot's paper employs an interesting and useful representational technique, originally inspired by work on semantic nets (see [Kowalski, 1979, pp. 31–37]), in which event descriptions are decomposed into binary relationships. Here's how the technique might be applied to the Blocks World.

$$\text{Initiates}(e,\text{On}(x,y)) \leftarrow \text{Act}(e,\text{Move}) \wedge \text{Object}(e,x) \wedge \text{Destination}(e,y) \wedge$$
$$\text{Time}(e,t) \wedge \text{HoldsAt}(\text{Clear}(x),t) \wedge \text{HoldsAt}(\text{Clear}(y),t) \wedge$$
$$\text{Diff}(x,y) \wedge \text{Diff}(x,\text{Table})$$

This clauses correspond to the situation calculus Axiom (BW8) in Section 11.4. The Diff predicate is defined in the usual way. Preconditions appear as HoldsAt atoms in the body of a clause. Event occurrences are described in terms of the Act, Object, and Destination predicates. Each event (occurrence) is given a unique name. For example, a simple narrative in which A is moved onto D at time 5, and then B is moved onto A at time 10 would be represented as follows.

Act(E1,Move)	Act(E2,Move)
Object(E1,A)	Object(E2,B)
Destination(E1,D)	Destination(E2,A)
Time(E1,5)	Time(E2,10)

However, the use of this technique isn't a genuine difference between the event calculus and situation calculus. Many later variants of the event calculus don't use the technique at all. Moreover, the same technique can easily be employed with the situation calculus. Here's the full set of clauses for the Blocks World, using a parameterised Move action instead of the Object and Destination predicates.

$$\text{Initiates}(e,\text{On}(x,y)) \leftarrow \text{Act}(e,\text{Move}(x,y)) \wedge \text{Time}(e,t) \wedge \qquad \text{(KSB1)}$$
$$\text{HoldsAt}(\text{Clear}(x),t) \wedge \text{HoldsAt}(\text{Clear}(y),t) \wedge$$
$$\text{Diff}(x,y) \wedge \text{Diff}(x,\text{Table})$$

$$\text{Terminates}(e,\text{On}(x,z)) \leftarrow \text{Act}(e,\text{Move}(x,y)) \wedge \text{Time}(e,t) \wedge \qquad \text{(KSB2)}$$
$$\text{HoldsAt}(\text{Clear}(x),t) \wedge \text{HoldsAt}(\text{Clear}(y),t) \wedge \text{Diff}(x,y) \wedge$$
$$\text{HoldsAt}(\text{On}(x,z),t) \wedge \text{Diff}(y,z)$$

$$\text{Incompatible}(\text{On}(x,y),\text{On}(x,z)) \leftarrow \text{Diff}(y,z) \qquad\qquad\qquad \text{(KSB3)}$$

$$\text{Initiates}(e,\text{Clear}(z)) \leftarrow \text{Act}(e,\text{Move}(x,y)) \wedge \text{Time}(e,t) \wedge \qquad \text{(KSB4)}$$
$$\text{HoldsAt}(\text{Clear}(x),t) \wedge \text{HoldsAt}(\text{Clear}(y),t) \wedge \text{Diff}(x,y) \wedge$$
$$\text{HoldsAt}(\text{On}(x,z),t) \wedge \text{Diff}(y,z)$$

$$\text{Terminates}(e,\text{Clear}(y)) \leftarrow \text{Act}(e,\text{Move}(x,y)) \wedge \text{Time}(e,t) \wedge \qquad \text{(KSB5)}$$
$$\text{HoldsAt}(\text{Clear}(x),t) \wedge \text{HoldsAt}(\text{Clear}(y),t) \wedge$$
$$\text{Diff}(x,y) \wedge \text{Diff}(x,\text{Table})$$

$$\text{Incompatible}(\text{Clear}(y),\text{On}(x,y)) \qquad\qquad\qquad\qquad\qquad \text{(KSB6)}$$

The narrative description is correspondingly simpler without the Object and Destination predicates.

$$\text{Act}(\text{E1},\text{Move}(\text{A},\text{D})) \qquad\qquad (\text{KSB7})$$

$$\text{Time}(\text{E1},5) \qquad\qquad (\text{KSB8})$$

$$\text{Act}(\text{E2},\text{Move}(\text{B},\text{A})) \qquad\qquad (\text{KSB9})$$

$$\text{Time}(\text{E2},10) \qquad\qquad (\text{KSB10})$$

The initial situation can be described via a "genesis" event at time 0. Here's a description of the initial situation familiar from previous examples (see Figure 11.5).

$$\text{Initiates}(\text{E0},\text{On}(\text{C},\text{Table})) \qquad\qquad (\text{KSB11})$$

$$\text{Initiates}(\text{E0},\text{On}(\text{B},\text{C})) \qquad\qquad (\text{KSB12})$$

$$\text{Initiates}(\text{E0},\text{On}(\text{A},\text{B})) \qquad\qquad (\text{KSB13})$$

$$\text{Initiates}(\text{E0},\text{On}(\text{D},\text{Table})) \qquad\qquad (\text{KSB14})$$

$$\text{Initiates}(\text{E0},\text{Clear}(\text{A})) \qquad\qquad (\text{KSB15})$$

$$\text{Initiates}(\text{E0},\text{Clear}(\text{D})) \qquad\qquad (\text{KSB16})$$

$$\text{Initiates}(\text{E0},\text{Clear}(\text{Table})) \qquad\qquad (\text{KSB17})$$

$$\text{Time}(\text{E0},0) \qquad\qquad (\text{KSB18})$$

The whole narrative is illustrated in Figure 12.4.

Let Σ be the conjunction of (KS1) to (KS14) with (KSB1) to (KSB18), plus the usual definition of Diff. Now SLDNF-resolution (augmented with some mechanism for dealing with the $<$ predicate) can be used to derive HoldsAt information from Σ. For example, the search space for the goal $\leftarrow$ HoldsAt(On(x,y),7) is depicted in Figures 12.5 and 12.6.

Much detail has been omitted from these figures, and in various places several resolution steps have been collapsed into one. The successful branch labelled A in Figure 12.5 is of particular interest, and is expanded in Figure 12.6.

The search space shown in these two figures exhibits a good deal of redundant computation, which would have to be reduced in a serious implementation. Furthermore, PROLOG would loop if given the same clauses. But these concerns are of secondary interest here. The two figures also illustrate the subtle way in which the original event calculus works, and in particular the way default persistence is achieved and the frame problem is overcome.

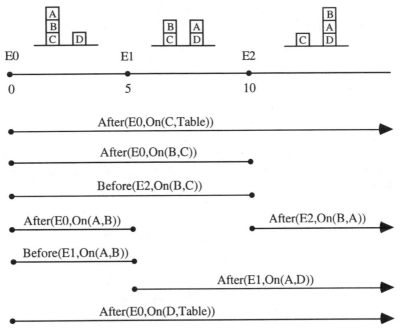

Figure 12.4: The Blocks World Narrative

Four answer substitutions are obtained, in three separate ways, via Axiom (KS10).

1. The answer substitutions {x/C, y/Table} and {x/D, y/Table} are obtained via the description of the initial situations, and Axiom (KS13). The fluents On(C,Table) and On(D,Table) start to hold at the time of E0. So we have Holds(After(E0,On(C,Table)) and Holds(After(E0,On(D,Table))). These two periods have no known end, so Axiom (KS13), using negation-as-failure, tells us that their respective fluents hold at time 7.

2. The answer substitution {x/A, y/D} is obtained via the description of the effects of E1, which is a successful Move(A,D) event, and Axiom (KS13). The fluent On(A,D) is initiated by E1, so we have Holds(After(E1,On(A,D))). This period has no known end, so (KS13) tells us that its fluent holds at time 7.

3. The answer substitution {x/B, y/C} is obtained via the description of the initial situation, and Axioms (KS7) and (KS12). The derivation of this answer substitution is depicted in Figure 12.6. The fluent On(B,C) is initiated by E0

at time 0 and then terminated by E2 at time 10. So we have Holds(After(E0,On(B,C))) and Holds(Before(E2,On(B,C))). Axiom (KS7) equates these two periods, using negation-as-failure, since there's no known event between 0 and 10 that affects On(B,C). Through Axiom (KS6), this sets the end point of the period After(E0,On(B,C)) to 10. This in turn enables us to use Axiom (KS12) to conclude that the period's fluent holds at time 7.

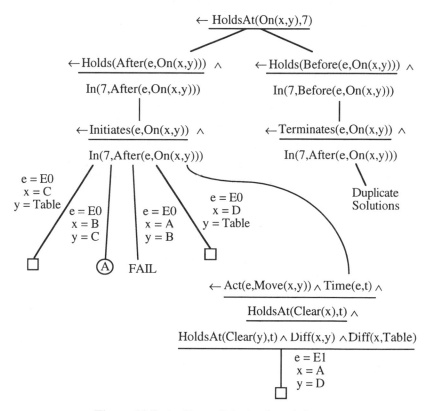

Figure 12.5: An Event Calculus Search Space

In addition, the answer substitution {x/B, x/C} is obtained independently via Axiom (KS11), in a manner that is symmetrical to the last of the above cases. The attempt to construct a refutation of ← Holds(On(A,B),7) fails (Figure 12.5) because E1 initiates the period After(E1,On(A,D)), and the fluent On(A,D) is incompatible with the fluent On(A,B), according to Axiom (KSB3). Note that this failure is not, as one might expect, because E1 terminates the fluent On(A,B).

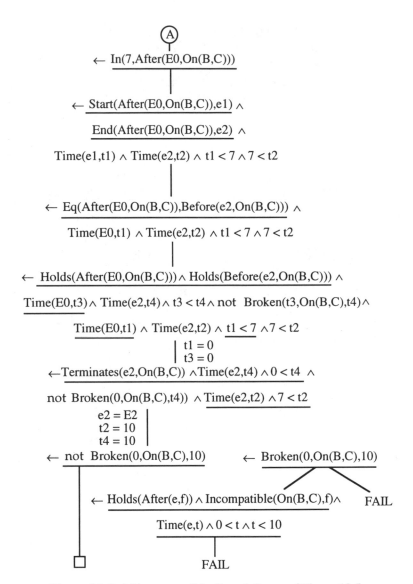

Figure 12.6: A Fragment of the Search Space of Figure 12.5

Notes

1. As already noted, Kowalski's book doesn't use negation-as-failure to express the common sense law of inertia, although the technique was known at the time.

However, I distinctly recall Kowalski presenting a version using negation-as-failure in his undergraduate lectures in 1981. The formulation given in this section corresponds more or less with my recollection.

2. The formal definition of the principle of directionality given in Chapter 5 has to be modified in the present case to deal with completion instead of circumscription.

3. A logic programming version of the situation calculus with narratives has been developed by Miller [1995b, Chapter 4].

4. Most literature on the event calculus employs the word "property" instead of "fluent".

5. In Kowalski and Sergot's formulation, the ordering of events was considered as more primitive than the ordering of time points. In their formulation, Axioms (KS7) to (KS9) don't mention time points at all, but instead employ a < predicate which ranges over events. This potentially allows for a more liberal ordering relation between events than that between time points. For example, events could have a branching structure like the tree of situations in situation calculus. Unfortunately, this possibility hasn't yet been properly explored in the literature.

6. Axiom (KS14) was absent from Kowalski and Sergot's formulation.

13 Simplifying and Extending the Event Calculus

Much of the representational power of Kowalski and Sergot's original event calculus can be retained in a much simpler variant, which is the one most commonly found in the literature. This chapter opens by presenting this simplified event calculus, an important feature of which is that it can be extended, without too much difficulty, so that it can represent continuous change. This extension, which is described in this chapter, allows the event calculus to deal with some benchmark problems that are extremely hard to represent using the situation calculus.

Although the original event calculus and its most common variants were developed under the auspices of the logic programming research community, the essential representational ideas it embodies transcend the limitations of the logic programmer's medium. This chapter finishes by taking the first tentative steps towards a circumscriptive version of the calculus. A full circumscriptive version is presented in the next two chapters.

13.1 A Simplified Event Calculus

The original event calculus has some interesting features. But it's open to criticism on a number of counts. A number of researchers have developed variants of the event calculus that preserve what was best about the original while discarding its less attractive aspects. Let's review those features of the original event calculus that set it apart from the situation calculus.

To begin with, the event calculus incorporates the idea of a distinguished narrative of events. Event occurrences are described by the Act and Time predicates. Of course, as we saw in Chapter 9, the situation calculus can be extended to incorporate a distinguished narrative of events too. But, unlike the situation calculus, with the event calculus, HoldsAt information is derived directly from the narrative description. In particular, default persistence works at the level of the narrative.[1] All of Kowalski and Sergot's axioms appeal, directly or indirectly, to the distinguished history of event occurrences that comprises the narrative. In this sense, the event calculus is narrative-based while the situation calculus is not.

As a consequence of this commitment to the narrative, the event calculus is obliged to represent the effects of actions via predicates like Initiates and Terminates, which are analogous to the Causes predicate used in some versions of the situation calculus (see Chapter 5). In the event calculus, there are no states or situations over which it would make sense to define a successor function analogous to the Result function in the situation calculus. The fact that the event calculus axioms appeal directly to event occurrences rules out such an idea. Consequently, situation calculus style effect axioms are impossible.

The narrative basis of the event calculus is certainly one of it's most attractive features, and deserves preservation. In particular, as we'll see shortly, it facilitates the representation of continuous change. Less worthy of preservation are the periods of the original event calculus. As Pinto and Reiter have pointed out [1993], these periods have a questionable ontological status. Does the term After(e,f) denote a temporal interval? If so, then as Pinto and Reiter argue convincingly, the axioms of the event calculus supply unwanted conclusions. If not, then what exactly does it denote? It may be possible to clear up this ontological confusion. But since periods are unnecessary anyway, as will become clear, it seems reasonable to abandon them.

The original event calculus has another feature which both provokes semantic disquiet, and is unnecessary for many applications, namely the symmetric treatment of persistence. The provision of backwards persistence obviously violates the principle of directionality (Section 5.3), and accordingly makes it harder to prove useful theorems about the formalism.

These considerations motivate the construction of a simplified version of the event calculus [Kowalski, 1992],[2] [Eshghi, 1988], [Shanahan, 1989]. The simplified event calculus modifies the original event calculus in the following ways.

- Event tokens are dispensed with. The Act and Time predicates are combined into the single predicate Happens, which is already familiar from Chapters 9 and 10. The formula Happens(a,t) represents that an event of *type* a occurs at time point t.[3]

- Periods are eliminated altogether. A simplified set of axioms bypasses the need for them.

- Default persistence operates in a forwards direction only.

- The Incompatible predicate is omitted, because its role in the definition of Broken is subsumed by the Terminates predicate.

We have the following general clauses.

$$\text{HoldsAt(f,t2)} \leftarrow \text{Happens(a,t1)} \wedge \text{Initiates(a,f,t1)} \wedge \qquad \text{(SEC1)}$$
$$t1 < t2 \wedge \text{not Clipped(t1,f,t2)}$$

$$\text{Clipped(t1,f,t2)} \leftarrow \text{Happens(a,t)} \wedge \text{Terminates(a,f,t)} \wedge \qquad \text{(SEC2)}$$
$$t1 < t \wedge t < t2$$

The formula Clipped(t1,f,t2) represents an event occurs that terminates the fluent f between times t1 and t2. The Clipped predicate is closely related to the Broken predicate of the original calculus, but Clipped appeals to Terminates where Broken appeals to the now redundant predicate Incompatible. Notice that a fluent doesn't hold at the time of the event that initiates it, but does hold at the time of the event that terminates it.

It's convenient to make a special case of the initial situation, and to introduce the predicate Initially to represent it. The formula Initially(f) represents that the fluent f is initiated at time 0. Like Happens, the Initially predicate has already featured in Chapter 9, and is used in narrative descriptions in just the same way here. An extra clause for HoldsAt is included to cater for this.

$$\text{HoldsAt(f,t)} \leftarrow \text{Initially(f)} \wedge \text{not Clipped(0,f,t)} \qquad \text{(SEC3)}$$

As before, the effects of actions are described in terms of the predicates Initiates and Terminates. However, these predicates now take event types as arguments (which are the same as actions in the situation calculus) instead of event tokens. This means they need a third argument for the time of occurrence of an event whose effects they're describing. For the Blocks World example, we have,

$$\text{Initiates(Move(x,y),On(x,y),t)} \leftarrow \text{HoldsAt(Clear(x),t)} \wedge \qquad \text{(SEB1)}$$
$$\text{HoldsAt(Clear(y),t)} \wedge \text{Diff(x,y)} \wedge \text{Diff(x,Table)}$$

$$\text{Terminates(Move(x,y),On(x,z),t)} \leftarrow \text{HoldsAt(Clear(x),t)} \wedge \qquad \text{(SEB2)}$$
$$\text{HoldsAt(Clear(y),t)} \wedge \text{Diff(x,y)} \wedge \text{HoldsAt(On(x,z),t)} \wedge$$
$$\text{Diff(y,z)}$$

$$\text{Initiates(Move(x,y),Clear(z),t)} \leftarrow \text{HoldsAt(Clear(x),t)} \wedge \qquad \text{(SEB3)}$$
$$\text{HoldsAt(Clear(y),t)} \wedge \text{Diff(x,y)} \wedge \text{HoldsAt(On(x,z),t)} \wedge$$
$$\text{Diff(y,z)}$$

$$\text{Terminates(Move(x,y),Clear(y),t)} \leftarrow \text{HoldsAt(Clear(x),t)} \wedge \qquad \text{(SEB4)}$$
$$\text{HoldsAt(Clear(y),t)} \wedge \text{Diff(x,y)} \wedge \text{Diff(x,Table)}.$$

These clauses are analogous to Axioms (KSB1), (KSB2), (KSB4) and (KSB5). Narratives are described using the Happens predicate in a way that's familiar from Chapters 9 and 10. Here's the description of the narrative for the example used in the last section.

$$\text{Initially(On(C,Table))} \qquad \text{(SEB5)}$$

$$\text{Initially(On(B,C))} \qquad \text{(SEB6)}$$

$$\text{Initially(On(A,B))} \qquad \text{(SEB7)}$$

$$\text{Initially(On(D,Table))} \qquad \text{(SEB8)}$$

$$\text{Initially(Clear(A))} \qquad \text{(SEB9)}$$

$$\text{Initially(Clear(D))} \qquad \text{(SEB10)}$$

$$\text{Initially(Clear(Table))} \qquad \text{(SEB11)}$$

$$\text{Happens(Move(A,D),5)} \qquad \text{(SEB12)}$$

$$\text{Happens(Move(B,A),10)} \qquad \text{(SEB13)}$$

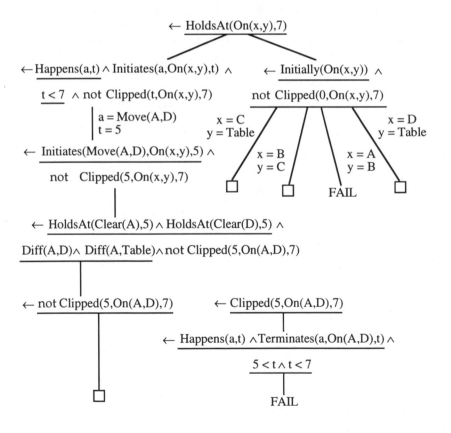

Figure 13.1: A Search Space for the Simplified Event Calculus

Now let Σ be the conjunction of (SEC1) to (SEC3) with (SEB1) to (SEB13) plus the usual definition of Diff. The search space for the goal ← HoldsAt(On(x,y),7) from Σ, using SLDNF-resolution augmented with a suitable mechanism for dealing with <, is depicted in Figure 13.1.

Much more detail of this search space is depicted than it was possible to show of the corresponding search space for the original event calculus, reflecting the degree of simplification that has taken place.

A more sophisticated logic programming formulation of the simplified event calculus is presented in [Miller, 1995a] and [Miller, 1995b, Chapter 4], which is shown to be sound and complete with respect to a situation calculus style specification based on the approach to narratives described in [Miller & Shanahan, 1994] (see Section 9.6).

13.2 Event Calculus Semantic Issues

In Section 12.2, a class of situation calculus programs was defined which are guaranteed to have consistent completions. The same exercise can be carried out for the simplified event calculus. As with the class of situation calculus programs, none of the standard theorems that guarantees a consistent completion is applicable, since HoldsAt is defined indirectly in terms of not Initiates and not Terminates, which in turn can be defined in terms of HoldsAt.

Definition 13.2.1. An *event calculus program* is the conjunction of,

- A finite set of Initially clauses of the form,

$$\text{Initially}(\beta)$$

- A finite set of Happens clauses of the form,

$$\text{Happens}(\alpha,\tau)$$

- A finite set of Initiates clauses of the form,

$$\text{Initiates}(\alpha,\beta_1,t) \leftarrow \Pi$$

and a finite set of Terminates clauses of the form,

$$\text{Terminates}(\alpha,\beta_1,t) \leftarrow \Pi$$

where Π doesn't mention the predicates Initially, Happens, Initiates, or Terminates, and every occurrence of the HoldsAt predicate is of the form HoldsAt(β_2,t),

- The simplified event calculus axioms (SEC1) to (SEC3), and

- A finite set of general clauses (*background sentences*) not mentioning the predicates Initially, Happens, Initiates, Terminates, HoldsAt, or <.   □

Theorem 13.2.2. Let Σ be an event calculus program including a set of background sentences Δ. If Δ has a consistent completion then so does Σ.

Proof. Let L be the language of Δ. (L doesn't include the predicates Initially, Happens, Initiates, Terminates, Clipped, HoldsAt, or <.) Let M1 be an interpretation of L that satisfies COMP[Δ], and in which time points are interpreted as natural numbers. Let Σ' be Σ with all occurrences of not replaced by "$\neg$".

Let $\Pi1(f,t2)$ be,

$$[\text{Initially}(f) \wedge \neg\,\text{Clipped}(0,f,t2)] \vee \exists\, a, t1\, [\text{Happens}(a,t1) \wedge$$
$$\text{Initiates}(a,f,t1) \wedge t1 < t2 \wedge \neg\,\text{Clipped}(t1,f,t2)].$$

In other words, $\Pi1$ stands for the disjoined bodies of the Axioms (SEC1) and (SEC3), which define HoldsAt. Let $\Pi2(t1,f,t2)$ be,

$$\exists\, a, t\, [\text{Happens}(a,t) \wedge \text{Terminates}(a,f,t) \wedge t1 < t \wedge t < t2].$$

In other words, $\Pi2$ stands for the body of Axiom (SEC2), which defines Clipped.

Let N_i be an interpretation of Happens, Initiates, Terminates, Clipped, and HoldsAt defined as follows for all $i \in \mathbb{N}$.[4]

- $N_i[\![\text{Happens}]\!] = \{\langle M1[\![\alpha]\!], M1[\![\tau]\!]\rangle \mid \text{Happens}(\alpha,\tau)$ is in $\Sigma'\}$

- $N_0[\![\text{Initiates}]\!] =$
    $\{\langle M1[\![\alpha]\!], M1[\![\beta]\!], 0\rangle \mid$
        $\text{Initiates}(\alpha,\beta,t) \leftarrow \Pi$ is in Σ' and $M1 \Vdash \Pi(0)\}$

where $\Pi(0)$ is Π with every occurrence of t replaced by 0

- $N_{i+1}[\![\text{Initiates}]\!] = N_i[\![\text{Initiates}]\!] \cup$
    $\{\langle M1[\![\alpha]\!], M1[\![\beta]\!], i+1\rangle \mid$
        $\text{Initiates}(\alpha,\beta,t) \leftarrow \Pi$ is in Σ' and $M1 + N_{i+1} \Vdash \Pi(i+1)\}$

where $\Pi(j)$ is Π with every occurrence of t replaced by j

- $N_0[\![\text{Terminates}]\!] =$
    $\{\langle M1[\![\alpha]\!], M1[\![\beta]\!], 0\rangle \mid$
        $\text{Terminates}(\alpha,\beta,t) \leftarrow \Pi$ is in Σ' and $M1 \Vdash \Pi(0)\}$

where $\Pi(0)$ is Π with every occurrence of t replaced by 0

- $N_{i+1}[\![\text{Terminates}]\!] = N_i[\![\text{Terminates}]\!] \cup$
  $\{\langle M1[\![\alpha]\!], M1[\![\beta]\!], i+1\rangle \mid$
  $\qquad \text{Terminates}(\alpha,\beta,t) \leftarrow \Pi \text{ is in } \Sigma' \text{ and } M1+N_{i+1} \Vdash \Pi(i+1)\}$

where $\Pi(j)$ is Π with every occurrence of t replaced by j

- $N_0[\![\text{Clipped}]\!] = \{\}$

- $N_{i+1}[\![\text{Clipped}]\!] = N_i[\![\text{Clipped}]\!] \cup \{\langle M1[\![\tau]\!], M1[\![\beta]\!], i\rangle \mid M1+N_i \Vdash \Pi2(\tau,\beta,i)\}$

- $N_0[\![\text{HoldsAt}]\!] = \{\langle M1[\![\beta]\!], 0\rangle \mid \text{Initially}(\beta) \text{ is in } \Sigma' \}$

- $N_{i+1}[\![\text{HoldsAt}]\!] = N_i[\![\text{HoldsAt}]\!] \cup \{\langle M1[\![\beta]\!], i+1\rangle \mid M1+N_i \Vdash \Pi1(\beta,i+1)\}$

Notice that $N_{i+1}[\![\text{Initiates}]\!]$ is defined in terms of N_{i+1}. This is possible because the body of an Initiates clause cannot mention the predicates Initiates or Terminates, and any mention it makes of HoldsAt will have the same time point argument as the head. The same argument applies to the definition of $N_{i+1}[\![\text{Terminates}]\!]$. Let M2 be defined as follows.

- $M2[\![\text{Initially}]\!] = \{M1[\![\beta]\!] \mid \text{Initially}(\beta) \text{ is in } \Sigma' \}$

- $M2[\![\text{Happens}]\!] = \{\langle M1[\![\alpha]\!], M1[\![\tau]\!]\rangle \mid \text{Happens}(\alpha,\tau) \text{ is in } \Sigma'\}$

- $M2[\![\rho]\!] = \bigcup_{i \in \mathbb{N}} N_i[\![\rho]\!]$ if ρ is Initiates, Terminates, Clipped, or HoldsAt

- M2 interprets the < predicate in the usual way for natural numbers

It can be verified that M1+M2 is a model of COMP[Σ]. $\qquad \square$

Unsurprisingly, the proof of this theorem relies on the fact that the simplified event calculus conforms to the principle of directionality. Any SLD-refutation for a HoldsAt formula will proceed backwards in time. To determine whether a fluent holds at time t, it is only ever necessary to examine which fluents hold at times earlier than t. Likewise, to determine $N_i[\![\text{HoldsAt}]\!]$ we only need to know about $N_j[\![\text{HoldsAt}]\!]$ for j<i.

It's a corollary of this theorem that the Blocks World example used in the last section has a consistent completion, since it's an event calculus program. The theorem also guarantees the consistency of the conjunction of (SEC1) to (SEC3) with the following general clauses, which represent the Yale shooting scenario.

$$\text{Initiates}(\text{Load},\text{Loaded},t) \qquad\qquad (\text{SEY1})$$

$$\text{Terminates}(\text{Shoot},\text{Alive},t) \leftarrow \text{HoldsAt}(\text{Loaded},t) \qquad\qquad (\text{SEY2})$$

$$\text{Initially(Alive)} \qquad\qquad \text{(SEY3)}$$

$$\text{Happens(Load,5)} \qquad\qquad \text{(SEY4)}$$

$$\text{Happens(Sneeze,10)} \qquad\qquad \text{(SEY5)}$$

$$\text{Happens(Shoot,15)} \qquad\qquad \text{(SEY6)}$$

There's no Wait action in this representation of the Yale shooting scenario, since waiting is much better represented simply as a pause in the narrative. Its place is taken by a Sneeze action, which fulfils the same function in that it supplies an opportunity for persistence to fail.

As Figure 13.2 shows, if we take for granted the interpretation of the < predicate, there exists an SLDNF-refutation for the general goal ← not HoldsAt(Alive,20).

So the Yale shooting scenario is dealt with correctly by the simplified event calculus. In contrast, as we'll see shortly, if we render the same clauses into predicate calculus with classical negation, and apply circumscription in the obvious way to address the frame problem, the Hanks-McDermott problem arises. As with the situation calculus formulation in Chapter 12, the frame problem has been overcome here using negation-as-failure. Naturally, we're led to ask how the Hanks-McDermott problem been avoided.

Much of the discussion of this question in the context of the situation calculus (Section 12.3) carries over to the simplified event calculus. Negation-as-failure is defined in such a way that the contrapositive of Axiom (SEC1) is blocked. It cannot be used to infer the backwards persistence of negative information. As in the situation calculus, this means that negation-as-failure effectively encodes a form of chronological minimisation: the last negation in a chain of SLDNF inferences is dominant. In the case of the simplified event calculus, this will be the earliest not Clipped. In this way, the logic programming versions of both formalisms conform to the principle of directionality.

13.3   Continuous Change in the Event Calculus

One of the most attractive features of the simplified event calculus is that it can be straightforwardly extended to represent continuous change, as in the variation in the height of a falling ball or the water level in a filling vessel.

Needless to say, continuous change is ubiquitous, and any serious attempt to formalise the effects of actions must take it into account. An early logical account of continuous change was supplied by McDermott [1982], and a fairly comprehensive treatment of the issue was given by Sandewall [1989a], [1989b].

Neither author uses the situation calculus or the event calculus, which are our main concern here.

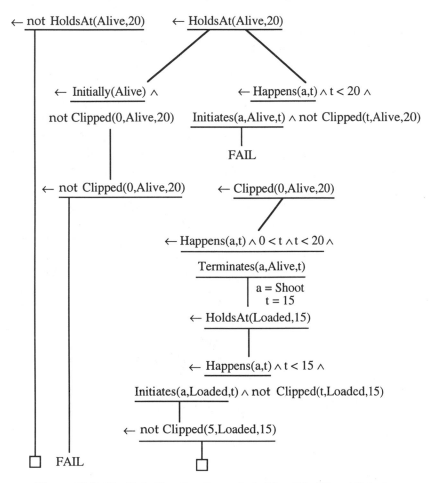

Figure 13.2: The Yale Shooting Scenario in Simplified Event Calculus

Some sketchy accounts of how to represent continuous change in the situation calculus were published in the early Nineties [Schubert, 1990, Section 5], [Gelfond, Lifschitz & Rabinov, 1991]. As well as being sketchy, none of these situation calculus accounts satisfactorily handles the phenomenon of events that are triggered when a continuously varying quantity reaches a threshold value. For example, consider a kitchen sink that's filling with water. When the water reaches the brim, the sink overflows.[5] In other words, an event occurs which is triggered because the water attains a particular level. This event in turn initiates and terminates various fluents. One of its effects, for example, is that the water level is no longer rising.[6]

Very recently, two accounts of continuous change in the situation calculus have been published that can handle triggered events [Reiter, 1996], [Miller, 1996]. Both are influenced by the earlier work of Pinto [1994, Chapter 6]. The phenomenon of triggered events seems naturally to be associated with the idea of a narrative, since a triggered event is an addition to the narrative. Accordingly, triggered events can be represented very naturally in the event calculus. Miller's situation calculus formulation is also narrative-based. However, Reiter's formulation shows that it is possible to do without a distinguished narrative time line and still represent continuous change and triggered events in the situation calculus.

The formalisation of continuous change with triggered events presented here follows that in [Shanahan, 1990].[7] The first step is to distinguish between *discrete* fluents, which hold over intervals of time of non-zero duration and *continuous* fluents, which hold instantaneously. This distinction only makes sense, of course, in the context of the real numbers, so I will assume that the $<$ predicate is interpreted accordingly. An example of a discrete fluent would be the fact that a ball is falling, while its height during the fall would be an example of a continuous fluent. The distinction is conceptual rather than formal. Indeed, the same fluent could be discrete at one time and continuous at a later time. After it lands (and stops bouncing), the ball's height becomes a discrete fluent.

Now, following [Shanahan, 1990], we introduce the predicate Trajectory.[8] The formula Trajectory(f1,t,f2,d) represents that if discrete fluent f1 is initiated at time t then continuous fluent f2 holds at time t + d. We have the following HoldsAt clause in addition to (SEC1) and (SEC3).

$$\text{HoldsAt(f2,t2)} \leftarrow \text{Happens(a,t1)} \wedge \text{Initiates(a,f1,t1)} \wedge \qquad \text{(SEC4)}$$
$$\text{Trajectory(f1,t1,f2,d)} \wedge \text{t2} = \text{t1} + \text{d} \wedge$$
$$\text{not Clipped(t1,f1,t2)}$$

I'll assume that arithmetic constraints such as the one that appears in this clause are accounted for, both semantically and computationally, by some framework such as that of Constraint Logic Programming [Jaffar & Lassez, 1987].

A domain description now includes a collection of Trajectory clauses. As an example, imagine a car that moves in straight line at fixed velocity of 10 units of distance per unit of time. The fluent Distance(x) represents that the car is x units away from its starting point. The fluent Moving represents that the car is moving.[9] There are two actions StartCar and StopCar, which respectively set the car in motion and bring it to a halt. We have the following clauses.

$$\text{Initiates(StartCar,Moving,t)} \qquad \text{(Car1)}$$

$$\text{Terminates(StopCar,Moving,t)} \qquad \text{(Car2)}$$

$$\text{Trajectory(Moving,t,Distance(x2),d)} \leftarrow \qquad \text{(Car3)}$$
$$\text{HoldsAt(Distance(x1),t)} \wedge x2 = x1 + 10 * d$$

These clauses are self-explanatory. But in addition, we need to represent what takes place when the fluent Distance(x) undergoes the transition from a discrete fluent to a continuous one, and vice versa.

$$\text{Terminates(StartCar,Distance(x),t)} \qquad \text{(Car4)}$$

$$\text{Initiates(StopCar,Distance(x),t)} \leftarrow \text{HoldsAt(Distance(x),t)} \qquad \text{(Car5)}$$

Clauses in the above style are usually required, whatever the domain. Narrative descriptions have the usual form. For example, we might have,

$$\text{Initially(Distance(0))} \qquad \text{(Car6)}$$

$$\text{Happens(StartCar,10)} \qquad \text{(Car7)}$$

$$\text{Happens(StopCar,20)} \qquad \text{(Car8)}$$

Now let Σ be the conjunction of Axioms (SEC1) to (SEC4) with (Car1) to (Car8). Figure 13.3 shows fragments of the SLDNF search space for the goal clause $\leftarrow$ HoldsAt(Distance(x),15) from Σ. The figure shows how the attempt to find an SLDNF-refutation of the goal fails using Axioms (SEC1) and (SEC3). The successful branch using the new axiom (SEC4) is labelled A.

13.4 Triggered Events and Continuous Change

Recall the example of the kitchen sink filling with water. When the water reaches the top of the sink, the level stops rising, and the water starts spilling onto the floor. With the apparatus of the last section, it's possible to represent the continuous variation in water level as the sink fills, but it's not clear how to represent the fact that an event occurs when the water reaches the top. Of course, it's possible to include this event explicitly in the narrative description via a Happens clause. But we would like the burden of inferring the occurrence of such events to fall to the logical apparatus we've provided, through the inclusion in our domain description of appropriate sentences which capture the requisite causal relations between continuous fluents and the events they trigger.

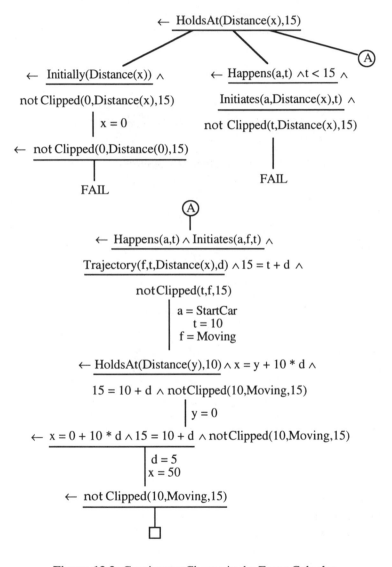

Figure 13.3: Continuous Change in the Event Calculus

Fortunately, triggered events can be incorporated into the formalism without very much difficulty. We simply need to include in our domain description formulae of the form,

$$\text{Happens}(\alpha,t) \leftarrow \text{HoldsAt}(\beta 1,t) \wedge \text{HoldsAt}(\beta 2,t)$$

where (at time t) $\beta 1$ is a continuous fluent and $\beta 2$ is a discrete fluent.[10] In general, $\beta 1$ will be on the trajectory of $\beta 2$. The second conjunct is included because α might terminate $\beta 2$, turning $\beta 1$ into a discrete fluent. Without the second conjunct, this would lead to infinitely many occurrences of α.

For the kitchen sink example, suppose that the brim is at level 10, and that the level increases at the rate of one unit of height per unit of time. Then we have the following clauses, which resemble those in the car example. The domain includes the fluents Filling and Height(x), and the actions TapOn and TapOff, whose intended meaning should be obvious.

$$\text{Initiates(TapOn,Filling,t)} \tag{Sk1}$$

$$\text{Terminates(TapOff,Filling,t)} \tag{Sk2}$$

$$\text{Trajectory(Filling,t,Height(x2),d)} \leftarrow \tag{Sk3}$$
$$\text{HoldsAt(Height(x1),t)} \wedge x2 = x1 + d$$

$$\text{Terminates(TapOn,Height(x),t)} \tag{Sk4}$$

$$\text{Initiates(TapOff,Height(x),t)} \leftarrow \text{HoldsAt(Height(x),t)} \tag{Sk5}$$

In addition, we require the following clauses to cater for the triggered event that occurs when the sink overflows. The event type (action) Overflow is introduced for this purpose.

$$\text{Happens(Overflow,t)} \leftarrow \text{HoldsAt(Height(10),t)} \wedge \tag{Sk6}$$
$$\text{HoldsAt(Filling,t)}$$

$$\text{Terminates(Overflow,Filling,t)} \tag{Sk7}$$

$$\text{Initiates(Overflow,Height(10),t)} \tag{Sk8}$$

$$\text{Initiates(Overflow,Spilling,t)} \tag{Sk9}$$

The fluent Spilling, which is initiated when an Overflow event occurs, could in turn be a continuous fluent, leading to the occurrence of other triggered events. (Imagine a cascade of champagne glasses, for example.)

Here's an example narrative description for this domain.

$$\text{Initially(Height(0))} \tag{Sk10}$$

Happens(TapOn,5)   (Sk11)

Let Σ be the conjunction of Axioms (SEC1) to (SEC4) with (Sk1) to (Sk11). Figures 13.4 and 13.5 show the structure of the SLDNF search space for the goal clause ← Holds(Height(x),20) from Σ.

The key difference between this example and that of the car is, of course, the fact that the Overflow event at time 15 is inferred rather than included explicitly in the narrative description. The SLDNF-refutation that proves that this event occurs is sketched in Figure 13.5.

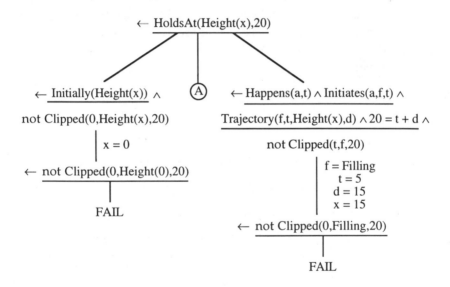

Figure 13.4: A Search Space with a Triggered Event

As usual, we would like to establish that a suitable class of event calculus programs extended for continuous change have consistent completions. Intuitively we should expect a counterpart to Theorem 13.2.2 to hold, since the modified event calculus conforms to the principle of directionality. To determine whether a fluent holds at time t, it is only ever necessary to examine which fluents hold at times earlier than t. Indeed, the construction presented in the proof of Theorem 13.2.2 can be suitably extended to cater for the continuous case for programs in which all Trajectory and Happens clauses are of a suitable form.

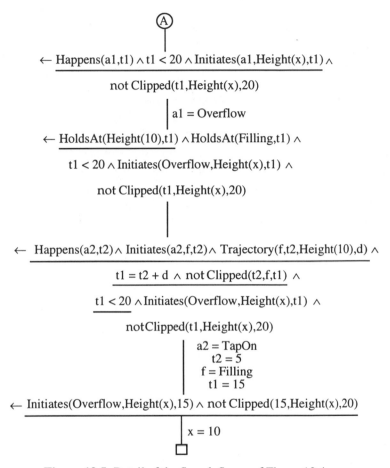

Figure 13.5: Detail of the Search Space of Figure 13.4

Notes

1. This difference between the event calculus and the situation calculus is greatly emphasised in [Kowalski & Sadri, 1994].

2. An earlier version of Kowalski's paper was published in 1986 as an Imperial College Department of Computing technical report, and contained the first version of the simplified event calculus.

3. In fact, several of the papers cited above preserve the event tokens of the original calculus.

4. Recall the definition of M1+M2 where M1 and M2 are interpretations (Definition 9.4.5).

5. Hayes [1985b] represents a similar example using his histories formalism. But since his formulation doesn't include a fluent for the level of liquid, it can't truly be said to address the issue of continuous change in the way that [Sandewall, 1989a], [Sandewall, 1989b] and [Shanahan, 1990] do.

6. This is called *autotermination* in [Shanahan, 1990].

7. The main difference is that the formulation in [Shanahan, 1990] retains event tokens. This has repercussions for the treatment of triggered events, which are given a simpler formulation here.

8. The problem of representing continuous change in the event calculus is also tackled by Van Belleghem, *et al.* [1994] in a somewhat different way. Their approach, like Miller's [1996], facilitates the representation of multiple influences on a continuously varying quantity.

9. Obviously, in any serious representation of such a domain, the fluent Moving would be parameterised with the vehicle's velocity.

10. A different approach to representing an overflow event is taken in [Van Belleghem, *et al.*, 1994].

14 A Circumscriptive Calculus of Events

This chapter draws together much of the material presented in previous chapters to form a calculus of events, based on the simplified event calculus presented in the last chapter, but which uses circumscription instead of negation-as-failure to overcome the frame problem [Shanahan, 1995b]. Based on the principles of separation and directionality, a combination of causal and state-based minimisation is used. This combination permits a powerful separation theorem to be proved, which guarantees that the Hanks-McDermott problem doesn't arise for a large class of domain theories. The various domain features permitted by the theorem are explored in the next chapter.

14.1 The Simplified Event Calculus with Circumscription

The simplified event calculus presented in the last chapter, especially with the extension for continuous change, is an attractive alternative to the situation calculus. However, the reduced expressive power of logic programs compared to full first-order predicate calculus with circumscription, plus the fact that the semantics of negation-as-failure is still not fully understood, mitigate against the wholesale adoption of the formalism in its logic programming guise. On the other hand, although research on the event calculus has largely been carried out in the context of logic programming, the essential features of the formalism aren't in any way tied down to the logic programming paradigm. These considerations lead us naturally to ask whether a circumscriptive version of the calculus can be constructed.

A circumscriptive calculus of events is presented in this chapter and the next which answers this question affirmatively. However, a good deal of modification of the formulation in the present chapter is required to achieve this. It turns out that the endeavour to overcome the frame problem for the simplified event calculus using circumscription recapitulates that endeavour for the situation calculus. If we adopt the most obvious circumscription policy, we get the Hanks-McDermott problem. If we modify the formalism in a way that makes the analogue of causal minimisation possible, we find that it suffers a corresponding loss of expressive power. However, a solution is possible that is inspired by state-based minimisation, but that incorporates elements of causal minimisation as well.

Let's see how the Hanks-McDermott problem arises if we attempt to use circumscription in a naive way to overcome the frame problem with the simplified event calculus. We begin by importing Axioms (SEC1) to (SEC3). They need to be modified slightly. First, negation-as-failure's not symbol has to be replaced by the classical negation symbol ¬. Second, we have to consider how negative HoldsAt information is to be dealt with in the absence of negation-as-failure. The most obvious way to adapt the axioms is to use the completions of the HoldsAt and Clipped predicates.

$$\text{HoldsAt}(f,t2) \leftrightarrow [\text{Happens}(a,t1) \wedge \text{Initiates}(a,f,t1) \wedge \quad \text{(EHM1)}$$
$$t1 < t2 \wedge \neg \text{Clipped}(t1,f,t2)] \vee [\text{Initially}(f) \wedge$$
$$\neg \text{Clipped}(0,f,t2)]$$

$$\text{Clipped}(t1,f,t2) \leftrightarrow \exists t \, [\text{Happens}(a,t) \wedge \text{Terminates}(a,f,t) \wedge \quad \text{(EHM2)}$$
$$t1 < t \wedge t < t2]$$

The Yale shooting scenario can be represented exactly as in Section 13.2.

$$\text{Initiates}(\text{Load},\text{Loaded},t) \qquad\qquad \text{(SEY1)}$$

$$\text{Terminates}(\text{Shoot},\text{Alive},t) \leftarrow \text{HoldsAt}(\text{Loaded},t) \qquad\qquad \text{(SEY2)}$$

$$\text{Initially}(\text{Alive}) \qquad\qquad \text{(SEY3)}$$

$$\text{Happens}(\text{Load},5) \qquad\qquad \text{(SEY4)}$$

$$\text{Happens}(\text{Sneeze},10) \qquad\qquad \text{(SEY5)}$$

$$\text{Happens}(\text{Shoot},15) \qquad\qquad \text{(SEY6)}$$

Since we're now back in the realm of full predicate calculus, we also require uniqueness-of-names axioms for actions and fluents.

$$\text{UNA}[\text{Load},\text{Sneeze},\text{Shoot}] \qquad\qquad \text{(SEY7)}$$

$$\text{UNA}[\text{Alive},\text{Loaded}] \qquad\qquad \text{(SEY8)}$$

We'll consider only models in which time points are interpreted by the natural numbers, and in which the < predicate is interpreted accordingly.

Now, intuitively it seems that the required circumscription policy to overcome the frame problem is to minimise Initiates and Terminates in parallel with Happens. This corresponds to the two assumptions that,

• The known effects of an action are all the effects of an action, and

• The known event occurrences are the only event occurrences.

HoldsAt and Clipped clearly have to be allowed to vary. So, if we let Σ be the conjunction of (EHM1) and (EHM2) with (SEY1) to (SEY6), then we're interested in,

$$\text{CIRC}[\Sigma \, ; \text{Happens}, \text{Initiates}, \text{Terminates} \, ; \text{HoldsAt}, \text{Clipped}].$$

Our hope is that the circumscription will entail ¬ HoldsAt(Alive,20). This ought to follow from Axiom (EHM1) since, if the minimisation works properly, the Alive fluent will be clipped by the Shoot action. However, our hope is frustrated by the existence of an anomalous model in which the Sneeze action unloads the gun.

Proposition 14.1.1. (The Hanks-McDermott Problem for Simplified Event Calculus)

$$\text{CIRC}[\Sigma \text{ ; Happens, Initiates, Terminates ; HoldsAt, Clipped}] \not\models$$
$$\neg \text{ HoldsAt(Alive,20)}$$

Proof. Consider any model M of Σ that meets the following criteria.

- M ⊩ Happens(a,t) ↔
  [a = Load ∧ t = 5] ∨ [a = Sneeze ∧ t = 10] ∨ [a = Shoot ∧ t = 15]

- M ⊩ Initiates(Load,Loaded,5)

- M ⊩ Terminates(Sneeze,Loaded,10)

- M ⊩ ¬ HoldsAt(Loaded,15)

- M ⊩ ¬ Terminates(Shoot,,Alive,15)

It's easy to see that such models exist. Furthermore, some of these models will be minimal with respect to the circumscription policy, because we cannot remove Terminates(Sneeze,Loaded,10) without introducing another Terminates sentence. The proposition follows from the fact that in all such minimal models, we have,

$$\text{M} \Vdash \text{HoldsAt(Alive,20)}. \qquad \square$$

This proposition is directly analogous to Proposition 3.3.2, which establishes the same result for the situation calculus. The insights behind the proposed solutions to this difficulty for the situation calculus are equally applicable here.

For example, we could try causal minimisation. Initiates and Terminates already resemble Lifschitz's predicate Causes (see Chapter 5), but with one crucial difference. The Causes predicate doesn't include any analogue of the third argument of Initiates and Terminates, which gives Initiates and Terminates clauses access to the time point at which an event occurs, thus permitting preconditions to be incorporated in their bodies.

To achieve the same effect as causal minimisation, we need to drop the temporal argument from Initiates and Terminates, and introduce a Precond predicate to cope with preconditions.

Success(a,t) $\equiv_{def}$ $\forall$ f [Precond(f,v,a) $\rightarrow$ [HoldsAt(f,t) $\leftrightarrow$ v = True]]

HoldsAt(f,t2) $\leftrightarrow$ [Happens(a,t1) $\wedge$ Success(a,t1) $\wedge$ Initiates(a,f) $\wedge$
t1 < t2 $\wedge$ $\neg$ Clipped(t1,f,t2)] $\vee$ [Initially(f) $\wedge$ $\neg$ Clipped(0,f,t2)]

Clipped(t1,f,t2) $\leftrightarrow$ $\exists$ t [Happens(a,t) $\wedge$ Success(a,t) $\wedge$ Terminates(a,f) $\wedge$
t1 < t $\wedge$ t < t2]

There's no need to go into more detail here. Suffice to say this manoeuvre works to the extent that causal minimisation works for the situation calculus, and fails in exactly the same way that it fails for situation calculus. In other words, we can indeed formalise the Yale shooting scenario using causal minimisation and get the desired results. But this is at the expense of expressive power. The resulting formalism has trouble representing actions with context-sensitive effects, and gives rise to similar difficulties with ramifications.

Can the Initiates and Terminates predicates be parameterised in such a way that they have full access to the fluents that hold when an event occurs, and yet in a way that doesn't leave their minimisation at the mercy of changes in the extension of HoldsAt? Inspired by the success of state-based minimisation (Chapters 6 and 7), it turns out that we can get this effect by introducing states into the ontology, and substituting a state argument for the time point argument in Initiates and Terminates.[1]

The formal details of the circumscriptive event calculus begin in the next section. First I'll present some of the intuition behind the formalism. The key idea is this. It's safe to index Initiates and Terminates on states because a state is just a collection of fluents, and is therefore a timeless entity. To see this more clearly, let's represent a state as a set of fluents, and assume that a fluent holds in a state s if and only if it's a member of s. For example, if σ = {Alive, Loaded} then Alive and Loaded hold in σ and Dead doesn't. Now we can write Initiates and Terminates formulae such as the following.

Terminates(Shoot,Alive,s) $\leftarrow$ Loaded $\in$ s

Irrespective of what fluents hold at what time points, we have Terminates(Shoot,Alive,σ). Contrast this with Axiom (SEY2) above, from which we were unable to show that Terminates(Shoot,Alive,15).

It remains to write an axiom that links states to time points, and yields the HoldsAt information we expect as the outcome of temporal projection. The state at a given time point t will be a set of fluents including those that have been made to hold before t by events in the narrative (and still hold), and excluding those that have been made not to hold before t by events in the narrative (and still don't hold). By making states intermediate between the domain description and the narrative, we have enforced the principle of separation, and cut the feedback loop that gives rise to the Hanks-McDermott problem.

Does the new style of Initiates and Terminates formula have the required expressive power? It should be clear that actions with context-sensitive effects can be represented in the new style, since Initiates and Terminates formulae have full access to the fluents that hold in the relevant state. But what about domain constraints?

We could simply write domain constraints as in the following example.

$$\text{HoldsAt(Alive,t)} \leftrightarrow \neg \text{HoldsAt(Dead,t)}$$

However, it's easy to see that this won't work properly. If this style of formula is used, the indirect effects of actions — fluents derivable through domain constraints — won't be accessible to Initiates and Terminates formulae, since Initiates and Terminates are indexed on states not time points. Instead, we need to introduce a new predicate HoldsIn. We write,

$$\text{HoldsIn(Alive,s)} \leftrightarrow \neg \text{HoldsIn(Dead,s)}.$$

Now, in order to give Initiates and Terminates formulae full access to the fluents that hold in the relevant state, they have to use HoldsIn instead of set membership. So we write,

$$\text{Terminates(Shoot,Alive,s)} \leftarrow \text{HoldsIn(Loaded,s)}.$$

But there's a further complication. The members of a set s are now only a subset of the fluents that hold in s. The members of s are the fluents that were initiated directly by events. Other fluents may be derivable through domain constraints. Unfortunately, this means that simple sets of fluents are no longer adequate for representing states, because we've assumed so far that a fluent holds in s if *and only if* it's a member of s. In other words, it has been assumed that s completely captures the fluents that hold in s. With the introduction of HoldsIn and domain constraints, this is no longer true.

This leads to the final step in designing the formalism, which is to modify the representation of a state. First, positive and negative fluents are distinguished. (Below, I write Not(f) for the negation of f.) A state is now represented by a set of fluents, *some of which may be negated*. Then, a fluent holds in a state s if it's a member of s, while a fluent does not hold in s if it's negation is a member of s. The set s only partially captures the fluents that hold and don't hold in s. Further information about the state is derivable through domain constraints.

Although the final product is complicated, each step in the design of the formalism follows with the inevitability of a sequence of moves in a chess end game. The formal presentation now follows.

14.2 States

The circumscriptive event calculus uses variables for time points (t, t1, t2, etc.), fluents (f, f1, f2, etc.), and states (s, s1, s2, etc.). The first part of the formalism to be presented concerns the properties of states.[2] A state is represented as a set of (possibly negated) fluents. To capture this, the predicate In is defined as follows, where the formula In(f,s) represents that fluent f is a member of the set s.

$$s1 = s2 \leftrightarrow \forall f \, [In(f,s1) \leftrightarrow In(f,s2)] \tag{S1}$$

$$\forall s1,f1 \, \exists s2 \, \forall f2 \, [In(f2,s2) \leftrightarrow [In(f2,s1) \vee f2 = f1]] \tag{S2}$$

$$\exists s \, \forall f \, [\neg \, In(f,s)] \tag{S3}$$

We've already seen a very similar collection of axioms in Section 7.2. Axiom (S1) says that two sets are equal if they contain the same fluents. Axiom (S2) says that any fluent can be added to any set to give another set. Axioms (S2) and (S3) guarantee that a set exists for every combination of fluents, and are analogous to the existence-of-situations axioms in Chapter 7.

Standard notation will be used for sets. In other words, if we have,

$$In(f,\sigma) \leftrightarrow [f = \beta_1 \vee f = \beta_2 \vee \ldots \vee f = \beta_n]$$

then σ can be written $\{\beta_1, \beta_2, \ldots, \beta_n\}$.

The fluents in a set can be negated. As in Baker's generalised fluents (see Section 7.2), the term Not(f) stands for the negation of the fluent f. The Not function's only role is in the circumscriptive event calculus's analogue of Baker's existence-of-situations axioms. As in Baker's work, it doesn't have a knowledge representation role. However, we need a uniqueness-names-of names axiom for fluents which covers it. For example, if our domain includes fluents $\beta_1, \beta_2, \ldots, \beta_n$, we include the axiom,

$$UNA[\beta_1, \beta_2, \ldots, \beta_n, Not].$$

In Chapter 7, since we needed to quantify independently over simple fluents and generalised fluents, a hierarchy of sorts had to be introduced. No such device is required here. We can safely include terms of the form Not(f) in the sort of fluents, so long as domain descriptions don't mention the Not function.

The fluents that hold in a given state s are partially captured by the members of s. The formula HoldsIn(f,s) represents that fluent f holds in state s. We have the following axioms.

$$\text{HoldsIn(f,s)} \leftarrow [\text{In(f,s)} \wedge \neg \text{AbState(s)}] \tag{E1}$$

$$\neg \text{HoldsIn(f,s)} \leftarrow [\text{In(Not(f),s)} \wedge \neg \text{AbState(s)}] \tag{E2}$$

If f is a member of s then f holds in the state s. Conversely, if Not(f) is a member of s then f does not hold in the state s. If neither f nor Not(f) are members of s then, in the absence of further information, we cannot say whether or not the fluent f holds in state s. However, further information of this kind may be present in the form of domain constraints expressed as extra HoldsIn formulae. Such formulae can be admitted without giving rise to contradiction because of the AbState conditions on (E1) and (E2). The predicate AbState will be minimised, making Axioms (E1) and (E2) into defaults. Abnormal states are those ruled out by domain constraints. The predicate AbState fulfils exactly the same role here as the AbSit predicate in the existence-of-situations axioms presented in Chapter 7.

For example, consider the state s = {F1, Not(F2)}. We have HoldsIn(F1,s) and ¬ HoldsIn(F2,s). But we don't have either HoldsIn(F3,s) or ¬ HoldsIn(F3,s). However, if we include the domain constraint,

$$\text{HoldsIn(F1)} \rightarrow \neg \text{HoldsIn(F3)}$$

then we have AbState({F1, Not(F2), F3}), as well as ¬ HoldsIn(F3,s).

Although there is no overall partitioning of fluents into primitive and derived,[3] the members of a set can be thought of as the primitive fluents that hold/don't hold in the corresponding state. As we'll see in the next section, the primitive fluents are those that are made to hold (or not hold) by events. Domain constraints in the form of extra HoldsIn formulae can then be thought of as yielding "derived" fluents. In the above example, F1 is primitive and F3 is derived. As spelt out at the end of the last section, it's because of domain constraints that states must be represented by *partial* descriptions of the fluents that hold in them, and (E1) and (E2) cannot be replaced by a simple biconditional.

The primitive/derived distinction parallels closely the distinction between frame and non-frame fluents introduced by Lifschitz [1990] (see Section 5.6). According to Lifschitz, the common sense law of inertia applies only to the frame fluents. Analogously, in the circumscriptive event calculus, the common sense law of inertia only applies to those fluents that have been initiated or terminated directly by events. In Lifschitz's situation calculus formulation, the frame fluents are fixed for all time.[4] In the circumscriptive event calculus, however, the frame fluents are a dynamically changing set. I'll adopt Lifschitz's terminology from now on, and refer to those fluents mentioned in the set representing a state as the *frame fluents*, and those not mentioned in the set as the *non-frame fluents*.

14.3   A Calculus of Events

Now the main axiom of the formalism is presented in a form that is suitable for domains that involve only discrete change. Later, it will be modified to cater for the continuous case. The axiom defines the predicate State. The formula State(t,s) represents that time point t is associated with state s. Each time point is associated with a single, characterising state s,[5] such that the fluent f is in s if and only if f was initiated by some event before t and still holds at t, and Not(f) is in s if and only if f was terminated by some event before t and still doesn't hold at t. The axiom we require is the following.

$$\text{State(t,s)} \leftrightarrow \forall \text{ f1 [In(f1,s)} \leftrightarrow \text{[Initiated(f1,t)} \vee \qquad \text{(E3)}$$
$$\exists \text{ f2 [f1 = Not(f2)} \wedge \text{Terminated(f2,t)]]]}$$

The formulae Initiated(f,t) and Terminated(f,t) are not part of the language, but are just abbreviations, which are defined as follows.[6] Several more predicates are introduced here, along with variables for the new sort of actions (event types) (a, a1, a2, etc.).

$$\text{Initiated(f,t2)} \equiv_{\text{def}} \exists \text{ a,t1,s [Happens(a,t1)} \wedge \text{t1} < \text{t2} \wedge \text{State(t1,s)} \wedge$$
$$\text{Initiates(a,f,s)} \wedge \neg \text{Clipped(t1,f,t2)]}$$

$$\text{Terminated(f,t2)} \equiv_{\text{def}} \exists \text{ a,t1,s [Happens(a,t1)} \wedge \text{t1} < \text{t2} \wedge \text{State(t1,s)} \wedge$$
$$\text{Terminates(a,f,s)} \wedge \neg \text{Declipped(t1,f,t2)]}$$

Again, the formulae Clipped(t1,f,t2) and Declipped(t1,f,t2) are not part of the language, but are abbreviations, which are defined as follows.

$$\text{Clipped(t1,f,t3)} \equiv_{\text{def}} \exists \text{ a,t2,s [Happens(a,t2)} \wedge \text{t1} < \text{t2} \wedge \text{t2} < \text{t3} \wedge$$
$$\text{State(t2,s)} \wedge \text{Terminates(a,f,s)]}$$

$$\text{Declipped(t1,f,t3)} \equiv_{\text{def}} \exists \text{ a,t2,s [Happens(a,t2)} \wedge \text{t1} < \text{t2} \wedge \text{t2} < \text{t3} \wedge$$
$$\text{State(t2,s)} \wedge \text{Initiates(a,f,s)]}$$

The Initiates and Terminates predicates are used in domain descriptions just as in the simplified event calculus of the last chapter. The formula Initiates(a,f,s) represents that, in state s, the fluent f is initiated by an event of type a, and the formula Terminates(a,f,s) represents that, in state s, the fluent f is terminated by an event of type a. Initiates and Terminates will be minimised. The formula Happens(a,t) represents that an event of type a happens at time t. The formula t1 < t2 represents that time t1 is before time t2. For the discrete case, time points can be interpreted by the naturals, and for now I'll assume that we're considering only models in which < is interpreted accordingly.

The Initially predicate, used in the simplified event calculus, has been dispensed with here. In the simplified event calculus, no distinction is made between knowing the value of a fluent in the initial situation and knowing that a fluent does not hold in the initial situation. This distinction is present in the circumscriptive version of the calculus, which rules out the naive use of an Initially predicate.[7] The initial situation will be described using a notional first event. This technique will become clear in the examples.

It's important to note here that, for reasons set out at the end of Section 14.1, the state s that is associated with a time t is not the set of *all* fluents that hold (or don't hold) at t. Rather, s is a *subset* of those fluents — the frame fluents. The presence of domain constraints, expressed in terms of HoldsIn, means that further "derived" (non-frame) fluents might hold (or not hold) at t. The last axiom of the formalism defines the predicate HoldsAt, which takes into account this possibility. The formula HoldsAt(f,t) represents that fluent f holds at time t.

$$\text{HoldsAt}(f,t) \leftrightarrow \exists s \ [\text{State}(t,s) \wedge \text{HoldsIn}(f,s)] \qquad \text{(E4)}$$

The HoldsAt predicate is still not defined so as to supply a complete description of which fluents hold at what times, because there may be non-deterministic actions, or an incompletely described initial situation. However, it takes into account all that is known about each time point. In the rest of the chapter, the conjunction of Axioms (S1) to (S3) with (E1) to (E4) will be denoted by EC. In general, a temporal projection problem will be captured by the conjunction of EC with a conjunction of Happens formulae representing a narrative, and a conjunction of Initiates, Terminates and HoldsIn formulae comprising the domain theory. The answer to the temporal projection problem resides in the set of HoldsAt formulae that are consequences.

The circumscription policy for overcoming the frame problem, representing the assumptions that the only domain constraints are the known domain constraints, that the only events that occur are those that are known to occur, and that the only effects of events are the known effects, is to minimise AbState at a high priority, and to minimise Happens, Initiates and Terminates at a lower priority, allowing HoldsAt and State to vary. In other words, given a formula Σ, we're interested in,

CIRC[Σ ; AbState > Happens, Initiates, Terminates ; HoldsAt, State].

It's necessary to prioritise the minimisation of AbState in order to exclude models in which a larger than necessary extension of AbState is traded for a smaller than desired extension of Initiates or Terminates. The circumscription of a formula Σ according to this policy will be written $\text{CIRC}_{ec}[\Sigma]$.

As pointed out in Section 10.1, a blanket minimisation of Happens, as conducted here, isn't always appropriate. The tentative solution to the problem of over-zealous event occurrence minimisation offered in that chapter is also pertinent here.

14.4   The Blocks World

Fortunately, the foregoing machinery is mostly transparent to anyone who uses the formalism, and descriptions of domains and histories are intuitive and elegant. In the next section, the mathematical properties of the event calculus are investigated, and a result is developed that supports the claim that the frame problem has been solved for a large class of examples. But first, I will show how the formalism could be used to represent the Blocks World example. The ontology of this world includes blocks and locations. A new sort is introduced for these, with variables x, y and z.[8] An event of type Move(x,y) is an attempt to move block x to location or block y. The fluent On(x,y) represents that block x is at location y or on block y. The domain of time points is assumed to be the natural numbers.[9] We have the following formulae.

$$\text{Initiates}(\text{Move}(x,y),\text{On}(x,y),s) \leftarrow \text{HoldsIn}(\text{Clear}(x),s) \land$$
$$\text{HoldsIn}(\text{Clear}(y),s) \land x \neq y \land x \neq \text{Table}$$

$$\text{Terminates}(\text{Move}(x,y),\text{On}(x,z),s) \leftarrow \text{HoldsIn}(\text{Clear}(x),s) \land$$
$$\text{HoldsIn}(\text{Clear}(y),s) \land x \neq y \land \text{HoldsIn}(\text{On}(x,z),s) \land y \neq z$$

$$\text{Initiates}(\text{Move}(x,y),\text{Clear}(z),s) \leftarrow \text{HoldsIn}(\text{Clear}(x),s) \land$$
$$\text{HoldsIn}(\text{Clear}(y),s) \land x \neq y \land \text{HoldsIn}(\text{On}(x,z),s) \land y \neq z$$

$$\text{Terminates}(\text{Move}(x,y),\text{Clear}(y),s) \leftarrow \text{HoldsIn}(\text{Clear}(x),s) \land$$
$$\text{HoldsIn}(\text{Clear}(y),s) \land x \neq y \land x \neq \text{Table}$$

The key feature of these formulae, which otherwise correspond very closely with those in Section 13.1, is that no mention is made of the HoldsAt predicate. No mention is made of actual times at all. Instead, the HoldsIn predicate is used to give access to the fluents that hold when an event occurs, by referring to the corresponding state. Because states are timeless, the formulae are timelessly true. This style of representation permits the vital separation of minimisation from temporal projection.

Instead of explicitly specifying the conditions under which an event initiates or terminates the Clear fluent, a domain constraint could be used. This would be achieved by writing HoldsIn formulae that related the Clear fluent to the On fluent, and that constrained every block or location to have at most one block on it.

As usual, a narrative is described using Happens formulae. For example, the following formulae represent that block A is moved onto block B at time 5, then block C is moved onto the table at time 8.

$$Happens(Move(A,B),5)$$

$$Happens(Move(C,Table),8)$$

Concurrent events, such as moving two blocks at the same time, are easily represented as Happens formulae with identical time arguments, so long as the events are independent, that is to say so long as their effects are not cumulative (as in putting two weights on one pan of a pair of scales at the same time) or cancelling (as in trying to lift an object and pressing down on it at the same time). In the next chapter, a version of the calculus is described that can cope with cumulative and cancelling concurrent events. Note that it's easy to write formulae that represent events whose exact order of occurrence is not known, using disjunctions of Happens formulae, or using Happens formulae with existentially quantified time arguments, as described in Section 10.1.

To illustrate a different approach to describing the initial situation, I will assume the occurrence of an event at time 0 which initiates (terminates) all the fluents that initially hold (don't hold). These would have been described by the Initially predicate in the simplified event calculus.[10] As a convention, the type of this initial event will be denoted by Start (and the uniqueness-of-names axiom for actions must always take it into account). Suppose blocks A, B and C are initially clear and on the table. Then we have,

$$Happens(Start,0)$$

$$Initiates(Start,On(A,Table),s)$$

$$Initiates(Start,On(B,Table),s)$$

$$Initiates(Start,On(C,Table),s)$$

$$\text{Initiates(Start,Clear(A),s)}$$

$$\text{Initiates(Start,Clear(B),s)}$$

$$\text{Initiates(Start,Clear(C),s)}.$$

The initial event can also terminate fluents, of course, thus making them not hold from time 0. Notice that, according to Axiom (E3), the state at time 0 is the empty set of fluents.

For each domain, a set of uniqueness-of-names axioms is required for fluents and actions (event types). It might also be necessary to include other uniqueness-of-names axioms, in this case for blocks and locations.

$$\text{UNA[Move, Start]}$$

$$\text{UNA[Clear, On, Not]}$$

$$\text{UNA[A, B, C, Table]}$$

If the conjunction of EC with all the above formulae is denoted by Σ, then in all models of $\text{CIRC}_{ec}[\Sigma]$, we have, for example, HoldsAt(On(A,B),12). I won't attempt to prove this here, but the results of the next section will provide a basis for proving which fluents hold at what times for any domain theory and narrative description.

Before moving on to the formal justification for the claim that the Hanks-McDermott problem has been avoided, let me recap on the intuition behind the formalism's approach to the frame problem. Note that the only predicates needed to capture the Blocks World domain and to represent a narrative are Initiates, Terminates, HoldsIn and Happens. The circumscription policy for overcoming the frame problem minimises only these domain and narrative predicates.

The results of temporal projection, on the other hand, are expressed in terms of the predicate HoldsAt, which doesn't appear in domain and history formulae. So, the principle of separation has been observed, and temporal projection is independent of minimisation. This has been achieved by using HoldsIn in the representation of the domain, a predicate indexed on states. It would have been tempting to use HoldsAt instead, obviating the need for states altogether. But then the extensions of Initiates and Terminates would vary according to the outcome of temporal projection. The strong result of the next section would not then be applicable, and the Hanks-McDermott problem would arise.

14.5 A Separation Theorem for the Calculus

As a number of authors have emphasised, such as Lifschitz [1991] and Sandewall [1993], we would like to be able to demonstrate that an approach to the frame problem yields correct results, not just with a single example, but with a significant class of examples. General results of this sort have been produced for the situation calculus by Lifschitz [1991] and Lin and Shoham [1991], but neither of these papers addresses continuous change, concurrent events, or events with non-deterministic effects. Lin and Shoham have extended their work to deal with concurrent events [1992], but the general result they prove is built on a criterion of epistemological completeness which apparently excludes the possibility of events with non-deterministic effects.

In this section, I present a separation theorem that says that any domain theory and narrative description of a certain form can be circumscribed independently from the axioms of the circumscriptive event calculus. The demands on the form of domain and narrative formulae are very liberal. Concurrent events are allowed, and in later sections I show that domains involving non-deterministic events and continuous change can also be represented in the required form. The theorem is very general, and applies not only to the calculus above, but also to any calculus having the right form. I will write $\bar{x}$ to denote a tuple of variables, and x_i to denote the ith variable in such a tuple.

Definition 14.5.1. A formula is *chronological in argument* k if it has the form $\forall \bar{x} \, \rho(\bar{x}) \leftrightarrow \phi(\bar{x})$, where ρ is a predicate whose k^{th} argument is a time point and $\phi(\bar{x})$ is a formula in which $\bar{x}$ is free, and all occurrences of ρ in $\phi(\bar{x})$ are in conjunctions of the form $\rho(\bar{z}) \wedge z_k < x_k$. □

For example, Axiom (E3) is chronological in argument 1. Under certain conditions, it's easy to work out the consequences of circumscribing the conjunction of a formula with a chronological formula.

Theorem 14.5.2. Consider only models in which the time points are interpreted by the naturals, and in which $<$ is interpreted accordingly. Let $\Delta = \forall \bar{x} \, \rho(\bar{x}) \leftrightarrow \phi(\bar{x})$ be a formula that is chronological in some argument. Let Σ be a formula that doesn't mention the predicate symbol ρ. If $\sigma 1^*$ and $\sigma 2^*$ are tuples of predicates such that $\sigma 2^*$ includes ρ then,

$$\text{CIRC}[\Sigma \wedge \Delta \, ; \sigma 1^*; \sigma 2^*]$$

is equivalent to,

$$\text{CIRC}[\Sigma \; ; \sigma 1^*; \sigma 2^*] \wedge \Delta.$$

Proof. The proof is given in Appendix B.   ☐

Since both Axioms (E3) and (E4) are chronological in one of their arguments, Theorem 14.5.2 ensures that any domain theory and narrative description can be circumscribed independently from the axioms of the circumscriptive event calculus, so long as the domain and narrative formulae don't mention HoldsAt or State. After this minimisation, the axioms of the circumscriptive event calculus can be used classically (in other words, monotonically) to derive which fluents hold at what times. Appendix C contains another theorem, related to Theorem 14.5.2, which facilitates the construction of temporal projection algorithms.

It's important to see that meeting the conditions for applying Theorem 14.5.2 is not in itself sufficient to solve the frame problem. It's still necessary to get the minimisation right before (E3) and (E4) are added. Axioms (S1) to (S3) and (E1) and (E2) play a crucial role in this respect. Theorem 14.5.2 simply supplies certain conditions under which projection is guaranteed not to interfere with minimisation. This sort of interference is what gives rise to the Hanks-McDermott problem.

In order to circumscribe domain theories and narrative descriptions, two other properties of circumscription will be useful. Theorems 14.5.3 and 14.5.4 are due to Vladimir Lifschitz. Let Σ be any formula and $\phi(\overline{x})$ be any formula with only $\overline{x}$ free.

Theorem 14.5.3. $\text{CIRC}[\Sigma \wedge \forall \, \overline{x} \, \rho(\overline{x}) \leftarrow \phi(\overline{x}); \rho]$ is equivalent to $\Sigma \wedge \forall \, \overline{x} \, \rho(\overline{x}) \leftrightarrow \phi(\overline{x})$ if Σ and $\phi(\overline{x})$ don't mention the predicate ρ.

Proof. See [Lifschitz, 1994].   ☐

In effect, Theorem 14.5.3 describes conditions under which circumscription implies the completion of a predicate (see Section 11.6).

Definition 14.5.4. An occurrence of a predicate symbol in a formula ϕ is *positive* if it is in the scope of an even number of negations in the equivalent formula ψ that is obtained by eliminating the connectives $\rightarrow$ and $\leftrightarrow$ from ϕ.   ☐

Theorem 14.5.5. Let ρ^* be the tuple of predicate symbols $\rho_1, \rho_2, ..., \rho_n$. If all occurrences in Σ of the predicate symbols in ρ^* are positive, then $\text{CIRC}[\Sigma \; ; \rho^*]$ is equivalent to,

$$\text{CIRC}[\Sigma \; ; \rho_1] \wedge \text{CIRC}[\Sigma \; ; \rho_2] \wedge \ldots \wedge \text{CIRC}[\Sigma \; ; \rho_n]$$

Proof. See [Lifschitz, 1994].   ☐

14.6 The Yale Shooting Scenario

With the results above, it's easy to show that the circumscriptive event calculus correctly formalises the Yale shooting scenario. The domain comprises three types of event — Load, Sneeze and Shoot — and two fluents — Alive and Loaded. These events and fluents are represented by the following formulae. Note that there are no axioms for the Sneeze event, since it doesn't affect any fluent.

$$\text{Initiates(Load,Loaded,s)} \qquad \text{(CEY1)}$$

$$\text{Terminates(Shoot,Alive,s)} \leftarrow \text{HoldsIn(Loaded,s)} \qquad \text{(CEY2)}$$

The Yale shooting scenario can be represented by the following narrative formulae, describing three events — Load then Sneeze then Shoot. The Sneeze event here serves the same purpose as waiting in the original formulation: it provides an opportunity for the minimisation to go wrong.

$$\text{Happens(Load,10)} \qquad \text{(CEY3)}$$

$$\text{Happens(Sneeze,15)} \qquad \text{(CEY4)}$$

$$\text{Happens(Shoot,20)} \qquad \text{(CEY5)}$$

The initial situation is described as follows.

$$\text{Happens(Start,0)} \qquad \text{(CEY6)}$$

$$\text{Initiates(Start,Alive,s)} \qquad \text{(CEY7)}$$

The following uniqueness-of-names have to be included.

$$\text{UNA[Load, Sneeze, Shoot, Start]} \qquad \text{(CEY8)}$$

$$\text{UNA[Alive, Loaded, Not]} \qquad \text{(CEY9)}$$

Let Σ be the conjunction of EC with (CEY1) to (CEY9).

Proposition 14.6.1. $\text{CIRC}_{ec}[\Sigma] \vDash \neg \text{HoldsAt(Alive,25)}$.

Proof. Let Φ be the conjunction of (CEY1) to (CEY9) with EC minus Axioms (E3) and (E4). $\text{CIRC}_{ec}[\Phi]$ is defined as the conjunction of,

$$\text{CIRC}[\Phi \text{ ; Happens, Initiates, Terminates ; State, HoldsAt}]$$

with,

$$\text{CIRC}[\Phi \text{ ; AbState ; Happens, Initiates, Terminates, State, HoldsAt}].$$

We'll consider each conjunct in turn.

Take the first conjunct. Since all occurrences of Happens, Initiates and Terminates in Φ are positive, CIRC[Φ ; Happens, Initiates, Terminates] is equivalent to,

CIRC[Φ ; Happens] ∧ CIRC[Φ ; Initiates] ∧ CIRC[Φ ; Terminates]

from Theorem 14.5.5. By applying Theorem 14.5.3 to each conjunct in this formula, we can show that the completions of Happens, Initiates and Terminates are true in all of its models. In particular, we have the following.

$$\text{Terminates(a,f,s)} \leftrightarrow a = \text{Shoot} \wedge f = \text{Alive} \wedge \qquad [14.6.2]$$
$$\text{HoldsIn(Loaded,s)}$$

$$\text{Happens(a,t)} \leftrightarrow [a = \text{Load} \wedge t = 10] \vee [a = \text{Sneeze} \wedge t = 15] \vee \quad [14.6.3]$$
$$[a = \text{Shoot} \wedge t = 20]$$

Since there are no occurrences of State or HoldsAt in Φ, [14.6.2] and [14.6.3] are also true in all models of CIRC$_{ec}$[Φ], where these predicates are allowed to vary.

Now let's look at the second conjunct of CIRC$_{ec}$[Φ]. In the absence of any domain constraints, the only abnormal combinations of fluents are those that include both f and Not(f) for some f. So, in all models of,

CIRC[Φ ; AbState ; Happens, Initiates, Terminates]

we have,

$$\text{AbState(s)} \leftrightarrow \exists f \, [\text{In(Not(f),s)} \wedge \text{In(f,s)}] \qquad [14.6.4]$$

Since there are no occurrences of State or HoldsAt in Φ, allowing these predicates to vary does not affect the outcome of the circumscription, so [14.6.4] is also true in all models of CIRC$_{ec}$[Φ].

Now, since (E3) and (E4) are chronological, by applying Theorem 14.5.2, first to add (E3) and then to add (E4), we can show that [14.6.2] to [14.6.4] are also true in all models of CIRC$_{ec}$[Φ ∧ (E3) ∧ (E4)], in other words in CIRC$_{ec}$[Σ].

The rest of the proof is classical deduction. From Axiom (E3), we get,

$$\text{CIRC}_{ec}[\Sigma] \vDash \text{State(0,s)} \leftrightarrow \forall f \, [\neg \text{In(f,s)}].$$

From this and Axiom (S3), we have,

$$\text{CIRC}_{ec}[\Sigma] \vDash \exists s \, [\text{State(0,s)}]$$

which yields, from (CEY7),

$$CIRC_{ec}[\Sigma] \vDash \exists s \; [State(0,s) \wedge Initiates(Start,Alive,s)] \qquad [14.6.5]$$

From this, using [14.6.3] and Axiom (E3) again, we get,

$$CIRC_{ec}[\Sigma] \vDash State(10,s) \leftrightarrow \forall f \; [In(f,s) \leftrightarrow f = Alive].$$

Axioms (S1) to (S3) guarantee that a suitable s exists. In other words,

$$CIRC_{ec}[\Sigma] \vDash \exists s \; [State(10,s)].$$

Now we have, from (CEY1),

$$CIRC_{ec}[\Sigma] \vDash \exists s \; [State(10,s) \wedge Initiates(Load,Loaded,s)]. \qquad [14.6.6]$$

From [14.6.2], [14.6.3], and the definition of Clipped, we have,

$$CIRC_{ec}[\Sigma] \vDash \neg \; Clipped(0,Alive,20)$$

and,

$$CIRC_{ec}[\Sigma] \vDash \neg \; Clipped(10,Alive,20).$$

From these, [14.6.5], and [14.6.6], using Axiom (E3), we get,

$$CIRC_{ec}[\Sigma] \vDash State(20,s) \leftrightarrow \forall f \; [In(f,s) \leftrightarrow [f = Alive] \vee [f = Loaded]]$$

which, from (S1) to (S3), gives us,

$$CIRC_{ec}[\Sigma] \vDash \exists s \; [State(20,s) \wedge \forall f \; [In(f,s) \leftrightarrow [f = Alive] \vee [f = Loaded]].$$

From Axiom (E1) and [14.6.4], this gives,

$$CIRC_{ec}[\Sigma] \vDash \exists s \; [State(20,s) \wedge HoldsIn(Alive,s) \wedge HoldsIn(Loaded,s)].$$

Now Axiom (CEY2) tells us,

$$CIRC_{ec}[\Sigma] \vDash \exists s \; [State(20,s) \wedge Terminates(Shoot,Alive,s)]. \qquad [14.6.7]$$

Now we have, from this and the definition of Clipped,

$$CIRC_{ec}[\Sigma] \vDash Clipped(0,Alive,25)$$

as well as, from [14.6.3] and the definition of Declipped,

$$CIRC_{ec}[\Sigma] \vDash \neg \; Declipped(20,Alive,25).$$

Given this and [14.6.7], we can show from (E3),

$$CIRC_{ec}[\Sigma] \vDash \exists s \; [State(25,s) \wedge \neg \; HoldsIn(Alive,s)]$$

and therefore, from Axiom (E4),

$$\text{CIRC}_{ec}[\Sigma] \vDash \neg \text{ HoldsAt(Alive,25)}. \qquad \square$$

Because this proof is both important and typical, I've presented all the steps involved, although these are mostly quite mechanical. Future proofs will omit many of these steps.

Notes

1. In Chapter 16, we'll see how to restore temporal arguments without precipitating problems.

2. The axioms presented in this section are an ontologically cleaner version of the corresponding axioms presented in [Shanahan, 1995b].

3. This point will be discussed later.

4. This doesn't have to be the case, of course. The Frame predicate can be turned into a fluent.

5. In fact, this is not quite true. The improper use of domain constraints can lead to time points for which no corresponding state exists. Thus, State is a predicate rather than a function.

6. Because Initiated, Terminated, Clipped and Declipped don't have the status of predicates, we don't have to worry about them when designing circumscription policies.

7. The formalism in [Shanahan, 1995b] retains the Initially predicate.

8. Blocks and locations should really have different sorts, but this would complicate the example.

9. The axioms of the circumscriptive event calculus don't depend on this assumption, and in Section 15.4 on continuous change, I will consider the case in which time points are interpreted by the reals.

10. A similar method could be adopted here, and the approach of using special predicates to describe the initial situation will be employed again in Chapter 16.

15 Applying the Calculus of Events

The beauty of Baker's approach to the frame problem is its applicability to domains with complicated features, such as actions that have indirect effects (ramifications) through domain constraints. The circumscriptive event calculus of the last chapter also copes well with ramifications, and can be extended to deal with other phenomena such as concurrent action, non-deterministic action, and continuous change. This chapter describes the application of the calculus to domains with these features. Several different approaches to non-deterministic action are explored. The extension to deal with concurrent action is inspired by the work of Lin and Shoham [1992] (see Section 10.4), and the extension to deal with continuous change is in essence that of [Shanahan, 1990] which was presented in Sections 13.3 and 13.4.

15.1 Ramifications

No modifications to the axioms presented in the last chapter are required to handle actions with indirect effects, or ramifications. These are often represented through domain constraints similar to those we've already seen in the context of the situation calculus. In the circumscriptive event calculus, domain constraints can be expressed as HoldsIn formulae. For example, the fluent Dead can be defined in the following way.

$$\text{HoldsIn(Dead,s)} \leftrightarrow \neg \text{HoldsIn(Alive,s)} \qquad \text{(CED1)}$$

Recall that this domain constraint, like all domain constraints, is a problem for causal minimisation (see Section 5.6). If the usual Yale shooting scenario is extended with this domain constraint, we expect to get the same conclusions as before, plus the conclusion that Dead holds at time 25. The rest of the axioms are carried forward from the last chapter, with the exception of the uniqueness-of-names axiom for fluents, which has to be extended.

$$\text{Initiates(Load,Loaded,s)} \qquad \text{(CED2)}$$

$$\text{Terminates(Shoot,Alive,s)} \leftarrow \text{HoldsIn(Loaded,s)} \qquad \text{(CED3)}$$

$$\text{Happens(Load,10)} \qquad \text{(CED4)}$$

$$\text{Happens(Sneeze,15)} \qquad \text{(CED5)}$$

$$\text{Happens(Shoot,20)} \qquad \text{(CED6)}$$

$$\text{Happens(Start,0)} \qquad \text{(CED7)}$$

$$\text{Initiates(Start,Alive,s)} \qquad \text{(CED8)}$$

$$\text{UNA[Load, Sneeze, Shoot, Start]} \qquad \text{(CED9)}$$

$$\text{UNA[Alive, Loaded, Dead, Not]} \qquad \text{(CED10)}$$

Let Σ be the conjunction of EC with (CED1) to (CED10).

Proposition 15.1.1. $\text{CIRC}_{ec}[\Sigma] \models \text{HoldsAt(Alive,20)} \land \text{HoldsAt(Dead,25)}$.

Proof. The addition of (CED1) doesn't substantially affect the proof of Proposition 14.6.1. Instead of [14.6.4] we have,

$$\text{AbState(s)} \leftrightarrow \exists \text{ f } [\text{In(Not(f),s)} \land \text{In(f,s)}] \lor [\text{In(Alive,s)} \land \text{In(Dead,s)}] \lor$$
$$[\text{In(Not(Alive),s)} \land \text{In(Not(Dead),s)}]$$

We still get,

$$\exists \text{ s } [\text{State(20,s)} \land \text{HoldsIn(Alive,s)} \land \text{HoldsIn(Loaded,s)}]$$

and therefore,

$$\text{HoldsAt(Alive,20)}.$$

But we also get, using (CED1),

$$\exists \text{ s } [\text{State(25,s)} \land \text{HoldsIn(Dead,s)}]$$

and therefore HoldsAt(Dead,25). □

Here we'll only look at simple examples. But in general, a domain constraint could be any formula involving just the HoldsIn predicate in which the only situation term is a universally quantified variable. In addition, a domain constraint could involve any predicate apart from HoldsAt, Initiates, Terminates, and State. For example, to formalise a scenario involving a chess board in the next section, I will introduce two predicates Black and White to be used in domain constraints.

Note that (CED1) doesn't ensure that an event that initiates Dead also terminates Alive. A fluent that holds because it was initiated by an event, can only be terminated directly by an event, and not by an event that initiates or terminates a fluent on which it depends. What this amounts to is that once a fluent has been initiated or terminated by an event, it must be considered as a frame fluent from then on. Later, I'll be introducing a new predicate Releases which will allow this rule to be relaxed.

This principle can be illustrated with the walking Turkey shoot scenario. A new fluent Walking is introduced, along with a further constraint that if Walking holds then Alive must hold [Baker, 1991]. The obvious way to try to represent this is with a HoldsIn formula.

$$\text{HoldsIn(Walking,s)} \rightarrow \text{HoldsIn(Alive,s)} \qquad \text{(CEW1)}$$

However, this formula only yields intuitive conclusions under certain circumstances. With the addition of (CEW1), we can show ¬ HoldsAt(Walking,25). But suppose we add a new event type Walk and the following additional Initiates and Happens formulae.

$$\text{Initiates(Walk,Walking,s)} \qquad \text{(CEW2)}$$

$$\text{Happens(Walk,5)} \qquad \text{(CEW3)}$$

We'll retain the rest of the Yale shooting scenario. The only axioms that change are the uniqueness-of-names axioms.

$$\text{Initiates(Load,Loaded,s)} \qquad \text{(CEW4)}$$

$$\text{Terminates(Shoot,Alive,s)} \leftarrow \text{HoldsIn(Loaded,s)} \qquad \text{(CEW5)}$$

$$\text{Happens(Load,10)} \qquad \text{(CEW6)}$$

$$\text{Happens(Sneeze,15)} \qquad \text{(CEW7)}$$

$$\text{Happens(Shoot,20)} \qquad \text{(CEW8)}$$

$$\text{Happens(Start,0)} \qquad \text{(CEW9)}$$

$$\text{Initiates(Start,Alive,s)} \qquad \text{(CEW10)}$$

$$\text{UNA[Load, Sneeze, Shoot, Walk, Start]} \qquad \text{(CEW11)}$$

$$\text{UNA[Alive, Loaded, Walking, Not]} \qquad \text{(CEW12)}$$

Let Σ be the conjunction of EC with (CEW1) to (CEW12). Do we still have ¬ HoldsAt(Walking,25) in all models of $\text{CIRC}_{ec}[\Sigma]$? From Axiom (E3), we get,

$$\text{State(25,s)} \rightarrow [\text{In(Not(Alive),s)} \wedge \text{In(Walking,s)}].$$

Therefore, from (CEW1), (E1) and (E2), we have,

$$\text{State(25,s)} \rightarrow \text{AbState(s)}.$$

So we can no longer deduce anything interesting about time 25. A better way to represent a domain constraint like (CEW1) is to use Initiates and Terminates. This preserves the principle that a fluent that is initiated directly by an event must also be terminated directly by an event.

$$\text{Terminates(a,Walking,s)} \leftarrow \text{Terminates(a,Alive,s)} \qquad \text{(CEW13)}$$

Both (CEW1) and (CEW13) can be present in the same domain theory. Axiom (CEW1) would be used to deduce that Alive holds when Walking holds, given an event that initiates Walking but none that initiates Alive, and Axiom (CEW13) would be used to deduce that Walking does not hold after an event that terminates Alive. Let Σ be the conjunction of EC with (CEW2) to (CEW13).

Proposition 15.1.2. $\text{CIRC}_{ec}[\Sigma] \vDash \neg \text{HoldsAt(Walking,25)}$.

Proof. Theorem 14.5.2 is applied in the usual way. $\text{CIRC}_{ec}[\Sigma]$ yields [14.6.4] as in the proof of Proposition 14.6.1, but instead of [14.6.2] and [14.6.3], $\text{CIRC}_{ec}[\Sigma]$ now gives,

$$\text{Terminates(a,f,s)} \leftrightarrow [a = \text{Shoot} \wedge f = \text{Alive} \wedge \qquad [15.1.3]$$
$$\text{HoldsIn(Loaded,s)}] \vee [a = \text{Shoot} \wedge f = \text{Walking} \wedge$$
$$\text{HoldsIn(Loaded,s)}]$$

$$\text{Happens(a,t)} \leftrightarrow [a = \text{Walk} \wedge t = 5] \vee [a = \text{Load} \wedge t = 10] \vee \quad [15.1.4]$$
$$[a = \text{Sneeze} \wedge t = 15] \vee [a = \text{Shoot} \wedge t = 20]$$

From [14.6.4], [15.1.3] and [15.1.4], it's straightforward to show classically that $\neg$ HoldsAt(Walking,25). $\qquad \square$

As we saw in Section 7.3, the indirect effects of an action are not always straightforward to represent by domain constraints. However, in the circumscriptive event calculus, indirect effects that have a causal flavour are unproblematic. Let's consider the stuffy room scenario again. We have,

$$\text{Initiates(Close1,Blocked1,t)} \qquad \text{(CES1)}$$

$$\text{Initiates(Close2,Blocked2,t)}. \qquad \text{(CES2)}$$

$$\text{UNA[Close1, Close2]} \qquad \text{(CES3)}$$

$$\text{UNA[Blocked1, Blocked2, Stuffy, Not]} \qquad \text{(CES4)}$$

The natural way to express the constraint that if both vents are blocked the room is stuffy is with a domain constraint.

$$\text{HoldsAt(Stuffy,t)} \leftrightarrow \text{HoldsAt(Blocked1,t)} \wedge \qquad \text{(CES5)}$$
$$\text{HoldsAt(Blocked2,t)}$$

Now consider the following narrative.

$$\text{Happens(Start,0)} \qquad \text{(CES6)}$$

$$\text{Initiates(Start,Blocked1)} \qquad \text{(CES7)}$$

$$\text{Terminates(Start,Blocked2)} \qquad \text{(CES8)}$$

$$\text{Happens(Close2,10)} \qquad \text{(CES9)}$$

It can easily be verified that, in combination with the usual axioms, these formulae yield, for example,

$$\neg \text{HoldsAt(Stuffy,5)}.$$

This is what we would expect. But consider any time after the Close2 action. Recall that, using state-based minimisation naively, two outcomes were possible here. Closing the vent could cause the room to get stuffy, as we would expect, or it could mysteriously cause the other vent to open. In the circumscriptive event calculus, only the former outcome is possible. In effect, this is because Stuffy is a non-frame fluent, since it is never initiated or terminated by an event.

Let Σ be the conjunction of EC with (CES1) to (CES9).

Proposition 15.1.5. $\text{CIRC}_{ec}[\Sigma] \models \text{HoldsAt(Stuffy,10)}$.

Proof. The proof is a straightforward variation on that of the previous propositions in this section. □

Scenarios like the stuffy room aren't the only kind of tricky benchmark involving indirect effects. Giunchiglia and Lifschitz [1995], following Myers and Smith [1988], draw attention to two scenarios which, although superficially similar, have to be treated very differently.

In the first scenario, we are asked to consider the following implication. A toy is safe from a baby if it is on the table. Two actions are involved: PutOnFloor and PutOnTable, which have their obvious meanings. There are two fluents: OnTable and BabySafe. The PutOnTable action has the direct effect of making OnTable hold. From the implication, we conclude that it has the indirect effect of making BabySafe true. The PutOnFloor action has the direct effect of making OnTable not hold. Clearly we expect the BabySafe fluent to "track" the OnTable fluent, and for the PutOnFloor action to have the indirect effect of making BabySafe not hold.

Compare this scenario to the following one. A different implication is involved: a person is wet if they are in the lake. Two actions are involved: JumpIn and GetOut, which again have their obvious meanings. There are two fluents: InLake and Wet. The JumpIn action has the direct effect of making InLake hold. From the implication, we conclude that it has the indirect effect of making Wet true. The GetOut action has the direct effect of making InLake not hold. However, in contrast to the baby scenario, we don't expect the Wet fluent to track the InLake fluent. When the person gets out of the lake, they are still wet.

Although superficially similar, it is clear that these two examples demand a different formalisation. Any formalism for representing action should permit both kinds of indirect effect to be represented. Both kinds of ramification are straightforwardly dealt with in the circumscriptive event calculus. The first kind of ramification is represented by a domain constraint, and the second kind is represented by an Initiates formula. The baby example is rendered as follows.

$$Initiates(PutOnTable,OnTable,s)$$

$$Terminates(PutOnFloor,OnTable,s)$$

$$HoldsIn(BabySafe,s) \leftrightarrow HoldsIn(OnTable,s)$$

The lake example is represented as follows.

$$Initiates(JumpIn,InLake,s)$$

$$Terminates(GetOut,InLake,s)$$

$$Initiates(a,Wet,s) \leftarrow Initiates(a,InLake,s)$$

The form of the last of these formula ensures that the Wet fluent becomes a frame fluent when InLake is initiated. This gives it a "life of its own", and it is subsequently subject to the common sense law of inertia independently from the InLake fluent. In contrast, the BabySafe fluent in the first example is still a non-frame fluent after OnTable is initiated. Therefore when OnTable fluent ceases to hold, so does the BabySafe fluent.

15.2 Non-Deterministic Effects

The separation of temporal projection and minimisation permitted by Theorem 14.5.2 allows us to represent events whose effects are non-deterministic, knowing that this will not precipitate the Hanks-McDermott problem. Examples of events with non-deterministic effects are those that initiate a disjunction of fluents or a fluent that is existentially quantified. Consider the following scenario, due to Ray Reiter.[1] After the action of throwing an object onto a chess board, the object is either on black, or on white, or on both black and white at once (if it straddles two squares).

Can the effects of such an action be represented in the circumscriptive event calculus, while preserving the conditions for applying Theorem 14.5.2? There is a danger that minimising the effects of moving an object onto the board will exclude the possibility of moving it to a position where it is on both black and white, since such an action would initiate two fluents when it could have initiated only one. The circumscription should allow at least one model in which such an action initiates both fluents. Also, it's important to exclude models in which the object, once moved onto the board, flickers between black and white. If it is moved onto a particular location on the board, then it should stay there until it is moved again.

Events with non-deterministic effects, such as the one in this scenario, can often be represented as initiating an intermediate fluent, which has non-deterministic ramifications. This is the approach taken in the following solution. The variable c is introduced for locations. A location is either black, white or mixed. There is one event type Move. The fluent Loc(c) represents that the object is at location c. There are two other fluents: OnBlack and OnWhite.

$$\forall\, s\, \exists\, c\ [\text{Initiates}(\text{Throw},\text{Loc}(c),s)] \qquad (\text{CB1})$$

$$\forall\, c\ [\text{Black}(c) \vee \text{White}(c) \vee \text{Mixed}(c)] \qquad (\text{CB2})$$

$$\text{Black}(c) \leftrightarrow \forall\, s\ [\text{HoldsIn}(\text{Loc}(c),s) \rightarrow \text{HoldsIn}(\text{OnBlack},s) \wedge \qquad (\text{CB3})$$
$$\neg\, \text{HoldsIn}(\text{OnWhite},s)]$$

$$\text{White}(c) \leftrightarrow \forall\, s\ [\text{HoldsIn}(\text{Loc}(c),s) \rightarrow \text{HoldsIn}(\text{OnWhite},s) \wedge \qquad (\text{CB4})$$
$$\neg\, \text{HoldsIn}(\text{OnBlack},s)]$$

$$\text{Mixed}(c) \leftrightarrow \forall\, s\ [\text{HoldsIn}(\text{Loc}(c),s) \rightarrow \text{HoldsIn}(\text{OnWhite},s) \wedge \qquad (\text{CB5})$$
$$\text{HoldsIn}(\text{OnBlack},s)]$$

Suppose the object is initially not on the chess board, and that it's thrown onto the board at time 5.

$$\text{Happens}(\text{Throw},5) \qquad (\text{CB6})$$

$$\text{Happens}(\text{Start},0) \qquad (\text{CB7})$$

$$\text{Terminates}(\text{Start},\text{Loc}(c),s) \qquad (\text{CB8})$$

Finally, we have some uniqueness-of-names axioms.

$$\text{UNA}[\text{Throw}, \text{Start}] \qquad (\text{CB9})$$

$$\text{UNA}[\text{OnBlack}, \text{OnWhite}, \text{Loc}, \text{Not}] \qquad (\text{CB10})$$

Let Σ be the conjunction of EC with (CB1) to (CB10).

Proposition 15.2.1. Each of the following is true.

$CIRC_{ec}[\Sigma] \vDash HoldsAt(OnBlack,10) \lor HoldsAt(OnWhite,10)$ [15.2.2]

$CIRC_{ec}[\Sigma] \nvDash \neg [HoldsAt(OnBlack,10) \land$ [15.2.3]
$HoldsAt(OnWhite,10)]$

Proof. Applying Theorems 14.5.2, 14.5.3 and 14.5.5 in the usual way, we get the completions of Happens, Initiates, and Terminates. Given these completions, we can use Axiom (E3) to show,

$CIRC_{ec}[\Sigma] \vDash \exists s [State(5,s)].$

From (CB1), this gives,

$CIRC_{ec}[\Sigma] \vDash \exists s [State(5,s) \land \exists c [Initiates(Throw,Loc(c),s)]].$

From this and the completion of Happens, especially the contribution of (CB6), applying Axiom (E3) again, we get,

$CIRC_{ec}[\Sigma] \vDash \exists s [State(10,s) \land \exists c [In(Loc(c),s)]].$

This entails, from Axiom (E1),

$CIRC_{ec}[\Sigma] \vDash \exists s [State(10,s) \land \exists c [HoldsIn(Loc(c),s)]].$

From this, Axioms (CB2) to (CB5), and Axiom (E4), we have,

$CIRC_{ec}[\Sigma] \vDash [HoldsAt(OnBlack,10) \land \neg HoldsAt(OnWhite,10)] \lor$
$[HoldsAt(OnWhite,10) \land \neg HoldsAt(OnBlack,10)] \lor$
$[HoldsAt(OnBlack,10) \land HoldsAt(OnWhite,10)]$

which simplifies to [15.2.2].

To show [15.2.3], we need to exhibit a model of $CIRC_{ec}[\Sigma]$ in which,

$HoldsAt(OnBlack,10) \land HoldsAt(OnWhite,10).$ [15.2.4]

It's easy to show there are models of (CB1) to (CB10) in which,

$\exists s [State(10,s) \land HoldsIn(OnWhite,s) \land$ [15.2.5]
$HoldsIn(OnBlack,s)].$

We know that the circumscription doesn't affect HoldsIn, since HoldsIn is held fixed. Furthermore, (from the construction of F in the proof of Theorem 14.5.2), we know that any such model can be extended to satisfy EC without affecting the extension of HoldsIn in that model. So there are models of $CIRC_{ec}[\Sigma]$ that satisfy [15.2.5]. In any such model, [15.2.4] is also satisfied, from Axiom (E4).   □

Notice that Axioms (CB1) to (CB5) cannot simply be replaced by,

$$\forall \, s \, \exists \, c \, [\text{Initiates}(\text{Throw},\text{OnBoard},s)]$$

$$\text{HoldsIn}(\text{OnBoard},s) \rightarrow \text{HoldsIn}(\text{OnBlack},s) \vee \text{HoldsIn}(\text{OnWhite},s).$$

These axioms, while ensuring that an object is either on black or on white after being thrown onto the chess board, don't guarantee the stability of either colour after the occurrence of further irrelevant events. Suppose the domain includes further fluents and events, and that the narrative description includes an additional event occurrence at time 15 (a Shoot event, say), which changes some fluents, but which doesn't affect the fluents OnBlack, OnWhite or OnBoard. Then models exist in which the fluent OnBlack holds up to time 15 while the fluent OnWhite doesn't, and then the fluent OnWhite holds from time 15 while the fluent OnBlack doesn't.

The following simplification of Axioms (CB1) to (CB5) is inadequate for similar reasons.

$$\forall \, s \, \exists \, c \, [\text{Initiates}(\text{Throw},\text{Loc}(c),s)] \qquad \text{(CBU1)}$$

$$\forall \, c \, [\text{Black}(c) \vee \text{White}(c)] \qquad \text{(CBU2)}$$

$$\text{Black}(c) \leftrightarrow \forall \, s \, [\text{HoldsIn}(\text{Loc}(c),s) \rightarrow \text{HoldsIn}(\text{OnBlack},s)] \quad \text{(CBU3)}$$

$$\text{White}(c) \leftrightarrow \forall \, s \, [\text{HoldsIn}(\text{Loc}(c),s) \rightarrow \text{HoldsIn}(\text{OnWhite},s)] \quad \text{(CBU4)}$$

The fluents OnBlack and OnWhite are even less stable with these axioms. If these axioms are substituted for Axioms (CB1) to (CB5) in Σ then the resulting theory has models in which, for example, the Throw event at time 5 initiates the fluent OnBlack but where the fluent OnWhite holds at time $5+2i$ and doesn't hold at time $5+2i+1$ for all $i \in \mathbb{N}$. The Black and White predicates have to pin down the status of the OnBlack and OnWhite fluents more precisely to eliminate such models, and the predicate Mixed is needed to account for the combination of both OnBlack and OnWhite.

Even Axioms (CB1) to (CB10) only offer a partial solution to the chess board scenario. There's one further complication that has to be dealt with. As things stand, within any given model, the same event will always have the same effect when the same fluents hold, even though that effect can be different in different models. Suppose we have a model in which,

$$\text{Initiates}(\text{Throw},\text{Loc}(c),s) \wedge \text{Black}(c)$$

for some location c and state s. If there are two distinct times t such that State(t,s) $\wedge$ Happens(Throw,t), then the outcome of both Throw events will be the same — the fluent OnBlack will hold. The intention, of course, was to make each Throw event uniquely non-deterministic. Even in the same model, we want a Throw event to have different outcomes at different times.

One way out of this difficulty is to omit Axiom (S1), which identifies states with the fluents that hold in them, and add an axiom that insists that there is at most one state for each time point. With a larger space of possible states for each time point, models can exist in which the same event has a different outcome at two different time points, even though exactly the same fluents hold.

But I won't explore this option, because there's an alternative approach which doesn't require any alteration of the axioms of the circumscriptive event calculus. The key idea is to suppose that the actual outcome of an action with a non-deterministic effect in reality depends on a *determining fluent* whose value is unknown. But it's crucial that the value of this determining fluent is potentially different for each occurrence of the non-deterministic action. This will mean that the each Throw action in a sequence can have a different effect.

In the following formalisation of the chess board scenario, the determining fluent is Determined(c). If Determined(c) holds then a Throw action will make the fluent Loc(c) hold.

$$\text{Initiates(Throw,Loc(c),s)} \leftarrow \text{HoldsIn(Determined(c),s)} \qquad \text{(CBD1)}$$

$$\forall \, s \, \exists \, c \, [\text{HoldsIn(Determined(c),s)}] \qquad \text{(CBD2)}$$

The above two axioms replace Axiom (CB1) in the original formulation. In addition, we'll introduce a PickUp action, which represents picking the object from the board ready for another throw.

$$\text{Terminates(PickUp,Loc(c),s)} \qquad \text{(CBD3)}$$

The rest of the domain theory, except the uniqueness-of-names axiom for fluents, is the same.

$$\forall \, c \, [\text{Black(c)} \lor \text{White(c)} \lor \text{Mixed(c)}] \qquad \text{(CBD4)}$$

$$\text{Black(c)} \leftrightarrow \forall \, s \, [\text{HoldsIn(Loc(c),s)} \rightarrow \text{HoldsIn(OnBlack,s)} \land \qquad \text{(CBD5)}$$
$$\neg \, \text{HoldsIn(OnWhite,s)}]$$

$$\text{White(c)} \leftrightarrow \forall \, s \, [\text{HoldsIn(Loc(c),s)} \rightarrow \text{HoldsIn(OnWhite,s)} \land \qquad \text{(CBD6)}$$
$$\neg \, \text{HoldsIn(OnBlack,s)}]$$

$$\text{Mixed(c)} \leftrightarrow \forall \, s \, [\text{HoldsIn(Loc(c),s)} \rightarrow \text{HoldsIn(OnWhite,s)} \land \qquad \text{(CBD7)}$$
$$\text{HoldsIn(OnBlack,s)}]$$

$$\text{UNA[Throw, PickUp, Start]} \qquad \text{(CBD8)}$$

$$\text{UNA[OnBlack, OnWhite, Loc, Determined, Not]} \quad \text{(CBD9)}$$

This time, we'll consider a narrative with two Throw events.

$$\text{Happens(Throw,5)} \quad \text{(CBD10)}$$

$$\text{Happens(PickUp,10)} \quad \text{(CBD11)}$$

$$\text{Happens(Throw,15)} \quad \text{(CBD12)}$$

The initial situation is the same as before.

$$\text{Happens(Start,0)} \quad \text{(CBD13)}$$

$$\text{Terminates(Start,Loc(c),s)} \quad \text{(CBD14)}$$

The determining fluent, like the fluents OnBlack and OnWhite in the incorrect formalisation of the scenario in Axioms (CBU1) to (CBU4), is unstable, and its value can fluctuate. This is because it's a non-frame fluent, and is therefore not subject to inertia.

Let Σ be the conjunction of EC with (CBD1) to (CBD14).

Proposition 15.2.6. Each of the following propositions is true.

$$\text{CIRC}_{ec}[\Sigma] \vDash \text{HoldsAt(OnBlack,10)} \vee \text{HoldsAt(OnWhite,10)} \quad [15.2.7]$$

$$\text{CIRC}_{ec}[\Sigma] \nvDash \neg [\text{HoldsAt(OnBlack,10)} \wedge \quad [15.2.8]$$
$$\text{HoldsAt(OnWhite,10)}]$$

$$\text{CIRC}_{ec}[\Sigma] \vDash \text{HoldsAt(OnBlack,20)} \vee \text{HoldsAt(OnWhite,20)} \quad [15.2.9]$$

$$\text{CIRC}_{ec}[\Sigma] \nvDash \neg [\text{IIoldsAt(OnBlack,20)} \wedge \quad [15.2.10]$$
$$\text{HoldsAt(OnWhite,20)}]$$

$$\text{CIRC}_{ec}[\Sigma] \nvDash \text{HoldsAt(OnBlack,10)} \leftrightarrow \text{Holds(OnBlack,20)} \quad [15.2.11]$$

Proof. Applying Theorems 14.5.2, 14.5.3 and 14.5.5 in the usual way, we get the completions of Happens, Initiates, and Terminates. Given these completions, we can use Axiom (E3) to show,

$$\text{CIRC}_{ec}[\Sigma] \vDash \exists \, s \, [\text{State(5,s)}]. \quad [15.2.12]$$

From this and (CBD2), we get,

$$\text{CIRC}_{ec}[\Sigma] \vDash \exists \, s \, [\text{State(5,s)} \wedge \quad [15.2.13]$$
$$\exists \, c \, [\text{HoldsIn(Determined(c),s)}]].$$

From this and (CBD1), we get,

CIRC$_{ec}$[Σ] ⊨ ∃ s [State(5,s) ∧ ∃ c [Initiates(Throw,Loc(c),s)]].

From this and the completion of Happens, especially the contribution of (CBD12), applying Axiom (E3) again, we get,

CIRC$_{ec}$[Σ] ⊨ ∃ s [State(10,s) ∧ ∃ c [In(Loc(c),s)]].   [15.2.14]

This entails, from Axiom (E1),

CIRC$_{ec}$[Σ] ⊨ ∃ s [State(10,s) ∧ ∃ c [HoldsIn(Loc(c),s)]].

From this, Axioms (CB2) to (CB5), and Axiom (E4), we have,

CIRC$_{ec}$[Σ] ⊨ [HoldsAt(OnBlack,10) ∧ ¬ HoldsAt(OnWhite,10)] ∨
[HoldsAt(OnWhite,10) ∧ ¬ HoldsAt(OnBlack,10)] ∨
[HoldsAt(OnBlack,10) ∧ HoldsAt(OnWhite,10)]

which simplifies to [15.2.7].

To show [15.2.8], it suffices to exhibit a model of CIRC$_{ec}$[Σ] in which,

HoldsAt(OnBlack,10) ∧ HoldsAt(OnWhite,10).   [15.2.15]

It's easy to show there are models of (CBD1) to (CDB14) in which,

∃ s [State(10,s) ∧ HoldsIn(OnWhite,s) ∧   [15.2.16]
HoldsIn(OnBlack,s)].

We know that the circumscription doesn't affect HoldsIn, since HoldsIn is held fixed. Furthermore, (from the construction of F in the proof of Theorem 14.5.2), we know that any such model can be extended to satisfy EC without affecting the extension of HoldsIn in that model. So there are models of CIRC$_{ec}$[Σ] that satisfy [15.2.16]. In any such model, [15.2.15] is also satisfied, from Axiom (E4).

The proofs of [15.2.9] and [15.3.10] are analogous to those for [15.2.7] and [15.2.8], taking as their starting point,

CIRC$_{ec}$[Σ] ⊨ ∃ s [State(15,s)]   [15.2.17]

instead of [15.2.12]. Proposition [15.2.17] can be shown from [15.2.14], using Axiom (E3) and the completion of Happens, especially the contribution of (CBD11).

To show [15.2.11], it suffices to exhibit a model that satisfies,

HoldsAt(OnBlack,10) ∧ ¬ HoldsAt(OnBlack,20).

To do this, it's sufficient to find a model that satisfies both,

$$\exists \, s \, [\text{State}(5,s) \wedge \exists \, c \, [\text{HoldsIn}(\text{Determined}(c),s) \wedge \text{Black}(c)]]$$

and,

$$\exists \, s \, [\text{State}(15,s) \wedge \exists \, c \, [\text{HoldsIn}(\text{Determined}(c),s) \wedge \text{White}(c)]].$$

From [15.2.17] and (CBD2) we get,

$$\text{CIRC}_{ec}[\Sigma] \vDash \exists \, s \, [\text{State}(15,s) \wedge \qquad\qquad [15.2.18]$$
$$\exists \, c \, [\text{HoldsIn}(\text{Determined}(c),s)]]$$

It's clear from the form Axioms (CBD4) to (CBD7) that a model of the required form can be constructed, given [15.2.13] and [15.2.18]. □

This proposition shows that successive Throw events can have different outcomes. In this case, the proof shows that a Throw that makes OnBlack hold can be followed by one that makes OnWhite hold.

The final approach I want to explore in this section involves the introduction of *disjunctive events*. Instead of attempting to define Initiates and Terminates clauses with non-deterministic outcomes, this approach adopts the idea that the occurrence of an action with a non-deterministic effect is really the occurrence of one or more actions with deterministic effects. The non-determinism arises because we don't know which of these deterministic events occurs.

For the chess board scenario, we introduce three new event types: ThrowBlack, ThrowWhite and ThrowMixed. Then we have the following formula.

$$\text{Happens}(\text{Throw},t) \rightarrow [\text{Happens}(\text{ThrowBlack},t) \vee \qquad (\text{CDE1})$$
$$\text{Happens}(\text{ThrowWhite},t) \vee \text{Happens}(\text{ThrowMixcd},t)]$$

In other words, the occurrence of a Throw event is really the occurrence of either a ThrowBlack event, a ThrowWhite event or a ThrowMixed event. Initiates and Terminates formulae concern only these three types of throw event.

$$\text{Initiates}(\text{ThrowBlack},\text{OnBlack},s) \qquad\qquad (\text{CDE2})$$

$$\text{Initiates}(\text{ThrowWhite},\text{OnWhite},s) \qquad\qquad (\text{CDE3})$$

$$\text{Initiates}(\text{ThrowMixed},\text{OnBlack},s) \qquad\qquad (\text{CDE4})$$

$$\text{Initiates}(\text{ThrowMixed},\text{OnWhite},s) \qquad\qquad (\text{CDE5})$$

$$\text{Terminates}(\text{PickUp},\text{OnBlack},s) \qquad\qquad (\text{CDE6})$$

$$\text{Terminates}(\text{PickUp},\text{OnWhite},s) \qquad\qquad (\text{CDE7})$$

UNA[Throw, PickUp, ThrowBlack, ThrowWhite, ThrowMixed] (CDE8)

UNA[OnBlack, OnWhite, Not]   (CDE9)

Narrative descriptions will only mention Throw events, reflecting the incompleteness of our knowledge about which type of event actually takes place.

Happens(Pickup,0)   (CDE10)

Happens(Throw,5)   (CDE11)

Happens(PickUp,10)   (CDE12)

Happens(Throw,15)   (CDE13)

No modifications to EC are required for this method. Let Σ be the conjunction of EC with (CDE1) to (CDE13).

Proposition 15.2.19. Each of the following propositions is true.

$CIRC_{ec}[\Sigma] \models HoldsAt(OnBlack,10) \vee HoldsAt(OnWhite,10)$

$CIRC_{ec}[\Sigma] \not\models \neg [HoldsAt(OnBlack,10) \wedge HoldsAt(OnWhite,10)]$

$CIRC_{ec}[\Sigma] \models HoldsAt(OnBlack,20) \vee HoldsAt(OnWhite,20)$

$CIRC_{ec}[\Sigma] \not\models \neg [HoldsAt(OnBlack,20) \wedge HoldsAt(OnWhite,20)]$

$CIRC_{ec}[\Sigma] \not\models HoldsAt(OnBlack,10) \leftrightarrow Holds(OnBlack,20)$

Proof. Theorem 14.5.2 is applied in the usual way to separate the axioms of the event calculus from Σ. The completions of Initiates and Terminates are obtained in the usual way. Unfortunately though, Theorems 14.5.3 and 14.5.5 are no longer applicable to the Happens predicate, because of the form of (CDE1). However, it can be shown that in all models M of Σ that are minimal with respect to Happens, we have one (and only one) of the following.

$M \Vdash Happens(ThrowBlack,5)$

$M \Vdash Happens(ThrowWhite,5)$

$M \Vdash Happens(ThrowMixed,5)$

A similar observation applies to time 15. Altogether there are nine possible extensions for Happens, reflecting the possible combinations of events at times 5 and 15. Applying the event calculus axioms in the usual way then yields each of the propositions in question in each of these classes of model.   □

15.3 Releasing Fluents

In Section 14.3, it was claimed that there is no overall partitioning of fluents into primitive and derived (or frame and non-frame). But in Section 15.1, it was pointed out that, once a fluent has been initiated or terminated by an event, it must be considered as a frame fluent from then on. This apparent contradiction motivates the introduction a useful new predicate Releases, after Kartha and Lifschitz [1994], which is related to Sandewall's idea of occlusion [Sandewall, 1994] (see Section 4.7).

The formula Releases(a,f,s) represents that it's not known whether or not the fluent f holds after an event of type a in state s. In effect, the Releases predicate turns a frame fluent into a non-frame fluent.[2] Non-frame fluents are not subject to the common sense law of inertia, so their values can fluctuate.[3] (Recall the instability of the OnWhite and OnBlack fluents in Axioms (CBU1) to (CBU4) of the last section).

The use of Releases can be illustrated with the Russian turkey shoot scenario [Sandewall, 1991], which is like the Yale shooting scenario, except that after the Load action, the gun's chamber is spun (as in Russian roulette). Following this Spin action, the value of the Loaded fluent is unknown. Accordingly, we write,

$$\text{Releases(Spin,Loaded,s).}$$

After the sequence Load, Spin, then Shoot, we don't expect to be able to conclude whether or not the victim is alive. With just the Initiates and Terminates predicates, an event can only make a fluent hold or make it not hold.[4] The Russian turkey shoot can be represented using just Initiates and Terminates formulae, but the Releases predicate offers the possibility of an alternative formulation. First, the axioms of the circumscriptive event calculus have to be altered to accommodate the Releases predicate. The modifications affect the definitions of Clipped and Declipped. We have,

$$\text{Clipped(t1,f,t3)} \equiv_{\text{def}} \exists \text{ a,t2,s [Happens(a,t2)} \wedge \text{t1} < \text{t2} \wedge \text{t2} < \text{t3} \wedge$$
$$\text{State(t2,s)} \wedge \text{[Terminates(a,f,s)} \vee \text{Releases(a,f,s)]]}$$

$$\text{Declipped(t1,f,t3)} \equiv_{\text{def}} \exists \text{ a,t2,s [Happens(a,t2)} \wedge \text{t1} < \text{t2} \wedge \text{t2} < \text{t3} \wedge$$
$$\text{State(t2,s)} \wedge \text{[Initiates(a,f,s)} \vee \text{Releases(a,f,s)]].}$$

The effect of these modifications should be clear from an inspection of Axiom (E3). For example, consider a state s where State(t,s) for some time t. If a fluent f is a member of s (in other words, a frame fluent) then, according to the old definitions, either f or Not(f) has to be a member of the corresponding state for any time after t. The Releases predicate enables a fluent to be lifted out of the set of frame fluents altogether. Releases will have to be minimised in the circumscription, along with Happens, Initiates, and Terminates.

Here are the axioms for the Russian turkey shoot in full.

$$\text{Initiates(Load,Loaded,s)} \qquad \text{(CER1)}$$

$$\text{Terminates(Shoot,Alive,s)} \leftarrow \text{HoldsIn(Loaded,s)} \qquad \text{(CER2)}$$

$$\text{Releases(Spin,Loaded,s)} \qquad \text{(CER3)}$$

$$\text{Happens(Load,10)} \qquad \text{(CER4)}$$

$$\text{Happens(Spin,15)} \qquad \text{(CER5)}$$

$$\text{Happens(Shoot,20)} \qquad \text{(CER6)}$$

$$\text{Happens(Start,0)} \qquad \text{(CER7)}$$

$$\text{Initiates(Start,Alive,s)} \qquad \text{(CER8)}$$

$$\text{UNA[Load, Shoot, Spin, Start]} \qquad \text{(CER9)}$$

$$\text{UNA[Alive, Loaded, Not]} \qquad \text{(CER10)}$$

Let ECN be the conjunction of Axioms (S1) to (S3) with Axioms (E1) to (E4), modified according to the above prescription. Let $\text{CIRC}_{ecn}[\Sigma]$ denote the following circumscription.

CIRC[Σ ; AbState > Happens, Initiates, Terminates, Releases ; HoldsAt, State]

Let Σ be the conjunction of ECN with (CER1) to (CER10).

Proposition 15.3.1. Each of the following propositions is true.

$$\text{CIRC}_{ecn}[\Sigma] \vDash \text{HoldsAt(Loaded,15)} \qquad [15.3.2]$$

$$\text{CIRC}_{ecn}[\Sigma] \nvDash \text{HoldsAt(Alive,25)} \qquad [15.3.3]$$

$$\text{CIRC}_{ecn}[\Sigma] \nvDash \neg \text{HoldsAt(Alive,25)} \qquad [15.3.4]$$

Proof. Axioms (E3) and (E4) are chronological, as before. The circumscription yields the completions of the predicates Happens, Initiates, Terminates and Releases (Theorems 14.5.2, 14.5.3 and 14.5.5). The proof of [15.3.2] proceeds along familiar lines, applying the axioms of ECN classically, and doesn't involve the Releases predicate. From ECN we obtain,

$$\exists \ s \ [\text{State(15,s)} \wedge [\text{In(f,s)} \leftrightarrow [f = \text{Alive} \vee f = \text{Loaded}]]].$$

In other words, the state at time 15 is {Alive, Loaded}. [15.3.2] follows directly from this and Axioms (E4) and (E1).

Now, taking into account the Spin action at time 15, from ECN and Axiom (CER3), we get,

$$\text{Clipped}(15,\text{Loaded},20)$$

and therefore,

$$\exists\, s\, [\text{State}(20,s) \wedge [\text{In}(f,s) \leftrightarrow f = \text{Alive}]].$$

In other words, the state at time 20 is {Alive}. Given this and the form of Axiom (E1), it's easy to see that there are models of $\text{CIRC}_{ecn}[\Sigma]$ that satisfy HoldsIn(Loaded,s) as well as models that satisfy $\neg$ HoldsIn(Loaded,s), where State(20,s). Therefore, from the form of Axiom (E4), there are models of $\text{CIRC}_{ecn}[\Sigma]$ that satisfy HoldsAt(Alive,25) as well as models that satisfy $\neg$ HoldsAt(Alive,25). [15.3.3] and [15.3.4] follow directly from this ☐

The same effect is achieved using the following axiom instead of Axiom (CER3).

$$\text{Terminates}(\text{Spin},\text{Loaded},s) \leftarrow \text{HoldsIn}(\text{Lucky},s)$$

The fluent Lucky is a determining fluent. In a sense, this formulation is a more accurate representation of the Russian turkey shoot scenario as it's usually described. The formulation using Releases is more accurate if the gun's chamber is still spinning when the Shoot action occurs. Then, the Loaded fluent can be thought of as in a state of constant flux, its value unstable. The formulation using Terminates assumes that the fluent does acquire a stable value after the Spin action, even though that value is unknown.

15.4 Concurrent Events

A straightforward modification to the axioms of the circumscriptive event calculus, which I'll describe in this section, permits the representation of concurrent events whose effects are cumulative or cancelling. Two or more events are *cumulative* if their simultaneous occurrence has effects that none of them has on its own. One event *cancels* the effect of another if their simultaneous occurrence prevents the second event from having an effect that it does have if it occurs on its own. (See Section 10.4.) It should be noted that, as with the suggestions in the previous section, none of the amendments I propose affects the applicability of Theorem 14.5.2, as Axioms (E3) and (E4) will remain chronological.

With the axioms of Section 14.3, it's possible to represent the simultaneous occurrence of two events, but not the fact that their effects are in any way dependent on each other. Let's see this with an example. Suppose we want to formalise the following. If we push a supermarket trolley then it will move forwards. If we pull on it will go backwards. But if we push on it at the same time as pulling on it, then it will spin around.[5] The first two facts are easily represented by the following event calculus formulae.

$$Initiates(Push,Forwards,s) \qquad (ST1)$$

$$Terminates(Push,Backwards,s) \qquad (ST2)$$

$$Initiates(Pull,Backwards,s) \qquad (ST3)$$

$$Terminates(Pull,Forwards,s) \qquad (ST4)$$

Suppose we push the trolley at time 5 and then pull it at time 10.

$$Happens(Push,5) \qquad (ST5)$$

$$Happens(Pull,10) \qquad (ST6)$$

If the conjunction of EC with all the above formulae and the requisite uniqueness-of-names axioms is denoted by Σ, then in all models of $CIRC_{ec}[\Sigma]$ we have, for example, HoldsAt(Forwards,7) and HoldsAt(Backwards,12). Now consider what happens if we try to represent the additional information that we pull the trolley at time 5 as well as pushing it, and that we push the trolley at time 10 as well as pulling it.

$$Happens(Pull,5) \qquad (ST7)$$

$$Happens(Push,10) \qquad (ST8)$$

If we let Δ denote the conjunction of Σ with these formulae, then in all models of $CIRC_{e\,c}[\Delta]$, we still have HoldsAt(Forwards,7) and HoldsAt(Backwards,12). How can we represent the fact that simultaneously pushing and pulling on the trolley makes it spin around instead of moving either forwards or backwards? Two steps are required. First, we need to be able to write Initiates and Terminates formulae that describe the effect of two or more events occurring together. Then we need to be able to express the fact that one event can cancel the effect of another occurring at the same time. To achieve the first aim, an extra axiom is introduced, along with the infix function & which maps a pair of event types onto a third event type. A compound event of type a1 & a2 happens if events of type a1 and a2 happen concurrently.[6]

$$\text{Happens(a1 \& a2,t)} \leftarrow \text{Happens(a1,t)} \wedge \text{Happens(a2,t)} \wedge \text{a1} \neq \text{a2} \quad \text{(E5)}$$

Note that this axiom will accumulate any number of concurrent events into a single event type.[7] Now, to represent the cumulative effect of two concurrent events, it's only necessary to write the appropriate Initiates and Terminates formulae in the usual manner. For the supermarket trolley example, the following extra Initiates and Terminates formulae will suffice.

$$\text{Initiates(Push \& Pull,Spinning,s)} \quad \text{(ST9)}$$

$$\text{Terminates(Push \& Pull,Forwards,s)} \quad \text{(ST10)}$$

$$\text{Terminates(Push \& Pull,Backwards,s)} \quad \text{(ST11)}$$

For completeness there should be two further formulae representing the fact that Push and Pull cach terminate Spinning. Now we will get the desired cumulative effect of both events, but we will still retain the unwanted previous conclusions about their individual effects. To overcome this problem, following Gelfond, Lifschitz and Rabinov [1991] and Lin and Shoham [1992], I'll introduce a new predicate Cancels. (See also Section 10.4). The formula Cancels(a1,a2) represents that if an event of type a1 occurs then it cancels the effects of any event of type a2 occurring at the same time. Now we have to modify the definitions of Initiated and Terminated to take account of Cancels.

$$\text{Initiated(f,t2)} \equiv_{\text{def}} \exists \text{ a,t1,s [Happens(a,t1)} \wedge \text{t1} < \text{t2} \wedge \text{State(t1,s)} \wedge$$
$$\text{Initiates(a,f,s)} \wedge \neg \text{Clipped(t1,f,t2)} \wedge \neg \text{Cancelled(a,t1)]}$$

$$\text{Terminated(f,t2)} \equiv_{\text{def}} \exists \text{ a,t1,s [Happens(a,t1)} \wedge \text{t1} < \text{t2} \wedge \text{State(t1,s)} \wedge$$
$$\text{Terminates(a,f,s)} \wedge \neg \text{Declipped(t1,f,t2)} \wedge$$
$$\neg \text{Cancelled(a,t1)]}$$

$$\text{Cancelled(a1,t)} \equiv_{\text{def}} \exists \text{ a2 [Happens(a2,t)} \wedge \text{Cancels(a2,a1)]}$$

Similar modifications are required for Clipped and Declipped. (Note that I haven't retained the modifications proposed in the last section to take account of the Releases predicate. Combining all the modifications of this chapter into one formalism is a straightforward exercise.)

$$\text{Clipped(t1,f,t3)} \equiv_{\text{def}} \exists \text{ a,t2,s [Happens(a,t2)} \wedge \text{t1} < \text{t2} \wedge \text{t2} < \text{t3} \wedge$$
$$\text{State(t2,s)} \wedge \text{Terminates(a,f,s)} \wedge \neg \text{Cancelled(a,t2)]}$$

Declipped(t1,f,t3) ≡$_{def}$ ∃ a,t2,s [Happens(a,t2) ∧ t1 < t2 ∧ t2 < t3 ∧
State(t2,s) ∧ Initiates(a,f,s) ∧ ¬ Cancelled(a,t2)]

Finally, Cancels must be minimised at the same priority as Happens, Initiates and Terminates, representing the assumption that events don't cancel each other's effects unless they are known to. It's interesting to note that there's no need for an axiom to ensure that a compound event inherits the effects of its component events, as required in the approach of Lin and Shoham [1992]. Instead, a narrative of events is described entirely in terms of the separate occurrences of individual events, even if they're concurrent. Cancellation formulae may now be included in the description of a domain.

Cancels(Push,Pull)   (ST12)

Cancels(Pull,Push)   (ST13)

To complete the supermarket trolley example, we have to add the following uniqueness-of-names axioms. Note that the & function must be taken into account in the uniqueness-of-names axioms for event types.

UNA[Push, Pull, &]   (ST14)

UNA[Spinning, Forwards, Backwards, Not]   (ST15)

Let ECC denote the conjunction of the modified axioms of the circumscriptive event calculus including Axiom (E5), and let CIRC$_{ecc}$[Σ] denote the circumscription of Σ according to the policy defined above.

Let Σ denote the conjunction of ECC with (ST1) to (ST15).

Proposition 15.4.1. Each of the following propositions is true.

CIRC$_{ecc}$[Σ] ⊨ ¬ HoldsAt(Forwards,7)

CIRC$_{ecc}$[Σ] ⊨ ¬ HoldsAt(Backwards,12)

CIRC$_{ecc}$[Σ] ⊨ HoldsAt(Spinning,7)

CIRC$_{ecc}$[Σ] ⊨ HoldsAt(Spinning,12)

Proof. From the minimisation of Cancels, the circumscription yields,

Cancels(a1,a2) ↔ [a1 = Push ∧ a2 = Pull] ∨ [a1 = Pull ∧ a2 = Push].

Given [15.4.2], the proofs of the four propositions proceed long familiar lines, except that [15.4.2] blocks the initiation of the fluents Forwards and Backwards at times 5 and 10.   □

15.5 Continuous Change

This section extends the event calculus of Section 14.3 to deal with continuous as well as discrete change, as in [Shanahan, 1990] (see Section 13.3). This is achieved through the introduction of two new predicates, Trajectory and Triggers.

A new sort for elapsed time is introduced, with variables d, d1, d2, etc. The formula Trajectory(f1,s,f2,d) represents that, if the discrete fluent f1 is initiated in state s, then after a period of time d the continuous fluent f2 holds. For example, fluent f1 could represent that a ball is moving at a certain velocity and fluent f2 could represent that the ball has travelled a certain distance from its starting point.

The Trajectory predicate facilitates the representation of continuous change, such as the height of a falling object or the level of liquid in a filling vessel, but it doesn't supply any means of representing that events occur when certain continuous fluents hold. For example, when the level of liquid in a vessel reaches the vessel's rim, an overflow event occurs. A second new predicate is introduced for to represent such examples. The formula Triggers(s,a) represents that an event of type a happens in state s.

There are now two ways in which a fluent can be caused directly by an event. I will write $Initiated_d(f,t)$ to represent that the discrete fluent f holds at time t and was initiated by an event, and $Initiated_c(f,t)$ to represent that the continuously varying fluent f holds at time t and was initiated by an event. The same fluent can be continuous at some times and discrete at others. The location of a ball, for instance, can be considered continuous while the ball is moving but discrete while it's stationary. We have the following replacement definitions for Initiated.

$$Initiated_d(f,t2) \equiv_{def} \exists\ t1,a,s\ [t1 < t2 \wedge State(t1,s) \wedge [Happens(a,t1) \vee$$
$$[t1 > 0 \wedge Triggers(s,a)]] \wedge Initiates(a,f,s) \wedge \neg\ Clipped(t1,f,t2)]$$

$$Initiated_c(f2,t2) \equiv_{def} \exists\ t1,a,s,f1\ [t1 < t2 \wedge State(t1,s) \wedge [Happens(a,t1) \vee$$
$$[t1 > 0 \wedge Triggers(s,a)]] \wedge Initiates(a,f1,s) \wedge \neg\ Clipped(t1,f1,t2) \wedge$$
$$d = t2{-}t1 \wedge Trajectory(f1,s,f2,d)]$$

$$Initiated(f,t) \equiv_{def} Initiated_d(f,t) \vee Initiated_c(f,t)$$

Notice that the axioms exclude the occurrence of triggered events at time 0. This is because the state at time 0 is always the empty set (from Axiom (E3)). In other words all fluents are non-frame fluents at time 0. This means that, for any combination of fluents not excluded by domain constraints, there will be a model in which that combination holds at time 0. Since this will include combinations that trigger events, we need to include the condition t1 > 0 in the axioms wherever Triggers appears, in order to prevent phantom event occurrences.[8]

The rest of the definitions of Section 14.3 are modified to cope with Triggers, but are otherwise the same, apart from the incorporation of the Releases predicate, as described in Section 15.3.

$$\text{Clipped}(t1,f,t3) \equiv_{\text{def}} \exists \ a,t2,s \ [t1 < t2 \wedge t2 < t3 \wedge \text{State}(t2,s) \wedge [\text{Happens}(a,t2) \vee \\ \text{Triggers}(s,a)] \wedge [\text{Terminates}(a,f,s) \vee \text{Releases}(a,f,s)]]$$

$$\text{Declipped}(t1,f,t3) \equiv_{\text{def}} \exists \ a,t2,s \ [t1 < t2 < t3 \wedge \text{State}(t2,s) \wedge [\text{Happens}(a,t2) \vee \\ \text{Triggers}(s,a)] \wedge [\text{Initiates}(a,f,s) \vee \text{Releases}(a,f,s)]]$$

$$\text{Terminated}(f,t2) \equiv_{\text{def}} \exists \ a,t1,s \ [t1 < t2 \wedge \text{State}(t1,s) \wedge [\text{Happens}(a,t1) \vee \\ [t1 > 0 \wedge \text{Triggers}(s,a)]] \wedge \text{Terminates}(a,f,s) \wedge \neg \ \text{Declipped}(t1,f,t2)]$$

Apart from these modifications, the axioms of EC are retained from Section 14.3. The conjunction of Axioms (S1) to (S3) with Axioms (E1) to (E4), given the modified definitions above, will be denoted CEC. The circumscription policy to overcome the frame problem is to minimise AbState with high priority, then Triggers, Happens, Initiates, Terminates, and Releases, allowing HoldsAt and State to vary. There's no need to minimise Trajectory, because this predicate can only affect non-frame fluents, whose values don't matter anyway. The circumscription of a formula Σ according to this policy will be written $\text{CIRC}_{\text{cec}}[\Sigma]$.

The statement of Theorem 14.5.2 and its proof in Appendix B assume that time points are interpreted by the natural numbers. To accommodate genuinely continuous change, time points need to be interpreted by the reals. A variant of Theorem 14.5.2 can be proved when time points are interpreted by the reals, but the proof is more complicated than that for the naturals. Also, a certain condition must hold. Intuitively, this condition states that it must be possible to map the real time line onto a well-founded structure (known as a marker set) in such a way that the recursive formula $\forall x \, q(\overline{x}) \leftrightarrow \phi(\overline{x})$ is also well-founded with respect to that structure. In the case of the circumscriptive event calculus axioms, this structure is the set of time points at which events occur. This condition clearly holds, for example, if there is a finite number of events.

Shortly I'll illustrate the use of the axioms presented above with an example. But first I'll present the extended version of Theorem 14.5.2.

Definition 15.5.1. A *marker set* is a subset S of $\mathbb{R}$ such that for all τ_1 in $\mathbb{R}$, the set of τ_2 in S such that $\tau_2 < \tau_1$ is finite. $\qquad \qquad \square$

From the definition, a marker set can be finite or infinite, but must be countable. Furthermore, the definition ensures that we can speak of the nth element of a marker set and that this will be less than the $n+1^{th}$ element.

Definition 15.5.2. A formula Δ is *real-chronological in argument* k with respect to a formula Σ and a marker set S if,

a) It has the form $\forall \bar{x} \rho(\bar{x}) \leftrightarrow \phi(\bar{x})$, where ρ is a predicate whose k^{th} argument is a time point and $\phi(\bar{x})$ is a formula in which $\bar{x}$ is free, and

b) All occurrences of ρ in $\phi(\bar{x})$ are in conjunctions of the form $\rho(\bar{z}) \wedge z_k < x_k \wedge \psi$, where $\Sigma \wedge \Delta \vDash \neg \psi$ if $z_k \notin S$. $\square$

Under the right conditions, Axiom (E3) will be real-chronological in argument 1 with respect to the circumscription of a conjunction of domain and narrative formulae, and a marker set corresponding to the set of time points at which events (including triggered events) occur.

Theorem 15.5.3. Consider only models in which time points are interpreted by the reals, and in which < is interpreted accordingly. Let $\sigma1^*$ and $\sigma2^*$ be tuples of predicate symbols where $\sigma2^*$ includes the predicate symbol ρ. Let Σ be a formula that doesn't mention ρ. Let $\Delta = \forall \bar{x} \rho(\bar{x}) \leftrightarrow \phi(\bar{x})$ be a formula that is real-chronological in some argument with respect to CIRC$[\Sigma ; \sigma1^*; \sigma2^*]$, and a marker set S. We have,

$$\text{CIRC}[\Sigma \wedge \Delta ; \sigma1^*; \sigma2^*]$$

is equivalent to,

$$\text{CIRC}[\Sigma ; \sigma1^*; \sigma2^*] \wedge \Delta.$$

Proof. The proof is given in Appendix D. $\square$

Now let Σ be the conjunction of a domain theory and a narrative description with CEC, but without Axioms (E3) and (E4). Let S be the set of time points at which events occur according to CIRC$_{cec}[\Sigma]$. It can be seen that (E3) is real-chronological in argument 1 with respect to CIRC$_{cec}[\Sigma]$ and S, so long as S is a marker set. So Theorem 15.5.3 can be used in exactly the same way as Theorem 14.5.2 to add (E3) and (E4) to a circumscribed Σ without affecting the minimisation.

Under what circumstances does S constitute a marker set? Here are some examples. It's clear that S is a marker set if there is a finite number of events. It can easily be shown that it's also a marker set if there exists a smallest non-zero interval size between any two non-concurrent events. On the other hand, S is clearly not a marker set if an event occurs at every time point in the infinite series $0, \frac{1}{2}, \frac{1}{4}, \frac{1}{8}, \frac{1}{16}$, and so on. Examples of this kind actually do arise, as in the idealised description of a bouncing ball (see [Davis, 1992]), and it might be possible to generalise the proof of Theorem 15.5.3 to cope with these cases, using transfinite induction.

To illustrate this approach to the representation of continuous change, I'll formalise Sandewall's "ball and shaft" example [Sandewall, 1989a]. A ball is moving horizontally along a surface towards a vertical shaft. When it reaches the shaft, it starts to fall, bouncing back and forth between the walls of the shaft, until it reaches the bottom where it comes to rest (see Figure 15.1).

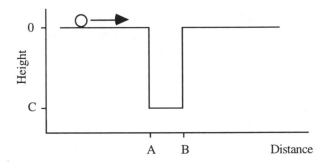

Figure 15.1: The Ball and Shaft Scenario

The "ball and shaft" can be represented as follows. New sorts are introduced for velocities and distances, and I will consider only interpretations in which these sorts are interpreted by the reals.[9] There are four types of event: Propel(v), Drop, Bounce and Stop. A Propel(v) event sets the ball in motion with velocity v. A Drop event, which occurs when the ball is no longer supported, starts the ball falling. A Bounce event, which occurs when the ball hits a vertical surface, reverses the ball's direction of motion. A Stop event occurs when the ball comes to rest. The fluent Moving(v) represents that the ball is moving horizontally with velocity v, Falling represents that the ball is in free fall, Distance(x) represents that the ball is distance x from its starting point which is assumed to be 0, and Height(x) represents that the ball is at height x. The horizontal surface is assumed to be at height 0. The near wall of the shaft is at distance A, the far wall is at distance B and the bottom is at height C. I will consider only interpretations in which the arithmetic functions have their usual meanings.

The first pair of axioms concerns horizontal movement.

$$\text{Initiates(Propel(v),Moving(v),s)} \qquad\qquad \text{(BS1)}$$

$$\text{Releases(Propel(v),Distance(x),s)} \qquad \text{(BS2)}$$

$$\text{Trajectory(Moving(v),s,Distance(x),d)} \leftarrow \qquad \text{(BS3)}$$
$$\text{HoldsIn(Distance(y),s)} \wedge x = y + v*d$$

Notice that Distance's transition from a discretely varying fluent to a continuously varying fluent is described by the Releases predicate. If Terminates is used in place of Releases in such cases, it prevents the possibility of the continuously varying fluent passing instantaneously back through the value it had when it started on its trajectory. This is not a problem in the present example, but it would be problematic if it was necessary to represent, say, a fluent with a sinusoidal trajectory.

When the ball reaches the near wall of the shaft, it starts to fall. It continues to move horizontally, of course, until it hits the opposite wall.

$$\text{Triggers(s,Drop)} \leftarrow \text{HoldsIn(Distance(x),s)} \wedge x = A \wedge \qquad \text{(BS4)}$$
$$\text{HoldsIn(Moving(v),s)} \wedge v > 0$$

$$\text{Initiates(Drop,Falling,s)} \qquad \text{(BS5)}$$

$$\text{Releases(Drop,Height(x),s)} \qquad \text{(BS6)}$$

$$\text{Trajectory(Falling,s,Height(x),d)} \leftarrow \text{HoldsIn(Height(y),s)} \wedge \qquad \text{(BS7)}$$
$$x = y - 4.9*d^2$$

When the ball reaches the far wall of the shaft, a Bounce event is triggered. It then bounces back and forth between the two walls.

$$\text{Triggers(s,Bounce)} \leftarrow \text{HoldsIn(Distance(x),s)} \wedge \qquad \text{(BS8)}$$
$$\text{HoldsIn(Moving(v),s)} \wedge [x = B \wedge v > 0] \vee$$
$$[x = A \wedge v < 0]$$

$$\text{Initiates(Bounce,Moving(v2),s)} \leftarrow \text{HoldsIn(Moving(v1),s)} \wedge \qquad \text{(BS9)}$$
$$v1 = -v2$$

$$\text{Terminates(Bounce,Moving(v),s)} \leftarrow \text{HoldsIn(Moving(v),s)} \qquad \text{(BS10)}$$

Finally, the ball comes to a complete halt when it hits the bottom of the shaft.

$$\text{Triggers(s,Stop)} \leftarrow \text{HoldsIn(Height(x),s)} \wedge x = C \wedge \qquad \text{(BS11)}$$
$$\text{HoldsIn(Falling,s)}$$

$$\text{Terminates(Stop,Moving(v),s)} \qquad \text{(BS12)}$$

$$\text{Terminates(Stop,Falling,s)} \qquad \text{(BS13)}$$

$$\text{Initiates(Stop,Distance(x),s)} \leftarrow \text{HoldsIn(Distance(x),s)} \qquad \text{(BS14)}$$

$$\text{Initiates(Stop,Height(x),s)} \leftarrow \text{HoldsIn(Height(x),s)} \qquad \text{(BS15)}$$

Two domain constraints are required to ensure that the ball's height and distance from its starting point are unique. Without these domain constraints, phantom triggered events can occur.

$$\text{HoldsIn(Height(x),s)} \wedge \text{HoldsIn(Height(y),s)} \rightarrow x = y \qquad \text{(BS16)}$$

$$\text{HoldsIn(Distance(x),s)} \wedge \text{HoldsIn(Distance(y),s)} \rightarrow x = y \qquad \text{(BS17)}$$

As usual, uniqueness-of-names axioms are required for actions and fluents.

$$\text{UNA[Propel, Drop, Bounce, Stop]} \qquad \text{(BS18)}$$

$$\text{UNA[Distance, Moving, Height, Falling, Not]} \qquad \text{(BS19)}$$

Initially the ball is at height 0 and distance 0. The only event in the narrative apart from the initial even is a Propel event at time 10.

$$\text{Happens(Start,0)} \qquad \text{(BS20)}$$

$$\text{Initiates(Start,Distance(0))} \qquad \text{(BS21)}$$

$$\text{Initiates(Start,Height(0))} \qquad \text{(BS22)}$$

$$\text{Happens(Propel(5),10)} \qquad \text{(BS23)}$$

Let Σ be the conjunction of CEC with (BS1) to (BS23).

Proposition 15.5.4. $\text{CIRC}_{cec}[\Sigma] \vDash \exists$ s, t [State(t,s) $\wedge$ Triggers(s,Stop)]. In other words, the ball eventually reaches the bottom of the shaft.

Proof. Let Φ be the conjunction of (BS1) to (BS23) with CEC minus Axioms (E3) and (E4). Applying Theorem 14.5.5 and then Theorem 14.5.3 to Φ, we get the completions of Happens, Initiates, Terminates, Trajectory, and Triggers. We need to show that Axiom (E3) is real chronological, given the modified definitions, with respect to $\text{CIRC}_{cec}[\Phi]$ and some marker set. Then, by Theorem 15.5.3, the completions are also consequences of $\text{CIRC}_{cec}[\Phi \wedge (E3)]$.

To show that Axiom (E3) is real-chronological with respect to $\text{CIRC}_{cec}[\Phi]$ and some marker set, we need to examine the consequences of $\text{CIRC}_{cec}[\Phi] \wedge (E3)$. In particular, given that Axiom (E3) has the form State(t1,s1) $\leftrightarrow$ ϕ(t1,s1), we need to find a marker set S such that all occurrences of State in ϕ(t1,s1) are in conjunctions of the form State(t2,s2) $\wedge$ t2 < t1 $\wedge$ ψ, where $\text{CIRC}_{cec}[\Phi] \wedge (E3) \vDash \neg \psi$ if t2 $\notin$ S.

Examining Axiom (E3), we see that it suffices to find a marker set S such that, for any t, if t $\notin$ S then,

CIRC$_{cec}$[Φ] $\wedge$ (E3) $\vDash \neg$ [State(t,s) $\wedge$ [Happens(a,t) $\vee$ [t > 0 $\wedge$ Triggers(s,a)]]].

Suppose we have CIRC$_{cec}$[Φ] $\wedge$ (E3). Then from Axioms (E3) and (S3) and the completion of Happens we get,

$$t \le 10 \to \exists\, s\, [\text{State}(t,s) \leftrightarrow \forall\, f\, [\neg\, \text{In}(f,s)]]$$

which yields, from (BS1),

$$\exists\, s\, [\text{State}(10,s) \wedge \text{Initiates}(\text{Propel}(5),\text{Moving}(5),s)]. \qquad [15.5.5]$$

We can show,

$$\neg \exists\, s, t\, [10 < t \le 10 + \frac{A}{5} \wedge \text{State}(t,s) \wedge \text{Triggers}(a,s)].$$

From this along with [15.5.5], the completion of Happens, Axiom (BS3), Axiom (E3), and Axioms (S1) to (S3) we get,

$$10 < t \le 10 + \frac{A}{5} \to \exists\, s\, [\text{State}(t,s) \leftrightarrow \forall\, f\, [\text{In}(f,s) \leftrightarrow [f = \text{Moving}(5)\ \vee$$
$$\exists\, x\, [f = \text{Distance}(x) \wedge x = 10+5*t]]]].$$

This yields, from Axiom (BS4),

$$\exists\, s, t\, [t = 10 + \frac{A}{5} \wedge \text{State}(t,s) \wedge \text{Triggers}(\text{Drop},s)]. \qquad [15.5.6]$$

Now let N be the largest integer smaller than,

$$\frac{5}{A - B} \sqrt{\frac{C}{4.9}}.$$

(N is the number of times the ball is expected to bounce before reaching the bottom of the shaft.) Suppose N is 0. Given [15.5.6] we can show,

$$\neg \exists\, s, t\, [10 + \frac{A}{5} < t \le 10 + \frac{A}{5} - \sqrt{\frac{C}{4.9}} \wedge \text{State}(t,s) \wedge \text{Triggers}(a,s)].$$

Similarly, if N is 1, we can show,

$$\neg \exists\, s, t\, [10 + \frac{A}{5} < t \le 10 + \frac{A}{5} + \frac{B\text{-}A}{5} \wedge \text{State}(t,s) \wedge \text{Triggers}(a,s)]$$

and,

$$\neg \exists\, s, t\, [10 + \frac{A}{5} + \frac{B\text{-}A}{5} < t \le 10 + A/5 - \sqrt{\frac{C}{4.9}} \wedge \text{State}(t,s) \wedge \text{Triggers}(a,s)].$$

In general we can show,

$$\neg \exists \, s, t \, [10 + \frac{A}{5} + N\frac{B-A}{5} < t \leq 10 + A/5 - \sqrt{\frac{C}{4.9}} \wedge State(t,s) \wedge Triggers(a,s)]$$

and, if $0 < M \leq N$,

$$\neg \exists \, s, t \, [10 + \frac{A}{5} + (M-1)\frac{B-A}{5} < t \leq 10 + \frac{A}{5} + M\frac{B-A}{5} \wedge State(t,s) \wedge Triggers(a,s)].$$

Finally, we can show,

$$\neg \exists \, s, t \, [t > 10 + \frac{A}{5} - \sqrt{\frac{C}{4.9}} \wedge State(t,s) \wedge Triggers(a,s)].$$

From all of this, it can be seen that, for any t,

$$CIRC_{cec}[\Phi] \wedge (E3) \vDash \neg \, [State(t,s) \wedge [Happens(a,t) \vee [t > 0 \wedge Triggers(s,a)]]]$$

if t is not a member of the marker set,

$$\{10, \, 10 + \frac{A}{5}, \, 10 + \frac{A}{5} - \sqrt{\frac{C}{4.9}}\} \cup \{10 + \frac{A}{5} + M\frac{B-A}{5} \mid M \leq N\}. \quad [15.5.7]$$

Therefore,

$$CIRC_{cec}[\Phi \wedge (E3)]$$

is equivalent to,

$$CIRC_{cec}[\Phi] \wedge (E3)$$

by Theorem 15.5.3. Given this and [15.5.7], we can show that

$$CIRC_{cec}[\Sigma] \vDash \exists \, s, t \, [t = 10 + \frac{A}{5} - \sqrt{\frac{C}{4.9}} \wedge State(t,s) \wedge Triggers(Stop,s)]. \quad \square$$

The same example is formalised by Sandewall [1989a] using a form of chronological minimisation extended to cope with continuous change, in which discontinuities are postponed until as late as possible. Sandewall's formulation, although it has a comparable number of axioms, is more concise. It uses temporal modalities and doesn't introduce events where there are discontinuities. It's arguable whether this succinctness is achieved at the expense of expressive power. Indeed, when Sandewall tries to combine reasoning about action with reasoning about continuous change, a much more complex formalisation results [Sandewall, 1989b].

Furthermore, as shown by Rayner [1991], Sandewall's technique of chronologically minimising discontinuities is problematic. Rayner asks us to consider a small extension of the ball-and-shaft scenario in which the lower half of the shaft is bathed in infra-red radiation. While the ball is in this radiation field, its temperature increases. So when the falling ball reaches the edge of the field, a discontinuity is inevitable. Either the ball's temperature must start to go up, or it has to bounce off the radiation field, thus avoiding the radiation field altogether. Obviously the first option is what we are looking for. Unfortunately, the chronological minimisation of discontinuities doesn't have a preference. Thus, by "trading abnormalities" in a familiar fashion, we obtain an anomalous model.[10]

No analogous problem can arise with the present formalisation. A separate Trajectory formula for temperature can be introduced, along with a suitable event which is triggered when the ball reaches the edge of the radiation field. Thanks to Theorem 15.5.3, no trading of abnormalities is made possible by such additions.

Notes

1. Ray Reiter described this problem to me in conversation in 1992. He must have had a similar conversation with Kartha or Lifschitz, since they tackle the same problem in one of their papers [Kartha & Lifschitz, 1994].
2. This doesn't correspond exactly with Kartha and Lifschitz's use of the predicate.
3. In Lifschitz's terms (see Section 5.6), the Releases predicate lifts a fluent out of the frame of fluents which are subject to the common sense law of inertia.
4. Terminates has a slightly different role in each of the versions of the event calculus presented in this book. In the simplified event calculus (Section 13.1), Terminates has a role similar to Releases in the circumscriptive event calculus. However, in the simplified calculus, no distinction is made between knowing that a fluent does not hold after an action and not knowing whether a fluent holds after an action. In the circumscriptive calculus, where this distinction is clearly made, the role of Terminates has to be symmetrical with that of Initiates.
5. This example is the same, in essence, as the soup bowl scenario in Section 10.4.
6. The use of the & function is slightly different here from its use in the concurrent version of the situation calculus in Section 10.4. There it was necessary to introduce a separate sort for generalised fluents (in effect sets of fluents), and effect axioms had to be written using a membership predicate (In). No such predicate is required in the event calculus formalisation.
7. Axioms for the associativity and commutativity of the & operator are unnecessary.

8. I neglected to consider this possibility in [Shanahan, 1995b].

9. The set of fluents is now as large as the reals. However, note that Axioms (S1) to (S3) only insist on the existence of states with finitely many fluents. In practice, only states with finitely many fluents will usually arise.

10. [Miller & Shanahan, 1996] presents another approach to continuous change in the event calculus which, like Sandewall's approach, appeals to the idea of minimising discontinuities, but doesn't suffer from Rayner's problem.

16 Forced Separation

A tacit assumption in many of the circumscriptive approaches to the frame problem, including the circumscriptive event calculus presented in the last two chapters, is that circumscription should be applied to whole theories, and not just to parts of them. For example, if $\Sigma_1 \wedge \Sigma_2$ is a formula describing the effects of actions, we should look for some ρ^* and σ^* such that $CIRC[\Sigma_1 \wedge \Sigma_2 ; \rho^* ; \sigma^*]$ solves the frame problem. It might then be desirable to prove a separation theorem to the effect that this circumscription is equivalent to $\Sigma_1 \wedge CIRC[\Sigma_2 ; \rho^* ; \sigma^*]$. But it would be illegitimate to consider $\Sigma_1 \wedge CIRC[\Sigma_2 ; \rho^* ; \sigma^*]$ as an object of study in its own right.

There are good reasons for taking this stand. (These are reviewed in the middle of this chapter.) But it has been challenged by a number of authors who have proposed solutions to the frame problem that work by circumscribing only parts of theories [Crawford & Etherington, 1992], [Doherty, 1994], [Kartha & Lifschitz, 1995], [Lin, 1995]. This chapter explores this technique, which was first proposed in essence by Sandewall [1989b], who calls it *filtered preferential entailment*. (see also [Sandewall, 1994, Chapter 9]). In the context of circumscription, I will refer to the technique as *forced separation*. The application of forced separation to the situation calculus is studied first, using a formalisation developed by Kartha and Lifschitz. Inspired by their work, a much simpler version of the circumscriptive event calculus than that supplied in the previous two chapters is then defined.

16.1 Eliminating Existence-of-Situations Axioms

Kartha and Lifschitz have shown that, by exploiting the trick of circumscribing only part of a theory of action, a solution to the frame problem can be defined for the situation calculus which is as robust as state-based minimisation, but which doesn't require an existence-of-situations axiom [Kartha & Lifschitz, 1995].

Kartha and Lifschitz's solution works for standard situation calculus formulae, but the first step in their approach is to transform these formulae into a slightly different form, in which the Result function is eliminated everywhere except in observation sentences.[1] A new predicate Holds$_R$ is introduced for this purpose. The function RF (for Result Free) is defined as follows.

Definition 16.1.1. If Σ is a conjunction of effect axioms then RF$[\Sigma]$ is the formula obtained by replacing every formula in Σ of the form Holds(β,Result(α,σ)) by Holds$_R$(β,α,σ). $\qquad\qquad\square$

The relationship between Holds and Holds$_R$ is captured by the following axiom.

$$\text{Holds}_R(f,a,s) \leftrightarrow \text{Holds}(f,\text{Result}(a,s)) \qquad \text{(KL)}$$

The common sense law of inertia is expressed in the following Result-free version of the frame axiom.

$$[\text{Holds}_R(f,a,s) \leftrightarrow \text{Holds}(f,s)] \leftarrow \neg \text{Ab}(a,f,s) \qquad \text{(F5)}$$

which is equivalent to RF[(F2)].

A transformed version of the domain constraints is also required, in which Holds_R replaces Holds. The function NC (for New Constraints) is defined as follows.

Definition 16.1.2. If Σ is a conjunction of domain constraints then $NC[\Sigma]$ is the formula obtained by replacing every formula in Σ of the form $\text{Holds}(\beta,\sigma)$ by $\text{Holds}_R(\beta,a,\sigma)$. Note that the variable a will be universally quantified with maximum scope. $\qquad\Box$

Let Σ_C be the conjunction of a set of effect axioms, let Σ_R be the conjunction of a set of domain constraints, and let Δ be the conjunction of a set of observation sentences. Let U be the conjunction of a set of uniqueness-of-names axioms for actions and fluents. We are interested in the following formula.[2]

$$\text{CIRC}[U \wedge \text{RF}[\Sigma_C] \wedge \text{NC}[\Sigma_R] \wedge \text{(F5)} ; \text{Ab} ; \text{Holds}_R] \wedge \text{(KL)} \wedge \Delta \wedge \Sigma_R$$

To see how this works, let's examine the Yale shooting scenario. The unmodified axioms are as follows.

$$\text{Holds}(\text{Loaded},\text{Result}(\text{Load},s)) \qquad \text{(Y1)}$$

$$\neg \text{Holds}(\text{Alive},\text{Result}(\text{Shoot},s)) \leftarrow \text{Holds}(\text{Loaded},s) \qquad \text{(Y2)}$$

$$\text{Holds}(\text{Alive},S0) \qquad \text{(Y3)}$$

$$\neg \text{Holds}(\text{Loaded},S0) \qquad \text{(Y4)}$$

$$\text{UNA}[\text{Load}, \text{Wait}, \text{Shoot}] \qquad \text{(Y5)}$$

$$\text{UNA}[\text{Alive}, \text{Loaded}] \qquad \text{(Y6)}$$

Let Σ_C be (Y1) $\wedge$ (Y2). Let Δ be (Y3) $\wedge$ (Y4). Let U be (Y5) $\wedge$ (Y6). There are no domain constraints, so we don't need to consider Σ_R.

Proposition 16.1.3. Let Φ be,

$$\text{CIRC}[U \wedge \text{RF}[\Sigma_C] \wedge \text{(F5)} ; \text{Ab} ; \text{Holds}_R] \wedge \text{(KL)} \wedge \Delta.$$

We have,

$$\Phi \vDash Holds(Alive,Result(Wait,Result(Load,S0)))$$

$$\Phi \vDash \neg\ Holds(Alive,Result(Shoot,Result(Wait,Result(Load,S0)))).$$

Proof. The Result-free forms of (Y1) and (Y2) are,

$$Holds_R(Loaded,Load,s) \qquad\qquad (YR1)$$

$$\neg\ Holds_R(Alive,Shoot,s) \leftarrow Holds(Loaded,s). \qquad (YR2)$$

So RF[Σ_C] is equivalent to (YR1) $\wedge$ (YR2). From this we show that,

$$CIRC[U \wedge (YR1) \wedge (YR2) \wedge (F5)\ ;\ Ab\ ;\ Holds_R] \vDash \qquad [16.1.4]$$
$$Ab(a,f,s) \leftrightarrow [a = Load \wedge f = Loaded \wedge \neg\ Holds(Loaded,s)] \vee$$
$$[a = Shoot \wedge f = Alive \wedge Holds(Loaded,s) \wedge Holds(Alive,s)].$$

The if half of this biconditional follows directly from (YR1), (YR2), and (F5). To see that the only-if half follows, consider that any model of U $\wedge$ (YR1) $\wedge$ (YR2) $\wedge$ (F5) that doesn't satisfy the only-if half can easily be transformed into a model that is identical except that the extension of Ab is smaller.

It's clear that (Y1) and (Y2) follow from Φ, since they follow from (YR1), (YR2), and (KL). Given (Y1), (Y2), and [16.1.4], it's easy to show that the proposition follows. $\qquad\qquad\qquad\qquad\qquad\qquad\qquad\qquad\qquad \Box$

To see how the approach deals with domain constraints, consider the walking turkey shoot scenario.

$$Holds(Walking,s) \rightarrow Holds(Alive,s). \qquad (WF1)$$

$$Holds(Loaded,Result(Load,s)) \qquad (WF2)$$

$$\neg\ Holds(Alive,Result(Shoot,s)) \leftarrow Holds(Loaded,s) \qquad (WF3)$$

$$Holds(Walking,S0) \qquad (WF4)$$

$$\neg\ Holds(Loaded,S0) \qquad (WF5)$$

$$UNA[Load, Wait, Shoot] \qquad (WF6)$$

$$UNA[Alive, Loaded, Walking] \qquad (WF7)$$

Let Σ_C be (WF2) $\wedge$ (WF3). Let Δ be (WF4) $\wedge$ (WF5). Let U be (WF6) $\wedge$ (WF7). Let Σ_R be (WF1).

Proposition 16.1.5. Let Φ be,

$$CIRC[U \wedge RF[\Sigma_C] \wedge NC[\Sigma_R] \wedge (F5)\ ;\ Ab\ ;\ Holds_R] \wedge (KL) \wedge \Delta \wedge \Sigma_R.$$

We have,

$$\Phi \vDash \text{Holds(Alive,Result(Wait,Result(Load,S0)))}$$

$$\Phi \vDash \neg \text{Holds(Walking,Result(Shoot,Result(Wait,Result(Load,S0))))}.$$

Proof. $RF[\Sigma_C] \wedge NC[\Sigma_R]$ is equivalent to the conjunction of the following formulae.

$$\text{Holds}_R(\text{Walking,s}) \rightarrow \text{Holds}_R(\text{Alive,s}) \qquad \text{(WFR1)}$$

$$\text{Holds}_R(\text{Loaded,Load,s}) \qquad \text{(WFR2)}$$

$$\neg \text{Holds}_R(\text{Alive,Shoot,s}) \leftarrow \text{Holds(Loaded,s)} \qquad \text{(WFR3)}$$

From this we show that,

$$CIRC[U \wedge (YR1) \wedge (YR2) \wedge (F5) ; Ab ; \text{Holds}_R] \vDash \qquad [16.1.6]$$
$$Ab(a,f,s) \leftrightarrow [a = \text{Load} \wedge f = \text{Loaded} \wedge \neg \text{Holds(Loaded,s)}] \vee$$
$$[a = \text{Shoot} \wedge f = \text{Alive} \wedge \text{Holds(Loaded,s)} \wedge \text{Holds(Alive,s)}] \vee$$
$$[a = \text{Shoot} \wedge f = \text{Walking} \wedge \text{Holds(Loaded,s)} \wedge$$
$$\text{Holds(Walking,s)}].$$

The if half of this biconditional follows directly from (WFR2), (WFR3), and (F5). To see that the only-if half follows, consider that any model of $U \wedge RF[\Sigma_C] \wedge NC[\Sigma_R] \wedge$ (F5) which doesn't satisfy the only-if half can easily be transformed into a model which is identical except that the extension of Ab is smaller.

Given [16.1.6], it's easy to show that the proposition holds.   □

Kartha [1995, Chapter 8] has established a soundness and completeness result which relates the above situation calculus formalisation to a variant of the language $\mathcal{A}$ that can represent domain constraints (see Section 8.6). This result suggests that the technique works at least as well as state-based minimisation.

16.2   The Intuition Behind Forced Separation

One way to think of this approach to frame problem is to note that, with the introduction of the Holds_R predicate, only pairs of successive situations are taken into account to establish an abnormalities. Each such pair is considered in isolation from each other pair. As emphasised by Kartha and Lifschitz, this likens their approach to the Possible Models Approach of Winslett [1988].

One way to see how this solution works at an intuitive level is to pay careful attention to the difference between $CIRC[\Sigma_1 \wedge \Sigma_2 ; \rho^*]$ and $\Sigma_1 \wedge CIRC[\Sigma_2 ; \rho^*]$, where Σ_1 and Σ_2 are any formulae and ρ^* is a tuple of predicate symbols.

Suppose we have three models M_1, M_2, and M_3 of Σ_2, such that M_1 and M_2 are also models of Σ_1, while M_3 is not, and where $M_3 \sqsubseteq_\rho M_2$ but there are no other preference relations among the models. If we conjoin Σ_1 to Σ_2 before circumscribing, M_3 plays no role in the minimisation process because it's not a model of Σ_1. So both M_1 and M_2 are models of the whole formula. On the other hand, if we circumscribe Σ_2 before conjoining Σ_1 to it, then M_3 does take part in the minimisation process, ruling out M_2. M_3 itself is then ruled out by the conjunction of Σ_1, leaving M_1 as the only model of the whole formula.

In the present case, the crucial formula that's lifted out of the circumscription is Axiom (KL). The familiar anomalous models of the Yale shooting scenario are analogous to M_2 in the above description. They are ruled out in the minimisation process because models of the effect axioms exist which are smaller in Ab, but which are themselves eventually ruled out by the addition of Axiom (KL), which links the effect axioms to the Result function.

Let's see how this works in the case of the anomalous model of the Yale shooting scenario in which the victim dies while the gun is being loaded (see Figure 6.4). In this model, there is no situation in which Alive and Loaded hold, thus motivating the introduction of an existence-of-situations-axiom.

However, although this interpretation would be a model of,

$$CIRC[U \wedge RF[\Sigma_C] \wedge (F5) \wedge (KL) \wedge \Delta \ ; Ab \ ; Holds_R]$$

it isn't a model of,

$$CIRC[U \wedge RF[\Sigma_C] \wedge (F5) \ ; Ab \ ; Holds_R]$$

and is therefore not a model of,

$$CIRC[U \wedge RF[\Sigma_C] \wedge (F5) \ ; Ab \ ; Holds_R] \wedge (KL) \wedge \Delta.$$

This is because there exists a model of $U \wedge RF[\Sigma_C] \wedge (F5)$ that is smaller in Ab. Although this preferable interpretation, which is illustrated in Figure 16.1, rules out the anomalous model, it's eventually ruled out itself by (KL) and Δ.

Notice that, in illustrating this model, there's no mention of the Result function, in contrast to the pictures used to illustrate state-based minimisation. This is crucial, of course, because it's only in the absence of a Result function that the interpretation in Figure 16.1 does its job. Since there is no link between $\sigma 1$ and $\sigma 2$, there doesn't have to be any abnormality with respect to Alive, thus barring the familiar trade in abnormalities that gives rise to the Hanks-McDermott problem.

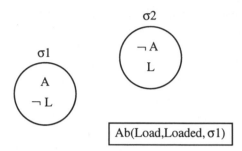

Figure 16.1: A Preferable Model to one of the Anomalous Models

It's interesting to note that this method conforms to the principle of separation in exactly the opposite way to state-based minimisation. There, the abnormalities that are included in the minimisation process are maximised because of the existence-of-situations axiom. Here they are minimised. The effect is the same in both cases: trading of abnormalities is impossible, and the minimisation used to overcome the frame problem is shielded from the outcome of temporal projection, which in situation calculus terms means the interpretation of the Result function.

Although it results in a solution to the frame problem that is at least as expressively flexible as state-based minimisation, and that doesn't require existence-of-situations axioms, there are a number of possible objections to the very idea of circumscribing only part of the theory, as mentioned at the beginning of the chapter. Here is a list of such objections.

- Intuitively, circumscription takes what is deductively known, and applies a non-monotonic rule of conjecture to it. According to this view, it's hard to see what could justify the application of the rule of conjecture to only part of what is deductively known. After all, if the rule of conjecture is correct, in the sense that it enshrines a default assumption we want to adopt, then it should be universally correct.

- By partitioning a theory, we are limiting the ways in which the different parts of the theory can be logically related together. Consider the following example, which is due to Tom Costello. I flick a switch and then enter a room, where I observe that the light is on. This observation leads me to conclude that either the light was already on, or that the effect of flicking the switch is to turn the light on. This conclusion can only be expressed as the disjunction of an observation sentence and an effect axiom. So, using the forced separation approach to the frame problem in which these two types of formulae are kept apart, it's impossible to add such information to a theory.

16.3 An Event Calculus Using Forced Separation

Those who are unimpressed by these objections to forced separation can exploit the idea to produce other elegant solutions to the frame problem. This section presents a version of the circumscriptive event calculus in which the forced separation approach is deployed. The result is a much simpler formulation than that of Chapters 14 and 15, and is closer in some respects to the logic programming formulation in Chapter 13.

As usual, the basic collection predicates for the calculus comprises Initiates, Terminates, Happens, and HoldsAt. In addition, we'll adopt the Releases predicate, as in Section 15.1. Unlike the circumscriptive event calculus of Chapters 14 and 15, Initiates, Terminates, and Releases will not be indexed on states but on time points, as in the logic programming version of the event calculus in Chapter 13. We'll get away with this by forcing the separation of minimisation from temporal projection, and this will be accomplished by lifting the main event calculus axioms outside the scope of any circumscription.

These axioms, which should be compared to those of Section 14.3, are as follows.[3] The approach to describing the initial situation is close to that used in Chapters 9 and 10. Instead of a Start event, two new predicates, Initially$_P$ and Initially$_N$, are introduced. The formula Initially$_P$(f) represents that the fluent f holds in the initial situation, and the formula Initially$_N$(f) represents that f does not hold in the initial situation.[4]

$$\text{HoldsAt(f,t2)} \leftarrow [\text{Initially}_P(f) \wedge \neg \text{Clipped(0,f,t2)}] \vee \qquad \text{(ECF1)}$$
$$[\text{Happens(a,t1)} \wedge \text{Initiates(a,f,t1)} \wedge t1 < t2 \wedge$$
$$\neg \text{Clipped(t1,f,t2)}]$$

$$\neg \text{HoldsAt(f,t2)} \leftarrow [\text{Initially}_N(f) \wedge \neg \text{Declipped(0,f,t2)}] \vee \qquad \text{(ECF2)}$$
$$[\text{Happens(a,t1)} \wedge \text{Terminates(a,f,t1)} \wedge t1 < t2 \wedge$$
$$\neg \text{Declipped(t1,f,t2)}]$$

$$\text{Clipped(t1,f,t2)} \leftrightarrow \exists \, a,t \, [\text{Happens(a,t)} \wedge [\text{Terminates(a,f,t)} \vee \qquad \text{(ECF3)}$$
$$\text{Releases(a,f,t)}] \wedge t1 < t \wedge t < t2]$$

$$\text{Declipped(t1,f,t2)} \leftrightarrow \exists \, a,t \, [\text{Happens(a,t)} \wedge [\text{Initiates(a,f,t)} \vee \qquad \text{(ECF4)}$$
$$\text{Releases(a,f,t)}] \wedge t1 < t \wedge t < t2]$$

Time points are assumed to be interpreted by the naturals or the reals, and the < predicate is assumed to be interpreted accordingly. The role of the Clipped and Declipped is the same here as in the formulation of Chapter 14, except that there they weren't awarded the status of predicates to simplify the circumscription policy. This isn't an issue here, since Axioms (ECF3) and (ECF4) will appear outside the scope of any circumscription.

Let the conjunction of (ECF1) to (ECF4) be denoted by Φ. The circumscription policy to overcome the frame problem is the following. Given a conjunction Δ of Happens, Initially$_P$, Initially$_N$ and temporal ordering formulae, a conjunction Σ of Initiates, Terminates, and Releases formulae, and a conjunction Ω of uniqueness-of-names axioms, we are interested in,

$$\text{CIRC}[\Delta ; \text{Happens}] \wedge \text{CIRC}[\Sigma ; \text{Initiates, Terminates, Releases}] \wedge \Omega \wedge \Phi.$$

In many cases, it will be possible to use Theorems 14.5.3 and 14.5.5 to show that the circumscriptions reduce to completions. Then the event calculus axioms Φ can be straightforwardly applied to show what fluents hold at which time points. No counterpart to the separation theorem developed in Chapter 14 (Theorem 14.5.2) is needed here, since the required separation is built in to the formulation from the start. The Hanks-McDermott problem simply cannot arise, because no interference is possible between temporal projection and the minimisation used to overcome the frame problem.

The following formulae are slightly modified from the Yale shooting scenario formulae of Section 14.6. The main difference is the substitution of a time point argument in Initiates and Terminates formulae where a state argument appeared before. As a consequence of this, preconditions like that in (FEY2) employ the HoldsAt predicate rather than HoldsIn, which can be completely dispensed with in this formulation.

$$\text{Initiates(Load,Loaded,t)} \tag{FEY1}$$

$$\text{Terminates(Shoot,Alive,t)} \leftarrow \text{HoldsAt(Loaded,t)} \tag{FEY2}$$

$$\text{Happens(Load,10)} \tag{FEY3}$$

$$\text{Happens(Sneeze,15)} \tag{FEY4}$$

$$\text{Happens(Shoot,20)} \tag{FEY5}$$

$$\text{Initially}_P\text{(Alive)} \tag{FEY6}$$

$$\text{UNA[Load, Sneeze, Shoot]} \tag{FEY7}$$

$$\text{UNA[Alive, Loaded]} \tag{FEY8}$$

According to the following proposition, this approach correctly formalises the Yale shooting scenario, using the formulae above. Let Δ be the conjunction of

(FEY3) to (FEY6). Let Σ be (FEY1) $\wedge$ (FEY2). Let Ω be the conjunction of (FEY7) and (FEY8). And let Φ be the conjunction of (ECF1) to (ECF4).

Proposition 16.3.1.

CIRC[Δ ; Happens] $\wedge$ CIRC[Σ ; Initiates, Terminates, Releases] $\wedge$ Ω $\wedge$ Φ $\models$
$$\neg \text{HoldsAt(Alive,25)}$$

Proof. From Theorem 14.5.3 we know that CIRC[Δ ; Happens] is equivalent to,

$$\text{Happens(a,t)} \leftrightarrow [a = \text{Load} \wedge t = 10] \vee [a = \text{Sneeze} \wedge t = 15] \vee \quad [16.3.2]$$
$$[a = \text{Shoot} \wedge t = 20].$$

Similarly, applying Theorem 14.5.5 and Theorem 14.5.3 to,

CIRC[Σ ; Initiates, Terminates, Releases]

yields,

$$\text{Initiates(a,f,t)} \leftrightarrow a = \text{Load} \wedge f = \text{Loaded} \qquad [16.3.3]$$

$$\text{Terminates(a,f,t)} \leftrightarrow a = \text{Shoot} \wedge f = \text{Alive} \wedge \qquad [16.3.4]$$
$$\text{HoldsAt(Loaded,t)}$$

$$\neg \exists \, a, f, t \, [\text{Releases(a,f,t)}]. \qquad [16.3.5]$$

From Axiom (ECF3), [16.3.2], and [16.3.4] we get $\neg$ Clipped(10,Loaded,20). From this, (FEY1), (FEY5), and Axiom (ECF1) we get HoldsAt(Loaded,20). From Axiom (ECF4) and [16.3.2] we get $\neg$ Declipped(20,Alive,25). Given this, (ECF2), [16.3.2], [16.3.4], and HoldsAt(Loaded,20) we get $\neg$ HoldsAt(Alive,25). $\qquad \square$

Domain constraints are very straightforwardly accommodated in this framework. These are expressed as universally quantified HoldsAt formulae, such as the following.

$$\text{HoldsAt(Dead,t)} \leftrightarrow \neg \text{HoldsAt(Alive,t)}$$

Domain constraints like these are conjoined to the theory outside of the scope of either of the circumscriptions.

In general, given,

- The conjunction Φ of (ECF1) to (ECF4),

- A conjunction Δ of Happens, Initially$_P$, Initially$_N$, and temporal ordering formulae,

- A conjunction Σ of Initiates, Terminates, and Releases formulae

- A conjunction Ω of uniqueness-of-names axioms, and

- A conjunction Ψ of domain constraints,

we are interested in,

$\quad$ CIRC[Δ ; Happens] $\wedge$ CIRC[Σ ; Initiates, Terminates, Releases] $\wedge \Omega \wedge \Psi \wedge \Phi$.

For example, the "dead or alive" variant of the Yale shooting scenario is captured as follows.

$$\text{Initiates(Load,Loaded,t)} \qquad \text{(FED1)}$$

$$\text{Terminates(Shoot,Alive,t)} \leftarrow \text{HoldsAt(Loaded,t)} \qquad \text{(FED2)}$$

$$\text{Happens(Load,10)} \qquad \text{(FED3)}$$

$$\text{Happens(Sneeze,15)} \qquad \text{(FED4)}$$

$$\text{Happens(Shoot,20)} \qquad \text{(FED5)}$$

$$\text{Initially}_P\text{(Alive)} \qquad \text{(FED6)}$$

$$\text{UNA[Load, Sneeze, Shoot]} \qquad \text{(FED7)}$$

$$\text{UNA[Alive, Loaded, Dead]} \qquad \text{(FED8)}$$

$$\text{HoldsAt(Dead,t)} \leftrightarrow \neg\, \text{HoldsAt(Alive,t)} \qquad \text{(FED9)}$$

If we let Δ be the conjunction of (FED3) to (FED6), Σ be (FED1) $\wedge$ (FED2), Ω be the conjunction of (FED7) and (FED8), Ψ be (FED9), and Φ be the conjunction of (ECF1) to (ECF4), we have the following proposition.

Proposition 16.3.6.

$\quad$ CIRC[Δ ; Happens] $\wedge$ CIRC[Σ ; Initiates, Terminates, Releases] $\wedge$
$\quad \Omega \wedge \Psi \wedge \Phi \models$ HoldsAt(Alive,20) $\wedge$ HoldsAt(Dead,25).

Proof. The proof is essentially the same as for Proposition 16.3.1. The addition of the domain constraint doesn't affect the circumscriptions in any way. Applying Axiom (FED9) to $\neg$ HoldsAt(Alive,25) gives HoldsAt(Dead,25). $\quad\square$

As before, care must be taken to observe the principle that a fluent, once it has been initiated/terminated should be considered as a frame fluent until it is clipped/declipped (Section 15.1). So, for the walking turkey shoot, we should write,

$$\text{Terminates(a,Walking,t)} \leftarrow \text{Terminates(a,Alive,t)}$$

rather than,

$$\text{HoldsAt(Walking,t)} \rightarrow \text{HoldsAt(Alive,t).}$$

So much for ramifications. What about non-determinism? How does the new version of the event calculus fare with actions whose effects are not completely known? Recall the chess board scenario from Section 15.2. The following formulae are almost identical to (CB1) to (CB5), the only difference being the time argument in place of the state argument in (CBF1).

$$\forall \, s \, \exists \, c \, [\text{Initiates(Throw,Loc(c),t)}] \qquad \text{(CBF1)}$$

$$\forall \, c \, [\text{Black(c)} \vee \text{White(c)} \vee \text{Mixed(c)}] \qquad \text{(CBF2)}$$

$$\text{Black(c)} \leftrightarrow \forall \, s \, [\text{HoldsIn(Loc(c),s)} \rightarrow \text{HoldsIn(OnBlack,s)} \wedge \quad \text{(CBF3)}$$
$$\neg \, \text{HoldsIn(OnWhite,s)}]$$

$$\text{White(c)} \leftrightarrow \forall \, s \, [\text{HoldsIn(Loc(c),s)} \rightarrow \text{HoldsIn(OnWhite,s)} \wedge \quad \text{(CBF4)}$$
$$\neg \, \text{HoldsIn(OnBlack,s)}]$$

$$\text{Mixed(c)} \leftrightarrow \forall \, s \, [\text{HoldsIn(Loc(c),s)} \rightarrow \text{HoldsIn(OnWhite,s)} \wedge \quad \text{(CBF5)}$$
$$\text{HoldsIn(OnBlack,s)}]$$

Recall that (CB1) to (CB5) weren't quite satisfactory since one of their consequences is that, in any given model, a Throw event always has the same effect when the same fluents hold. In Section 15.2, a determining fluent was introduced to avoid this problem. With the present formulation, in which Initiates, Terminates and Releases all take time arguments instead of state arguments, a determining fluent isn't required to permit models in which different occurrences of a Throw event can have different outcomes even when exactly the same fluents hold.

We've now considered ramifications and non-determinism. I won't present the details here, but the techniques of Section 15.4 for dealing with concurrent actions with cumulative or cancelling effects carry over cleanly to the new calculus. The only remaining phenomenon to consider in the context of the new event calculus is that of continuous change, which is the topic of the next section.

16.4 Continuous Change and Triggered Events

The forced separation approach can be extended to deal with continuous change and triggered events. As with discrete change, circumscribing only part of the theory yields a formulation that is close to the logic programming formulation (Sections 13.3 and 13.4).

Time points are assumed to be interpreted by the reals. As in previous formulations, the Trajectory predicate is the main addition. As in the logic programming version of Chapter 13, the Trajectory predicate can take a time point argument, rather than the state argument required in the formulation of Section 15.5. The following extra axiom is all we need.

$$\text{HoldsAt}(f2,t2) \leftarrow \text{Happens}(a,t1) \wedge \text{Initiates}(a,f1,t1) \wedge \qquad \text{(ECF5)}$$
$$t1 < t2 \wedge t2 = t1 + d \wedge \text{Trajectory}(f1,t1,f2,d) \wedge$$
$$\neg \text{Clipped}(t1,f1,t2)$$

Like domain constraints, Trajectory formulae are included outside the scope of the circumscriptions.

In general, given,

- The conjunction Φ of (ECF1) to (ECF5),

- A conjunction Δ of Happens, Initially$_P$, Initially$_N$, and temporal ordering formulae,

- A conjunction Σ of Initiates, Terminates, and Releases formulae

- A conjunction Ω of uniqueness-of-names axioms,

- A conjunction Ψ of domain constraints, and

- A conjunction Π of Trajectory formulae,

we are interested in,

$$\text{CIRC}[\Delta \; ; \text{Happens}] \wedge \text{CIRC}[\Sigma \; ; \text{Initiates, Terminates, Releases}] \wedge$$
$$\Omega \wedge \Psi \wedge \Pi \wedge \Phi.$$

As in the logic programming formulation of continuous change in the event calculus (Section 13.4), triggered events are easily represented via formulae of the form,

$$\text{Happens}(\alpha,t) \leftarrow \text{HoldsAt}(\beta1,t) \wedge \text{HoldsAt}(\beta2,t)$$

where $\beta1$ is a continuous fluent at time t and $\beta2$ is a discrete fluent, and $\beta1$ is on the trajectory of $\beta2$. Such formulae are included in Δ, and as such are within the scope of the circumscription that minimises Happens.

The following formulae representing the continuous variation in the water level in a kitchen sink are similar to those in Section 13.4.

$$\text{Initiates(TapOn,Filling,t)} \qquad \text{(SkF1)}$$

$$\text{Terminates(TapOff,Filling,t)} \qquad \text{(SkF2)}$$

$$\text{Releases(TapOn,Height(x),t)} \qquad \text{(SkF3)}$$

$$\text{Initiates(TapOff,Height(x),t)} \leftarrow \text{HoldsAt(Height(x),t)} \qquad \text{(SkF4)}$$

$$\text{Terminates(Overflow,Filling,t)} \qquad \text{(SkF5)}$$

$$\text{Initiates(Overflow,Height(10),t)} \qquad \text{(SkF6)}$$

$$\text{Initiates(Overflow,Spilling,t)} \qquad \text{(SkF7)}$$

$$\text{Trajectory(Filling,t,Height(x2),d)} \leftarrow \qquad \text{(SkF8)}$$
$$\text{HoldsAt(Height(x1),t)} \wedge x2 = x1 + d$$

$$\text{HoldsAt(Height(x1),t)} \wedge \text{HoldsAt(Height(x2),t)} \rightarrow x1 = x2 \qquad \text{(SkF9)}$$

$$\text{Happens(Overflow,t)} \leftarrow \text{HoldsAt(Height(10),t)} \wedge \qquad \text{(SkF10)}$$
$$\text{HoldsAt(Filling,t)}$$

$$\text{Initially}_P\text{(Height(0))} \qquad \text{(SkF11)}$$

$$\text{Happens(TapOn,5)} \qquad \text{(SkF12)}$$

This formulation differs very little from the logic program version in Section 13.4. (SkF3) has to be a Releases formula instead of a Terminates formula so that the Height fluent is not subject to the common sense law of inertia after the tap is turned on. The domain constraint (SkF9) ensures that the water always has a unique level.

Two uniqueness-of-names axioms are required.

$$\text{UNA[TapOn, TapOff, Overflow]} \qquad \text{(SkF13)}$$

$$\text{UNA[Filling, Height, Spilling]} \qquad \text{(SkF14)}$$

Care must be taken to put each of these formula in the right place relative to the circumscription. Let Φ be the conjunction of (ECF1) to (ECF5). Let Δ be the conjunction of (SkF10) to (SkF12). Let Σ be the conjunction of (SkF1) to (SkF7). Let Ω be the conjunction of (SkF13) and (SkF14). Let Ψ be (SkF9). Finally let Π be (SkF8).

Proposition 16.4.1.

$$\text{CIRC}[\Delta ; \text{Happens}] \wedge \text{CIRC}[\Sigma ; \text{Initiates, Terminates, Releases}] \wedge$$
$$\Omega \wedge \Psi \wedge \Pi \wedge \Phi \vDash \text{HoldsAt(Height(10),20)}.$$

Proof. From Theorem 14.5.3 we see that CIRC[Δ ; Happens] is equivalent to,

$$\text{Happens(a,t)} \leftrightarrow [a = \text{TapOn} \wedge t = 5] \vee [a = \text{Overflow} \wedge \qquad [16.4.2]$$
$$\text{HoldsAt(Height(10),t)} \wedge \text{HoldsAt(Filling,t)}].$$

By applying Theorem 14.5.5 and Theorem 14.5.3 to,

$$\text{CIRC}[\Sigma \; ; \text{Initiates, Terminates, Releases}]$$

we get,

$$\text{Initiates(a,f,t)} \leftrightarrow [a = \text{TapOn} \wedge f = \text{Filling}] \vee \exists \, x \; [a = \text{TapOff} \wedge \qquad [16.4.3]$$
$$f = \text{Height(x)} \wedge \text{HoldsAt(Height(x),t)}] \vee [a = \text{Overflow} \wedge$$
$$[f = \text{Height(10)} \vee f = \text{Spilling}]]$$

$$\text{Terminates(a,f,t)} \leftrightarrow [a = \text{TapOff} \wedge f = \text{Filling}] \vee \qquad [16.4.4]$$
$$[a = \text{Overflow} \wedge f = \text{Filling}]$$

$$\text{Releases(a,f,t)} \leftrightarrow \exists \, x \; [a = \text{TapOn} \wedge f = \text{Height(x)}]. \qquad [16.4.5]$$

From (ECF3), [16.4.2], [16.4.4] and [16.4.5] we get ¬ Clipped(0,Height(0),5). From this, (SkF11), and Axiom (ECF1) we get HoldsAt(Height(0),5). (SkF8) then yields,

$$\text{Trajectory(Filling,5,Height(d),d)}.$$

Given this, (SkF1) and (SkF12), applying Axiom (ECF5) yields,

$$\text{HoldsAt(Height(t1–5),t1)} \leftarrow 5 < t1 \wedge \neg \text{Clipped(5,Filling,t1)}. \quad [16.4.6]$$

From [16.4.2] we have,

$$\text{Happens(Overflow,t)} \rightarrow \text{HoldsAt(Height(10),t)} \wedge \qquad [16.4.7]$$
$$\text{HoldsAt(Filling,t)}.$$

Next we note that there can be at most one t such that,

$$[\text{Happens(Overflow,t)} \wedge 5 < t < 15].$$

To see this, consider that Filling must hold at the time of an Overflow event (from [16.4.7]), and that Overflow events terminate Filling (from (SkF5)). Therefore, between any two Overflow events there must be a TapOn event, since only TapOn events initiate Filling. But according to [16.4.2], the only TapOn event occurs at time 5.

Now suppose there is a time τ such that [Happens(Overflow,τ) ∧ 5 < τ < 15]. Since at most one such time can exist, we have ¬ Clipped(,Filling,τ). Therefore, from [16.4.6] we have HoldsAt(Height(τ–5),τ). Since $\tau < 15$, this means that the height of the water at τ is less than 10. But from [16.4.7], we have HoldsAt(Height(10),τ), which is a contradiction. Therefore τ doesn't exist, and we have $\neg$ Clipped(5,Filling,15).

Given $\neg$ Clipped(5,Filling,15), [16.4.6] yields HoldsAt(Height(10),15). From (SkF10), this in turn gives,

$$\text{Happens(Overflow,15).} \qquad [16.4.8]$$

Using (SkF6), we have,

$$\text{Initiates(Overflow,Height(10),15).} \qquad [16.4.9]$$

Now it's easy to show,

$$\neg \text{ Clipped(15,Height(x),20)} \qquad [16.4.10]$$

since no further TapOn events occur, and TapOn is the only type of event that can terminate or release the Height fluent. Given [16.4.8] to [16.4.10] we can use Axiom (ECF1) to derive HoldsAt(Height(10),20).　　　　□

Needless to say, the continuous change formulation presented here can also cope with Sandewall's ball-and-shaft scenario, which is represented using suitably modified versions of the formulae in Section 15.5. As with the state-based formalisation presented in that section, the difficulties described by Rayner [1991] do not arise using the techniques of this chapter.

Notes

1. Kartha and Lifschitz's version of the situation calculus is superficially different to the one used this book. They use unreified fluents, and employ a Poss predicate (see Section 8.4).

2. Kartha and Lifschitz use the formalism of nested abnormality theories, which is a generalisation of circumscription [Lifschitz, 1995]. The formulation used here is equivalent.

3. Although I haven't worked out the details, I believe something like the following simplification of the event calculus in this section is possible. First, the Not function is reintroduced, and we include the axiom,

$$\neg \text{ HoldsAt(f,t)} \leftrightarrow \text{HoldsAt(Not(f),t).}$$

Next we dispense with axioms (ECF2) and (ECF4) and do away with the predicates Initially$_N$, Releases and Declipped. The Releases disjunct of Axiom (ECF3) is removed. The Initially$_P$ predicate can be renamed Initially. Wherever we would formerly have written Initially$_N$(f) we now write Initially(Not(f)). Wherever we would formerly have written Terminates(a,f,t) we now also write Initiates(a,Not(f),t). Wherever we would formerly have written Initiates(a,f,t) we now also write Terminates(a,Not(f),t). Finally, wherever we would formerly have written Releases(a,f,t) we now write Terminates(a,f,t).

4. If a single Initially predicate were used, as in Chapters 9 and 10, every fluent would be a frame fluent from time 0, and would be subject to inertia.

CIRC[Σ ; AbSit > Ab > Follows ; Holds, Result, S0, S2] $\vDash$
$\exists$ s1,s2 [s1 = Result(Steal,s2) $\wedge$ Follows(s1,S0) $\wedge$
Follows(S2,s2)].

Proof. Let M be a model of the circumscription. The extension of Follows in M cannot be empty, because then S0 = S2, which contradicts Axioms (SCA1) and (SCA2). On the other hand, it's clear that the extension of Follows in M has finitely many members, because any model of Σ in which Follows has an infinite extension can be converted into one that is smaller according to the circumscription policy, and that has only finitely many members.

From Axiom (SCA4), this means that, in any model of the circumscription,

S2 = Result(α_1, Result(α_2, . . ., Result(α_n,S0) . . .)).

for some finite non-empty sequence of actions α_1 to α_n. Given this and Axiom (F2), we have,

$\exists$ a,s1,s2 [Ab(a,CarParked) $\wedge$ s1 = Result(a,s2) $\wedge$ [17.2.2]
Follows(s1,S0) $\wedge$ Follows(S2,s2)].

From (SCA5) and the minimisation of Ab, we get,

Ab(a,f,s) $\leftrightarrow$ a = Steal $\wedge$ f = CarParked $\wedge$ Holds(CarParked,s).

The proposition follows from this and [17.2.2]. $\square$

So far, the new style of representation seems fine. But recall that state-based minimisation also worked with the original style of representation for the stolen car scenario. When one additional fluent was added, however, anomalous models arose (see Section 7.4). The problem, as reported by Baker [1989], is that the assertion that the car is not in the car park in S2 forces a new abnormality (see Proposition 7.4.3). There is a variety of choices for this abnormality, each of which satisfies Axiom (F2) while allowing the car to disappear. Unfortunately, in a domain with just one extra fluent (Alive, say), some of them are both counter-intuitive and minimal.

With the alternative style of representation, this problem simply doesn't arise, because no new abnormalities are introduced. Instead, new actions are introduced into the unknown sequence between S0 and S2. To see this, suppose we have the following additional formula in the stolen car scenario.

Holds(Alive,S0)   (SCA6)

17 Explanation: The Assimilation of Observations

Most of the material presented up to now has been concerned with prediction problems, in other words problems of reasoning forwards in time from causes to effects. This chapter presents various methods for doing explanation, that is reasoning backwards in time from effects to causes. Explanation problems arise with the need to assimilate observation sentences.

Two main techniques are presented: the deductive approach and the abductive approach. Both the situation calculus and the event calculus are discussed. To begin with, a number of situation calculus representation issues are addressed. Then some difficult benchmark examples are investigated. Among other things, these reveal that the interaction between observation sentences and non-determinism is a significant issue for both the deductive and abductive approaches.

17.1 Explanation in the Situation Calculus

Explanation problems, otherwise called postdiction problems, were encountered in several places in the foregoing text. In particular, we've seen two prominent benchmark scenarios for explanation problems from the literature: the stolen car scenario [Kautz, 1986] (see Sections 4.6, 5.5, and 7.4), and the Stanford murder mystery [Baker, 1989] (see Sections 5.5 and 7.4). None of the approaches to representing and reasoning about action presented so far has incorporated a satisfactory treatment of explanation problems such as these.

Recall that, in the stolen car scenario, someone parks their car in the morning, goes away for a while, and returns to find their car no longer there. While they're away, the victim of this misfortune reasonably concludes that their car is still where they left it. Having observed the empty space where the car should have been, they are forced to retract this conclusion, and find an explanation for its disappearance. The car could have been taken at any time during the owner's absence, and this should be reflected in the explanation.

Here are the axioms that have been used for the stolen car scenario so far in this book. They're taken from [Baker, 1989].

$\neg$ Holds(Stolen,S0)   (SC1)

S2 = Result(Wait,Result(Wait,S0))   (SC2)

Holds(Stolen,S2)   (SC3)

Using this representation of the stolen car scenario, both chronological and causal minimisation yield counter-intuitive results (see Sections 4.6 and 5.5, respectively), and the scenario only has to be modestly enhanced for even state-based minimisation to fall down (see Section 7.4).

A similar style of representation is employed in their attempts to deal with explanation problems by [Lifschitz & Rabinov, 1989] and [Crawford & Etherington, 1992]. These authors overcome the difficulties attendant on this style of representation by different means. Lifschitz and Rabinov's proposal is presented within the framework of causal minimisation (see Chapter 5), but the basic idea is independent of any particular approach to the frame problem. Their approach is to permit miracles to occur, where a *miracle* is an event that takes place concurrently with other actions, and without which inconsistency arises. In the stolen car scenario represented as above, a miracle would have to occur concurrently with one of the Wait actions. This miracle (which is unlikely to be perceived as such by the car's owner) would cause the observed change in the fluent Stolen. Obviously miracles need to be minimised, and Lifschitz and Rabinov do this using prioritised circumscription.

Crawford and Etherington also tackle the problem with miracles, but using a technique for overcoming the frame problem that is close to Baker's state-based minimisation (see Chapters 6 and 7). In addition, they introduce a further innovation. In order to avoid the problems with explanation encountered by Baker (described in Section 7.4), they isolate observations from the minimisation process used to overcome the frame problem. Observations are only added to the theory after this minimisation has been done, and only then are miracles minimised. So the incorporation of an observation sentence will never interfere with the minimisation process used to overcome the frame problem. Accordingly, this approach could be said to adhere to the principle of separation (see Section 5.3).

Further problems with the application of state-based minimisation to explanation problems were uncovered by Kartha [1994]. These relate primarily to non-deterministic action, and will be discussed later. However, as we are about to see, the difficulties encountered with state-based minimisation are largely due to inadequate knowledge representation [Shanahan, 1993]. Using a better style of representation for explanation problems, a wide class of domains and scenarios can be dealt with correctly by unmodified state-base minimisation, and without the introduction of miracles, as such.

17.2 Towards a Narrative-Based Approach

Do Axioms (SC1) to (SC3) constitute a good representation of the stolen car scenario? Let's consider exactly what knowledge we're trying to capture. The

meaning of Result(Wait,Result(Wait,S0)) is the situation that results when two successive Wait actions are performed in situation S0. The assertion that S2 equals this situation means that the only two actions that occur between S0 and S2 are the two Wait actions. It's implicit in this assertion that nothing else happens between S0 and S2.

However, the whole point of the stolen car scenario is that we *do not know* what actions take place between S0 and S2. In other words, we don't know what S2 equals in terms of the Result function. Since the intended meaning of Wait is an action that has no effect, then it doesn't seem likely that S2 equals Result(Wait,Result(Wait,S0)).[1] However, since it's only by default that waiting has no effect, it is still possible to conclude that one of the wait actions is responsible for the car's disappearance.

Rather than half-heartedly asserting that nothing happens between S0 and S2 and allowing default reasoning to override this assertion to conclude that Wait actions sometimes have strange effects, a more intuitive representation of the stolen car scenario asserts nothing about S2 beyond the fact that it is the result of a sequence of actions that starts in situation S0. Then the aim of explanation is to characterise S2 in terms of the result function, that is to characterise the sequence of actions that starts in S0 and leads to a situation S2 in which the car is gone. Here's an alternative representation of the stolen car scenario along these lines.[2]

$$\text{Holds(CarParked,S0)} \qquad \text{(SCA1)}$$

$$\neg\,\text{Holds(CarParked,S2)} \qquad \text{(SCA2)}$$

$$\text{Follows(S2,S0)} \qquad \qquad \text{(SCA3)}$$

The predicate Follows is defined thus.

$$\text{Follows(s1,s2)} \leftrightarrow [\text{s1} = \text{s2} \vee \exists\ \text{a,s3}\ [\text{s1} = \text{Result(a,s3)} \wedge \text{Follows(s3,s2)}]]$$

Finally we have one effect axiom.

$$\neg\,\text{Holds(CarParked,Result(Steal,s))} \qquad \text{(SCA5)}$$

Let's adopt Baker's approach to the frame problem, including the second-order existence-of-situations axiom from Section 7.5, and see how this alternative representation fares. In addition to the usual predicates, Follows will be minimised at a low priority in order to obtain its transitive closure.

Proposition 17.2.1. If Σ is the conjunction of (SCA1) to (SCA5), plus Axioms (EoS9), (EoS10) and (F2), then,

Since there's now more than one fluent, we need a uniqueness-of-names axiom.

$$\text{UNA[CarParked, Alive]} \qquad \text{(SCA7)}$$

Proposition 17.2.3. If Σ is the conjunction of (SCA1) to (SCA7) with Axioms (EoS9), (EoS10) and (F2), then,

$$\text{CIRC}[\Sigma \; ; \text{AbSit} > \text{Ab} > \text{Follows} \; ; \text{Holds, Result, S0, S2}] \models$$
$$\exists \, s1,s2 \, [s1 = \text{Result(Steal,s2)} \wedge \text{Follows(s1,S0)} \wedge$$
$$\text{Follows(S2,s2)}].$$

Proof. The minimisation of Ab is unchanged with the additional formulae, and the proof is unaltered from that of Proposition 17.2.1. □

As already pointed out, the corresponding proposition doesn't obtain for the original style of representation, since the introduction of a new fluent perturbs the minimisation of Ab.

In a sense, this approach is not very different from the approach using miracles. In both cases, the course of events between S0 and S2 is incompletely known. With miracles, the source of this incompleteness is unknown actions occurring in parallel with known actions. With the Follows predicate, there are no parallel actions, and instead the source of the incompleteness is unknown actions in the linear sequence between S0 and S2. Both techniques contrast with an approach in which incompleteness only arises with respect to the effects of actions.

17.3 Narratives and Explanation

Miracles can be thought of as a gesture towards the idea of a distinguished course of actions or events about which we have incomplete information, in other words a narrative. As such, they are not particularly successful. Suppose, for example, that the only possible explanation of the car's disappearance involves a sequence of three actions (for example: smash the glass, hotwire the ignition, then drive away). The miracles approach would try to superimpose this sequence of three actions onto the sequence of two Wait actions that, according to Axiom (SC2), have occurred between S0 and S2. Unfortunately, the style of representation deployed by believers in miracles forbids a sequence of three actions from occurring in parallel with a sequence of two.

The Follows predicate goes a step further in the direction of incorporating the idea of a narrative into the representation of an explanation problem. It permits the length and contents of a distinguished sequence of actions to be incompletely known, and filled in by whatever apparatus is used to address explanation problems. It even incorporates a primitive form of event occurrence minimisation, in the form of the minimisation of Follows. So why not go the whole hog, and use the representational techniques developed for narratives in Chapter 9?

Recall the axioms for associating a situation with every time point, adapted from [Miller & Shanahan, 1994] (see Section 9.6).

$$\text{Initially}(f) \leftrightarrow \text{Holds}(f,\text{State}(0)) \tag{MS1}$$

$$\text{State}(t1) = \text{State}(0) \leftarrow \neg \exists a,t2 \ [\text{Happens}(a,t2) \wedge t2 < t1] \tag{MS2}$$

$$\text{State}(t1) = \text{Result}(a1,\text{State}(t2)) \leftarrow [\text{Happens}(a1,t2) \wedge t2 < t1 \wedge \tag{MS3}$$
$$\neg \exists a2,t3 \ [\text{Happens}(a2,t3) \wedge t2 < t3 < t1]]$$

$$\text{HoldsAt}(f,t) \leftrightarrow \text{Holds}(f,\text{State}(t)) \tag{MS4}$$

In a temporal projection problem, if Σ is the conjunction of,

- A linear simple narrative description,

- A collection of effect axioms and domain constraints,

- Axioms (MS1) to (MS4),

- Axioms (EoS9), (EoS10) and (F2), and

- Uniqueness-of-names axioms for actions and fluents,

then we're interested in the circumscription,

$$\text{CIRC}[\Sigma \ ; \text{AbSit} > \text{Happens}, \text{Ab} \ ; \text{State}, \text{HoldsAt}, \text{Holds}, \text{Result}]$$

which is denoted $\text{CIRC}_{MS}[\Sigma]$. Among the logical consequences of $\text{CIRC}_{MS}[\Sigma]$, we expect to see HoldsAt facts.

In an explanation problem, Σ can also include a number of observation sentences of the form,

$$\text{HoldsAt}(\beta,\tau)$$

where β is a fluent and τ is a time point. Among the consequences of $\text{CIRC}_{MS}[\Sigma]$, as well as further HoldsAt facts, we expect to find Happens facts, which explain the observation sentences.

For example, the stolen car scenario, including the extra Alive fluent, could be represented as follows.

$$\text{HoldsAt}(\text{CarParked},T1) \tag{SCN1}$$

$$\neg \text{ HoldsAt(CarParked,T2)} \qquad \text{(SCN2)}$$

$$\text{T1} < \text{T2} \qquad \text{(SCN3)}$$

$$\neg \text{ Holds(CarParked,Result(Steal,s))} \qquad \text{(SCN4)}$$

$$\text{Initially(Alive)} \qquad \text{(SCN5)}$$

$$\text{UNA[CarParked, Alive]} \qquad \text{(SCN6)}$$

Notice that the inclusion of the observation sentences (SCN1) and (SCN2) violates the conditions for applying the separation theorems 9.6.1 and 9.6.3. But we can still prove useful propositions.

Proposition 17.3.1. If Σ is the conjunction of (SCN1) to (SCN6), plus Axioms (MS1) to (MS4), and Axioms (EoS9), (EoS10) and (F2), then,

$$\text{CIRC}_{\text{MS}}[\Sigma] \vDash \exists \text{ t } [\text{T1} \leq \text{t} < \text{T2} \wedge \text{Happens(Steal,t)}].$$

Proof. From (SCN1) and (MS4), we have,

$$\text{Holds(CarParked,State(T1))}.$$

From this and (MS1) to (MS3), we can show,

$$\text{Initially(CarParked)} \vee \exists \text{ a,t } [\text{Happens(a,t)} \wedge \text{t} < \text{T1} \wedge$$
$$\text{Ab(a,CarParked,State(t))}].$$

The minimisation of Happens and Ab eliminates the second disjunct, leaving us with,

$$\text{Initially(CarParked)} \wedge \neg \exists \text{ a,t } [\text{Happens(a,t)} \wedge \text{t} < \text{T1} \wedge \qquad [17.3.2]$$
$$\text{Ab(a,CarParked,State(t))}].$$

(This is a surprisingly strong conclusion, which I will discuss below.) Furthermore, the minimisation of Ab and Happens will prevent the occurrence of any events between time 0 and time T1, so we have State(T1) = State(0).

But clearly, from (SCN2), State(T2) $\neq$ State(T1). Therefore, from the contrapositive of (MS2), we have,

$$\exists \text{ a,t } [\text{Happens(a,t)} \wedge \text{t} < \text{T2}]$$

and furthermore,

$$\exists \text{ a,t } [\text{Happens(a,t)} \wedge \text{T1} \leq \text{t} \wedge \text{t} < \text{T2}].$$

The minimisation of Happens ensures that only one such event occurs between T1 and T2. From (MS3), this means we have,

$\exists$ a,t [Happens(a,t) $\wedge$ T1 $\leq$ t $\wedge$ t < T2 $\wedge$ State(T2) = Result(a,T1)].

From this, the frame axiom (F2), and (SCN1) and (SCN2), we can see that,

$\exists$ a,t [Happens(a,t) $\wedge$ T1 $\leq$ t $\wedge$ t < T2 $\wedge$ Ab(a,CarParked,State(t))].

The minimisation of Ab tells us that the abnormality must concern a Steal action, from which the proposition follows. $\square$

So explanation via narratives duplicates the results obtained using the Follows predicate, and seems like a plausible idea. But the presence of [17.3.2] illustrates an important feature of the deductive approach to explanation using circumscription, namely that explanation is constrained by the circumscription policy. Since Ab is minimised in CIRC$_{MS}$, the option of an event between time 0 and time T1 to explain the fact that the car was parked at T1 was not open.

The same point is illustrated more forcefully in the following example, in which the stolen car problem is enhanced with a single irrelevant event between times T1 and T2. Four extra formulae are required, as follows.[3]

Happens(Sneeze,T3)   (SCN7)

T1 < T3   (SCN8)

T3 < T2   (SCN9)

UNA[Steal, Sneeze]   (SCN10)

Because the minimisation of Happens is in parallel with that of Ab, the addition of these two formulae weakens the strongest conclusion the deductive approach to explanation can offer for the car's disappearance. If Σ is the conjunction of (SCN1) to (SCN10), plus Axioms (MS1) to (MS4), and Axioms (EoS9), (EoS10) and (F2), then the strongest thing we can show is,

$$\text{CIRC}_{MS}[\Sigma] \vDash \exists t [T1 \leq t < T2 \wedge \text{Happens(Steal,t)}] \vee$$
$$\text{Ab(Sneeze,CarParked,State(T3)).}$$

The reason for this should be clear. We now have a choice for how to account for the car's disappearance: maybe the car was stolen between T1 and T2, or maybe the Sneeze event known to occur between T1 and T2 had an unexpected effect. Minimal models of Σ exist incorporating both these explanations.

We could alter the circumscription policy so that Happens is minimised at a lower priority than Ab. This would eliminate the rogue explanation involving the

Sneeze action. Alternatively, in some circumstances, explanations in terms of unknown effects of known events might be exactly what we require, in which case the prioritisation could be switched, and Ab minimised at a lower priority than Happens.

Whichever policy is chosen, when we conjoin observation sentences to our theory we violate the principles of separation and directionality. In effect, this means we have lost control of the minimisation process. But why should the need to tackle explanation problems interfere with our efforts to overcome the frame problem at all? Shortly I'll present the abductive approach to explanation, which doesn't interfere with minimisation in any way. First, I would like to present two more examples of tricky explanation problems.

17.4 A Hard Example for State-Based Minimisation

The first example is from [Kartha, 1994], and concerns a bus ride. Rather than being a general difficulty for any approach to explanation, the bus ride scenario throws up a problem with state-based minimisation.

The difficulty is most easily illustrated using the standard representation, without appealing to narratives. Exactly the same problem arises whichever style of representation is deployed. The problem that arises is very subtle, and is due to the interplay of observation sentences and actions with non-deterministic effects.

In the bus ride scenario, a commuter buys a ticket and boards a bus. Non-determinism arises from the fact that, in general, the bus could either be red or yellow. On the particular day in question, the bus turns out to be red, and this fact supplies the troublesome observation sentence.

To begin with, we have a collection of domain constraints. It's impossible to be on board both a red and a yellow bus simultaneously, and being on board either bus is only possible if the commuter has a ticket. We have the following formulae. The intended meanings of the terms standing for fluents and actions should be obvious.

$$\neg \, [\text{Holds}(\text{OnRed,s}) \wedge \text{Holds}(\text{OnYellow,s})] \qquad \text{(BR1)}$$

$$\text{Holds}(\text{OnRed,s}) \rightarrow \text{Holds}(\text{HasTicket,s}) \qquad \text{(BR2)}$$

$$\text{Holds}(\text{OnYellow,s}) \rightarrow \text{Holds}(\text{HasTicket,s}) \qquad \text{(BR3)}$$

Two effect axioms are required. The term Buy denotes the action of buying a ticket.

$$\text{Holds}(\text{HasTicket,Result}(\text{Buy,s})) \leftarrow \neg \, \text{Holds}(\text{HasTicket,s}) \qquad \text{(BR4)}$$

$$[\text{Holds(OnRed,Result(Board,s))} \vee \qquad \text{(BR5)}$$
$$\text{Holds(OnYellow,Result(Board,s))}] \leftarrow \text{Holds(HasTicket,s)} \wedge$$
$$\neg \text{Holds(OnRed,s)} \wedge \neg \text{Holds(OnYellow,s)}$$

The commuter, who initially has no ticket, buys one and then boards a bus, which on this occasion turns out to be a red one.

$$\neg \text{Holds(HasTicket,S0)} \qquad \text{(BR6)}$$

$$\text{Holds(OnRed,S2)} \qquad \text{(BR7)}$$

$$\text{S2 = Result(Board,Result(Buy,S0))} \qquad \text{(BR8)}$$

Finally we have the usual uniqueness-of-names axioms for fluents and actions.

$$\text{UNA[OnRed, OnYellow, HasTicket]} \qquad \text{(BR9)}$$

$$\text{UNA[Buy, Board]} \qquad \text{(BR10)}$$

Let Σ be the conjunction of (BR1) to (BR10) with Axioms (EoS9), (EoS10) and (F2), and consider,

$$\text{CIRC}[\Sigma \,;\, \text{AbSit} > \text{Ab} \,;\, \text{Holds, Result, S0, S2}].$$

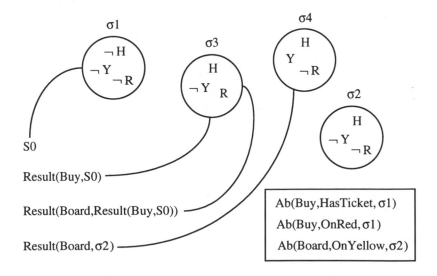

Figure 17.1: An Anomalous Model of the Bus Ride Scenario

Figure 17.1 depicts an anomalous model of this circumscription. Where a term Result(a,s) is not shown, its denotation equals that of s. In this model, the commuter is mysteriously transported on to the bus at the time of buying a ticket. It's easy to see that a model of Σ of this form is possible, and Kartha shows that such a model will be minimal with respect to the circumscription policy [1994].

How is this minimal model possible? To see this, compare it with the expected model depicted in Figure 17.2.

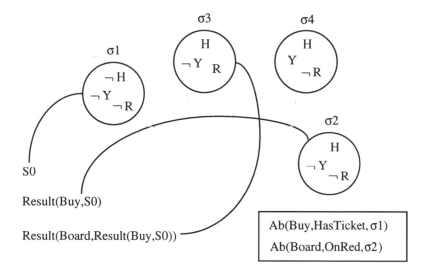

Figure 17.2: The Expected Model of the Bus Ride Scenario

We can obtain the anomalous model from the expected one in two steps.

- First, we disconnect the line emanating from Result(Buy,S0), and reattach it to σ3. This removes one abnormality, namely Ab(Board,OnRed,σ2), at the expense of introducing another, namely Ab(Buy,OnRed,σ1).

- Next, to obtain a model, we have to decide on the denotation of Result(Board,σ2), which is now undetermined. If we attach it to σ3, we'll reintroduce the same abnormality we just got rid of, and the result would not be a minimal model. But according to (BR5), we have a choice. We can attach it to σ4, which introduces another new abnormality, namely Ab(Board,OnYellow,σ2).

Notice that the observation sentence (BR7) plays a crucial role here, by anchoring the denotation of Result(Board,Result(Buy,S0)) firmly to σ3. Without it, the anomalous model would not be minimal, since Result(Buy,S0) could then be attached to σ2, eliminating Ab(Buy,OnRed,σ1) without introducing any new abnormalities. (The commuter would then end up on the yellow bus.)

Moving to a narrative-based representation doesn't alleviate the problem. (Although, as we'll see shortly, it's one step on the road to a solution.) The following formulae are the narrative-based replacements for (BR6) to (BR8).

$$\neg \, \text{Initially(HasTicket)} \qquad \text{(BRN1)}$$

$$\text{Happens(Buy,T1)} \qquad \text{(BRN2)}$$

$$\text{Happens(Board,T2)} \qquad \text{(BRN3)}$$

$$\text{HoldsAt(OnRed,T3)} \qquad \text{(BRN4)}$$

$$T1 > 0 \qquad \text{(BRN5)}$$

$$T2 > T1 \qquad \text{(BRN6)}$$

$$T3 > T2 \qquad \text{(BRN7)}$$

Let Σ be the conjunction of (BR1) to (BR5) with (BR9), (BR10), (BRN1) to (BRN7), and Axioms (EoS9), (EoS10), (F2) and (MS1) to (MS4). From $\text{CIRC}_{MS}[\Sigma]$ we get,

$$\neg \, \text{Holds(HasTicket,S0).} \qquad [17.4.1]$$

We also get,

$$\text{Holds(OnRed,State(T3))}$$

and, with the minimisation of Happens,

$$\text{State(T3)} = \text{Result(Board,Result(Buy,S0)).}$$

This yields,

$$\text{Holds(OnRed,Result(Board,Result(Buy,S0))).} \qquad [17.4.2]$$

With [17.4.1] and [17.4.2], we're back in exactly the same position we were in with (BR6) to (BR8).

However, by adopting the "disjunctive events" approach to non-determinism (see Section 15.2), we obtain a solution to the problem. With this approach, the occurrence of an action with a non-deterministic effect is considered as implying a disjunction of event occurrences. This method presupposes the ability to represent narratives with concurrent action. For this purpose, we import the techniques of Sections 10.4 and 10.5.

Two new actions are introduced: BoardRed and BoardYellow. The occurrence of a Board event implies either the occurrence of a BoardRed event or the occurrence of a BoardYellow event. Since the events that can occur concurrently never interfere with each other, we can forget about the Cancels predicate. Otherwise, the style of representation we use is inherited directly from that in Section 10.5. The Result function now takes a generalised action as an argument. Replacing (BR5), we have the following formulae.

$$\text{Holds(OnRed,Result(g,s))} \leftarrow \text{In(BoardRed,g)} \wedge \qquad \text{(BRN8)}$$
$$\text{Holds(HasTicket,s)} \wedge \neg \text{Holds(OnRed,s)} \wedge$$
$$\neg \text{Holds(OnYellow,s)}$$

$$\text{Holds(OnYellow,Result(g,s))} \leftarrow \text{In(BoardYellow,g)} \wedge \qquad \text{(BRN9)}$$
$$\text{Holds(HasTicket,s)} \wedge \neg \text{Holds(OnRed,s)} \wedge$$
$$\neg \text{Holds(OnYellow,s)}$$

In addition, we have,

$$\text{Happens(Board,t)} \rightarrow \text{Happens(BoardRed,t)} \vee \qquad \text{(BRN10)}$$
$$\text{Happens(BoardYellow,t)}$$

The rest of the formalisation is more or less as before.

$$\text{Holds(HasTicket,Result(Buy,s))} \leftarrow \neg \text{Holds(HasTicket,s)} \qquad \text{(BRN11)}$$

$$\neg [\text{Holds(OnRed,s)} \wedge \text{Holds(OnYellow,s)}] \qquad \text{(BRN12)}$$

$$\text{Holds(OnRed,s)} \rightarrow \text{Holds(HasTicket,s)} \qquad \text{(BRN13)}$$

$$\text{Holds(OnYellow,s)} \rightarrow \text{Holds(HasTicket,s)} \qquad \text{(BRN14)}$$

$$\text{UNA[OnRed, OnYellow, HasTicket]} \qquad \text{(BRN15)}$$

$$\text{UNA[Buy, Board, BoardRed, BoardYellow]} \qquad \text{(BRN16)}$$

Let Σ be the conjunction of (BRN1) to (BRN16) with Axioms (GA1) to (GA3), Axioms (CMS1) to (CMS4), and Axioms (CN), (EoS9), (EoS10) and (F3).

We are interested in,

$$\text{CIRC}[\Sigma ; \text{Happens, AbSit} > \text{Ab} ;$$
$$\text{Happens}\dagger, \text{State, HoldsAt, Holds, Result]}.$$

The following proposition says that the anomalous model of Figure 17.1 has been eliminated. Without the non-deterministic effect axiom (BR5), the anomalous model cannot arise.

Proposition 17.4.3.

$$\text{CIRC}[\Sigma \; ; \text{Happens}, \text{AbSit} > \text{Ab} \; ;$$
$$\text{Happens}\dagger, \text{State}, \text{HoldsAt}, \text{Holds}, \text{Result}] \models \neg \text{HoldsAt}(\text{OnRed}, \text{T2}) \wedge$$
$$\neg \text{HoldsAt}(\text{OnYellow}, \text{T2})$$

Proof. Because the effect axioms are deterministic, the minimisation of Ab is straightforward. We get,

$$\text{Ab}(a,f,s) \leftrightarrow [a = \text{Buy} \wedge f = \text{HasTicket} \wedge \qquad\qquad [17.4.4]$$
$$\neg \text{Holds}(\text{HasTicket},s)] \vee [\neg \text{Holds}(\text{OnRed},s) \wedge$$
$$\neg \text{Holds}(\text{OnYellow},s) \wedge [[a = \text{BoardRed} \wedge f = \text{OnRed}] \vee$$
$$[a = \text{BoardYellow} \wedge f = \text{OnYellow}]]$$

Notice that the Board action has no (direct) effects. From the minimisation of Happens, it can be shown that any model of the circumscription must satisfy either,

$$\text{Happens}(a,t) \leftrightarrow [a = \text{Buy} \wedge t = \text{T1}] \vee [a = \text{Board} \wedge t = \text{T2}] \vee \quad [17.4.5]$$
$$[a = \text{BoardRed} \wedge t = \text{T2}]$$

or,

$$\text{Happens}(a,t) \leftrightarrow [a = \text{Buy} \wedge t = \text{T1}] \vee [a = \text{Board} \wedge t = \text{T2}] \vee \quad [17.4.6]$$
$$[a = \text{BoardYellow} \wedge t = \text{T2}].$$

Suppose M is a model that satisfies [17.4.6]. From Axiom (CN), we get,

$$\text{Happens}\dagger(g,t) \leftrightarrow [t = \text{T1} \wedge \forall a \, [\text{In}(a,g) \leftrightarrow a = \text{Buy}]] \vee [t = \text{T2} \wedge$$
$$\forall a \, [\text{In}(a,g) \leftrightarrow a = \text{Board} \vee a = \text{BoardYellow}]].$$

Given this and Axioms (CMS1) to (CMS4), we can show,

$$\text{State}(\text{T3}) = \text{Result}(\text{BoardYellow}, \text{Result}(\text{Buy}, \text{S0})).$$

But then, applying [17.4.4], [17.4.6] and Axioms (CMS1) to (CMS4), we can show,

$$\neg \text{HoldsAt}(\text{OnRed}, \text{T3})$$

which contradicts the observation sentence (BRN2). Therefore M cannot be a model, and every model of the circumscription has to satisfy [17.4.5]. The proposition follows straightforwardly from here. □

An alternative approach to the problem of combining observation sentences with non-determinism, as recommended by Kartha [1994], is to adopt the method of forced separation described in Chapter 16. However, as I argue in the next section, there are reasons to prefer a different approach altogether.

17.5 A Hard Example for the Deductive Approach

This example is from [Shanahan, 1993], and is an enhancement of the stolen car scenario. In this version, it's a precondition of the Steal action that the car park is unguarded. If a lazy security guard comes on duty, he immediately falls asleep, leaving the car park vulnerable to theft. A new fluent, Guarded, is introduced, along with the action Guard(x) representing that security guard x comes on duty.

$$\neg\, \text{Holds(CarParked,Result(Steal,s))} \leftarrow \neg\, \text{Holds(Guarded,s)} \quad \text{(ESC1)}$$

$$\text{Holds(Guarded,Result(Guard(x),s))} \leftrightarrow \neg\, \text{Lazy(x)} \quad \text{(ESC2)}$$

As before, the car is parked at time T1, when it is also guarded. By time T2, it has disappeared. The only lazy security guard we know of is Fred.

$$\text{HoldsAt(CarParked,T1)} \quad \text{(ESC3)}$$

$$\text{HoldsAt(Guarded,T1)} \quad \text{(ESC4)}$$

$$\neg\, \text{HoldsAt(CarParked,T2)} \quad \text{(ESC5)}$$

$$\text{T1} < \text{T2} \quad \text{(ESC6)}$$

$$\text{Lazy(Fred)} \quad \text{(ESC7)}$$

$$\text{UNA[CarParked, Guarded]} \quad \text{(ESC8)}$$

$$\text{UNA[Guard, Steal]} \quad \text{(ESC9)}$$

Now, what can we conclude from the fact that the car is not parked at time T2? The only plausible explanation, given the knowledge we have, is that Fred came on duty and fell asleep, leaving the car park unguarded. But what do we get from the above formulae? Let Σ be the conjunction of (ESC1) to (ESC9), plus Axioms (MS1) to (MS4), and Axioms (EoS9), (EoS10) and (F2), and consider $\text{CIRC}_{\text{MS}}[\Sigma]$.

As in the proof of Proposition 17.3.1, we can show,

$$\exists\ a,t\ [Happens(a,t) \wedge T1 \leq t < T2].$$

In contrast to the proof of Proposition 17.3.1, if we assume only one such event between T1 and T2, it cannot be a Steal action, since then Guarded would still hold, and the car would remain parked. A single event occurrence has to involve a new type of action, one that affects CarParked without the Guarded precondition. This is one type of minimal model, but it can be eliminated with a different circumscription policy, namely one in which Ab is minimised at a higher priority than Happens.

A second type of minimal model exists, which is not eliminated in this way, in which there are two event occurrences between T1 and T2: a Guard(x) action where Lazy(x) is true, followed by a Steal action. Indeed, using the stronger circumscription policy,

$$CIRC[\Sigma\ ;\ AbSit > Ab > Happens\ ;\ State, HoldsAt, Holds, Result]$$

which reflects a preference for explanations expressed in terms of unknown event occurrences rather than in terms of unexpected effects of known actions, all minimal models include these two events. So we can show,

$$\exists\ t1,t2\ [Happens(Guard(x),t1) \wedge T1 \leq t1 \wedge Lazy(x) \wedge \qquad [17.5.1]$$
$$Happens(Steal,t2) \wedge t1 < t2 < T2].$$

This is very nearly the desired result, but not quite because no mention is made of Fred, the only lazy security guard we know of. Of course, in a sense, this is quite correct, since nowhere have we said explicitly that Fred is the *only* lazy guard. On the other hand, if it was Fred that came on duty, that would explain the fact that the car park was unguarded at the crucial time.

To see that this indifference to Fred could be a serious shortcoming, let's introduce a further complication to the story. In addition to the car park's being unguarded, there's another precondition to a successful theft. The alarm mustn't be on. Instead of (ESC1), we have,

$$\neg\ Holds(CarParked,Result(Steal,s)) \leftarrow \qquad (ESC10)$$
$$\neg\ Holds(Guarded,s) \wedge \neg\ Holds(Alarm,s).$$

Initially the alarm is indeed off, but if Fred comes on duty he always turns it on, knowing he's likely to fall asleep. However, after someone smashes the alarm, it isn't on any longer.

$$\neg\ Holds(Alarm,S0) \qquad (ESC11)$$

$$Holds(Alarm,Result(Guard(Fred),s)) \qquad (ESC12)$$

Since for any explanation Δ of Γ we have $\Delta \models$ [17.6.4], we know that if Δ is minimal then [17.6.4] $\models \Delta$. So all minimal explanations are logically equivalent to [17.6.4]. □

Recall from Section 17.3 that the addition of a Sneeze event between T1 and T2 precipitated a weakening of the explanation for (SCN2) produced by the deductive approach. To restore the stronger explanation, a modification of the circumscription policy was required in which Happens was minimised at a lower priority than Ab. No such weakening takes place with the abductive approach, whatever position Happens occupies in the prioritisation.

The potentially troublesome additional formulae are the following.

$$\text{Happens(Sneeze,T3)} \qquad \text{(SCN7)}$$

$$\text{T1} < \text{T3} \qquad \text{(SCN8)}$$

$$\text{T3} < \text{T2} \qquad \text{(SCN9)}$$

$$\text{UNA[Steal, Sneeze]} \qquad \text{(SCN10)}$$

Proposition 17.6.5. Let Σ be the conjunction of (SCN1) with (SCN3) to (SCN10), plus Axioms (MS1) to (MS4), and Axioms (EoS9), (EoS10) and (F2). All members of,

$$\text{ABD}_{sc}[(\text{SCN2}) ; \Sigma]$$

are logically equivalent to,

$$\exists\, t\, [\text{T1} \leq t < \text{T2} \wedge \text{Happens(Steal,t)}].$$

Proof. The addition of the extra formulae doesn't affect the proof of Proposition 17.6.3 in any way. □

The reason for the difference between the approaches is simple. In the abductive approach, the terms in which an explanation are expressed are specified by an abduction policy which is entirely separate from the circumscription policy used to overcome the frame problem. Indeed, using the deductive approach, there's no way to distinguish explanations from other logical consequences of a theory.

This brings us to the important question of the relationship between abduction and deduction [Console, *et al.*, 1991], [Konolige, 1992]. When do they coincide? In essence, abduction finds sufficient conditions for a fact to hold, while deduction only finds necessary conditions. In certain circumstances, necessary conditions are also sufficient conditions. This is the case when the knowledge involved is expressed in terms of biconditionals. The frame axiom (F2), for example, makes it a necessary and sufficient condition for a fluent to hold in Result(a,s) that the fluent holds in s, given that a isn't abnormal in this context. Furthermore, one-way implications can sometimes behave like biconditionals in this way when minimisation is involved, because minimisation often has the effect of "completing" the implication, that is to say turning it into a biconditional. This was the case with Ab in the stolen car scenario. However, there's no reason to suppose that necessary and sufficient conditions will always coincide, even in the presence of minimisation, as we saw with the extended stolen car scenario, in which deduction failed because the predicate Lazy was not completed.

17.7   Abduction and Knowledge Assimilation

As hinted at by the title of the present chapter, throughout this book explanation is viewed as an aspect of knowledge assimilation rather than as a form of reasoning in its own right. Of particular interest here is the kind of knowledge whose assimilation leads to a process of reasoning backwards in time from effects to causes, namely observation sentences. How are such sentences to be assimilated? The straightforward answer offered by the deductive approach is that they should simply be conjoined to the theory like any other sort of sentence to be assimilated. Indeed, for other types of sentence this works perfectly well. However, when it comes to observation sentences, the deductive approach has certain disadvantages.

Several of these disadvantages have already been discussed.

- With the deductive approach, a working solution to the frame problem sometimes has to be modified to cater for the possibility of the addition of observation sentences, as demonstrated at the end Section 17.3.

- The deductive approach often stops short of providing a satisfactory explanation, as illustrated by the example of Section 17.5.

- The deductive approach often leads to a violation of the principle of directionality, which in turn makes useful theorems hard to prove.

The abductive approach has none of these disadvantages.

On another level, the view that the deductive approach is wrong appeals to our intuitions about causality and the arrow of time. Observing the principle of directionality means that, in some sense, the logical consequence relation mirrors the arrow of time. It points forwards only.[5] In the context of the assimilation of observation sentences, the principle of directionality has the following corollary.

Prediction is deduction but explanation is abduction.

But what exactly does the abductive assimilation of an observation sentence involve when there are many explanations of that sentence, as there usually are according to the definition offered in the previous section? The most straightforward answer is this. Given an observation sentence Γ and a background theory Σ, conjoin the disjunction of all minimal explanations of Γ to Σ.

Let Σ and Γ be any formulae of first-order predicate calculus with equality. Let $\rho*$ be a (possibly partitioned) tuple of predicate symbols, let $\sigma*$ be a tuple of predicate, constant and function symbols, and let $\eta*$ be a tuple of predicate symbols.

Let $ABD^+[\Gamma ; \Sigma ; \rho* ; \sigma* ; \eta*]$ denote the set of all explanations of Γ in terms of $\eta*$ given a background theory Σ and a circumscription policy that minimises $\rho*$ and allows $\sigma*$ to vary. The difference between ABD and ABD^+ is that ABD^+ includes non-minimal explanations.

Definition 17.7.1. The result of assimilating Γ into Σ, given the circumscription policy of minimising $\rho*$ and allowing $\sigma*$ to vary, and given the set $\eta*$ of abducibles, written $ASM[\Gamma ; \Sigma ; \rho* ; \sigma* ; \eta*]$, is,

- $CIRC[\Sigma \wedge \Gamma ; \rho* ; \sigma*]$ if Γ is not an observation sentence,

- $CIRC[\Sigma \wedge \bigvee_{\Delta \in E} \Delta ; \rho* ; \sigma*]$ if Γ is an observation sentence

where E is the set $ABD^+[\Gamma ; \Sigma ; \rho* ; \sigma* ; \eta*]$. $\square$

ASM can be thought of as a kind of *revision* operator, in the sense of Alchourrón, Gärdenfors and Makinson [1985]. The following theorem shows that, under certain conditions, ASM conforms to Alchourrón, Gärdenfors and Makinson's first postulate, which says that if a knowledge base is revised by a sentence Γ then the result should entail Γ.[6]

Theorem 17.7.2. If $ABD^+[\Gamma ; \Sigma ; \rho* ; \sigma* ; \eta*]$ is non-empty then,

$$ASM[\Gamma ; \Sigma ; \rho* ; \sigma* ; \eta*] \vDash \Gamma.$$

Proof. From Definition 17.7.1, the theorem trivially holds if Γ is not an observation sentence. If Γ is an observation sentence then,

$$\text{ASM}[\Gamma ; \Sigma ; \rho^* ; \sigma^* ; \eta^*] \vDash \bigvee_{\Delta \in E} \text{CIRC}[\Sigma \wedge \Delta ; \rho^* ; \sigma^*] \qquad [17.7.3]$$

where E is the set $\text{ABD}^+[\Gamma ; \Sigma ; \rho^* ; \sigma^* ; \eta^*]$. This follows from the general property of circumscription that, for any Δ_1 and Δ_2,

$$\text{CIRC}[\Delta_1 \vee \Delta_2 ; \rho^* ; \sigma^*] \vDash \text{CIRC}[\Delta_1 ; \rho^* ; \sigma^*] \vee \text{CIRC}[\Delta_2 ; \rho^* ; \sigma^*].$$

Since E is non-empty and, for each Δ in E, we have,

$$\text{CIRC}[\Sigma \wedge \Delta ; \rho^* ; \sigma^*] \vDash \Gamma$$

we also have,

$$\bigvee_{\Delta \in E} \text{CIRC}[\Sigma \wedge \Delta ; \rho^* ; \sigma^*] \vDash \Gamma.$$

The theorem follows from this and [17.7.3]. □

The following theorem establishes that the definition of ASM doesn't have to appeal to the idea of a minimal explanation.

Theorem 17.7.4. $\text{ASM}[\Gamma ; \Sigma ; \rho^* ; \sigma^* ; \eta^*]$ is logically equivalent to,

- $\text{CIRC}[\Sigma \wedge \Gamma ; \rho^* ; \sigma^* ; \eta^*]$ if Γ is not an observation sentence,

- $\text{CIRC}[\Sigma \wedge \bigvee_{\Delta \in E} \Delta ; \rho^* ; \sigma^*]$ if Γ is an observation sentence

where E is the set $\text{ABD}[\Gamma ; \Sigma ; \rho^* ; \sigma^* ; \eta^*]$.

Proof. The proposition follows from the fact that,

$$\bigvee_{\Delta \in E1} \Delta$$

where E1 is the set $\text{ABD}^+[\Gamma ; \Sigma ; \rho^* ; \sigma^* ; \eta^*]$, is logically equivalent to,

$$\bigvee_{\Delta \in E2} \Delta$$

where E2 is the set $\text{ABD}[\Gamma ; \Sigma ; \rho^* ; \sigma^* ; \eta^*]$. To see that this equivalence holds, consider that, in the first disjunction, every non-minimal explanation Δ is disjoined with some minimal explanation Δ' such that $\Delta \vDash \Delta'$. If $\Delta \vDash \Delta'$ then $\Delta \vee \Delta'$ is equivalent to Δ', so the incorporation of non-minimal explanations has no effect. □

Naturally, the definition of ASM can be specialised for the situation calculus. Given two formulae Γ and Σ, the formula,

$$\text{ASM}[\Gamma ; \Sigma ; \text{AbSit} > \text{Ab, Happens} ;$$
$$\text{State, HoldsAt, Holds, Result ; Happens, Initially}, <, \leq]$$

will be denoted $\text{ASM}_{sc}[\Gamma ; \Sigma]$.

Let's revisit the lazy security guard scenario of Section 17.5. Let Σ be the conjunction of (ESC2) to (ESC4) with (ESC6) to (ESC13), plus Axioms (MS1) to (MS4), and Axioms (EoS9), (EoS10) and (F2). Note the crucial omission of the observation sentence (ESC5). Let Δ be,

$$\exists\, t1,t2,t3\; [\text{Happens(Guard(Fred)},t1) \wedge T1 \leq t1 \wedge \text{Happens(Smash},t2) \wedge$$
$$t1 < t2 \wedge \text{Happens(Steal},t3) \wedge t2 < t3 \wedge t3 < T2].$$

We have the following proposition.

Proposition 17.7.5.

$$\text{ASM}_{sc}[(\text{ESC5}) ; \Sigma] \vDash \Delta.$$

Proof. Using familiar techniques, it's easy to verify that,

$$\text{CIRC}[\Sigma \wedge \Delta ; \text{AbSit} > \text{Ab, Happens} ;$$
$$\text{State, HoldsAt, Holds, Result}] \vDash (\text{ESC5}).$$

Therefore, since $\Sigma \wedge \Delta$ is consistent and mentions only abducible predicates, Δ is an explanation of (ESC5). By inspection, it can be confirmed that any sequence of events that leads to the car's disappearance by time T2 has to include a Guard(Fred) event, a Smash event and a Steal event, in that order. So Δ will follow from every explanation of (ESC5). Δ therefore follows from the disjunction of all such explanations, and the proposition holds.　　□

In other words, the abductive approach yields the full explanation of the car's disappearance, where the deductive approach was unable to identify Fred's unwitting role in the theft.

17.8　Non-Determinism and the Abductive Approach

Actions with non-deterministic effects are a potential source of trouble for the abductive approach to the assimilation of observation sentences. To see this, consider the bus ride scenario again. After a Board action, the commuter is either on a red bus or a yellow bus. In addition, we have an observation sentence that says that, on a given occasion, the commuter in fact ended up on a red bus after a

Board action. According to the abductive approach, any explanation of this fact has to entail it when conjoined with the background theory. But, if the bus ride scenario is represented using formulae (BR1) to (BR10) of Section 17.4, the background theory is too weak to yield the colour of the commuter's bus as a logical consequence. The strongest conclusion it's capable of is a disjunction.

More formally, if we let Σ be the conjunction of (BR1) to (BR6) and (BR8) to (BR10) with Axioms (EoS9), (EoS10) and (F2), then we have the following proposition.

Proposition 17.8.1. $ABD_{sc}[(BR7) ; \Sigma]$ is empty.

Proof. The proposition follows from the fact that for every Δ, if there exists a model of $CIRC_{MS}[\Delta \wedge \Sigma]$ that satisfies HoldsAt(OnRed,S2), then there also exists a model of $CIRC_{MS}[\Delta \wedge \Sigma]$ that satisfies HoldsAt(OnYellow,S2), and that therefore doesn't satisfy HoldsAt(OnRed,S2).   □

Fortunately, the manoeuvre that enabled state-based minimisation to cope with domains like the bus ride scenario also rescues the abductive approach, namely the deployment of the method of disjunctive events for representing non-determinism (see Sections 15.2 and 17.4).

Let Σ be the conjunction of (BRN1) to (BRN3) and (BRN5) to (BRN16) with Axioms (GA1) to (GA3), Axioms (CMS1) to (CMS4), and Axioms (CN), (EoS9), (EoS10) and (F3). We have the following proposition.

Proposition 17.8.2. The set,

$$ABD[(BRN4) ; \Sigma ; Happens, AbSit > Ab ;$$
$$Happens\dagger, State, HoldsAt, Holds, Result ; Happens, Initially, <, \leq]$$

is non-empty.

Proof. Let Δ be,

$$Happens(BoardRed,T2).$$

Δ is consistent with Σ, and, using the same method as in the proof of Proposition 17.4.3, we can show,

$$CIRC[\Sigma \wedge \Delta ; Happens, AbSit > Ab ;$$
$$Happens\dagger, State, HoldsAt, Holds, Result] \models HoldsAt(OnRed,T3).$$

Therefore Δ is an explanation of (BRN4).   □

As in Section 17.4, problems with non-determinism have been avoided by viewing non-determinism as incomplete information about the narrative. In the case of state-based minimisation, this meant that it couldn't interfere with the minimisation used to overcome the frame problem. In the case of abduction, the technique works in a different way. With non-determinism confined to the narrative, the abductive process itself can fill in the resulting gaps in knowledge.

Other ways of combining non-determinism and abduction are possible. For example, in [Shanahan, 1996b], following [Reiter, 1987], a weaker form of *consistency-based abduction* is used in order to provide explanations for triggered events in the presence of non-deterministic continuous change. The following definition of weak abduction should be compared to Definition 17.6.1.

Definition 17.8.3. A formula Δ is a *weak explanation* of Γ *in terms of* η^* given a *background theory* Σ and a *circumscription policy* that minimises ρ^* and allows σ^* to vary if,

- $CIRC[\Sigma \wedge \Delta ; \rho^*; \sigma^*]$ is consistent,

- Δ mentions only predicates in η^*, and

- $CIRC[\Sigma \wedge \Delta ; \rho^*; \sigma^*] \not\models \neg \Gamma.$ $\square$

This form of abduction is not useful for examples like the bus ride scenario. Its main application is to problems in which the negation of the fact to be explained is a logical consequence in the absence of an explanation. The work reported in [Shanahan, 1996b] concerns a mobile robot whose sensor data is to be explained in terms of the existence of obstacles in its environment. In the absence of any information about obstacles, the theory describing the robot's relationship to its environment predicts the absence of any sensor data. So Definition 17.8.3 is applicable. The stronger form of abduction of Definition 17.6.1 is inappropriate because the theory also incorporates a non-deterministic Trajectory formula to describe the robot's motion, which is uncertain due to motor noise.

17.9 Abduction and the Circumscriptive Event Calculus

The abductive approach to explanation can be straightforwardly adapted to both versions of the circumscriptive event calculus, namely the state-based version of Chapters 14 and 15 and the forced separation version of Chapter 16. The task is least straightforward for the forced separation version, so that's the one I'll concentrate on here.

Following Section 16.3, let,

- Δ_1 be a conjunction of Happens, Initially$_P$, Initially$_N$, and temporal ordering formulae,

- Σ be a conjunction of Initiates, Terminates and Releases formulae, and

- Φ be the conjunction of,

  - Axioms (ECF1) to (ECF4), with

  - A conjunction of uniqueness-of-names axioms, and

  - A conjunction of domain constraints.

Definition 17.9.1. A formula Δ_2 is an *explanation* of the observation sentence (HoldsAt formula) Γ in the *forced separation version* of the *circumscriptive event calculus* if,

- CIRC[$\Delta_1 \wedge \Delta_2$; Happens] is consistent,

- Δ_2 mentions only the predicates Happens, Initially$_P$, Initially$_N$, $<$ and $\leq$, and

- $\quad$ CIRC[$\Delta_1 \wedge \Delta_2$; Happens] $\wedge$
  CIRC[Σ ; Initiates, Terminates, Releases] $\wedge \Phi \vDash \Gamma$. $\qquad\qquad$ □

The set of all such explanations of Γ will be denoted $ABD_{ec}{}^+[\Gamma, \Phi, \Delta_1, \Sigma]$. The following definition is analogous to Definition 17.7.1.

Definition 17.9.2. If Γ is an observation sentence, then $ASM_{ec}[\Gamma, \Phi, \Delta_1, \Sigma]$ denotes,

$$\text{CIRC}[\Delta_1 \wedge \bigvee_{\Delta \in E} \Delta \ ; \text{Happens}] \wedge$$
$$\text{CIRC}[\Sigma \ ; \text{Initiates, Terminates, Releases}] \wedge \Phi$$

where E is the set $ABD_{ec}{}^+[\Gamma, \Phi, \Delta_1, \Sigma]$. If Γ is an Initiates, Terminates or Releases formula, then $ASM_{ec}[\Gamma, \Phi, \Delta_1, \Sigma]$ denotes,

$$\text{CIRC}[\Delta_1 \ ; \text{Happens}] \wedge$$
$$\text{CIRC}[\Sigma \wedge \Gamma \ ; \text{Initiates, Terminates, Releases}] \wedge \Phi.$$

If Γ is a Happens formula, then $ASM_{ec}[\Gamma, \Phi, \Delta_1, \Sigma]$ denotes,

$$\text{CIRC}[\Delta_1 \wedge \Gamma \ ; \text{Happens}] \wedge$$
$$\text{CIRC}[\Sigma \ ; \text{Initiates, Terminates, Releases}] \wedge \Phi.$$

Otherwise $ASM_{ec}[\Gamma, \Phi, \Delta_1, \Sigma]$ denotes,

$$\text{CIRC}[\Delta_1 \text{ ; Happens]} \wedge$$
$$\text{CIRC}[\Sigma \text{ ; Initiates, Terminates, Releases]} \wedge \Phi \wedge \Gamma. \qquad \Box$$

Counterparts to Theorems 17.7.2 and 17.7.4 can easily be established for ASM_{ec}.

Let's consider the stolen car scenario first.

$$\text{Initiates(Park,CarParked,t)} \qquad \text{(SCE1)}$$

$$\text{Terminates(Steal,CarParked,t)} \qquad \text{(SCE2)}$$

$$\text{Happens(Park,T1)} \qquad \text{(SCE3)}$$

$$\text{UNA[Steal, Park]} \qquad \text{(SCE4)}$$

$$\text{T1} < \text{T2} \qquad \text{(SCE5)}$$

$$\neg \ \text{HoldsAt(CarParked,T2)} \qquad \text{(SCE6)}$$

Let Δ_1 be (SCE3), let Σ be (SCE1) $\wedge$ (SCE2), and let Φ be the conjunction of Axioms (ECF1) to (ECF4) with (SCE4) and (SCE5). Let Γ be the observation sentence (SCE6).

Proposition 17.9.3.

$$\text{ASM}_{ec}[\Gamma, \Phi, \Delta_1, \Sigma] \models \exists \ t \ [\text{Happens(Steal,t)} \wedge \text{T1} < t \wedge t < \text{T2}].$$

Proof. Let Δ_2 be,

$$\exists \ t \ [\text{Happens(Steal,t)} \wedge \text{T1} < t \wedge t < \text{T2}].$$

Using the same method as in the proof of Proposition 16.3.1, it can be shown that,

$$\text{CIRC}[\Delta_1 \wedge \Delta_2 \text{ ; Happens]} \wedge$$
$$\text{CIRC}[\Sigma \text{ ; Initiates, Terminates, Releases]} \wedge \Phi \models \neg \ \text{HoldsAt(CarParked,T2)}.$$

This means that Δ_2 is an explanation of Γ. Furthermore, since the only event that can make the car disappear is a Steal event, we know that every explanation of Γ implies Δ_2. Therefore,

$$\bigvee_{\Delta \in E} \Delta \rightarrow \Delta_2$$

where E is the set $\text{ABD}_{ec}{}^+[\Gamma, \Phi, \Delta_1, \Sigma]$. The proposition then follows directly. $\Box$

The bus ride scenario also succumbs to the abductive approach with the event calculus. As in Section 17.4, the method of disjunctive events is used to capture the non-deterministic effect of a Board event. To begin with, we have a group of narrative formulae.

$$\text{Initially}_N(\text{HasTicket}) \qquad \text{(BRE1)}$$

$$\text{Happens}(\text{Buy},\text{T1}) \qquad \text{(BRE2)}$$

$$\text{Happens}(\text{Board},\text{T2}) \qquad \text{(BRE3)}$$

$$\text{T1} > 0 \qquad \text{(BRE4)}$$

$$\text{T2} > \text{T1} \qquad \text{(BRE5)}$$

$$\text{T3} > \text{T2} \qquad \text{(BRE6)}$$

$$\text{Happens}(\text{Board},t) \rightarrow \text{Happens}(\text{BoardRed},t) \vee \qquad \text{(BRE7)}$$
$$\text{Happens}(\text{BoardYellow},t)$$

Let Δ_1 be the conjunction of (BRE1) to (BRE7). Next we have a group of Initiates and Terminates formulae.

$$\text{Initiates}(\text{Buy},\text{HasTicket},t) \qquad \text{(BRE8)}$$

$$\text{Initiates}(\text{BoardRed},\text{OnRed},t) \leftarrow \text{HoldsAt}(\text{HasTicket},t) \qquad \text{(BRE9)}$$

$$\text{Initiates}(\text{BoardYellow},\text{OnYellow},t) \leftarrow \text{HoldsAt}(\text{HasTicket},t) \qquad \text{(BRE10)}$$

Let Σ be the conjunction of (BRE7) to (BRE10). Domain constraints come next.

$$\neg\,[\text{HoldsAt}(\text{OnRed},t) \wedge \text{HoldsAt}(\text{OnYellow},t)] \qquad \text{(BRE11)}$$

$$\text{HoldsAt}(\text{OnRed},t) \rightarrow \text{HoldsAt}(\text{HasTicket},t) \qquad \text{(BRN12)}$$

$$\text{HoldsAt}(\text{OnYellow},t) \rightarrow \text{HoldsAt}(\text{HasTicket},t) \qquad \text{(BRN13)}$$

Finally we require some uniqueness-of-names axioms.

$$\text{UNA}[\text{OnRed, OnYellow, HasTicket}] \qquad \text{(BRE14)}$$

$$\text{UNA}[\text{Buy, Board, BoardRed, BoardYellow}] \qquad \text{(BRE15)}$$

Let Φ be the conjunction of Axioms (ECF1) to (ECF4) with (BRE11) to (BRE15). Let Γ be the following observation sentence.

$$\text{HoldsAt}(\text{OnRed},\text{T3}) \qquad \text{(BRE16)}$$

Proposition 17.9.3. The following two propositions hold.

$$\text{ASM}_{ec}[\Gamma,\,\Phi,\,\Delta_1,\,\Sigma] \vDash \text{Happens}(\text{BoardRed},\text{T2}) \qquad [17.9.4]$$

$$\text{ASM}_{ec}[\Gamma, \Phi, \Delta_1, \Sigma] \vDash \neg \text{ HoldsAt(OnRed,T2)} \wedge \qquad [17.9.5]$$
$$\neg \text{ HoldsAt(OnYellow,T2)}$$

Proof. The circumscription $\text{CIRC}[\Delta_1 ; \text{Happens}]$ admits two classes of model, one whose members satisfy,

$$\text{Happens(a,t)} \leftrightarrow [a = \text{Buy} \wedge t = \text{T1}] \vee [a = \text{Board} \wedge t = \text{T2}] \vee \quad [17.9.6]$$
$$[a = \text{BoardRed} \wedge t = \text{T2}]$$

and one whose members satisfy,

$$\text{Happens(a,t)} \leftrightarrow [a = \text{Buy} \wedge t = \text{T1}] \vee [a = \text{Board} \wedge t = \text{T2}] \vee \quad [17.9.7]$$
$$[a = \text{BoardYellow} \wedge t = \text{T2}].$$

(Recall the proof of Proposition 17.4.3.) Now, it can be verified that any model of,

$$\text{CIRC}[\Delta_1 ; \text{Happens}] \wedge \text{CIRC}[\Sigma ; \text{Initiates, Terminates, Releases}] \wedge \Phi$$

which satisfies [17.9.7] also satisfies,

$$\text{HoldsAt(OnYellow,T3)}$$

and cannot therefore satisfy Γ because of (BRE11). So we are left with [17.9.6]. Given this, we can prove [17.9.4] and [17.9.5]. $\qquad \square$

A similar exercise, using similar formalisations of both the stolen car scenario and the bus ride scenario, can be carried out for the state-based version of the circumscriptive event calculus.

The subject of explanation, in the context of any formalism, deserves a great deal more attention than I have been able to give it here. Of particular interest is the issue of preference relations among explanations, touched on in Section 17.6. The only kinds of explanation we have looked at here have been in terms of the narrative. But explanations in terms of extra effect axioms or Initiates and Terminates formulae are also possible.[7] The best choice may be a framework in which narrative explanations are preferred, but that allows explanations in terms of previously unknown effects of actions where necessary.

Notes

1. In fact, the very idea of a "wait" action seems rather strange here, and the idea of a sequence of two wait actions seems stranger still. Surely waiting is a pause between actions rather than an action in its own right. In other examples involving a Wait action, this can readily be replaced by a Sneeze action fulfilling

the same role of an action that has no effect. Here, no such substitution is possible, since by a Wait action, we genuinely mean a pause in the narrative.

2. I prefer the formula ¬ Holds(CarParked,s) to Baker's Holds(Stolen,s), although they fulfil the same role.

3. A uniqueness-of-names axiom for actions is now needed. This was unnecessary with just a single Steal action in the domain.

4. In [Shanahan, 1989] and [Denecker, *et al.,* 1992], a logic programming approach is taken to explanation, following the work of [Eshghi, 1988]. The present chapter concentrates on approaches using circumscription.

5. Schubert questions our "deep-seated prejudices against the idea of reasoning deductively against the causal arrow" [Schubert, 1994], citing the efficacy of explanation closure axioms (see Sections 8.1 and 8.2), which seem to violate this idea, as a reason for overcoming these prejudices. However, even theories of action based on explanation closure axioms conform to the principle of directionality if they do not include observation sentences.

6. ASM doesn't conform to all the so-called AGM postulates. A more thorough investigation of the properties of abductive revision operators like ASM can be found in [Boutilier & Becher, 1995] and [Boutilier, 1996].

7. The topic of induction is relevant here.

Bibliography

The bracketed numbers at the end of a reference indicate the pages on which the work is cited. Where the citation is in an endnote, the number of the page containing the endnote reference is given.

[Allen, 1984] J.F.Allen, Towards a General Theory of Action and Time, *Artificial Intelligence*, vol. 23 (1984) pp. 123–154. (7)

[Allen, *et al.*, 1991] J.F.Allen, H.A.Kautz, R.N.Pelavin and J.D.Tenenberg, *Reasoning about Plans*, Morgan Kaufmann (1991). (347, 364)

[Alchourrón, Gärdenfors & Makinson, 1985], C.Alchourrón, P.Gärdenfors and D.Makinson, On the Logic of Theory Change: Partial Meet Contraction and Revision Functions, *Journal of Symbolic Logic*, vol. 50 (1985), pp. 510–530. (353)

[Apt, Blair & Walker, 1987] K.R.Apt, A.Blair and A.Walker, Towards a Theory of Declarative Knowledge, in *Foundations of Deductive Databases and Logic Programming*, ed. J.Minker, Morgan Kaufmann (1987), pp. 89–148. (228)

[Apt & Bol, 1994] K.R.Apt and R.N.Bol, Logic Programming and Negation: A Survey, *Journal of Logic Programming*, vol. 19 (1994), pp. 9–71. (230)

[Baker, 1989] A.B.Baker, A Simple Solution to the Yale Shooting Problem, *Proceedings 1989 Knowledge Representation Conference (KR 89)*, pp. 11–20. (58, 65, 80, 93, 97, 111, 126, 127, 331, 334, 347)

[Baker, 1991] A.B.Baker, Nonmonotonic Reasoning in the Framework of the Situation Calculus, *Artificial Intelligence*, vol. 49 (1991), pp. 5–23. (99, 108, 111, 121, 125, 131, 150, 287)

[Baker & Ginsberg, 1989] A.B.Baker and M.L.Ginsberg, Temporal Projection and Explanation, *Proceedings IJCAI 89*, pp. 906–911. (99)

[Baral & Gelfond, 1993] C.Baral and M.Gelfond, Representing Concurremt Actions in Extended Logic Programming, *Proceedings IJCAI 93*, pp. 866–871. (153)

[Baral, Gelfond & Provetti, 1997] C.Baral, M.Gelfond and A.Provetti, Representing Actions: Laws, Observations and Hypotheses, *The Journal of Logic Programming* (1997), to appear. (153)

[Birnbaum, 1991] L.Birnbaum, Rigor Mortis: A Response to Nilsson's "Logic and Artificial Intelligence", *Artificial Intelligence*, vol. 47 (1991), pp. 57–77. (xxxii)

[Boutilier, 1996] C.Boutilier, Abduction to Plausible Causes: An Event-Based Model of Belief Update, *Artificial Intelligence* vol. 83 (1996), pp. 143–166. (347, 353)

[Boutilier & Becher, 1995] C.Boutilier and V.Becher, Abduction as Belief Revision, *Artificial Intelligence*, vol. 77 (1995), pp. 43–94. (347, 353)

[Brooks, 1991a] R.A.Brooks, Intelligence Without Representation, *Artificial Intelligence*, vol. 47 (1991), pp. 139–159. (xxvi, 6)

[Brooks, 1991b] R.A.Brooks, Intelligence Without Reason, *Proceedings IJCAI 91*, pp. 569–595. (xxvi, xxix, 6)

[Buvač & Mason, 1993] S.Buvač and I.A.Mason, Propositional Logic of Context, *Proceedings AAAI 93,* pp. 412–419. (190)

[Clark, 1978] K.L.Clark, Negation as Failure, in *Logic and Databases*, ed. H.Gallaire and J.Minker, Plenum Press (1978), pp. 293–322. (17, 47, 218, 219, 225, 227)

[Clark, 1979] K.L.Clark, Predicate Logic as a Computational Formalism, Research Report DOC 79/59, Imperial College Department of Computing (1979). (209)

[Clocksin & Mellish, 1987] W.F.Clocksin and C.Mellish, *Programming in Prolog* (Third Edition), Springer-Verlag, 1987. (215)

[Cohn, 1985] A.G.Cohn, On the Solution of Schubert's Steamroller in Many Sorted Logic, *Proceedings IJCAI 85*, pp. 1169–1174. (31)

[Colmerauer, *et al.*, 1973] A.Colmerauer, H.Kanoui, R.Pasero, and P.Roussel, Un Systeme de Comunication Homme-Machine en Francais, Techniocal Report, Groupe de Recherche en Intelligence Artificielle, Université d'Aix Marseille, 1973. (203, 212)

[Console *et al.*, 1991] L.Console, D.Dupré and P.Torasso, On the Relationship between Abduction and Deduction, *Journal of Logic and Computation*, vol. 1 (1991), pp. 661–690. (351)

[Crawford & Etherington, 1992] J.M.Crawford and D.W.Etherington, Formalizing Reasoning about Change: A Qualitative Reasoning Approach, *Proceedings AAAI 92*, pp. 577–583. (315, 332, 347)

[Crockett, 1994] L.Crockett, *The Turing Test and the Frame Problem: AI's Mistaken Understanding of Intelligence*, Ablex (1994). (24)

[Davies & Russell, 1987] T.R.Davies and S.J.Russell, A Logical Approach to Reasoning by Analogy, *Proceedings IJCAI 87*, pp. 264–270. (xxxii)

[Davis, 1990] E.Davis, *Representations of Commonsense Knowledge*, Morgan Kaufmann (1990). (30)

[Davis, 1992] E.Davis, Infinite Loops in Finite Time: Some Observations, *Proceedings 1992 Knowledge Representation Conference (KR 92)*, pp. 47–58. (308)

[Denecker & De Schreye, 1993] M.Denecker and D.De Schreye, Representing Incomplete Knowledge in Abductive Logic Programming, *Proceedings of the 1993 International Symposium on Logic Programming*, pp. 147–163. (150)

[Denecker, *et al.*, 1992] M.Denecker, L.Missiaen and M.Bruynooghe, Temporal Reasoning with Abductive Event Calculus, *Proceedings ECAI 92*, pp. 384–388. (238, 241, 347)

[Dennett, 1978] D.Dennett, *Brainstorms: Philosophical Essays on Mind and Psychology*, Harvester Press (1978). (23)

[Dennett, 1987] D.Dennett, Cognitive Wheels: The Frame Problem of AI, in *The Robots Dilemma: The Frame Problem in Artificial Intelligence*, ed. Z.W.Pylyshyn, Ablex (1987), pp. 41–64. (23)

[Doherty, 1994] P.Doherty, Reasoning about Action and Change Using Occlusion, *Proceedings ECAI 94*, pp. 401–405. (315)

[Dung, 1993] P.M.Dung, Representing Actions in Logic Programming and its Applications in Database Updates, *Proceedings of the Tenth International Conference on Logic Programming* (1993), pp. 222–238. (150)

[Elkan, 1992] C.Elkan, Reasoning about Action in First-Order Logic, *Proceedings Ninth Biennial Conference of the Canadian Society for Computational Studies of Intelligence (CSCSI 92)*, pp. 221–227. (144)

[Eshghi, 1988] K.Eshghi, Abductive Planning with Event Calculus, *Proceedings of the Fifth International Conference on Logic Programming* (1988), pp. 562–579. (252, 347, 364)

[Eshghi & Kowalski, 1989] K.Eshghi and R.A.Kowalski, Abduction Compared with Negation by Failure, *Proceedings of the Sixth International Conference on Logic Programming*, pp. 234–255. (347)

[Etherington, Mercer & Reiter, 1985] D.Etherington, R.Mercer and R.Reiter, On the Adequacy of Circumscription for Closed-World Reasoning, *Computational Intelligence*, vol. 1 (1985), pp. 11–15. (51, 228)

[Evans, 1989] C.Evans, Negation as Failure as an Approach to the Hanks and McDermott Problem, *Proceedings 2nd International Symposium on Artificial Intelligence*. (236, 239)

[Fetzer, 1991] J.H.Fetzer, The Frame Problem: Artificial Intelligence Meets David Hume, in *Reasoning Agents in a Dynamic World: The Frame Problem*, ed. K.M.Ford and P.J.Hayes, JAI Press (1991), pp. 55–69. (24)

[Fikes & Nilsson, 1971] R.E.Fikes and N.J.Nilsson, STRIPS: A New Approach to the Application of Theorem Proving to Problem Solving, Artificial Intelligence, vol. 2 (1971), pp. 189–208. (xxvi, 6)

[Finger, 1987] J.J.Finger, *Exploiting Constraints in Design Synthesis*, PhD thesis, Stanford University, 1987. (94)

[Fodor, 1983] J.A.Fodor, *The Modularity of Mind*, MIT Press (1983). (xxiv, xxv)

[Fodor, 1987] J.A.Fodor, Modules, Frames, Fridgeons, Sleeping Dogs, and the Music of the Spheres, in *The Robots Dilemma: The Frame Problem in Artificial Intelligence*, ed. Z.W.Pylyshyn, Ablex (1987), pp. 139–149. (23, 24)

[Ford & Pylyshyn, 1996] K.Ford and Z.Pylyshyn, eds., *The Robot's Dilemma Revisited*, Ablex (1996). (23)

[Galton, 1991] A.Galton, Reified Temporal Theories and How to Unreify Them, *Proceedings IJCAI 91*, pp. 1177–1182. (38)

[Gardin & Meltzer, 1989] Analogical Representations of Naive Physics, *Artificial Intelligence*, vol. 38 (1989), pp. 139–159. (xxxi)

[Gelfond & Lifschitz, 1992] M.Gelfond and V.Lifschitz, Representing Actions in Extended Logic Programming, *Proceedings of the 1992 Joint International Conference and Symposium on Logic Programming*, pp. 559–573. (150)

[Gelfond & Lifschitz, 1993] M.Gelfond and V.Lifschitz, Representing Action and Change by Logic Programs, *The Journal of Logic Programming*, vol. 17 (1993), pp. 301–322. (150)

[Gelfond, Lifschitz & Rabinov, 1991] M.Gelfond, V.Lifschitz and A.Rabinov, What Are the Limitations of the Situation Calculus? in *Essays in Honor of Woody Bledsoe*, ed R.Boyer, Kluwer Academic (1991), pp. 167–179. (11, 44, 185, 194, 259, 303)

[Genesereth & Nilsson, 1987] M.R.Genesereth and N.J.Nilsson, *Logical Foundations of Artificial Intelligence*, Morgan Kaufmann (1987). (xix, 30)

[Georgeff, 1987] M.P.Georgeff, Many Agents Are Better than One, *Proceedings of the 1987 Workshop on the Frame Problem*, ed. F.M.Brown, pp. 59–75. (186)

[Ginsberg & Smith, 1987] M.L.Ginsberg and D.E.Smith, Reasoning about Action I: A Possible Worlds Approach, *Proceedings of the 1987 Workshop on the Frame Problem*, pp. 233–258. (94, 122)

[Giunchiglia & Lifschitz, 1995] E.Giunchiglia and V.Lifschitz, Dependent Fluents, *Proceedings IJCAI 95*, pp. 1964–1969. (122, 289)

[Glymour, 1987] C.Glymour, Android Epistemology and the Frame Problem: Comments on Dennett's "Cognitive Wheels", in *The Robots Dilemma: The Frame Problem in Artificial Intelligence*, ed. Z.W.Pylyshyn, Ablex (1987), pp. 65–75. (23)

[Green, 1969] C.Green, Applications of Theorem Proving to Problem Solving, *Proceedings IJCAI 69*, pp. 219–240. (6, 216, 231, 364)

[Haas, 1987] A.R.Haas, The Case for Domain-Specific Frame Axioms, *Proceedings of the 1987 Workshop on the Frame Problem*, pp. 343–348. (9, 135, 136, 140)

[Hamilton, 1988] A.G.Hamilton, *Logic for Mathematicians* (Revised Edition), Cambridge University Press (1988). (30, 118)

[Hanks & McDermott, 1986] S.Hanks and D.McDermott, Default Reasoning, Nonmonotonic Logics, and the Frame Problem, *Proceedings AAAI 86*, pp. 328–333. (60, 69)

[Hanks & McDermott, 1987] S.Hanks and D.McDermott, Nonmonotonic Logic and Temporal Projection, *Artificial Intelligence*, vol. 33 (1987), pp. 379–412. (17, 41, 60)

[Harnad, 1990] S.Harnad, The Symbol Grounding Problem, *Physica D*, vol. 42 (1990), pp. 335–346. (23)

[Haugh, 1987] B.A.Haugh, Simple Causal Minimizations for Temporal Persistence and Projection, *Proceedings AAAI 87*, pp. 218–223. (83)

[Hayes, 1971] P.J.Hayes, A Logic of Actions, in *Machine Intelligence 6*, ed. D.Michie and B.Meltzer, Edinburgh University Press (1969), pp. 495–520. (8)

[Hayes, 1973] P.J.Hayes, The Frame Problem and Related Problems in Artificial Intelligence, in *Artificial and Human Thinking*, ed. A.Elithorn and D.Jones, Elsevier (1973). (8)

[Hayes, 1977] P.J.Hayes, In Defence of Logic, *Proceedings IJCAI 77*, pp. 559–565. (xxx, xxxi)

[Hayes, 1985a] P.J.Hayes, The Second Naive Physics Manifesto, in *Formal Theories of the Commonsense World*, ed. Hobbs J.R. and Moore R.C., Ablex (1985), pp. 1–36. (xxx, 7, 45, 185)

[Hayes, 1985b] P.J.Hayes, Naive Physics 1: Ontology for Liquids, in *Formal Theories of the Commonsense World*, ed. Hobbs J.R. and Moore R.C., Ablex (1985), pp. 71–107. (7, 260)

[Hayes, 1987] P.J.Hayes, What the Frame Problem Is and Isn't, in *The Robots Dilemma: The Frame Problem in Artificial Intelligence*, ed. Z.W.Pylyshyn, Ablex (1987), pp. 123–137. (7, 23)

[Hobbs, *et al.*, 1990] J.R.Hobbs, M.Stickel, D.Appelt and P.Martin, Interpretation as Abduction, SRI Technical Report no. 499 (1990), SRI, Menlo Park, California. (347)

[Jaffar & Lassez, 1987] J.Jaffar and J-L.Lassez, Constraint Logic Programming, *Proceedings 14th ACM Symposium on Principles of Programming Languages* (1987), pp. 111–119. (243, 260)

[Janlert, 1987] L-E.Janlert, Modeling Change — The Frame Problem, in *The Robots Dilemma: The Frame Problem in Artificial Intelligence*, ed. Z.W.Pylyshyn, Ablex (1987), pp. 1–40. (8)

[Kakas, Kowalski & Toni, 1993] A.C.Kakas, R.A.Kowalski and F.Toni, Abductive Logic Programming, *Journal of Logic and Computation*, vol. 2, no. 6 (1993), pp. 719–770. (230, 347)

[Kakas & Miller, 1997] A.Kakas and R.S.Miller, A Simple Declarative Language for Describing Narratives with Actions, *The Journal of Logic Programming* (1997), to appear. (153)

[Kartha, 1993] G.N.Kartha, Soundness and Completeness Theorems for Three Formalizations of Action, *Proceedings IJCAI 93*, pp. 724–729. (148, 150)

[Kartha, 1994] G.N.Kartha, Two Counterexamples Related to Baker's Approach to the Frame Problem, *Artificial Intelligence*, vol. 69 (1994), pp. 379–391. (128, 158, 332, 339, 341, 345)

[Kartha, 1995] G.N.Kartha, *A Mathematical Investigation of Reasoning about Actions*, PhD Thesis, Department of Computer Sciences, University of Texas at Austin (1995). (318)

[Kartha, 1996] G.N.Kartha, On the Range of Applicability of Baker's Approach to the Frame Problem, *Proceedings AAAI 96*, pp. 664–669. (132)

[Kartha & Lifschitz, 1994] G.N.Kartha and V.Lifschitz, Actions with Indirect Effects (Preliminary Report), *Proceedings 1994 Knowledge Representation Conference (KR 94)*, pp. 341–350. (153, 140, 290, 299)

[Kartha & Lifschitz, 1995] G.N.Kartha and V.Lifschitz, A Simple Formalization of Actions Using Circumscription, *Proceedings IJCAI 95*, pp. 1970–1975. (315)

[Kautz, 1986] H.Kautz, The Logic of Persistence, *Proceedings AAAI 86*, pp. 401–405. (22, 76, 77, 79, 80, 331)

[Konolige, 1992] K.Konolige, Abduction Versus Closure in Causal Theories, *Artificial Intelligence*, vol. 53 (1992), pp. 255–272. (351)

[Kowalski, 1974] R.A.Kowalski, Predicate Logic as a Programming Language, *Proceedings IFIP 74*, pp. 569–574. (203, 213)

[Kowalski, 1979] R.A.Kowalski, *Logic for Problem Solving*, Elsevier North Holland, 1979. (206, 215, 216, 243)

[Kowalski, 1992] R.A.Kowalski, Database Updates in the Event Calculus, *Journal of Logic Programming*, vol. 12 (1992), pp. 121–146. (6, 252)

[Kowalski & Kuehner, 1971] R.A.Kowalski and D.Kuehner, Linear Resolution with Selection Function, *Artificial Intelligence*, vol. 2, pp. 227–260. (203)

[Kowalski & Sadri, 1994] R.A.Kowalski and F.Sadri, The Situation Calculus and Event Calculus Compared, *Proceedings 1994 International Symposium on Logic Programming*, pp. 539–553. (251)

[Kowalski & Sergot, 1986] R.A.Kowalski and M.J.Sergot, A Logic-Based Calculus of Events, *New Generation Computing*, vol. 4 (1986), pp. 67–95. (7, 231, 241)

[Kunen, 1989] K.Kunen, Signed Data Dependencies in Logic Programs, *Journal of Logic Programming*, vol. 7 (1989), pp. 231–245. (229)

[Lemmon, 1965] E.J.Lemmon, *Beginning Logic*, Van Nostrand Reinhold (1965). (30)

[Lespérance, *et al.*, 1994] Y.Lespérance, H.J.Levesque, F.Lin, D.Marcu, R.Reiter, and R.B.Scherl, A Logical Approach to High-Level Robot Programming: A Progress Report, in *Control of the Physical World by Intelligent Systems: Papers from the 1994 AAAI Fall Symposium*, ed. B.Kuipers, New Orleans (1994), pp. 79–85. (xxx, 363)

[Levesque, *et al.*, 1997] H.Levesque, R.Reiter, Y.Lespérance, F.Lin and R.B.Scherl, GOLOG: A Logic Programming Language for Dynamic Domains, *The Journal of Logic Programming* (1997), to appear. (363)

[Lifschitz, 1985] V.Lifschitz, Computing Circumscription, *Proceedings IJCAI 85*, pp. 121–127. (112, 230)

[Lifschitz, 1986] V.Lifschitz, Pointwise Circumscription: Preliminary Report, *Proceedings AAAI 86*, pp. 406–411. (76, 77, 114)

[Lifschitz, 1987] V.Lifschitz, Formal Theories of Action, *Proceedings of the 1987 Workshop on the Frame Problem*, pp. 35–57. (83, 95)

[Lifschitz, 1990] V.Lifschitz, Frames in the Space of Situations, *Artificial Intelligence*, vol. 46 (1990), pp. 365–376. (95, 124, 273)

[Lifschitz, 1991] V.Lifschitz, Toward a Metatheory of Action, *Proceedings 1991 Knowledge Representation Conference (KR 91)*, pp. 376–386. (90, 132, 279)

[Lifschitz, 1994] V.Lifschitz, Circumscription, in *The Handbook of Logic in Artificial Intelligence and Logic Programming, Volume 3: Nonmonotonic Reasoning and Uncertain Reasoning*, ed. D.M.Gabbay, C.J.Hogger and J.A.Robinson, Oxford University Press (1994), pp. 297–352. (54, 114, 230, 280)

[Lifschitz, 1995] V.Lifschitz, Nested Abnormality Theories, *Artificial Intelligence*, vol. 74 (1995), pp. 351–365. (316)

[Lifschitz & Rabinov, 1989] V.Lifschitz and A.Rabinov, Miracles in Formal Theories of Action, *Artificial Intelligence*, vol. 38 (1989), pp. 225–237. (93, 332, 347)

[Lin, 1995] F.Lin, Embracing Causality in Specifying the Indirect Effects of Actions, *Proceedings IJCAI 95*, pp. 1985–1991. (122, 315)

[Lin & Reiter, 1994] F.Lin and R.Reiter, State Constraints Revisited, *The Journal of Logic and Computation* , vol. 4, no. 5 (1994), pp. 655–677. (2, 21, 86, 139, 140, 149)

[Lin & Shoham, 1991] F.Lin and Y.Shoham, Provably Correct Theories of Action, *Proceedings AAAI 91*, pp. 349–354. (132, 150, 195, 279)

[Lin & Shoham, 1992] F.Lin and Y.Shoham, Concurrent Actions in the Situation Calculus, *Proceedings AAAI 92*, pp. 590–595. (185, 194, 195, 279, 285, 303, 304)

[Lloyd, 1987] J.W.Lloyd, *Foundations of Logic Programming (Second Edition)*, Springer-Verlag, 1987. (203, 207, 209, 210, 211, 215, 227)

[Loui, 1987] R.P.Loui, Response to Hanks and McDermott: Temporal Evolution of Beliefs and Beliefs about Temporal Evolution, *Cognitive Science*, vol. 11 (1987), pp. 283–297. (140)

[McCain & Turner, 1995] N.McCain and H.Turner, A Causal Theory of Ramifications and Qualifications, *Proceedings IJCAI 95*, pp. 1978–1984. (122)

[McCarthy, 1959] J.McCarthy, Programs with Common Sense, *Proceedings of the Teddington Conference on the Mechanization of Thought Processes*, Her Majesty's Stationery Office, London (1959), pp. 75–91. (xxx)

[McCarthy, 1963] J.McCarthy, Situations, Actions and Causal Laws, Stanford Artificial Intelligence Project, Memo 2 (1963). (2, 36)

[McCarthy, 1977] J.McCarthy, Epistemological Problems of Artificial Intelligence, *Proceedings IJCAI 77*, pp. 1038–1044. (47, 83)

[McCarthy, 1980] J.McCarthy, Circumscription — A Form of Non-Monotonic Reasoning, *Artificial Intelligence*, vol. 13 (1980), pp. 27–39. (17, 20, 46, 47, 84)

[McCarthy, 1986] J.McCarthy, Applications of Circumscription to Formalizing Common Sense Knowledge, *Artificial Intelligence*, vol. 26 (1986), pp. 89–116. (17, 51, 58, 60, 99)

[McCarthy, 1988] J.McCarthy, Mathematical Logic in Artificial Intelligence, *Daedalus*, Winter 1988, pp. 297–311. (12, 45)

[McCarthy, 1989] J.McCarthy, Artificial Intelligence, Logic and Formalizing Common Sense, in *Philosophical Logic and Artificial Intelligence*, ed. R.Thomason, Kluwer Academic (1989), pp. 161–190. (19)

[McCarthy, 1993] J.McCarthy, Notes on Formalizing Context, *Proceedings IJCAI 93*, pp. 555–560. (189)

[McCarthy, 1996] J.McCarthy, Book Review of "What Computers Still Can't Do" by Hubert Dreyfus, *Artificial Intelligence*, vol. 80 (1996), pp. 143–150. (55)

[McCarthy & Hayes, 1969] J.McCarthy and P.J.Hayes, Some Philosophical Problems from the Standpoint of Artificial Intelligence, in *Machine Intelligence 4*, ed. D.Michie and B.Meltzer, Edinburgh University Press (1969), pp. 463–502. (1, 2, 7, 36, 37, 42, 57)

[McCarthy & Lifschitz, 1987] J.McCarthy and V.Lifschitz, Commentary on McDermott, *Computational Intelligence*, vol. 3 (1987), pp. 196–197. (xxxii)

[McDermott, 1982] D.McDermott, A Temporal Logic for Reasoning about Processes and Plans, *Cognitive Science*, vol. 6 (1982), pp. 101–155. (258)

[McDermott, 1987a] D.McDermott, We've Been Framed: Or Why AI Is Innocent of the Frame Problem, in *The Robots Dilemma: The Frame Problem in Artificial Intelligence*, ed. Z.W.Pylyshyn, Ablex (1987), pp. 113–122. (6)

[McDermott, 1987b] D.McDermott, A Critique of Pure Reason, *Computational Intelligence*, vol. 3 (1987), pp. 151–160. (xxxii, 7)

[Miller, 1995a] R.S.Miller, *Formal Reasoning about Actions and Narratives*, PhD Thesis, Department of Computing, Imperial College, London (1995). (238, 241, 255, 364)

[Miller, 1995b] R.S.Miller, Situation Calculus Specifications for Event Calculus Logic Programs, in *Proceedings of the Third International Conference on Logic Programming and Non-Monotonic Reasoning* (1995), pp. 217–230. (238, 241, 255)

[Miller, 1996] R.S.Miller, A Case Study in Reasoning about Actions and Continuous Change, *Proceedings ECAI 96*, pp. 624–628. (260)

[Miller & Shanahan, 1994] R.S.Miller and M.P.Shanahan, Narratives in the Situation Calculus, *The Journal of Logic and Computation*, vol. 4, no. 5 (1994), pp. 513–530. (156, 162, 175, 187, 198, 255, 236)

[Miller & Shanahan, 1996] R.S.Miller and M.P.Shanahan, Reasoning about Discontinuities in the Event Calculus, *Proceedings 1996 Knowledge Representation Conference (KR 96)*, pp. 63–74. (31)

[Minsky, 1975] M.Minsky, A Framework for Representing Knowledge, reprinted in *Readings in Knowledge Representation*, ed. R.Brachman and H.Levesque, Morgan Kaufmann (1985), pp. 245–262. (47)

[Missiaen, *et al.*, 1995] L.Missiaen, M.Bruynooghe and M.Denecker, CHICA, A Planning System Based on Event Calculus, *The Journal of Logic and Computation*, vol. 5, no. 5 (1995), pp. 579–602. (347, 364)

[Moore, 1982] R.C.Moore, The Role of Logic in Knowledge Representation and Commonsense Reasoning, *Proceedings AAAI 82*, pp. 428–433. (xxx, xxxi)

[Morgenstern & Stein, 1988] L.Morgenstern and L.A.Stein, Why Things Go Wrong: A Formal Theory of Causal Reasoning, *Proceedings AAAI 88*, pp. 518–523. (347)

[Morris, 1988] P.H.Morris, The Anomalous Extension Problem in Default Reasoning, *Artificial Intelligence*, vol. 35 (1988), pp. 383–399. (240)

[Muggleton, 1991] S.Muggleton, Inductive Logic Programming, *New Generation Computing*, vol. 8, no. 4 (1991), pp. 295–318. (xxxii)

[Myers & Smith, 1988] K.L.Myers and D.E.Smith, The Persistence of Derived Information, *Proceedings AAAI 88*, pp. 496–500. (289)

[Newell & Simon, 1976] A.Newell and H.A.Simon, Computer Science as Empirical Enquiry: Symbols and Search, *Communications of the ACM*, vol. 19, no. 3 (1976), pp. 113–126. (xxxiii, xxxiv)

[Nilsson, 1984] N.J.Nilsson, ed., *Shakey the Robot*, SRI Technical Note no. 323 (1984), SRI, Menlo Park, California. (xxvii)

[Nilsson, 1991] N.J.Nilsson, Logic and Artificial Intelligence, *Artificial Intelligence*, vol. 47 (1991), pp. 31–56. (xx, xxxi)

[Pednault, 1988] E.P.D.Pednault, Extending Conventional Planning Techniques to Handle Actions with Context-Dependent Effects, *Proceedings AAAI 88*, pp. 55–59. (92)

[Pednault, 1989] E.P.D.Pednault, ADL: Exploring the Middle Ground between STRIPS and the Situation Calculus, *Proceedings 1989 Knowledge Representation Conference (KR 89)*, pp. 324–332. (140, 148, 150)

[Pinto, 1994] J.Pinto, *Temporal Reasoning in the Situation Calculus*, PhD Thesis, Computer Science Department, University of Toronto (1994). (150, 260)

[Pinto & Reiter, 1993] J.Pinto and R.Reiter, Temporal Reasoning in Logic Programming: A Case for the Situation Calculus, *Proceedings of the Tenth International Conference on Logic Programming* (1993), pp. 203–221. (156, 252)

[Poole, 1988] D.Poole, A Logical Framework for Default Reasoning, *Artificial Intelligence*, vol. 36 (1988), pp. 27–47. (xxxii, 347)

[Provetti, 1996] A.Provetti, Hypothetical Reasoning about Actions: From Situation Calculus to Event Calculus, *Computational Intelligence*, to appear. (364)

[Pylyshyn, 1987] Z.W.Pylyshyn, ed., *The Robot's Dilemma: The Frame Problem in Artificial Intelligence*, Ablex (1987). (23)

[Quine, 1987] W.V.Quine, *Quiddities*, Harvard University Press (1987). (xxxii)

[Rayner, 1991] M.Rayner, On the Applicability of Nonmonotonic Logic to Formal Reasoning in Continuous Time, *Artificial Intelligence*, vol. 49 (1991), pp. 345–360. (313, 329)

[Reggia, 1983] J.Reggia, Diagnostic Expert Systems Based on a Set-Covering Model, *International Journal of Man-Machine Studies*, vol. 19, no. 5 (1983), pp. 437–460. (347)

[Reiter, 1978] R.Reiter, On Closed World Data Bases, in *Logic and Databases*, ed. H.Gallaire and J.Minker, Plenum Press (1978), pp. 55–76. (213, 220)

[Reiter, 1980] R.Reiter, A Logic for Default Reasoning, *Artificial Intelligence*, vol. 13 (1980), pp. 81–132. (17, 47, 71)

[Reiter, 1982] R.Reiter, Circumscription Implies Predicate Completion (Sometimes), *Proceedings AAAI 82*, pp. 418–420. (230)

[Reiter, 1987] R.Reiter, A Theory of Diagnosis from First Principles, *Artificial Intelligence*, vol. 32 (1987), pp. 57–95. (347, 357)

[Reiter, 1991] R.Reiter, The Frame Problem in the Situation Calculus: A Simple Solution (Sometimes) and a Completeness Result for Goal Regression, in *Artificial Intelligence and Mathematical Theory of Computation: Papers in Honor of John McCarthy*, ed. V.Lifschitz, Academic Press (1991), pp. 359–380. (21, 140, 143, 144, 146, 148, 150, 157)

[Reiter, 1993] R.Reiter, Proving Properties of States in the Situation Calculus, *Artificial Intelligence*, vol. 64 (1993), pp. 337–351. (43, 161)

[Reiter, 1996] R.Reiter, Natural Actions, Concurrency and Continuous Time in the Situation Calculus, *Proceedings 1996 Knowledge Representation Conference (KR 96)*, pp. 2–13. (260, 364)

[Reiter & Criscuolo, 1981] R.Reiter and G.Criscuolo, On Interacting Defaults, *Proceedings IJCAI 81*, pp. 270–276. (225)

[Robinson, 1965] J.A.Robinson, A Machine Oriented Logic Based on the Resolution Principle, *Journal of the ACM*, vol. 12 (1965), pp. 23–41. (203)

[Sandewall, 1972] E.Sandewall, An Approach to the Frame Problem and its Implementation, in *Machine Intelligence 7*, ed.B.Meltzer and D.Michie, Edinburgh University Press (1972), pp. 195–204. (46, 57)

[Sandewall, 1989a] E.Sandewall, Combining Logic and Differential Equations for Describing Real-World Systems, *Proceedings 1989 Knowledge Representation Conference (KR 89)*, pp. 412–420. (258, 260, 308, 312)

[Sandewall, 1989b] E.Sandewall, Filter Preferential Entailment for the Logic of Action in Almost Continuous Worlds, *Proceedings IJCAI 89*, pp. 894–899. (258, 260, 313, 315)

[Sandewall, 1991] E.Sandewall, *Features and Fluents*, Technical Report LiTH-IDA-R-91-29 (first review version), Department of Computer and Information Science, Linköping University, Sweden, 1991. (81, 185, 299)

[Sandewall, 1993] E.Sandewall, The Range of Applicability of Nonmonotonic Logics for the Inertia Problem, *Proceedings IJCAI 93*, pp. 738–743. (81, 279)

[Sandewall, 1994] E.Sandewall, *Features and Fluents: The Representation of Knowledge about Dynamical Systems, Volume 1*, Oxford University Press, 1994. (81, 132, 299, 315)

[Scherl & Levesque, 1993] R.Scherl and H.Levesque, The Frame Problem and Knowledge Producing Actions, *Proceedings AAAI 93*, pp. 689–695. (363)

[Schubert, 1990] L.K.Schubert, Monotonic Solution of the Frame Problem in the Situation Calculus, in *Knowledge Representation and Defeasible Reasoning*, ed. H.Kyburg, R.Loui and G.Carlson, Kluwer (1990), pp. 23–67. (136, 138, 140, 194, 259)

[Schubert, 1994] L.K.Schubert, Explanation Closure, Action Closure and the Sandewall Test Suite for Reasoning about Change, *Journal of Logic and Computation*, vol. 4, no. 5 (1994), pp. 679–700. (139, 353)

[Shanahan, 1989] M.P.Shanahan, Prediction Is Deduction but Explanation Is Abduction, *Proceedings IJCAI 89*, pp. 1055–1060. (xxxiii, 128, 252, 347)

[Shanahan, 1990] M.P.Shanahan, Representing Continuous Change in the Event Calculus, *Proceedings ECAI 90*, pp. 598–603. (260, 285, 305)

[Shanahan, 1993] M.P.Shanahan, Explanation in the Situation Calculus, *Proceedings IJCAI 93*, pp. 160–165. (127, 128, 332, 345, 347)

[Shanahan, 1995a] M.P.Shanahan, Default Reasoning about Spatial Occupancy, *Artificial Intelligence*, vol. 74 (1995), pp. 147–163. (128)

[Shanahan, 1995b] M.P.Shanahan, A Circumscriptive Calculus of Events, *Artificial Intelligence*, vol. 77 (1995), pp. 249–284. (267, 272, 275, 306, 391)

[Shanahan, 1996a] M.P.Shanahan, Robotics and the Common Sense Informatic Situation, *Proceedings ECAI 96*, pp. 684–688. (xxx)

[Shanahan, 1996b] M.P.Shanahan, Noise and the Common Sense Informatic Situation for a Mobile Robot, *Proceedings AAAI 96*, pp. 1098–1103. (357)

[Shoham, 1986] Y.Shoham, Chronological Ignorance: Time, Nonmonotonicity, Necessity and Causal Theories, *Proceedings AAAI 86*, pp. 389–393. (76)

[Shoham, 1988] Y.Shoham, *Reasoning About Change: Time and Causation from the Standpoint of Artificial Intelligence*, MIT Press (1988). (7, 47)

[Sussman & Winograd, 1970] G.J.Sussman and T.Winograd, MICROPLANNER Reference Manual, AI Memo 203, MIT AI Lab, Cambridge, Massachusetts (1970). (218)

[Thielscher, 1994] M.Thielscher, Representing Actions in Equational Logic Programming, *Proceedings of the Eleventh International Conference on Logic Programming* (1994), pp. 207–224. (150)

[Van Belleghem, *et al.*, 1994] K.Van Belleghem, M.Denecker and D.De Schreye, Representing Continuous Change in the Abductive Event Calculus, *Proceedings of the Eleventh International Conference on Logic Programming* (1994), pp. 225–239. (260, 263)

[Winslett, 1988] M.Winslett, Reasoning about Actions Using a Possible Models Approach, *Proceedings AAAI 88*, pp. 89–93. (318)

[Winston, 1992] P.H.Winston, *Artificial Intelligence* (Third Edition), Addison-Wesley (1992). (xix)

Appendix A: Proof of Theorem 9.7.5

Let Σ be the conjunction of,

- A collection of effect axioms and domain constraints not mentioning the predicates HoldsAt, Actual, Start, Happens, and Initially, the function State, or the constant S0,

- Axiom (Arb1)

- Axioms (EoS12), (EoS13) and (F2), and

- Uniqueness-of-names axioms for actions and fluents.

Let Δ_N be the conjunction of a linear simple narrative description and the uniqueness-of-names axioms for fluents and actions. Let Δ_{PR} be the conjunction of Axiom (Arb2) with Axioms (PR1) to (PR11), and the uniqueness-of-names axioms for fluents and actions. Let Δ_{MS} be the conjunction of Axioms (MS1) to (MS4) with the uniqueness-of-names axioms for fluents and actions. We'll consider only interpretations in which time points are interpreted by the naturals, and in which < has the corresponding usual meaning.

Two lemmas are required before Theorem 9.7.5 can be proved.

Lemma A.1. From

$$\Delta_{PR} \wedge Happens(a,t) \leftrightarrow \bigvee_{i=1}^{m} [a = \alpha_i \wedge t = \tau_i]$$

we can derive,

$$HoldsAt(f,t) \leftrightarrow [Initially(f) \wedge [m = 0 \vee t \leq \tau_1]] \vee$$
$$\bigvee_{i=1}^{m} [Holds(f,Result(\alpha_i, \ldots Result(\alpha_1,S0) \ldots)) \wedge \tau_i < t \leq \tau_{i+1}] \vee$$
$$[Holds(f,Result(\alpha_m, \ldots Result(\alpha_1,S0) \ldots)) \wedge \tau_m < t].$$

Proof. Suppose we have,

$$Happens(a,t) \leftrightarrow \bigvee_{i=1}^{m} [a = \alpha_i \wedge t = \tau_i] \qquad [A.2]$$

The first step in the proof is to obtain definitions of Actual and Start. From (PR10) and [A.2], we have,

$$\exists s\, [Actual(Result(a,s)) \wedge Start(Result(a,s),t)] \leftrightarrow \bigvee_{i=1}^{m} [a = \alpha_i \wedge t = \tau_i] \quad [A.3]$$

From (PR4) we get,

$$[Actual(s1) \wedge Start(s1,t)] \rightarrow s1 = S0 \vee \exists\, a,s2\ [s1 = Result(a,s2)]$$

which entails,

$$[Actual(s1) \wedge Start(s1,t)] \rightarrow s1 = S0 \vee \exists\, a,s2\ [s1 = Result(a,s2) \wedge$$
$$Actual(Result(a,s2) \wedge Start(Result(a,s2),t)].$$

From this and [A.3] we get,

$$[Actual(s1) \wedge Start(s1,t)] \rightarrow s1 = S0 \vee \exists\, a,s2\ [s1 = Result(a,s2) \wedge$$
$$\bigvee_{i=1}^{m}\ [a = \alpha_i \wedge t = \tau_i]].$$

Applying (PR8), we get,

$$[Actual(s1) \wedge Start(s1,t)] \rightarrow [s1 = S0 \wedge t = 0] \vee \qquad\qquad [A.4]$$
$$\exists\, a,s2\ [s1 = Result(a,s2) \wedge \bigvee_{i=1}^{m}\ [a = \alpha_i \wedge t = \tau_i]]$$

Now, we clearly have,

$$Actual(s) \wedge Start(s,t) \leftarrow [s = S0 \wedge t = 0]$$

We can also show,

$$Actual(s) \wedge Start(s,t) \leftarrow [s = Result(\alpha 1, S0) \wedge t = \tau 1] \qquad\qquad [A.5]$$

To see this, consider that we know

$$\exists\, s2[Actual(Result(\alpha 1,s2)) \wedge Start(Result(\alpha 1,s2),\tau 1)]$$

from [A.3], and hence we have Actual(s2) from (PR2), and $\exists\, t2\ [Start(s2,t2)]$ from (PR5). Therefore,

$$[s2 = S0 \wedge t = 0] \vee \exists\, a,s3\ [s2 = Result(a,s3) \wedge \bigvee_{i=1}^{m}\ [a = \alpha_i \wedge t = \tau_i]]$$

from [A.4]. But $t2 < \tau 1$ because Start(s2,t2) and Start(Result($\alpha 1$,s2),$\tau 1$) (Axiom (PR7)). So t2 must be 0. From Axiom (PR6), only one situation can start at 0, and this has to be S0. Hence we have [A.5].

An argument of the same form can be applied for s = Result($\alpha 2$,Result($\alpha 1$,S0)) and t = $\tau 2$, and so on. This gives, in general,

$$[Actual(s) \wedge Start(s,t)] \leftarrow [s = S0 \wedge t = 0] \vee$$
$$\bigvee_{i=1}^{m}\ [s = Result(\alpha_i, Result(\alpha_{i-1}, \ldots Result(\alpha_1, S0) \ldots)) \wedge t = \tau_i\ ]$$

This implication can be made into a biconditional. To see this, suppose the only-if half of the biconditional is not true. Then there is some s and t such that Actual(s) and Start(s,t), but where,

$$\bigwedge_{i=1}^{m} \quad \begin{array}{c} [s \neq S0 \vee t \neq 0] \wedge \\ [s \neq Result(\alpha_i, Result(\alpha_{i-1}, \ldots Result(\alpha_1, S0) \ldots) \vee t \neq \tau_i]. \end{array}$$

First note that if $t \neq 0$ then $s \neq S0$, since Start(S0,0), and there cannot be more than one start time for any actual situation (Axiom (PR6)). So the first conjunct entails that $s \neq S0$. This means that there must be some a and s' such that $s = Result(a,s')$. Since Actual(s) and Start(s,t), Axiom (PR10) then insists that Happens(a,t). Now, [A.2] says that $a = \alpha_i$ and $t = \tau_i$ for some i between 1 and m. But this contradicts the second conjunct above. Therefore no such s and t exist, and the biconditional form of [A.6] is true.

$$\bigvee_{i=1}^{m} \quad \begin{array}{c} [Actual(s) \wedge Start(s,t)] \leftrightarrow [s = S0 \wedge t = 0] \vee \\ [s = Result(\alpha_i, Result(\alpha_{i-1}, \ldots Result(\alpha_1, S0) \ldots) \wedge t = \tau_i] \end{array}$$

Axiom (PR5) permits us to split this definition as follows.

$$s = S0 \vee \bigvee_{i=1}^{m} \quad \begin{array}{c} Actual(s) \leftrightarrow \\ [s = Result(\alpha_i, Result(\alpha_{i-1}, \ldots Result(\alpha_1, S0) \ldots)] \end{array}$$

$$\bigvee_{i=1}^{m} \quad \begin{array}{c} Start(s,t) \leftrightarrow [s = S0 \wedge t = 0] \vee \\ [s = Result(\alpha_i, Result(\alpha_{i-1}, \ldots Result(\alpha_1, S0) \ldots) \wedge t = \tau_i] \end{array}$$

Now, by substituting these definitions into Axiom (PR11) and simplifying the result, we have,

$$HoldsAt(f,t) \leftrightarrow \exists s [Holds(f,s) \wedge \Pi \wedge [\Gamma \vee \Psi]]$$

where Π is,

$$s = S0 \vee \bigvee_{i=1}^{m} [s = Result(\alpha_i, \ldots Result(\alpha_1, S0) \ldots) \wedge \tau_i < t]$$

and Γ is,

$$\neg \exists a [\bigvee_{i=1}^{m} Result(a,s) = Result(\alpha_i, \ldots Result(\alpha_1, S0) \ldots)]$$

and Ψ is,

$$\exists a [\bigvee_{i=1}^{m} [Result(a,s) = Result(\alpha_i, \ldots Result(\alpha_1, S0) \ldots) \wedge t \leq \tau_i]].$$

Γ can be further simplified to,

$$s = Result(\alpha_m, \ldots Result(\alpha_1, S0) \ldots).$$

Ψ can also be further simplified to,

$$\bigvee_{i=1}^{m} [s = Result(\alpha_{i-1}, \ldots Result(\alpha_1, S0) \ldots) \wedge t \leq \tau_i].$$

The definition of HoldsAt then becomes,

$$HoldsAt(f,t) \leftrightarrow \exists s [Holds(f,s) \wedge [s = S0 \vee$$

$$\bigvee_{i=1}^{m} [s = Result(\alpha_i, \ldots Result(\alpha_1, S0) \ldots) \wedge \tau_i < t]] \wedge$$

$$[s = Result(\alpha_m, \ldots Result(\alpha_1, S0) \ldots) \vee$$

$$\bigvee_{i=1}^{m} [s = Result(\alpha_{i-1}, \ldots Result(\alpha_1, S0) \ldots) \wedge t \leq \tau_i]]].$$

Since Holds(f,S0) is equivalent to Initially(f) (Axiom (PR9)), this can be rewritten as follows.

$$HoldsAt(f,t) \leftrightarrow [Initially(f) \wedge [m = 0 \vee t \leq \tau_1]] \vee \exists s [Holds(f,s) \wedge$$

$$[\bigvee_{i=1}^{m} [s = Result(\alpha_i, \ldots Result(\alpha_1, S0) \ldots) \wedge \tau_i < t]] \wedge$$

$$[s = Result(\alpha_m, \ldots Result(\alpha_1, S0) \ldots) \vee$$

$$\bigvee_{i=1}^{m} [s = Result(\alpha_{i-1}, \ldots Result(\alpha_1, S0) \ldots) \wedge t \leq \tau_i]]]$$

Finally, redistributing the disjunction on the fourth line of this formula and simplifying the result yields,

$$HoldsAt(f,t) \leftrightarrow [Initially(f) \wedge [m = 0 \vee t \leq \tau_1]] \vee$$

$$\bigvee_{i=1}^{m} [Holds(f,Result(\alpha_i, \ldots Result(\alpha_1, S0) \ldots)) \wedge \tau_i < t \leq \tau_{i+1}] \vee$$

$$[Holds(f,Result(\alpha_m, \ldots Result(\alpha_1, S0) \ldots)) \wedge \tau_m < t]] \qquad \square$$

Lemma A.7. From

$$\Delta_{MS} \wedge Happens(a,t) \leftrightarrow \bigvee_{i=1}^{m} [a = \alpha_i \wedge t = \tau_i]$$

we can derive,

$$\text{HoldsAt(f,t)} \leftrightarrow [\text{Initially(f)} \land [m = 0 \lor t \le \tau_1]] \lor$$

$$\bigvee_{i=1}^{m} [\text{Holds(f,Result}(\alpha_i, \ldots \text{Result}(\alpha_1, \text{State}(0)) \ldots)) \land \tau_i < t \le \tau_{i+1}] \lor$$

$$[\text{Holds(f,Result}(\alpha_m, \ldots \text{Result}(\alpha_1, \text{State}(0)) \ldots)) \land \tau_m < t].$$

Proof. Suppose we have,

$$\text{Happens(a,t)} \leftrightarrow \bigvee_{i=1}^{m} [a = \alpha_i \land t = \tau_i] \qquad [A.8]$$

From Axioms (MS4) and (MS2), we have,

$$\text{HoldsAt(f,t1)} \leftarrow \text{Holds(f,State(0))} \land \neg \exists\, a,t2\ [\text{Happens(a,t2)} \land t2 < t1].$$

From this and Axiom (MS1), we get,

$$\text{HoldsAt(f,t1)} \leftarrow \text{Initially(f)} \land \neg \exists\, a,t2\ [\text{Happens(a,t2)} \land t2 < t1].$$

From this and [A.8], we have,

$$\text{HoldsAt(f,t)} \leftarrow [m = 0 \lor t \le \tau_1]. \qquad [A.9]$$

From (MS4) and (MS3), we get,

$$\text{HoldsAt(f,t1)} \leftarrow \text{Holds(f, Result(a1,State(t2)))} \land \text{Happens(a1,t2)} \land t2 < t1 \land$$
$$\neg \exists\, a2,t3\ [\text{Happens(a2,t3)} \land t2 < t3 < t1].$$

If we take a1 to be α_1, and t2 to be τ_1, then given [A.8], this becomes,

$$\text{HoldsAt(f,t)} \leftarrow \text{Holds(f,Result}(\alpha_1, \text{State}(\tau_1))) \land \tau_1 < t \le \tau_2.$$

Since, from [A.8], no events occur before τ_1, Axiom (MS2) permits us to rewrite this as follows.

$$\text{HoldsAt(f,t)} \leftarrow \text{Holds(f,Result}(\alpha_1, \text{State}(0))) \land \tau_1 < t \land t \le \tau_2.$$

In general, using the same argument, we can show for any i, $1 \le i < m$,

$$\text{HoldsAt(f,t)} \leftarrow \qquad\qquad [A.10]$$
$$\text{Holds(f,Result}(\alpha_i, \ldots \text{Result}(\alpha_1, \text{State}(0)) \ldots)) \land \tau_i < t \le \tau_{i+1}.$$

Using the same argument, we can also show,

$$\text{HoldsAt(f,t)} \leftarrow \qquad\qquad [A.11]$$
$$\text{Holds(f,Result}(\alpha_m, \ldots \text{Result}(\alpha_1, \text{State}(0)) \ldots)) \land \tau_m < t.$$

Putting [A.9], [A.10], and [A.11] together, we get,

$$\text{HoldsAt(f,t)} \leftarrow [\text{Initially(f)} \wedge [m = 0 \vee t \le \tau_1]] \vee$$

$$\bigvee_{i=1}^{m} [\text{Holds(f,Result}(\alpha_i, \ldots \text{Result}(\alpha_1, \text{State}(0)) \ldots)) \wedge \tau_i < t \le \tau_{i+1}] \vee$$

$$[\text{Holds(f,Result}(\alpha_m, \ldots \text{Result}(\alpha_1, \text{State}(0)) \ldots)) \wedge \tau_m < t].$$

Now all that remains is to turn this into a biconditional.

Suppose the only-if half of the biconditional doesn't hold. Then there is some f and t for which the biconditional doesn't hold. In other words, we have HoldsAt(f,t), but,

$$\neg [\text{Initially(f)} \wedge [m = 0 \vee t \le \tau_1]] \wedge \qquad\qquad [\text{A.12}]$$

$$\bigwedge_{i=1}^{m} \neg [\text{Holds(f,Result}(\alpha_i, \ldots \text{Result}(\alpha_1, \text{State}(0)) \ldots)) \wedge \tau_i < t \le \tau_{i+1}] \wedge$$

$$\neg [\text{Holds(f,Result}(\alpha_m, \ldots \text{Result}(\alpha_1, \text{State}(0)) \ldots)) \wedge \tau_m < t].$$

According to Axiom (MS4), we have Holds(f,State(t)). There are four cases, corresponding to the different parts of this formula. Either $m = 0$, or $t \le \tau_1$, or $\tau_i < t \le \tau_{i+1}$ for some i where $1 \le i < m$, or $\tau_m < t$.

Suppose either $m = 0$ or $t \le \tau_1$. Then no event occurs before t, from [A.8]. So State(t) is State(0) according to Axiom (MS2). Therefore Initially(f) according to Axiom (MS1). So, from the first conjunct of [A.12], $m \ne 0$ and $t > \tau_1$.

Suppose $\tau_i < t \le \tau_{i+1}$ for some i where $1 \le i < m$. Then, according to [A.8] and Axiom (MS3), State(t) = Result(α_i, . . . Result(α_1,State(0)) . . .). So, from the second conjunct of [A.12], $\tau_m < t$.

But if $\tau_m < t$, then State(t) = Result(α_m, . . . Result(α_1,State(0)) . . .), according to [A.8] and Axiom (MS3). This contradicts the third conjunct of [A.12]. So we cannot have HoldsAt(f,t) and [A.12]. Therefore,

$$\text{HoldsAt(f,t)} \leftrightarrow [\text{Initially(f)} \wedge [m = 0 \vee t \le \tau_1]] \vee$$

$$\bigvee_{i=1}^{m} [\text{Holds(f,Result}(\alpha_i, \ldots \text{Result}(\alpha_1, \text{State}(0)) \ldots)) \wedge \tau_i < t \le \tau_{i+1}] \vee$$

$$[\text{Holds(f,Result}(\alpha_m, \ldots \text{Result}(\alpha_1, \text{State}(0)) \ldots)) \wedge \tau_m < t] \qquad \square$$

Theorem 9.7.5. For any fluent β and time point τ,

$$\text{CIRC}_{\text{PR}}[\Sigma \wedge \Delta_N \wedge \Delta_{\text{PR}}] \vDash \text{HoldsAt}(\beta, \tau)$$

if and only if,

$$\text{CIRC}_{\text{MS}}[\Sigma \wedge \Delta_N \wedge \Delta_{\text{MS}}] \vDash \text{HoldsAt}(\beta, \tau).$$

Proof. From Theorem 9.5.1, $CIRC_{PR}[\Sigma \wedge \Delta_N \wedge \Delta_{PR}]$ is equivalent to,

$$CIRC[\Sigma \; ; \; AbSit > Ab \; ; \; Holds, Result] \wedge$$
$$CIRC[\Delta_N \wedge \Delta_{PR} \; ; \; Happens \; ; \; HoldsAt, Actual, Start, S0].$$

Theorem 9.6.1 is easily modified to give the same result if Axioms (EoS12), (EoS13) and (Arb1) are substituted for Axiom (EoS9) and (EoS10). Then, $CIRC_{MS}[\Sigma \wedge \Delta_N \wedge \Delta_{MS}]$ is equivalent to,

$$CIRC[\Sigma \; ; \; AbSit > Ab \; ; \; Holds, Result] \wedge$$
$$CIRC[\Delta_N \wedge \Delta_{MS} \; ; \; Happens \; ; \; State, HoldsAt].$$

From Theorem 9.6.3, we know that,

$$CIRC[\Delta_N \wedge \Delta_{MS} \; ; \; Happens \; ; \; State, HoldsAt]$$

is equivalent to,

$$CIRC[\Delta_N \; ; \; Happens] \wedge \Delta_{MS}.$$

Similarly, from Theorem 9.5.3,

$$CIRC[\Delta_N \wedge \Delta_{PR} \; ; \; Happens \; ; \; HoldsAt, Actual, Start, S0]$$

is equivalent to,

$$CIRC[\Delta_N \; ; \; Happens] \wedge \Delta_{PR}.$$

So we need to show that for any M, if M is a model of,

$$CIRC[\Sigma \; ; \; AbSit > Ab \; ; \; Holds, Result] \wedge CIRC[\Delta_N \; ; \; Happens]$$

then for any fluent β and time point τ,

$$M \Vdash \Delta_{PR} \rightarrow HoldsAt(\beta,\tau)$$

if and only if,

$$M \Vdash \Delta_{MS} \rightarrow HoldsAt(\beta,\tau).$$

Since M is a model of $CIRC[\Delta_N \; ; \; Happens]$, and since the simple narrative description in Δ_N is linear, M satisfies a formula of the form,

$$Happens(a,t) \leftrightarrow \bigvee_{i=1}^{m} [a = \alpha_i \wedge t = \tau_i] \qquad [A.13]$$

where $\tau_i < \tau_{i+1}$.

From [A.13] and Lemma A.1 we have,

$$M \Vdash \Delta_{PR} \rightarrow [\text{HoldsAt}(f,t) \leftrightarrow [\text{Initially}(f) \wedge [m = 0 \vee t \leq \tau_1]] \vee \quad [\text{A.14}]$$

$$\bigvee_{i=1}^{m} [\text{Holds}(f,\text{Result}(\alpha_i, \ldots \text{Result}(\alpha_1,S0) \ldots)) \wedge \tau_i < t \leq \tau_{i+1}] \vee$$

$$[\text{Holds}(f,\text{Result}(\alpha_m, \ldots \text{Result}(\alpha_1,S0) \ldots)) \wedge \tau_m < t]].$$

From [A.13] and Lemma A.7 we have,

$$M \Vdash \Delta_{MS} \rightarrow [\text{HoldsAt}(f,t) \leftrightarrow [\text{Initially}(f) \wedge [m = 0 \vee t \leq \tau_1]] \vee \quad [\text{A.15}]$$

$$\bigvee_{i=1}^{m} [\text{Holds}(f,\text{Result}(\alpha_i, \ldots \text{Result}(\alpha_1,\text{State}(0)) \ldots)) \wedge \tau_i < t \leq \tau_{i+1}] \vee$$

$$[\text{Holds}(f,\text{Result}(\alpha_m, \ldots \text{Result}(\alpha_1,\text{State}(0)) \ldots)) \wedge \tau_m < t].$$

From Axioms (PR9) and (MS1), we conclude that, for any fluent β,

$$M \Vdash \Delta_{PR} \rightarrow \text{Holds}(\beta,S0)$$

if and only if,

$$M \Vdash \Delta_{MS} \rightarrow \text{Holds}(\beta,\text{State}(0)).$$

Given this relationship between S0 and State(0), and given [A.14] and [A.15], we can see that, for any fluent β and time point τ,

$$M \Vdash \Delta_{PR} \rightarrow \text{HoldsAt}(\beta,\tau)$$

if and only if,

$$M \Vdash \Delta_{MS} \rightarrow \text{HoldsAt}(\beta,\tau). \qquad \qquad \square$$

Appendix B: Proof of Theorem 14.5.2

The proof relies on the fact that, because chronological formulae conform to the principle of directionality, a mapping can be constructed by working forwards in time which permits the application of Theorem 9.4.6, which yields the separation theorem we require.[1]

Let L1 be a language of many-sorted first-order predicate calculus with equality which does not include the predicate symbol ρ. Let L1 include a sort for time points, and the infix predicate symbol $<$ whose two arguments are time points. We'll consider only interpretations in which time points are interpreted by the naturals, and in which $<$ has the corresponding usual meaning.

Let Σ be a formula of L1. Let ρ be an n-ary predicate symbol, and let $\Delta = \forall\, \bar{x}\ \rho(\bar{x}) \leftrightarrow \phi(\bar{x})$ be a formula which is chronological in argument t. Let L1+L2 be the language of Δ. Note that L2 includes the predicate symbol ρ.

Let M be any interpretation of L1.

Definition B.1. Let $F_\alpha(M)$ be an interpretation of L2 defined for any $\alpha \in \mathbb{N}$ as follows.

$$F_0(M)[\![\rho]\!] = \{\,\}$$

$$F_{\alpha+1}(M)[\![\rho]\!] = \{\langle x_1, \ldots, x_n\rangle \mid M+F_\alpha(M) \Vdash \phi(x_1, \ldots, x_n)\} \qquad \square$$

Lemma B.2. For any $\alpha \in \mathbb{N}$, if for all x_i where $x_t < \alpha$,

$$F_{\alpha+1}(M) \Vdash \rho(x_1, \ldots, x_n) \text{ if and only if } F_\alpha(M) \Vdash \rho(x_1, \ldots, x_n).$$

then, for all x_i where $x_t < \alpha+1$,

$$M+F_{\alpha+1}(M) \Vdash \phi(x_1, \ldots, x_n) \text{ if and only if } M+F_\alpha(M) \Vdash \phi(x_1, \ldots, x_n).$$

Proof. Recall that Δ is chronological. So whether a given interpretation satisfies a given $\phi(x_1, \ldots, x_n)$ where $x_t \leq \alpha$ depends only on whether that interpretation satisfies certain $\rho(y_1, \ldots, y_n)$ where $y_t < \alpha$. Therefore, if the set of $\rho(y_1, \ldots, y_n)$ where $y_t < \alpha$ that are satisfied by $F_\alpha(M)$ is preserved in $F_{\alpha+1}(M)$, then the set of $\phi(x_1, \ldots, x_n)$ where $x_t \leq \alpha$ that are satisfied by $M+F_\alpha(M)$ must be preserved in $M+F_{\alpha+1}(M)$. $\qquad \square$

Lemma B.3. For any $\alpha \in \mathbb{N}$ and for all x_i where $x_t < \alpha$,

$$F_{\alpha+1}(M) \Vdash \rho(x_1, \ldots, x_n) \text{ if and only if } F_\alpha(M) \Vdash \rho(x_1, \ldots, x_n).$$

Proof. The proof is by induction. Clearly the lemma holds for the base case where α is 0.

Suppose the lemma holds for some β. So for all x_i where $x_t < \beta$,

$F_{\beta+1}(M) \Vdash \rho(x_1, \ldots, x_n)$ if and only if $F_\beta(M) \Vdash \rho(x_1, \ldots, x_n)$.

From this and Lemma B.2 we get, for all x_i where $x_t < \beta+1$,

$$M+F_{\beta+1}(M) \Vdash \phi(x_1, \ldots, x_n) \text{ if and only if } M+F_\beta(M) \Vdash \phi(x_1, \ldots, x_n). \quad [B.4]$$

From Definition B.1, for any $\gamma \in \mathbb{N}$ and for all x_i,

$$F_{\gamma+1}(M) \Vdash \rho(x_1, \ldots, x_n) \text{ if and only if } M+F_\gamma(M) \Vdash \phi(x_1, \ldots, x_n). \quad [B.5]$$

From [B.4] and [B.5] we get, for all x_i where $x_t < \beta+1$,

$$F_{\beta+2}(M) \Vdash \rho(x_1, \ldots, x_n) \text{ if and only if } F_{\beta+1}(M) \Vdash \rho(x_1, \ldots, x_n). \qquad \square$$

Lemma B.6. For any $\alpha \in \mathbb{N}$ and for all x_i where $x_t \leq \alpha$,

$$M+F_{\alpha+1}(M) \Vdash \phi(x_1, \ldots, x_n) \text{ if and only if } M+F_\alpha(M) \Vdash \phi(x_1, \ldots, x_n).$$

Proof. The lemma follows directly from Lemmas B.2 and B.3. $\qquad \square$

Lemma B.7. For any $\alpha \in \mathbb{N}$ and for all x_i, if $x_t < \alpha$ then,

$$F_\alpha(M) \Vdash \rho(x_1, \ldots, x_n) \text{ if and only if } M+F_\alpha(M) \Vdash \phi(x_1, \ldots, x_n).$$

Proof. (If half)

Clearly the if half of the lemma holds if α is 0.

Suppose $\alpha > 0$. From Definition B.1 we have, for all x_i,

$$F_\alpha(M) \Vdash \rho(x_1, \ldots, x_n) \text{ if } M+F_{\alpha-1}(M) \Vdash \phi(x_1, \ldots, x_n). \quad [B.8]$$

From Lemma B.6 we have, for all x_i where $x_t < \alpha$,

$$M+F_{\alpha-1}(M) \Vdash \phi(x_1, \ldots, x_n) \text{ if } M+F_\alpha(M) \Vdash \phi(x_1, \ldots, x_n).$$

From this and [B.8] we get, for all x_i where $x_t < \alpha$,

$$F_\alpha(M) \Vdash \rho(x_1, \ldots, x_n) \text{ if } M+F_\alpha(M) \Vdash \phi(x_1, \ldots, x_n).$$

(Only if half)

Clearly the only-if half of the lemma holds if α is 0.

Suppose $\alpha > 0$. From Definition B.1 we have, for all x_i,

$$M+F_{\alpha-1}(M) \Vdash \phi(x_1, \ldots, x_n) \text{ if } F_\alpha(M) \Vdash \rho(x_1, \ldots, x_n). \quad [B.9]$$

From Lemma B.6 we have, for all x_i where $x_t < \alpha$,

$$M+F_\alpha(M) \Vdash \phi(x_1, \ldots, x_n) \text{ if } M+F_{\alpha-1}(M) \Vdash \phi(x_1, \ldots, x_n).$$

From this and [B.9] we get, for all x_i where $x_t < \alpha$,

$$M+F_\alpha(M) \Vdash \phi(x_1, \ldots, x_n) \text{ if } F_\alpha(M) \Vdash \rho(x_1, \ldots, x_n). \qquad \square$$

Definition B.10. Let $F(M)$ be an interpretation of L2 defined as follows.

$$F(M)\llbracket \rho \rrbracket = \bigcup_{\alpha \in \mathbb{N}} \{ \langle x_1, \ldots, x_n \rangle \mid x_t = \alpha \text{ and } \langle x_1, \ldots, x_n \rangle \in F_{\alpha+1}(M)\llbracket \rho \rrbracket \} \qquad \square$$

Lemma B.11. For all x_i,

$$F(M) \Vdash \rho(x_1, \ldots, x_n) \text{ if and only if } M+F(M) \Vdash \phi(x_1, \ldots, x_n).$$

Proof. The lemma follows directly from Definition B.10 and Lemma B.7. $\qquad \square$

Theorem 14.5.2. Consider only models in which the time points are interpreted by the naturals, and in which $<$ is interpreted accordingly. If $\sigma 1^*$ and $\sigma 2^*$ are tuples of predicate symbols such that $\sigma 2^*$ includes ρ then,

$$\text{CIRC}[\Sigma \wedge \Delta \;;\; \sigma 1^* \;;\; \sigma 2^*]$$

is equivalent to,

$$\text{CIRC}[\Sigma \;;\; \sigma 1^* \;;\; \sigma 2^*] \wedge \Delta.$$

Proof. From Lemma B.11, F is a mapping from interpretations of L1 to interpretations of L2 such that, for any interpretation M of L1 that satisfies Σ, $M+F(M)$ is a model of Δ. The theorem follows from this and Theorem 9.4.6. $\qquad \square$

Notes

1. The proof in this appendix is a tidier version of the proof in [Shanahan, 1995b].

Appendix C: Temporal Projection Algorithms

Theorem C.6, presented here, facilitates the construction of algorithms for temporal projection. Let Σ be a formula which doesn't mention the n-ary predicate symbol ρ. Let $\Delta = \forall \, \overline{x} \, \rho(\overline{x}) \leftrightarrow \phi(\overline{x})$ be a formula which is chronological in argument t. We'll consider only interpretations in which time points are interpreted by the naturals, and in which $<$ has the corresponding usual meaning.

Let $\sigma1^*$ and $\sigma2^*$ be tuples of predicate symbols such that $\sigma2^*$ includes ρ. Let M^* be the set of all models of CIRC[Σ ; $\sigma1^*$; $\sigma2^*$].

Lemma C.1. For any model M+N of CIRC[$\Sigma \wedge \Delta$; $\sigma1^*$; $\sigma2^*$] where M $\in$ M* and N interprets only ρ, for any $\alpha \in \mathbb{N}$ and for all x_i where $x_t < \alpha$,

$$M+N \Vdash \rho(x_1, \ldots, x_n) \text{ if and only if } F_\alpha \Vdash \rho(x_1, \ldots, x_n).$$

Proof. CIRC[$\Sigma \wedge \Delta$; $\sigma1^*$; $\sigma2^*$] is equivalent to CIRC[Σ ; $\sigma1^*$; $\sigma2^*$] $\wedge \Delta$, from Theorem 14.5.2. So we can assume M+N is a model of CIRC[Σ ; $\sigma1^*$; $\sigma2^*$] $\wedge \Delta$.

The proof is by induction. The lemma is clearly true for the base case where α is 0. Suppose for some β we have, for all x_i where $x_t < \beta$,

$$M+N \Vdash \rho(x_1, \ldots, x_n) \text{ if and only if } F_\beta \Vdash \rho(x_1, \ldots, x_n).$$

Because Δ is chronological, we then have, for all x_i where $x_t < \beta+1$,

$$M+N \Vdash \phi(x_1, \ldots, x_n) \text{ if and only if } F_\beta \Vdash \phi(x_1, \ldots, x_n). \qquad \text{[C.2]}$$

(See the proof of Lemma B.2.) From the definition of Δ we have, for all x_i,

$$M+N \Vdash \rho(x_1, \ldots, x_n) \text{ if and only if } M+N \Vdash \phi(x_1, \ldots, x_n). \qquad \text{[C.3]}$$

We also have, from Definition B.1, for all x_i,

$$F_{\beta+1} \Vdash \rho(x_1, \ldots, x_n) \text{ if and only if } F_\beta \Vdash \phi(x_1, \ldots, x_n). \qquad \text{[C.4]}$$

From [C.2], [C.3], and [C.4], we have, for all x_i where $x_t < \beta+1$,

$$M+N \Vdash \rho(x_1, \ldots, x_n) \text{ if and only if } F_{\beta+1} \Vdash \rho(x_1, \ldots, x_n). \qquad \square$$

Definition C.5. Let C_α be an interpretation of L2 defined for any $\alpha \in \mathbb{N}$ as follows.

$$C_0[\![\rho]\!] = \{\,\}$$

$$C_{\alpha+1}[\![\rho]\!] = \{\langle x_1, \ldots, x_n\rangle \mid \text{for all } M \in M^*, M+C_\alpha \Vdash \phi(x_1, \ldots, x_n)\} \qquad \square$$

Theorem C.6. For any $\alpha \in \mathbb{N}$ and for all x_i where $x_t < \alpha$,

$$C_\alpha \Vdash \rho(x_1, \ldots, x_n)$$

if and only if,

$$CIRC[\Sigma \wedge \Delta \; ; \sigma 1^*; \sigma 2^*] \vDash \rho(x_1, \ldots, x_n).$$

Proof. From Definitions B.1 and C.5, for any $\alpha \in \mathbb{N}$,

$$C_\alpha [\![\rho]\!] = \bigcap_{M \in M^*} F_\alpha(M)[\![\rho]\!]. \qquad [C.7]$$

Since $CIRC[\Sigma \wedge \Delta \; ; \sigma 1^*; \sigma 2^*]$ is equivalent to $CIRC[\Sigma \; ; \sigma 1^*; \sigma 2^*] \wedge \Delta$, from Theorem 14.5.2, all models of $CIRC[\Sigma \wedge \Delta \; ; \sigma 1^*; \sigma 2^*]$ have the form M+N where $M \in M^*$ and N interprets only ρ.

The lemma follows from this, Lemma C.1 and [C.7].   □

Theorem C.6 facilitates the construction of algorithms for deciding whether $q(x_1,...,x_n)$ is true (or false) in all models of $CIRC[\Sigma \wedge \Delta \; ; \sigma 1^*; \sigma 2^*]$, given any x_i. Let α be x_t. An algorithm built according to the following schema will compute the set S_P of all tuples $\langle y_1, \ldots, y_n \rangle \in C_\alpha[\![\rho]\!]$ where $y_t < \alpha$, and the set S_N of all tuples $\langle y_1, \ldots, y_n \rangle \notin C_\alpha[\![\rho]\!]$ where $y_t < \alpha$. From Theorem C.6, to check whether $\rho(x_1, \ldots, x_n)$ is true (or false) in all models of $CIRC[\Sigma \wedge \Delta \; ; \sigma 1^*; \sigma 2^*]$, it is simply necessary to check for membership of S_P (or S_N).

$S_P := \{\}$
$S_N := \{\}$
For $Y_t := 0$ TO α
    $S_P := S_P \cup \{\langle y_1, \ldots, y_n \rangle \mid \text{TRUE}(y_1, \ldots, y_n)\}$
    $S_N := S_N \cup \{\langle y_1, \ldots, y_n \rangle \mid \text{FALSE}(y_1, \ldots, y_n)\}$
End For

$\text{TRUE}(y_1, \ldots, y_n)$ is shorthand for "$\phi(y_1, \ldots, y_n)$ is true in all models of $CIRC[\Sigma \; ; \sigma 1^*; \sigma 2^*]$", and $\text{FALSE}(y_1, \ldots, y_n)$ is shorthand for "$\phi(y_1, \ldots, y_n)$ is false in all models of $CIRC[\Sigma \; ; \sigma 1^*; \sigma 2^*]$". Another algorithm is required for computing the sets $\{\langle y_1, \ldots, y_n \rangle \mid \text{TRUE}(y_1, \ldots, y_n)\}$ and $\{\langle y_1, \ldots, y_n \rangle \mid \text{FALSE}(y_1, \ldots, y_n)\}$ at each iteration. The details of this second algorithm depend on χ and ϕ, but it can exploit the fact that all occurrences of ρ in $\phi(y_1, \ldots, y_n)$ are in conjunctions of the form $q(z_1, \ldots, z_n) \wedge z_t < y_t$. On any given iteration of the algorithm, a conjunction of that form is true in all models of $CIRC[\Sigma \; ; \sigma 1^*; \sigma 2^*]$ if and only if $\langle z_1, \ldots, z_n \rangle \in S_P$, and is false if and only if $\langle z_1, \ldots, z_n \rangle \in S_N$. In the case of (E3), since the definitions of Initiated and Terminated are clausal, resolution theorem proving techniques could be used to compute the required sets. Similarly, SLDNF-resolution (see Chapter 11) could be used to compute with Horn clause fragments of the domain and history formulae when their circumscription coincides with their completion.

There's nothing surprising about this algorithm schema, of course. It simply works forwards in time in the way we might expect. The purpose of Theorem C.6 is to endorse the use of the obvious algorithm. Effectively, Theorem C.6 allows us to forget about Δ computationally, in the same way that Theorems 14.5.2 and 15.5.3 allow us to forget about it from the point of view of minimisation.

$\phi(x_1, \ldots, x_n)$ where $x_t \leq S_{\alpha+1}$ that are satisfied by $M+F_\alpha(M)$ must be preserved in $M+F_{\alpha+1}(M)$. □

Lemma D.3. For any $\alpha \in \mathbb{N}$ where $\alpha > 0$, if S has α or more elements then, for all x_i where $x_t \leq S_\alpha$,

$$F_{\alpha+1}(M) \Vdash \rho(x_1, \ldots, x_n) \text{ if and only if } F_\alpha(M) \Vdash \rho(x_1, \ldots, x_n).$$

Proof. The proof is by induction. First let's consider the base case where α is 1. Suppose that S is non-empty. We have,

$$F_1(M)\llbracket \rho \rrbracket = \{\langle x_1, \ldots, x_n \rangle \mid M \Vdash \phi(x_1, \ldots, x_n)\}$$

$$F_2(M)\llbracket \rho \rrbracket = \{\langle x_1, \ldots, x_n \rangle \mid F_1(M)+M \Vdash \phi(x_1, \ldots, x_n)\}.$$

Because Δ is real-chronological with respect to CIRC[Σ ; $\sigma 1^*$; $\sigma 2^*$] and the marker set S, whether a given model of CIRC[Σ ; $\sigma 1^*$; $\sigma 2^*$] satisfies a given $\phi(x_1, \ldots, x_n)$ where $x_t \leq S_1$ doesn't depend at all on whether that model satisfies any $\rho(y_1, \ldots, y_n)$. Therefore, from the definitions above, the set of $\rho(x_1, \ldots, x_n)$ where $y_t \leq S_1$ that are satisfied by $F_1(M)$ is preserved in $F_2(M)$.

Now suppose the lemma holds for some $\beta > 0$, and suppose that S has β or more elements. So for all x_i where $x_t \leq S_\beta$,

$$F_{\beta+1}(M) \Vdash \rho(x_1, \ldots, x_n) \text{ if and only if } F_\beta(M) \Vdash \rho(x_1, \ldots, x_n).$$

From this and Lemma D.2 we get, for all x_i where $x_t \leq S_{\beta+1}$,

$$M+F_{\beta+1}(M) \Vdash \phi(x_1, \ldots, x_n) \text{ if and only if } M+F_\beta(M) \Vdash \phi(x_1, \ldots, x_n). \quad [D.4]$$

From Definition D.1, for any $\gamma \in \mathbb{N}$ and for all x_i,

$$F_{\gamma+1}(M) \Vdash \rho(x_1, \ldots, x_n) \text{ if and only if } M+F_\gamma(M) \Vdash \phi(x_1, \ldots, x_n). \quad [D.5]$$

From [D.4] and [D.5] we get, for all x_i where $x_t \leq S_{\beta+1}$,

$$F_{\beta+2}(M) \Vdash \rho(x_1, \ldots, x_n) \text{ if and only if } F_{\beta+1}(M) \Vdash \rho(x_1, \ldots, x_n). \quad □$$

Lemma D.6. For any $\alpha \in \mathbb{N}$ where $\alpha > 0$, if S has α or more elements then, for all x_i where $x_t \leq S_\alpha$,

$$M+F_{\alpha+1}(M) \Vdash \phi(x_1, \ldots, x_n) \text{ if and only if } M+F_\alpha(M) \Vdash \phi(x_1, \ldots, x_n).$$

Proof. The lemma follows directly from Lemmas D.2 and D.3. □

Lemma D.7. For any $\alpha \in \mathbb{N}$ where $\alpha > 0$, if S has α or more elements then, for all x_i where $x_t \leq S_\alpha$,

Appendix D: Proof of Theorem 15.5.3

Let L1 be a language of many-sorted first-order predicate calculus with equality which does not include the predicate symbol ρ. Let L1 include a sort for time points, and the infix predicate symbol $<$ whose two arguments are time points. We'll consider only interpretations in which time points are interpreted by the reals, and in which $<$ has the corresponding usual meaning.

Let Σ be a formula of L1. Let ρ be an n-ary predicate symbol, let $\sigma1^*$ and $\sigma2^*$ be tuples of predicate symbols such that $\sigma2^*$ includes ρ, and let $\Delta = \forall\,\overline{x}\,\rho(\overline{x}) \leftrightarrow \phi(\overline{x})$ be a formula which is real-chronological in argument t with respect to CIRC$[\Sigma\;;\sigma1^*;\sigma2^*]$ and a marker set S. Let L1+L2 be the language of Δ. Note that L2 includes the predicate symbol ρ.

Let M be a model of CIRC$[\Sigma\;;\sigma1^*;\sigma2^*]$.

The proof is a variation of the proof of Theorem 14.5.2 in Appendix B. There, induction took place over the naturals, while here induction takes place over the marker set S.

As in Appendix B, the task is to find a mapping F which permits the application of (a variant of) Theorem 9.4.6. Definition D.1 is the same as Definition B.1, but under the assumption that time points are interpreted by the reals instead of the naturals.

Definition D.1. Let $F_\alpha(M)$ be an interpretation of L2 defined for any $\alpha \in \mathbb{N}$ as follows.

$$F_0(M)[\![\rho]\!] = \{\,\}$$

$$F_{\alpha+1}(M)[\![\rho]\!] = \{\langle x_1, \ldots, x_n\rangle \mid M + F_\alpha(M) \Vdash \phi(x_1, \ldots, x_n)\}$$ □

Let S_α denote the αth element of S.

Lemma D.2. For any $\alpha \in \mathbb{N}$ where $\alpha > 0$, if S has α or more elements then, for all x_i where $x_t \leq S_\alpha$, if,

$$F_{\alpha+1}(M) \Vdash \rho(x_1, \ldots, x_n) \text{ if and only if } F_\alpha(M) \Vdash \rho(x_1, \ldots, x_n).$$

then, for all x_i where $x_t \leq S_{\alpha+1}$,

$$M + F_{\alpha+1}(M) \Vdash \phi(x_1, \ldots, x_n) \text{ if and only if } M + F_\alpha(M) \Vdash \phi(x_1, \ldots, x_n).$$

Proof. Recall that Δ is real-chronological with respect to CIRC$[\Sigma\;;\sigma1^*;\sigma2^*]$ and the marker set S. So whether a given model of CIRC$[\Sigma\;;\sigma1^*;\sigma2^*]$ satisfies a given $\phi(x_1, \ldots, x_n)$ where $x_t \leq S_{\alpha+1}$ depends only on whether that model satisfies certain $\rho(y_1, \ldots, y_n)$ where $y_t \leq S_\alpha$. Therefore, if the set of $\rho(y_1, \ldots, y_n)$ where $y_t \leq S_\alpha$ that are satisfied by $F_\alpha(M)$ is preserved in $F_{\alpha+1}(M)$, then the set of

$F_\alpha(M) \Vdash \rho(x_1, \ldots, x_n)$ if and only if $M+F_\alpha(M) \Vdash \phi(x_1, \ldots, x_n)$.

Proof. (If half)

Suppose S has α or more elements. From Definition D.1 we have, for all x_i,

$$F_\alpha(M) \Vdash \rho(x_1, \ldots, x_n) \text{ if } M+F_{\alpha-1}(M) \Vdash \phi(x_1, \ldots, x_n). \qquad [D.8]$$

From Lemma D.6 we have, for all x_i where $x_t \leq S_\alpha$,

$$M+F_{\alpha-1}(M) \Vdash \phi(x_1, \ldots, x_n) \text{ if } M+F_\alpha(M) \Vdash \phi(x_1, \ldots, x_n).$$

From this and [D.8] we get, for all x_i where $x_t \leq S_\alpha$,

$$F_\alpha(M) \Vdash \rho(x_1, \ldots, x_n) \text{ if } M+F_\alpha(M) \Vdash \phi(x_1, \ldots, x_n).$$

(Only if half)

Suppose S has α or more elements. From Definition D.1 we have, for all x_i,

$$M+F_{\alpha-1}(M) \Vdash \phi(x_1, \ldots, x_n) \text{ if } F_\alpha(M) \Vdash \rho(x_1, \ldots, x_n). \qquad [D.9]$$

From Lemma D.6 we have, for all x_i where $x_t \leq S_\alpha$,

$$M+F_\alpha(M) \Vdash \phi(x_1, \ldots, x_n) \text{ if } M+F_{\alpha-1}(M) \Vdash \phi(x_1, \ldots, x_n).$$

From this and [D.9] we get, for all x_i where $x_t \leq S_\alpha$,

$$M+F_\alpha(M) \Vdash \phi(x_1, \ldots, x_n) \text{ if } F_\alpha(M) \Vdash \rho(x_1, \ldots, x_n). \qquad \square$$

Lemma D.7 corresponds to Lemma B.7 in the proof of Theorem 14.5.2. Now we need the counterpart to Lemma D.7 for the case where S has fewer than α elements.

Lemma D.10. For any $\alpha \in \mathbb{N}$, if S has fewer than α elements then for all x_i,

$$F_\alpha(M) \Vdash \rho(x_1, \ldots, x_n) \text{ if and only if } M+F_\alpha(M) \Vdash \phi(x_1, \ldots, x_n).$$

Proof. Consider any $\alpha \in \mathbb{N}$. Let γ be the cardinality of S, and suppose $\alpha > \gamma$.

From Lemma D.7 we have, for all x_i where $x_t \leq S_\gamma$,

$$F_\gamma(M) \Vdash \rho(x_1, \ldots, x_n) \text{ if and only if } M+F_\gamma(M) \Vdash \phi(x_1, \ldots, x_n). \quad [D.11]$$

Recall that Δ is real-chronological with respect to $CIRC[\Sigma ; \sigma1*; \sigma2*]$ and the marker set S. So whether a given model of $CIRC[\Sigma ; \sigma1*; \sigma2*]$ satisfies any given $\phi(x_1, \ldots, x_n)$ depends only on whether that model satisfies certain $\rho(y_1, \ldots, y_n)$ where $y_t \leq S_\gamma$. So from [D.11] and Definition D.1, for all x_i,

$$F_\gamma(M) \Vdash \rho(x_1, \ldots, x_n) \text{ if and only if } M+F_\gamma(M) \Vdash \phi(x_1, \ldots, x_n).$$

Now it suffices to show that for any $\alpha \geq \gamma$,

$$F_\alpha(M) \Vdash \rho(x_1, \ldots, x_n) \text{ if and only if } F_\gamma(M) \Vdash \rho(x_1, \ldots, x_n).$$

The proof is by induction. Clearly the proposition holds for the base case where α is γ. Suppose it holds for some $\beta \geq \gamma$. So we have,

$$F_\beta(M) \Vdash \rho(x_1, \ldots, x_n) \text{ if and only if } F_\gamma(M) \Vdash \rho(x_1, \ldots, x_n).$$

Because Δ is real-chronological with respect to CIRC[Σ ; $\sigma1*$; $\sigma2*$] and the marker set S, whether a given model of CIRC[Σ ; $\sigma1*$; $\sigma2*$] satisfies a given $\phi(x_1, \ldots, x_n)$ depends only on whether that model satisfies certain $\rho(y_1, \ldots, y_n)$ where $y_t \leq S_\gamma$. Therefore, since the set of $\rho(y_1, \ldots, y_n)$ where $y_t \leq S_\gamma$ that are satisfied by $F_\beta(M)$ equals the set of such formulae satisfied by $F_\gamma(M)$, the set of $\phi(x_1, \ldots, x_n)$ that are satisfied by $M+F_\beta(M)$ must equal the set of such formulae that are satisfied by $M+F_\gamma(M)$. From Definition D.1, this means that the set of $\rho(x_1, \ldots, x_n)$ that are satisfied by $F_{\beta+1}(M)$ must equal the set of such formulae that are satisfied by $F_\gamma(M)$. $\square$

Definition D.12. Let F(M) be an interpretation of L2 defined as follows.

$$F(M)[\![\rho]\!] = P1 \cup P2$$

where P1 is,

$$\bigcup_{x_t \in \mathbf{R}} \{\langle x_1, \ldots, x_n \rangle \mid \text{for some } \alpha, S_\alpha < x_t \leq S_{\alpha+1} \text{ and}$$
$$\langle x_1, \ldots, x_n \rangle \in F_{\alpha+1}(M)[\![\rho]\!]\}$$

and P2 is,

$$\bigcup_{x_t \in \mathbf{R}} \{\langle x_1, \ldots, x_n \rangle \mid \text{for all } \alpha, x_t > S_\alpha \text{ and } \langle x_1, \ldots, x_n \rangle \in F_\gamma(M)[\![\rho]\!]\}$$

where γ is the cardinality of S. $\square$

   Note that, given the definition of a marker set, P2 is empty if S is infinite.

Lemma D.13. For all x_i,

$$F(M) \Vdash \rho(x_1, \ldots, x_n) \text{ if and only if } M+F(M) \Vdash \phi(x_1, \ldots, x_n).$$

Proof. The lemma follows directly from Lemma D.7, Lemma D.10, and Definition D.12, given that S is a marker set. $\square$

   Next, we need a minor generalisation of Theorem 9.4.6.

Theorem D.14. If there exists a mapping G from interpretations of L1 to interpretations of L2 such that, for any interpretation M of L1 that satisfies CIRC[Σ ; $\sigma 1^*$; $\sigma 2^*$], M+G(M) is a model of Δ, then,

$$\text{CIRC}[\Sigma \wedge \Delta ; \sigma 1^* ; \sigma 2^*]$$

is equivalent to,

$$\text{CIRC}[\Sigma ; \sigma 1^* ; \sigma 2^*] \wedge \Delta.$$

Proof. The proof is a simple adaptation of the proof of Theorem 9.4.6. $\square$

Theorem 15.5.3. Consider only models in which time points are interpreted by the reals, and in which < is interpreted accordingly. Let $\sigma 1^*$ and $\sigma 2^*$ be tuples of predicate symbols where $\sigma 2^*$ includes the predicate symbol ρ. Let Σ be a formula which doesn't mention ρ. Let $\Delta = \forall \bar{x} \rho(\bar{x}) \leftrightarrow \phi(\bar{x})$ be a formula which is real-chronological in some argument with respect to CIRC[Σ ; $\sigma 1^*$; $\sigma 2^*$], and a marker set S. We have,

$$\text{CIRC}[\Sigma \wedge \Delta ; \sigma 1^*; \sigma 2^*]$$

is equivalent to,

$$\text{CIRC}[\Sigma ; \sigma 1^*; \sigma 2^*] \wedge \Delta.$$

Proof. From Lemma D.13, F is a mapping from interpretations of L1 to interpretations of L2 such that, for any interpretation M of L1 that satisfies Σ, M+F(M) is a model of Δ. The theorem follows from this and Theorem D.14. $\square$

Index

When a word or phrase is mentioned in an endnote, the number of the page containing the endnote reference is given in the corresponding index entry.